Praise for *The Warner Brothers*

"Chris Yogerst gets it right! This lively biography of the brothers Warner—Jack, Harry, Samuel, and Albert—gives us the inside narrative. The brothers never tried to assimilate or erase their Jewish ethnicity. Instead, they made haste with what it gave them, chutzpah, seichel (meaning a head for business), and . . . a great respect for the written word. The Warners wooed the best writers and got the greatest scripts. They knew that life is a one-two punch and they brazenly put that up on the big screen. Yogerst's knowing bio seals the deal: it was chutzpah what made the movies!

—MARILYN ANN MOSS
author of *Raoul Walsh: The True Adventures
of Hollywood's Legendary Director*
and *The Farrows of Hollywood: Their Dark Side of Paradise*

"A fascinating, up-close portrait of the Warner brothers, whose passionate commitment to film made their namesake studio one of the great cultural, social, and political forces during Hollywood's dazzling golden age. Surveying Warner Bros.'s vast range of genres—from hard-bitten realism to uplifting entertainment to film noir to heart-wrenching romance—Yogerst unveils the behind-the-scenes drama of this tight-knit yet often combative family and spotlights the brothers' extraordinary sense of responsibility to reinforcing and repairing America's social fabric. *The Warner Brothers* explores weakness along with strength: the very human frailties that emerged especially when history turned against their generation of studio heads following World War II. Thoroughly researched and written in a lively and compelling style, this book adds a vital new dimension to film history."

—VANDA KREFFT
author of *The Man Who Made the Movies:
The Meteoric Rise and Tragic Fall of William Fox*

"Chris Yogerst provides a compelling, thoroughly researched account of the struggles and successes of Warner Bros. More than a book of Hollywood anecdotes, it is a business story for film buffs and business executives who want to know the wheelings and dealings behind the movies."

—GREG ORR
producer and grandson of Jack Warner

The Warner Brothers

The Warner Brothers

Chris Yogerst
Afterword by Michael Uslan

UNIVERSITY PRESS OF KENTUCKY

Scholarly publisher for the Commonwealth, serving Bellarmine University, Berea College, Centre College of Kentucky, Eastern Kentucky University, The Filson Historical Society, Georgetown College, Kentucky Historical Society, Kentucky State University, Morehead State University, Murray State University, Northern Kentucky University, Spalding University, Transylvania University, University of Kentucky, University of Louisville, University of Pikeville, and Western Kentucky University. All rights reserved.

Editorial and Sales Offices: The University Press of Kentucky
663 South Limestone Street, Lexington, Kentucky 40508-4008
www.kentuckypress.com

Unless otherwise noted, illustrations are courtesy of the Media History Digital Library.

Cataloging-in-Publication data is available from the Library of Congress.

ISBN 978-0-8131-9801-9 (hardcover : alk. paper)
ISBN 978-0-8131-9803-3 (epub)
ISBN 978-0-8131-9802-6 (pdf)

This book is printed on acid-free paper meeting
the requirements of the American National Standard
for Permanence in Paper for Printed Library Materials.

Manufactured in the United States of America

Member of the Association
of University Presses

To my daughter, June Rose,
whose curiosity of the world continues to inspire me.

Contents

Prologue: Put up or Shut Up   *1*

1   Manifest Destiny: Origins to 1923   *7*

2   Incorporation, Innovation, Triumph, and Tragedy: 1923-1929   *39*

3   Battling the Depression, Censors, and Stars: 1930-1936   *75*

4   Fighting Fascism, America Firsters, and the US Senate: 1937-1941   *114*

5   The War Years: 1942-1945   *146*

6   Postwar Politics, HUAC, and the Blacklist: 1946-1947   *179*

7   Last Gasp of Old Hollywood: 1948-1955   *211*

8   End of the Studio, End of the Family: 1956-1959   *248*

9   A New Hollywood Rises: 1960-1978   *267*

Coda: As Time Goes By   *294*

Afterword by Michael Uslan   *298*

Acknowledgments   *301*

Notes   *307*

Index   *337*

Prologue

Put up or Shut Up

On December 8, 1938, the Hollywood Anti-Nazi League met at the home of Warner Bros. star Edward G. Robinson. Warner Bros. was readying the production of *Confessions of a Nazi Spy* (1939), based on the anti-Nazi work of FBI agent Leon Turrou. Robinson would, of course, play Turrou. Up to that point, no major studio had tackled a film about the Nazis, but Warner Bros. had led the charge by being the first to pull its products from Germany after Hitler took power in 1933. Fifty-six members of the Hollywood community attended the gathering at Robinson's home five years later, including Groucho Marx, who "stood up and said, 'I want to propose a toast to Warners—the only studio with any guts.'"[1] There was something unique about the Warner brothers among studio moguls, all of whom were businessmen through and through. Jack and Harry Warner, especially, were shrewd businessmen but also expert communicators and showmen.

They differed in intention, of course. Jack liked to see his name in the papers. More self-centered, Jack enjoyed being a celebrity. He was a performer at heart, but not a very good one. His talents were better suited to his role as a flashy studio chief with his finger on the pulse of the audience, snatching up trending narratives primed for the big screen. Conversely, Harry was more interested in seeing his ideas in the papers. Instead of gallivanting with the stars, as Jack did, Harry spent time meeting with powerful world leaders, contemplating the universal impact of movies, and sharing the gleaned insight with everyone around him.

Jack's disagreements with his older brother were legendary, but he still followed Harry's lead when it came to addressing contemporary mores. Regarding Groucho's comment, the Warners' guts were twofold. Harry regularly consulted other studio bosses about the growing Nazi threat at home, in addition to speaking publicly about the dangers of radicalism more broadly.

At the studio, Jack often green-lit films that interlaced with Harry's messages. *Confessions of a Nazi Spy* was just one of many. The studio had a reputation for churning out courageous pictures, be it pushing against the Nazis or dancing on or beyond the lines of the Production Code.

The brothers' words always aligned with their production decisions, which led to the Warner Bros. tagline: "combining good citizenship with good picture making." For example, the Warner brothers promoted their studio's release schedule for 1931–1932 with an advertisement that read "Put up or Shut Up." Though not written or designed by the brothers directly, that ad is a perfect example of how their personalities seeped into every corner of the studio.

Coming off groundbreaking gangster films such as *Little Caesar* and *The Public Enemy* in 1931, Warner Bros. followed by combining the talents of Edward G. Robinson and James Cagney, who played a pair of gamblers in *Smart Money* (1931). Women's films included *Night Nurse* (1931), starring a young Barbara Stanwyck as a strong-willed nurse who foils a chauffeur's plot to murder two children in the hopes of landing an inheritance. Warner Bros. tackled the financial struggles of the Great Depression like no other studio, doubling down on stories that would entertain, engage, and even enrage audiences. The Warners took the lead in supporting World War II both on and off the screen.

In the aftermath of the blacklist in 1947, the studio tried to placate the government by making anticommunist films. Bryan Foy's B movie *I Was a Communist for the F.B.I.* (1951) was largely inconsequential, although censor Joseph Breen wrote many letters to Jack Warner asking for deletions. The questionable use of racial slurs and details of a race riot stayed in the film, despite Breen's objections. Others, such as *Storm Warning* (1951) starring Ronald Reagan, Ginger Rogers, and Doris Day, remain prescient tales of small communities battling racism. As cultural and political values changed, Warner Bros. continued to push controversial and socially liberal adult material such as *A Streetcar Named Desire* (1951) and *Who's Afraid of Virginia Woolf?* (1966), even after the brothers moved to the political right after the war. Warner Bros. was more than a film studio because its productions reflected the Warner brothers' brand of cultural insight and resilience, which had been cultivated over years of trials and failures.

This project began years ago as an idea to write a biography of Harry Warner, who is largely underappreciated in film history, at least compared

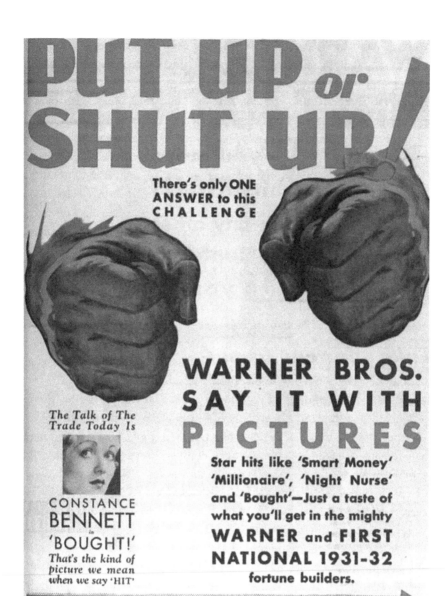

Warner Bros. advertisement, 1931.

with his younger brother Jack. Harry stands out not because of his determination and ability to weather adversity, which were necessary qualities
among all early Hollywood moguls, but because of his faithfulness to his
family, industry, and country. Unlike many other studio heads, Harry was
not a philanderer. He was the staunchest defender of his industry on national
platforms throughout his career and had a way of promoting nonideological
patriotism that can teach a great deal to readers in the twenty-first century.
The man was a towering presence known for his "tolerant friendliness," for
being "charitable to a fault," and for his "imperturbable calm."[2] Harry died
before the nostalgia for golden age Hollywood peaked, when Kevin Brownlow and Peter Bogdanovich were interviewing industry legends in the 1960s.
Jack, being one of the last living moguls of his era, enjoyed that glory. Harry
deserves his rightful place in film history, but his story is incomplete without
Sam, Jack, Albert, and scores of others who helped the Warners along the way.

Neal Gabler, author of *An Empire of Their Own: How the Jews Invented
Hollywood,* describes Hollywood's founders as "men who regarded themselves as marginal men trying to punch into the American mainstream," who
"embarked on an assimilation so ruthless and complete that they cut their
lives to the pattern of American respectability as they interpreted it."[3] This
was certainly true of many Hollywood moguls. The Warner brothers were
unique, in that they did not shy away from their Jewish background. Jack
was the least religious, but he never hid his Jewish roots. Harry, Albert, and
Sam remained devout Jews throughout their lives. Harry spoke regularly and
proudly about his faith, as well as calling for the acceptance of all faiths. Of
course, as a sign of the times, their Jewish identities took a backseat in the
early twentieth century in order to get business loans and mortgages. Sam
would find that getting a home loan was easier when the real estate agent or
banker saw his Catholic wife's crucifix.

Max Bercutt, a public relations man who worked at Warner Bros. from
1948 to 1968, referred to Jack as "the last of the great showmen." According to
Bercutt, Jack would "scream and holler and make your life miserable but he
won't kill you if he knows you're doing a job for Warner Bros." He labeled Jack
"debonair" and described the studio as "the product of good-housekeeping,
meticulously maintained, painted, paved, the lawns and shrubbery mani-
cured."[4] Warner did not even allow movie advertisements on the studio's
outside walls. Today, a very different policy regarding advertisements is evident when driving by the studio on Olive Avenue in Burbank.

More than any other studio chief in the 1920s, Harry was "a pioneer who did not succumb to the developments of a new industry because he set the pace for the revolutionizing process."[5] He was a calm and confident leader. Harry was an astute businessman, a generous human being, and an incredibly loyal family man. Albert was the quiet brother, shying away from the spotlight but seemingly liked by all. Sam was, by all accounts, a genius whose enthusiasm for technical advancements was contagious. He was closest to brother Jack; the two were a great team and shared the drive for success.

What follows is a story about four brothers and how their personal lives and beliefs drove the movies produced at Warner Bros. It is important to point out that while some historians have traditionally viewed movie moguls as businessmen, plain and simple, the Warners were deeply and personally invested in the content and impact of their product. In fact, Jack was so involved that when he eventually took over as Warner Bros. president, he remained in Los Angeles (instead of moving to New York, where most studio presidents resided) and continued to oversee production. The Warners aspired to be more than successful; they were purveyors of essential popular culture. It was not enough that people bought tickets. The goal was to show audiences something exciting that they would continue to think about after leaving the theater.

Many of the major studio bosses wanted to appear more politically connected than they were. For example, Louis B. Mayer often presented himself as the most powerful person at MGM, with a Rolodex of important political connections. We now know that these connections actually came from Ida Koverman, his personal secretary (who was, of course, much more than a secretary).[6] The Warners regularly landed meetings and communicated directly with US presidents such as Franklin D. Roosevelt, Harry Truman, and John F. Kennedy. Harry often traveled in Europe, meeting with world leaders prior to World War II. It is often said, accurately, that Sam was the technical genius and Albert was the wizard of distribution. Jack was the biggest showman of the group, but he also had a keen eye for film content that represented the brothers' interests. Harry's strength was connecting their brand to the political powers of the day—or, in some cases, defending Warner Bros. from those political powers, a role both Harry and Jack would play over the years.

In his 1975 biography of the brothers, Charles Higham writes that Warner Bros. studio was as "powerful as a major newspaper, dealing vigorously with crooked politics, with the mafia, with the prohibition gangs, with the lack of privileges for women in a male-dominated society, with the ugliness of theatrical life."[7] The Warner brothers, like the studio bearing their name, were different from Hollywood's other movie moguls. They were shrewd, brash, outspoken, and passionate in ways that deviated from the industry norm. The brothers' strong sense of civic responsibility was evident in their interviews, memos, public speeches, and films. They created and embodied their own brand of tough, gritty, bold Americanism. The most publicly consistent brother was Harry, a stoic businessman and proud immigrant. Sam was the technical visionary who was gone too soon. Albert largely avoided the public eye, although he served as a loyal ambassador to the family brand. Jack was the wild child, the entertainer, the sometimes unpredictable one.

The Warner brothers overcame obstacle after obstacle before finally finding a business they could excel at together. Even when Thomas Edison's thugs shut them down, the Warners found their way back into the film business. Their ability to prevail defined the brothers, who were, perhaps, more resilient than any other transformative group of businessmen in modern history. As Harry once said, "The Warner brothers have always construed themselves as one."[8] The brothers' story is one that has been told before, but mostly in fragments inserted into tales of stars and films. This book certainly features movie stars and famous films, but its focus is the Warners, who worked diligently to create films with a true and honest impact on society. Warner Bros. produced its share of fun, escapist films, yet the movies that mirrored and engaged contemporary culture were those that best represented the brothers' sense of social responsibility.

A Note on Language

A few of the quotations printed in this volume contain anti-Semitic slurs and racial epithets. I have chosen to reproduce the speakers' original words to accurately document instances of racism and prejudice and to provide context for some of the events under discussion. Discretion is advised.

1

Manifest Destiny

Origins to 1923

The Warners lived in a world of anti-Jewish violence in the shtetels of eastern Europe. The brothers' parents, Benjamin and Pearl, were constant pillars of resilience. Ben practiced his faith in a stable in Krasnosielc, Poland, near Warsaw. Worshipping for the Warners meant always being on the lookout for police. Many of the Warner children would be born there, including Harry, the eldest. Krasnosielc had a long history of Jewish oppression and would be effectively wiped out with Germany's invasion of Poland in 1939. The panzer division in Krasnosielc corralled Jews in the town's synagogue, which had stood strong since 1883, and gunned them down.

In his biography of Jack Warner, journalist Bob Thomas writes of the Warners' experience in the Old World: "the night-riding of Cossacks, the burning of houses, the raping of women was part of life's burdens for Jews of the shtetl."[1] Ben's dreams of a better life were roused by a fellow villager named Waleski, who had moved to the United States and wrote letters about the riches of America. Ben first journeyed to America in 1883 (some sources say as early as 1880), eager to find comfort and prosperity, but he found only more poverty. Waleski offered Ben shelter in a heatless basement and a job as a shoe repairman. Ben intended to send for his family as soon as he had saved enough money.

The family's surname was either Wonsal or Wonskolaser before it was changed to Warner. Harry (originally Hirsch) was born in 1881, Albert (originally Abraham) in 1884, and Sam in 1887. The concentration of Jews in Krasnosielc made it a target for religious persecution, so Harry, Albert, and Sam, along with their mother, headed to the United States in 1889, leaving from Germany aboard the steamship *Hermann*. Always ready to pursue a new opportunity, Ben then took the family to Canada in search of "the fortune to be made by trading tin wares to trappers for fur pelts."[2] Jack was born on August 2, 1892, in London, Ontario. Working the hard winters, Ben continued to collect pelts until his partner abandoned him. At that point, it was time to try the American Dream one more time.

Back in the United States, Ben made the decision to Americanize his children's names. That was when Hirsch became Harry and Abraham became Albert. There would be twelve Warner children in total. Ben also pushed the family to learn English, reverting to Yiddish only on Jewish holidays. He knew their future relied on some level of assimilation and worked hard to set an example. The Warners attempted to strike a balance between fitting into their adopted homeland and retaining their traditions from the Old World. Many Hollywood moguls shed their Jewish heritage sometime during their ascendancy in Tinseltown, but the Warner brothers would be known as the industry family that fearlessly retained their Judaism.

One source of strength was undoubtedly Ben, who once told Harry, "You're going to have to fight with the weapon you have at your command so that the children and their children may have a right to live and have a faith, no matter what their faith may be, in our great country, America."[3] Though Ben offered sound advice to all his children, his words were instilled most firmly in Harry, who had the ability to live by example and showcase his ambition and passion. Ben was known as a happy, funny, kind man, but he did not have the same drive that propelled Harry. Unfortunately, Harry did not have much of a childhood in the old country, and as the oldest, he quickly assumed the caretaker role, a position he maintained his entire life. Harry's daughter, Betty, remembered hearing stories of Harry and Albert selling newspapers on street corners in Baltimore at the age of six or seven.[4]

The older brothers were religiously observant and could speak Hebrew at an early age. The much younger Jack had no interest in Judaism, let alone in learning Hebrew. In his autobiography, Jack recalled his frustrations with a rabbi who came to teach the Warner children. "You are stupid," the rabbi reportedly told Jack, and poked him with a hatpin. Always the rebel, Jack threatened to pull the rabbi's beard. On the rabbi's next visit, Jack remembered, "I saw his hand go for the hatpin. I jumped, but he had a right like Sonny Liston and that pin must have gone in two inches. I clutched the whiskers as if they were a bell clapper and gave them a mighty yank."[5] The rabbi never returned. Jack remained a firebrand his whole life and was a constant irritation to Harry, but he worked with his brothers to create a studio that used movies to defend the right to pursue any way of life.

Though not as extreme as Jack, Sam too had little interest in Judaism. These two brothers, who had the least direct connection to the family's homeland, were the most rebellious. The Warners' newfound roots on the edges of the Midwest contributed to their disinterest in full assimilation. Many other Hollywood Jews experienced the United States in major cities, where there were more distinct class and cultural hierarchies. The Warner brothers, regardless of their level of faith, never bowed to the social pressures of assimilation. Each brother maintained his own unique identity within the family.

Youngstown, Ohio, was pivotal in shaping the Warner brothers. Youngstown had a reputation for being a rough burg. By the time the Warners arrived, the community's iron ore deposits had been depleted, and many steelworkers found themselves unemployed. According to Jack, J. Edgar Hoover later told him that turn-of-the-century Youngstown "was one of the toughest cities in America, and a gathering place for Sicilian thugs active in the mafia."[6] Jack told a few stories of his own about hoodlums robbing his father's store, getting held up at knifepoint, and watching the cops kill a Black man trying to break into the store. Recognizing that some of their clientele were truly dangerous, Ben had Jack carry a small pistol when he worked at the store. Anyone familiar with Jack knew that he liked to tell stories, true or not, but the fact that he was scared away from guns forever seems to corroborate the threat.

After the success of Warner Bros. gangster films in the 1930s, a journalist suggested that Jack may have been a gangster himself in his earlier years. "As a matter of fact, I was," he admitted, referring to the Westlake Crossing gang in Youngstown. It was really less of a gang and more of "a teen-age mob led by a junior Dillinger whose name was Toughy McElvey. I survived a couple of rumbles with a rival gang in which we belted one another with our fists or threw stones that never hit anyone. Toughy eventually vanished from the scene—perhaps he turned into a Hollywood agent—and the gang broke up."[7] In reality, the Warners were quite disciplined workhorses who had little time for trouble. When not working for the family, they were involved in both school and neighborhood sports.

The Warner family had two children who, unfortunately, were not long for this world. Henry was born in 1886 and died in 1890, and Fannie, born in 1891, died in 1894 while the family was living in Canada. High childhood mortality rates were a clear indication of the difficult living conditions endured by many in the late nineteenth century.

Ben Warner was continually searching for work that would provide his family safety and stability. The patriarch of the Warner family was a large, strong man who was friendly but could be a bit anxious, like many immigrants. Sometime in the late 1800s (sources give a range of dates from 1888 to 1894) Ben opened a shoe repair shop in Baltimore that he would eventually reestablish when the family moved to Ohio. His original storefront sign read "The Baltimore Repair Shop." Warner was an expert cobbler, and his promise that shoes would be "repaired while you wait" was his strongest advertisement. Harry helped his father build the shop and learned many lessons in frugality that he would carry over into the film business. Ben demonstrated how to straighten bent nails for reuse, as well as how to hold nails in your mouth to avoid having to search for a new one after each swing of the hammer. Later, this story would somehow morph into one that had Harry straightening nails with his teeth. Harry started managing the shop in 1890, when he was only nine.

According to local reporter Esther Hamilton, one day a handsome, sharply dressed man walked by the Warners' shoe repair shop.[8] That man was Henry Garlick, president of First National Bank. "Young man," Garlick said, looking down at Harry, "does that sign [the one that promised repairs while you wait] mean what it says?" Young Harry replied, "Indeed it does, sir."[9] The Warners took Garlick's boots while the banker sat down to wait. He was stunned when his boots were returned before he had finished reading his newspaper. That transaction was the beginning of an important relationship between the banker and the Warners. Garlick would become a good friend and a key partner, lending the family money in the early days. Years later, after the brothers struck it big in Hollywood, they gave Garlick a life pass to all Warner theaters.

The Warners soon made enough money to bring the rest of the family to Baltimore. Ben came up with the Warner family code: "all for one and one for all." This emphasis on collaboration helped the brothers' film business prevail in the twentieth century. As more shoe repair shops popped up in the Baltimore area, the family decided to move back to Youngstown. There, Ben opened a grocery store and butcher shop on Federal Street, in an area known as Spring Common. He stocked both kosher and nonkosher meats, often switching the two because he thought nonkosher tasted better. Seven-year-old Jack would wake up at 4:00 a.m. to ready the horse-drawn wagon to deliver orders around town. Sisters Sadie and Rose prepared the orders, and Albert (still called Abe by the family) worked behind the front counter. The Warners lived in a Polish neighborhood, where they encountered the anti-Semitism they had hoped to leave behind in Poland. Harry recalled, "Kids would come by and look in the window, laughing and wanting to see if Jews really had tails."[10]

Harry, the financial brains of the family, came up with the idea of purchasing meat in bulk to increase profit margins. Unfortunately, he purchased more pork loins than he could sell, and with a short shelf life, much of the meat spoiled. It was a tough lesson that would harden Harry and likely influenced his future frugality. That mistake was enough to bust the grocery business. Part of the Warners' resilience as a family was, according to journalist Bob Thomas, "instinctual from the ghetto centuries and further inbred from the years of bare-bone survival in the New Land," and it "was viewed by neighbors with awe and admiration."[11] All their earnings went into a shared fund that supported them all, and they confronted both success and failure together as a family.

The Warners engaged in several other ventures at the turn of the century. Harry and Abe operated a bicycle repair shop on Chestnut Street in Youngstown. The older brothers became involved in bicycle racing, and Harry cycled six days per week. The store rented bikes for fifteen cents an hour, taking advantage of the booming cycling craze. The bike boom in the United States was short-lived, however, starting in 1895 (when more than three hundred manufacturers were producing bicycles) and ending in 1900. Interest was fanned by major publications such as *Harper's*, *Scribner's*, and *Life* magazines. Ohio was home to one of the largest bicycle assembly plants, which may have prolonged the interest in bicycling in the region. Moving on from bicycles, the brothers opened a bowling alley (young Sam and Jack set the pins); it did well but eventually plateaued due to an influx of competition. The brothers soon latched on to a craze that would not fizzle out, despite predictions to the contrary.

Much of the brothers' resilience was due to their mother, Pearl. A Youngstown local who lived with the Warners at the time remembered that when the boys came home, each one stopped to hug his mother. "Mom," one would say, "we're going to be millionaires someday."[12] Pearl always responded gently and affirmatively, without breaking her momentum in the kitchen. No matter how tough things were, she never showed signs of intimidation, worry, insecurity, or hopelessness. Pearl also instilled a sense of hospitability in her children, arranging to house friends of the family when necessary. The Warners lived at numerous places around Youngstown, including Walnut Street, Belmont Avenue, Federal Street, and above a butcher shop. It was difficult for such a large family to find adequate living space. One home they rented was being demolished one room at a time. The family squeezed tight until they were left on the street. Eventually, Pearl had to lie about the size of her entourage because the homes they lived in became known as the "Warner hotel." The housing problem was resolved when Ben got a job building apartments at the corner of Elm and Bissell. Ben and Pearl lived there until 1924, when they moved to California.

In 1900 Albert Warner entered Rayen High School in Youngstown. Truth be told, Abe's only incentive to attend school was to play football, so he would enroll every fall, join the team, and then drop out when football season ended. When his younger brother Dave entered high school, he assumed the teachers thought as highly of Abe (a star halfback) as the coaches did. Dave was wrong. Abe's disinterest in academics gave the Warners an undesirable reputation among the Rayen faculty. It was actually Milton, the youngest Warner brother, who was the best athlete in the family. He excelled in football, baseball, track, and basketball. Milton's two no-hit, no-run games in the 1915 season became a Rayen legend. Sadly, after getting multiple offers from professional baseball teams that same year, Milton fell victim to a ruptured appendix and died at age nineteen. He would have been the first Warner to make it big.

The town's respect for the Warners was on display during Anna Warner's 1904 marriage to Dave Robbins. The wedding, held at Diamond Hall, was a major event for the locals. Friends of the family spent a week doing nothing but cooking and preparing for the big day. At the Ozersky Bakery, the Warner family was determined to construct the perfect wedding cake. On the day itself, every taxicab in town was commandeered to chauffer guests to the hall.

During this time, Albert was peddling soap door-to-door. His angle was to convince people that if they bought four bars of soap he would give them the fifth for free. Another story has the brothers selling ice cream wrapped in a cookie, possibly creating the first ice cream cone. "They were always manipulating their goods, as true hucksters, finding the best way to sell," said Albert's step-grandson. And, according to Jack, "Albert could sell a bathing suit to an Eskimo."[13] One of Jack's first jobs was singing at the Dome Theater on Federal Street in Youngstown (it may have operated under a different name at the time). He also sang at the opera house in Central Square.

The brothers had an assortment of early jobs, but one of the most important was Sam's summer job working at Idora Park with Hales Tours and Scenes of the World amusement company. Hales Tours was the brainchild of former Kansas City fire chief George C. Hale. Film and theater critic Edward Wagenknecht remembered that Hales Tours came through his hometown as a child. The company exhibited "travel films, showing in tiny theaters built to resemble railway coaches. The 'conductor' stood on the back platform to receive your ticket, and when you went inside and took your seat you really seemed to be settling down for a journey."[14] Sam sold tickets and narrated the films. According to journalist and historian Terry Ramsaye, bells would ring and the stationary car would move on rockers, providing the appearance and sense of movement. The projected film added to the illusion, as passengers watched the scenes seemingly pass by. Hales Tours provided "a moderately successful illusion of travel."[15]

Sam was the most beloved of the Warner brothers in Youngstown. He was always fascinated by technical gadgets and processes, which gave way to a creatively entrepreneurial mind-set. One of his first innovations was to set up an ice cream machine in front of Morgan's shooting gallery. At the time, the only other place to get a cone was at an ice cream parlor, and Sam's idea was fairly successful. But soon he was off in another direction. Sam worked as a railroad fireman for a brief time, until he got a job at a penny arcade at Cedar Point Amusement Park on the shore of Lake Erie. This is where Sam first saw a kinetoscope projecting a motion picture. By 1902, Sam was managing Cedar Point, an early endeavor of Frederick Ingersoll of future Luna Park fame.[16]

By the end of 1903, four theaters in Boston were exhibiting films with the primary projection systems of the day: vitagraph and kinetograph.[17] Each system used a different method of projecting moving images, or at least providing the sense of movement. As exhibition companies began to acquire projection equipment, the distribution of film reels increased. The first years of the twentieth century were problematic for early cinema because there was no standard equipment across the film industry. Patent and copyright problems lurked around every corner, and competition was ruthless. Meanwhile, demand soared as audiences quickly became bored with the bland, predictable offerings. The novelty of moving images was wearing thin, and viewers wanted something new. The Warner brothers' interest in film during these early days of cinema proved pivotal.

Myron Ponner, who knew the Warner family in New Castle, Pennsylvania, remembered when Sam acquired his first camera. He would walk around outside with his hat turned backward, photographing anything he could. One day he tried to capture the brothers' warm reception as they came home to their beloved mother. They must have been having an off day, because Sam said, "You're not at a funeral. You are home to welcome your mother."[18] Sam's friend Joe Marks (who would later become a casting director at Warner Bros.) also helped him investigate this new acquisition.

By this time, Sam was working at a Central Square machine shop owned by family friend George Olenhauser. Someone brought a kinetoscope—specifically, an Edison Kinetoscope Deluxe Traveling Model AA Projector—into the shop for repair, and Olenhauser called on Sam. Opening the brass and copper device, Sam "felt as if he had truly touched a magic lantern."[19] It was not long before Sam got a lead on where he could acquire a kinetoscope of his own. A local businesswoman knew someone who needed to offload one for some quick cash. Sam pitched the idea of investing in this new technology to his family. The projector cost $1,000, and it came with a copy of Edwin S. Porter's *The Great Train Robbery* (1903). The brothers pooled all their money, but it was not enough. Benjamin Warner hocked his gold watch to make up the difference.

The year 1903 marked a transition in filmmaking, moving from what Tom Gunning calls a "cinema of attractions," based on simple spectatorship of an event, to narrative storytelling, which allowed audiences to get lost in what they saw onscreen.[20] The Edison Manufacturing Company invested in a series of films, including urban drama, comedy, and romance. The most famous was based on Scott Marble's 1896 play *The Great Train Robbery*. Edwin S. Porter's adaptation of Marble's play caught the attention of early cinema audiences, including Sam Warner. Camera techniques such as panning, tilting, crosscutting, and location shooting pulled audiences into the story as they watched individual scenes unfold before their eyes. It did not hurt that the mythos of the Wild West was still recent, both in reality and in the imagination of many Americans. Other film companies, such as Biograph, soon made narrative films their standard output.

Nickel Madness

There was only one way to test the viability of this new trend: with an audience. The brothers set up a tent in their yard and invited neighbors and community members to witness the moving images emanating from Sam's projector. The attraction was a hit. Now the brothers needed a more permanent venue. Knowing that a carnival was coming to the town of Niles, northwest of Youngstown, they found a vacant store there and set up shop, hoping to take advantage of the influx of people attracted by the carnival. Abe sold tickets, and Sam worked the projector. There are conflicting reports regarding the whereabouts of Harry and Jack. According to the family history, Harry stayed in Youngstown and worked to ensure that the family had an income. Jack was still quite young, and he may or may not have tagged along to Niles. A history written by a Youngstown native claimed that Harry and Jack were also in Niles, with Harry tending to the finances and Jack running errands. During the shows, the seven hundred feet of tattered celluloid often broke or completely unraveled, but Sam quickly learned how to repair the film and stay on schedule. The Warners' show was a hit, being the first film ever projected in Niles.[21] Curious crowds filled the venue, proving the viability of a small cinema.

Once the carnival left Niles, Sam and Abe presented their show in other nearby towns until a massive snowstorm discouraged customers, who were unwilling to stand in the drafty and often unheated storefront theaters. The brothers had made $300 per week while on the road, after expenses. Harry recognized that the key to making a real profit was to lease their own venue and build a following. The brothers quickly found a former New Castle nickelodeon spacious enough to show films. As the story goes, the brothers ran out of money before they could purchase chairs for their theater, so they worked out a deal with a local funeral parlor to use its seats, provided they were not needed for a funeral. The theater seated ninety-nine; keeping the capacity under one hundred meant avoiding costly safety regulations such as fire extinguishers and emergency exits. Soon the brothers were running two theaters, the Cascade and the Bijou, which sat on opposite sides of a penny arcade just a short trolley ride from the Warner home.

The Cascade opened on May 28, 1905.[22] On Memorial Day, a funeral for the local school superintendent was scheduled, which meant the funeral

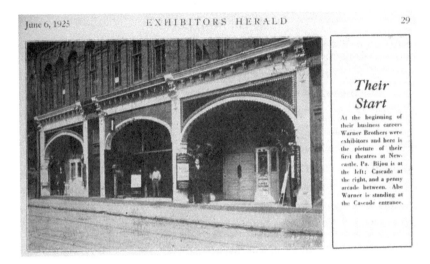

June 6, 1925 EXHIBITORS HERALD 29

Their Start

At the beginning of their business careers Warner Brothers were exhibitors and here is the picture of their first theatres at Newcastle, Pa. Bijou is at the left; Cascade at the right, and a penny arcade between. Abe Warner is standing at the Cascade entrance.

Warner's Features advertisement.

parlor needed its seats. Desperate to keep their operation running through the holiday, the brothers called the superintendent's widow and promised that if she postponed the service until the next day, her children could see free films all year. She agreed. The Cascade was an early success, both attracting the blue-collar community and offering a classy environment not yet associated with movie theaters, which were often located in the seedy areas of big cities. A sign outside the Warners' venue read: "Refined Entertainment for Ladies, Gentlemen and Children." Every woman who came to the theater was given a carnation. The Warners made filmgoing something of a social event.

Before the film started, Sam opened the show with some informative slides for the audience. The first stated, "Please read the titles [to] yourself. Loud reading annoys your neighbors." This was followed by "Ladies! Kindly remove your hats" and "Gentlemen! Please don't spit on the floor." When the first reel of the film ended, a slide appeared reading, "One moment please while the operator changes reels."[23]

Ben Warner was proud that his sons had brought this new cinema technology to the community, but he was even prouder when, on the second day of operation, there was a line down the block as patrons waited to see the show. Ben and Pearl closed the store for the day and watched the spectacle. After the first show, the audience was so stunned that no one stood up to leave when the house lights were turned on. In another well-known piece of

Warner history, Ben encouraged Jack to get up and sing his terrible version of "Sweet Adeline." "Jack's voice, skipping octaves from tenor to baritone, sounded like ice cracking from a glacial floe and drove customers from the place."[24] Sister Rose accompanied him on the piano, which she also played during film screenings.

The brothers capitalized on the period from 1895 to 1905, when nickelodeons made the transition from sideshows in saloons and amusement parks to main attractions. The timing was perfect to take advantage of cinema's improving social status. Movies became most popular outside of major cities, where traditional theater had less of a financial foothold on audiences. In rural areas and smaller cities, nickelodeons and storefront theaters took off. In nearby Pittsburgh, vaudeville mogul Harry Davis became interested in the nascent motion picture industry, and he opened the Nickelodeon on Smithfield Street. Given Pittsburgh's prosperity, Davis's operation benefited from the community's disposable income.[25] By the end of 1905, "movies were not simply gathering places . . . they were centers of communication and cultural diffusion."[26] The Warners' Cascade theater followed the trend by combining movies with vaudeville performances.

The early film business could be extremely dangerous, especially during an era when smoking was commonplace. As the film wound through the projector, it did not wind up onto another reel (that would come later). Instead, the film piled up on the floor or in a bin. In his autobiography, Jack relates a story about a safety inspector who had been advised not to smoke around the highly flammable celluloid but walked into the projection room with a lit cigarette. "There was a rumbling blast that blew part of the projector through the ceiling and into the sky. The windows and doors collapsed, and the unfortunate inspector was dead when we finally dragged him, clothes ablaze, out into the air."[27] Jack always had a penchant for the hyperbolic, but the story is a good reminder of the risky nature of early film exhibition.

By 1907, the term "nickel madness" described both the widespread popularity and the broad disapproval of these five-cent cinemas.[28] Some concerned citizens feared that these small theaters were ripe venues for pickpockets, while others were worried about moving images corrupting youth. Some thought that sitting in a dark theater was a "cloak for evil," and in fact, in some theaters customers sat in the light and watched the movie through holes in a curtain.[29] New York City police commissioner Theodore A. Bingham "denounced nickel madness as pernicious, demoralizing, and a direct menace to the young."[30] Trying to grow a business in the midst of such rhetoric would prepare the Warner brothers to deal with industry censors and moral crusaders.

The years following 1907 were momentous for the Warner family, both personally and professionally. Harry met his future wife, Rea Levinson, at a local dance. Harry was quite the dancer, having entered a series of dance contests with his sister Rose.[31] Like Harry, Rea came from a Jewish immigrant family, but her lineage was more intellectual, educated, and cultured. Given the class-consciousness of the era, one might have thought Rea would have no interest in a poor European Jew like Harry, but she was immediately attracted to his strong face, blue eyes, and blond hair. Harry was attracted to Rea's beauty, elegance, and brilliance. Unlike many Hollywood moguls, Harry married only once and remained with Rea until his death. In 1908 Abe met a Jewish girl named Bessie Krieger, and they married shortly thereafter.

As nickelodeons popped up in nearly every town, demand for films skyrocketed, and audiences were eager for new content. Harry quickly realized that the real money was in film distribution. The brothers went to Pittsburgh and opened the Duquesne Amusement Supply Company, named after a local college in the hope of adding a touch of class to the business.[32] Sam and Abe went to New York City and acquired films from theater magnate Marcus Loew. The future top man at MGM studios, Loew sold the brothers a backlog of used films for $500. While the three older brothers were increasingly busy with their film ventures, poor Jack was still relegated to kid brother status, but he would soon get his break in the family business. The Warner family continued to grow as Harry and Rea welcomed their son Lewis into the world on October 10, 1908.

From Exhibition to Exchange

The Warners' theaters were bringing in more than $2,000 a week, which told Harry it was time to reinvest in the next big step. They sold the Cascade theater for $40,000 and used that money to invest in a new film exchange, expanding the Duquesne Amusement Supply Company. *Variety* reported that management of the Cascade theater was taken over in November 1907 by Harvey Arlington of Youngstown, Ohio.[33] Arlington had previous experience managing the Temple theater with his wife, Clarice Templeton. The brothers continued to acquire films and rent their collection to other theaters. Jack recalled that sometimes a movie would be missing a section, where the film had snapped off, and he would simply attach whatever film was lying around to complete the reels. The audience rarely noticed.

Harry and Abe continued to manage the company in Pittsburgh, while Sam opened a new one in Norfolk, Virginia. Jack served as Sam's assistant. Close in age, Sam and Jack always got along well and became a great team. Norfolk was a logical place to open the next branch of Duquesne. The brothers followed the lead of successful southern exhibitors Jack and Otto Wells, who relocated their operation to Norfolk in 1908. They were quickly "viewed by the local press as upstanding and socially involved citizens" who "became a vital part of the middle and upper classes that brought together social respectability and moviegoing."[34] Movies were still in their infancy and were fighting for legitimacy among the upper classes and religious leaders, so working in a town with growing respect for the film industry was the right place to be.

While in Norfolk, Sam and Jack lived in a boardinghouse on Granby Street. "Nearly all of the boarders were young bachelors, avoiding the trap of matrimony," recalled Jack, "or unattached ladies waiting for some Lancelot to take them away from the gas plate and the washboard."[35] The two brothers made the most of their time away from their father's watchful eye. Although Jack was often the center of attention, Sam's energy provided the fuel for any party. To impress the ladies, Sam performed tricks, such as walking on his hands or wowing onlookers by landing a backflip. Sam did not have to resort to theatrics, however, as he spoke "as melodiously as Caruso sang."[36]

In Norfolk, the brothers started publishing a monthly magazine called the *Duquesne Film Noise*. Sam was the editor, and Jack served as assistant editor. Both men were pictured in "high collars, dark suits with serious expressions, seemingly trying to look older than they were."[37] Knowing that their forward thinking could change the industry, the brothers bragged, "We are the only film exchange issuing its own magazine, watch others follow." And they proudly exclaimed to exhibitors, "Give us an order and you will get the best—the firm with the goods will stand the test."[38] The magazine also included a schedule of local vaudeville bookings, as many people still preferred these comedic stage acts over films. The vaudeville acts attracted a predictable audience, most of whom came for their reserved seats, watched the show, and then left. However, some showed an interest in seeing the films that followed, and these "sitters-on" stayed put, forcing theater staff to turn on the house lights and pace the aisles to identify the squatters.

The family custom had always been for the children to give all their earnings to Ben and Pearl, keeping only fifty cents per week for themselves. But, being away from home, Sam and Jack were tempted to splurge on themselves. One day in 1909, after having some success in Virginia, the two drove back to Ohio in a white Buick roadster—a hot car at the time.[39] The only other Buick roadster in Youngstown was owned by a local doctor. While the younger brothers tended to spend their money quickly, Harry was an expert saver, and he often spent any extra money on his parents, eager to show his gratitude for their unflinching support. When Harry turned nineteen, Pearl gifted him with a piano, so he could play for guests. Rose too learned to play the piano, and her skills paid off as she accompanied the films shown in her brothers' first theaters. Esther Hamilton remembered that Rose was "one of the best piano thumpers . . . and although her accompaniment was largely improvised, it was loud, and she kept time, and the customers were satisfied."[40]

By 1910, Thomas Edison had organized his fiefdom into the General Film Company, complete with an intimidating army of powerful attorneys. Harry attempted to sidestep the company by quietly meeting with theater owners and sneaking reels of film into venues hidden under coats, in the pages of a newspaper, or in a briefcase.[41] Sam remembered one of Edison's thugs walking into the Warners' Pittsburgh film exchange and bluntly telling the brothers that they would no longer be supplied with any films. With the supply chain halted, the Warners had no choice but to sell their business. The price was $10,000 cash, $12,000 in preferred stock, and three years' worth of payments amounting to $52,000. The Warners wanted to stay in the film business, so Sam asked about a job running the exchange for General Film. The brothers went to New York to meet with General Film's president, only to learn that someone else had been hired to run the Pittsburgh exchange.

Instead, the brothers found work with the future founder of Universal Pictures, Carl Laemmle, who owned the Independent Motion Picture Distribution and Sales Company, known as IMP. The Warners were hired to run IMP in the Pittsburgh area. During this time, the industry was constantly caught up in Edison's lawsuits, and Hamilton remembered the brothers spending an inordinate amount of time in court, having been subpoenaed by the Edison attorneys or by one of the other independents.

Although Thomas Edison was an important and influential inventor, his work in the film industry created more divisions than bridges. By 1911, his General Film Company owned almost every film exchange in the country. The one holdout, the Greater New York Film Exchange, was owned by William Fox. Edison then created the Motion Picture Patents Corporation (MPPC), also known as the Edison Trust, to control film distribution and exhibition. The founding members of the MPPC were Edison, Biograph, Vitagraph, Essanay, Selig Polyscope, Lubin Manufacturing, Kalem Company, Star Film Paris, American Pathe, George Kleine, and Eastman Kodak. The Edison Trust chased after anyone who used Edison's inventions without a license, and the Warner brothers were among the many victims of these patent wars. The sheer power and menacing presence of the MPPC were intimidating, but that did not stop the Warners. William Fox initiated an antitrust lawsuit with the Justice Department, and Laemmle's outfit was known as an "enemy organization of the Trust."[42]

Exhausted from the endless legal battles, Harry decided it was time to bail out and start again. With the money left from the sale of their film exchange, Harry purchased a grocery store in Youngstown. He was familiar with the grocery business and knew it would keep the family afloat while they plotted a new way back into the film industry. As a side project, the brothers opened and operated the Rex theater, showing the film prints they had managed to keep. But after a few runs of each film, the audiences wanted something new, and the Rex shut down. Harry ran the grocery store while Sam, Abe, and Jack spread out looking for work. Abe got a job as a traveling salesman, and Jack went to New York, where he found work splicing films. Jack immersed himself in the entertainment business, reading the trade press every day, attending vaudeville shows at night, and seeing every new film available. Increasingly curious about the cost of production as well as the mechanics of direction, Jack was piecing together the skills of a top producer.

Sam's contribution was his discovery of an Italian film, *Dante's Inferno* (1911), which was not regulated by the Edison Trust. One of the first blockbusters and possibly the first feature-length film (beating Cecil B. DeMille's *The Squaw Man* by three years), *Dante's Inferno* captivated Sam and propelled the brothers to discover new exhibition practices. Their traveling exhibition featured alcoholic actor W. Stevens Bush (referred to as Professor Bush during shows), who read scenes from Dante's poem. Jack ran a wind machine while moving a piece of metal to imitate thunder. The film was tinted in different colors, which made this film experience different from others. Certainly, Sam channeled his days with Hales Tours to create an immersive viewing experience. Although the traveling show was fun, it was not a long-term

The first movie road show, as reported in the trades, was the Warners' exhibition of *Dante's Inferno*. This photograph was taken in Atlantic City, New Jersey. Sam and Jack Warner are on the far right; W. Stevens Bush is third from the left.

fix. *Exhibitors Herald* cited the *Dante's Inferno* road show as the first of its kind.[43] While on the road in Tiffin, Ohio, the brothers saw their show go up in flames. Sam had just stepped away from the projection machine when the floor beneath caught fire. The insulation of the machine's electric cable had worn bare in sections, sparking and setting the carpet aflame. Abe, who had come along for this stretch of the tour, had run the wire. The accident led to some unplanned vacation time, which allowed the family to plot their next venture in the film business.

The Warners had learned many hard lessons from nearly every angle of the film industry, and they were not about to give up. According to Hamilton, the brothers were defined by their work ethic. "They worked five times as hard as most men," she wrote, "their lives knew no eight-hour day, or 40-hour week. They took their chances with their money, put up their watches, their rings, even their clothing as security when they got into a tight spot."[44] Such a fearless mentality displayed not only their ambition but also their valiant approach to business. Many of the early moguls shared this drive, but perhaps none more so than the four Warner brothers.

Making Movies

The brothers were determined to stay in the film business. Harry knew there was money to be made with inexpensive two-reel films. The Warners rented space in an old foundry Harry had discovered in St. Louis. While there, Jack and Sam put together *The Covered Wagon*, a two-reel adventure about settlers attacked by Indians while crossing the plains. Sam remembered having only three wagons and a nearly dry river. The Missouri National Guard was somehow convinced to help by "blasting away with their (1910 Army issue) carbines at the marauding Indians, fording the Mississippi."[45] The brothers also made another film, *Raiders on the Mexican Border*. The movies were garbage, but it was a great learning experience. Film was still an experimental medium, and Sam and Jack loved learning on the job and enjoyed the freewheeling approach to filmmaking. The problem was that the brothers were broke again, with a total of a $1.65 between them. Always willing to support their boys' ventures, Ben and Pearl bailed them out with $400. Many years later, after Warner Bros. was a household name, Harry said, "Whatever we have today was built on the four hundred dollars our parents gave us at that time."[46]

Warner Feature Film Company soon began to expand, with offices in Chicago, Cleveland, Indianapolis, Dallas, Kansas City, St. Louis, Minneapolis, Omaha, Atlanta, Buffalo, Detroit, and Boston, in addition to San Francisco, New York, and Philadelphia. Albert sat as president, Harry served as secretary and treasurer, and H. M. Goetz was general auditor. The brothers also struck up partnerships with other film corporations. Showing a knack for recognizing innovative and industry-defining talent, the brothers partnered with Gauntier Feature Players. Gauntier's leading lady, Gene Gauntier, was a pivotal pioneer in the film industry. She was the Kalem Film Manufacturing Company's first "Kalem Girl" from 1907 to 1912. Gauntier worked as both an actress (*The Girl Spy*, 1909) and a screenwriter, authoring the script for *Ben Hur* (1907). Gauntier left Kalem in 1912 and founded the Gene Gauntier Feature Players Company, "a decision enthusiastically hailed by the *Moving Picture World*."[47]

Moving Picture World reported on the partnership between the Warners and Gauntier at the end of 1912. Her company had been considering many competitive offers, but in the end, it was Albert Warner's standing in the industry that won out. The respect he earned from everyone he worked with, as well as his plan to look after the interests of Gauntier's company, landed

Directors' Room, Warner's Features, Inc.   General Office, Warner's Features, Inc.

Warner's New York offices.

the partnership. No doubt the Warners were drawn to Gauntier's talents both onscreen and off, as she mirrored the brothers' drive for success in the growing film industry. Warner Feature Film Company began promoting itself as Warner's Features, putting its name below Gene Gauntier Feature Players, albeit in larger type.

Once again, the brothers split up to maximize opportunities around the country. Jack went to San Francisco, Sam went to Los Angeles, and Harry and Abe opened an office in New York. Things were looking up, as the Edison Trust had been busted by the end of 1912. Jack also met one of his closest friends, Sid Grauman, while setting up shop in San Francisco. Grauman later introduced Jack to his future wife, Irma Claire Salomon, the daughter of a prominent Jewish family in town. Sam traveled to Los Angeles to check out the growing film community in Southern California. Screenwriter Lenore Coffee, who came to Hollywood about a year later, remembered that "Hollywood Boulevard was a villagey street. There was a large market which served superb breakfasts at the counter . . . it was packed with movie people, for calls to work were early."[48] The mass influx of major studios was still to come.

By 1913, Warner Feature Film Company officially became Warner's Features Inc. The company's business plan was solid, but the brothers lacked the cash they needed to grow the business properly. They sold their stock in the company, while retaining the rights to their name.[49] New investors came on board, and the corporation was reorganized with P. A. (Pat) Powers as president, Albert as vice president, Harry as sales manager, and Goetz as assistant sales manager. Powers had a similar history to the Warners, selling phonographs in the early days of the century and then distributing films to

Warner's Features advertisement, December 1914.

nickelodeon exhibitors during the nickel madness days. Powers wound up working for Carl Laemmle when he merged with IMP in 1912. After Powers's time with Warner's Features, he brokered a merger that created Universal Pictures and another that created RKO Radio Pictures. By the late 1920s, he sold Walt Disney a Cinephone to make sound animation films that were distributed through Powers's Celebrity Pictures.

What drew Powers to Warner's Features was the brothers' drive to keep up with demand, and at that point, most exhibitors were looking for three-reel features. In addition, Powers was intrigued by the Warners' willingness to pay top dollar for talent to write, direct, and star in their films. As *Moving Picture World* observed, "the company's policy of paying the highest prices for features has served its purposes in attracting some of the best producers [and directors]."[50] The venture with Powers was another essential learning experience for the brothers. Powers had the capital, and the brothers had the ideas. If the Warners could secure funding, their tested methods of exhibition, distribution, and production were sure to provide big returns. The brothers continued to boast their brand: "Warner's Features have the appeal that fills houses—the 'punch' that builds business—the quality that spells success."[51]

After marrying in 1914, Irma and Jack welcomed a son, Jack Jr., into the world on March 27, 1916. Naming a son after his living father is a forbidden practice in Jewish households, but Jack did not care. After almost a year, Jack Jr. was taken to Youngstown to meet his grandparents, Ben and Pearl. The delay may have been caused by deference to Irma, whose prominent San Francisco family was quite different from the immigrant, working-class Warners. Meeting the large Warner family could not have been easy for Irma, and the Warner sisters proved to be trouble: "Sadie was a critic, Rose a dominant personality, and Annie a quiet lady."[52] It took time for the family to warm up to Irma, and it did not help that she was not a fan of Pearl's kosher cooking.

On to Los Angeles

One day in 1917 Sam walked by a bookstore in Los Angeles. The United States had been involved in World War I since April 6, but the war had been raging overseas since 1914. Sam spotted a poster for *My Four Years in Germany* by James W. Gerard. Under President Woodrow Wilson, Gerard had been the US ambassador to Germany from 1913 to 1917, after serving on the New York Supreme Court from 1907 to 1911. Leading up to and during the war in Europe, Gerard oversaw relations between Germany and Great Britain and fought for Belgian neutrality. Gerard was no stranger to tense politics, having risen through the ranks in New York's Tammany Hall political machine to become a front-running candidate for the US Senate. Early in his tenure as ambassador, Gerard dealt with the kaiser and the ramifications of Germany's attack on the British ocean liner the *Lusitania* in 1915. The attack killed 1,198 people and played a role in the United States' declaration of war on Germany. Gerard found himself in the middle of Germany during this time, making for a harrowing tale.

After reading half the book, Sam phoned his brother Harry and explained the sales potential for a film based on Gerard's story. Engrossed by this contemporary war saga, Sam told Harry, "It's about this big-deal guy's experiences trying to stop the country from getting into the war with the Germans. The story's got the Kaiser, Hindenburg, war speeches in the German Reichstag."[53] Filled with enthusiasm, Sam wired the ambassador in Washington and discovered that Gerard was scheduled to travel by train to California, so Harry hastily bought a ticket and hopped on the same train. Harry made his case during the trip: "Mr. Ambassador, film is the great founder of peace. When people understand each other, they need not fight. I feel it is our patriotic duty . . . to make a motion picture of your book."[54] Harry's words may have sounded overzealous, but there was nothing phony about his intent. Gerard had already had offers from William Fox and Lewis Selznick, but Harry's passion was impressive. He claimed the film "will help arouse the world at large as to why we must fight for civilization." Gerard was convinced and accepted Warner's offer.

The next problem was finding the money to make good on that offer. Harry caught the next train back east to seek backing for the film. Sam and Jack went to New York to rent space at the Biograph, as well as additional spaces in New Jersey. The funding came from Mark M. Dintenfass, who delivered $28,000 in a shoe box and would coproduce the film with the brothers. Dintenfass had previously owned a company that made early sound films with what was called the Cameraphone, later renamed the Actophone. Paranoid about the Edison Trust, Dintenfass had required that all studio guests be approved through a peephole by a watchman. The technology was top secret, and the onscreen talent was not allowed to get a close look at the camera. Such fear was not unwarranted, but Dintenfass slipped up one day while filming on location when a bystander began asking questions about the camera. The bystander was Al McCoy, an Edison employee, and an injunction was filed immediately.

The Warners likely got along with Dintenfass because they had experienced similar dealings with Edison. Dintenfass was taken to court three times and finally managed to avoid jail by promising to give up filmmaking. However, Dintenfass soon approached Sigmund Lubin, who had moved his production facility to the new Lubinville location in Indiana. Having had his own problems with Edison in the past, Lubin quietly rented his extra space on Arch Street to Dintenfass. Terry Ramsaye, who regularly covered the film industry in the trade press, maintained that Dintenfass was difficult to track during this time, but he continued to work without interference.[55] Whatever stability or success Dintenfass found, it allowed him to fund *My Four Years in Germany* and get the Warner brothers one step closer to making feature films. Harry found a screenwriter, Charles Logue, who penned the script and presented the final product to Gerard, who approved. Gerard and Harry finalized the paperwork so filming could begin. The brothers hired William Nigh, fresh off directing a string of dramas for William Fox.

As word of the film spread, more established studios wondered what the brothers were thinking. Who were they to try to step into the big leagues with a feature film of their own? The larger studios issued boycotts, refusing to show the film if it were booked in an affiliated theater. One day, while the brothers were sitting in their New York office, a man came in and offered a lowball price for the film. Assuming the man had been sent by the Edison Trust or even Edison himself, Abe stood up and threatened to throw him out the window. The man promptly left. Soon thereafter the brothers turned down an offer from William Fox, who was one of the most powerful men in the business, having weathered the corrupt Tammany Hall political machine as well as battles with Edison. Fox had one of the most powerful studios, so turning down his offer took chutzpah.

My Four Years in Germany was released through First National and played on a double bill with Charlie Chaplin's *A Dog's Life* (1918). An advertisement in *Exhibitors Herald and Motography* billed the Chaplin film as "the comedy that has made box office history" and hailed the Warners' film as "the screen classic that has put pep in our patriotism."[56] Once again, the Warners associated their brand with top talent. When the film premiered in New York at the end of 1917, the audience gave it a standing ovation, beginning a run that made $800,000 and landed the brothers $130,000 after debts were paid.

Advertisement for *My Four Years in Germany* alongside Charlie Chaplin's *A Dog's Life*.

My Four Years in Germany is significant not only because it was the first feature film produced by the Warner brothers but also because it prefigured the type of headline-driven filmmaking the studio would be known for in the decades to come. The film's depiction of war was so powerful that some audiences felt like they were watching actual newsreel footage. Gerard's story provided explicit details about the German prison camps. As historian Kevin Brownlow observes, "POWs and civilians were shown scrambling for scraps of bread, being attacked by guard dogs, and being repatriated 'the Hindenburg way'—through mass executions."[57] Gerard worked closely with director Nigh to ensure realistic imagery and fidelity to the atrocities taking place in Europe. Actual quotes from Kaiser Wilhelm II were used, and the film was regularly branded as "FACT NOT FICTION."[58] *My Four Years in Germany* is considered one of the first major propaganda films.

My Four Years in Germany elicited a fanatical response in many locations. One screening ended with a model of the kaiser hanging. An American senator stated, "Show these pictures to the American people and you will wipe Germanism from the earth."[59] Others who were less impressed with the film's anti-imperial stance rioted at screenings or cut cables in an attempt to stop the film. In some cities *My Four Years in Germany* outperformed the groundbreaking, albeit deeply racist, *Birth of a Nation* (1915). When the Chicago police censor, Major Metellus Lacullus Cicero Funkhouser, tried to remove scenes from *My Four Years in Germany,* Warner Bros. ultimately got him fired. This was probably for the best, because shortly after Funkhouser was removed, he was put on trial for a string of illegal activities that had occurred under his watch. The offenses included illegal wiretapping and the purchase of liquor (which may have been subject to wartime prohibition) in a variety of sordid locations.

Following *My Four Years in Germany,* the brothers found success with *Pershing's Crusaders.* Released in May 1918, this thirty-seven-minute documentary covered American troops in France during World War I. Albert Warner told *Motion Picture News* that the film had been shown in mining camps, "where formerly motion pictures were unheard of."[60] The film was also exhibited at schools, universities, and town halls and in places as far off the grid as northern Alaska. Warner boasted about the expansive nature of the new medium. In addition, he noted that "ministers in Los Angeles and elsewhere have used *Pershing's Crusaders* as a topical theme of powerful sermons." Warner was careful to note that these sermons were "for and not against motion pictures." The film was also welcomed at YMCA headquarters. Interestingly, it was not long before the clergy were speaking out against the film industry in droves.

In October 1918 Albert was interviewed by *Motion Picture News* about the changing exhibition landscape for feature films. The Warners did good business with *The Kaiser's Finish* (1918), a spy thriller about the last German emperor that included real war footage. The film ran for an unprecedented number of weeks. "A season ago," explained Warner, "arguments and the hardest kind of sales work was needed to convince them [exhibitors] that a booking could be profitable if it was for more than two or three days at most." This was good for the industry because theaters could stretch their investments in films and advertisements instead of shelling out top dollar for new films twice a week. Albert observed that buyers "want war pictures and . . . these will be in demand as long as the war lasts."[61] So, after the armistice on November 11, 1918, the prospect of making a new war film became obsolete. The following February, Albert told *Moving Picture World* he was proud of what *The Kaiser's Finish* said about the history of Germany. Regarding its relevance after the war, he said, "we have lost no sleep" and explained, "we are

The young Warner brothers.

accustomed to jolts in the picture business."[62] Albert told the interviewer how his brothers had survived a series of successes and failures since the dawn of cinema, each time responding with a new successful venture.

In the spirit of trial and error, Sam Warner cowrote a story titled *Open Your Eyes* (1919), which was produced with the cooperation of state health authorities. The film is a bold statement about venereal disease and the danger of sweeping social problems under the rug. The narrative, which follows several individuals with syphilis, was too direct for many audiences. For example, one scene in which a mother is having a sex talk with her daughter is intercut with images of a hen hatching chicks. *Wid's Daily* (the precursor to *Film Daily*) hammered the film, calling it "morbid and unpleasant." Although it was "correct enough in its argument and may act as a warning to young men and women, who are ignorant about the menace of social diseases," this type of picture "does not belong in theaters operated as places of amusement." *Open Your Eyes* was acceptable at a venue that "catered to transients in a downtown district."[63] *Variety* described the film as "plainly a picture tract on syphilis, against prostitution, which is blamed entirely for the inoculation of the unwary, and for the riddance of that scourge, the quack doctor, who poses as a specialist."[64]

Open Your Eyes played in a few cities before getting special treatment in Washington, DC. The president of the Board of Commissioners for the District of Columbia said while introducing the film, "one little streetwalker will spread more disease, cause more misery, ruin more lives, bring about more deaths . . . than all the lepers who have been in the District of Columbia since the foundation of the Government."[65] *Open Your Eyes* was a straightforward propaganda film, and the experience helped the brothers fine-tune their ability to work with government officials. That was not the last time they collaborated with the government on a production, and it certainly would not be the last time the studio made a film that split audiences on moral grounds.

Sam and Jack were operating near downtown Los Angeles at a makeshift studio near producer William Selig's zoo. The Selig zoo had opened in 1915, and one of its animals supposedly served as the iconic MGM lion (according to another report, it came from the Dublin zoo). The brothers made some inexpensive films featuring animals (cheaper to hire than human actors), correctly predicting that audiences would enjoy serials in which dangerous beasts threatened damsels in distress. For example, each episode of the fifteen-part serial *The Lost City* (1920) ended with a cliffhanger to ensure that the audience returned the following week. Another popular serial from the Warners was *The Tiger Band,* starring silent film actress Helen Holmes. Jack said of the popular cliffhanger endings, "The fade-out title CONTINUED NEXT WEEK left the audience in Freudian frustration. As a matter of fact, they really had something to worry about, because the biggest apes were always young guys dressed up in gorilla suits, and people knew very well they weren't going into the cave just to talk about heredity."[66] The serials were popular, but they were even more significant because they represented the earliest use of the abbreviated "Warner Bros." prior to the studio's 1923 incorporation.

Shortly after filming a number of serials, the brothers acquired a new space on Sunset Boulevard near Gower Street and the poverty-row studios. The studio on Sunset was so dilapidated that they refused to put their name out front. Still pinching pennies, Jack Warner got a loan from a young director named Howard Hawks. Though it is not clear how the two met, the professional relationship lasted many years.[67] Hawks directed films for Warner Bros. after it became a major studio. Because Warner had always paid up promptly in the past, Hawks was willing to help him again. The next time Warner was in a tight spot, Hawks agreed to oversee a series of Warner comedies featuring Italian comic Mario Bianchi (stage name Monty Banks). The Warners claimed the new films would "eclipse anything in the line of screen comedy that Mr. Banks has ever attempted."[68] The Welcome Comedies, as they were called, included about two dozen short films that ran from 1920 to 1921. Banks became the go-to comedian on the lot after Jack tried, unsuccessfully, to snatch Harold Lloyd from Hal Roach.[69] Jack recalled that after five Monty Banks films, Hawks "got tired of the rusty old comedy plots and wanted to make epics, and so Sam and I handled the Banks pictures alone."[70]

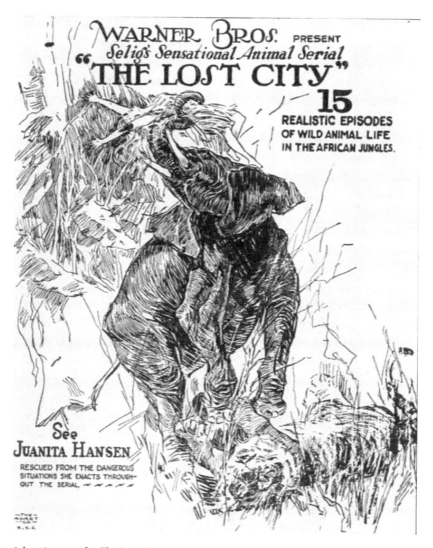

Advertisement for *The Lost City*.

Back in New York, Albert was on the trail of a pretty journalist who had caught his eye. In a 1919 letter from Harry to Jack, the eldest brother explained, "Hope to have some good news for you soon if I can bring Albert down from the clouds. He's nutty about a beautiful girl who writes a picture column in the *Morning Telegraph*. He wants to marry her, but she isn't interested. He takes her out all over New York, is with her all the time, so naturally he can't get his mind on business. No one in California knows much about this girl, but she seems well established here. Her name is Louella Parsons."[71] Jack recalled that Albert "came down [from the clouds] at supersonic speed and landed with a dull thud when Louella turned her big brown eyes on some other suitor." Of course, Parsons was an up-and-coming journalist who became one of the most influential gossip columnists in Hollywood. Her syndicated columns would soon be read around the country. "We never forgave Albert for goofing that courtship," Jack teased. "Just think of the great reviews we could have had all these years if Louella had become Mrs. Albert Warner."[72]

In June 1920 the brothers purchased a 250-by-600-foot property from film pioneer David Horsley, one of the first filmmakers to move to the West Coast. The studio was located at Nineteenth and Main Streets in Los Angeles.[73] The brothers were coy when pressed for details about the new studio, but they planned to build a new lot. Shortly thereafter, they acquired a ten-acre studio lot known as the Sunset Bronson Studios. At the time, its covered stage was the largest in the word, at 350 feet long and 200 feet wide.[74] The purchase price was $25,000, with nothing down and monthly installments of $1,500.

In 1921 Joseph Schenck, Jesse Lasky, Cecil B. DeMille, Carl Laemmle, Jack Warner, and Mary Pickford (among others) created the Motion Picture Relief Fund. The goal was to "take care of our own" by offering medical and hospital care to aging film industry employees.[75] In the studio's later years, Warner Bros. was known to quietly take care of its elder employees, which meant keeping on the payroll silent-era talent that had not made a successful transition into the sound era. It is important to note that this was long before Social Security and the types of pensions enjoyed in the late twentieth and early twenty-first centuries. The film industry recognized the need to take care of those who had helped build its empires. Although there is no shortage of stories about the victims of Hollywood oppression, it is worth noting that the Motion Picture Relief Fund, still in existence today, was a bright spot in this time of strict vertical integration.

The Warners obtained additional financial assistance from Motley Flint, a manager at the Security Bank of Los Angeles who first met the brothers during a rail trip to New York. Flint helped finance *The Tiger Band* and saw potential in the Warners' family business. At a time when the banking industry was experiencing a wave of anti-Semitism that affected many of the early Hollywood moguls, Flint was a trusted friend who treated the Warners fairly and without prejudice. In January 1921 auto manufacturer Henry Ford's *Dearborn Independent* featured columns that warned of "Jew-controlled" movies. "As soon as the Jew gained control of the movies," the article claimed, "we had a movie problem . . . it is the genius of that race to create problems of moral character in whatever business they achieve a majority." With feature films enjoying a prominent role in entertainment, "this simply means that millions of Americans every day place themselves voluntarily within range of Jewish ideas of life, love and labor, within range of Jewish propaganda."[76] Such threats to the Warners' way of life encouraged them to produce films about current events. In 1921 Harry decided to make a series of socially conscious dramas dealing with prejudice and corruption. The films tanked at the box office, but that did not deter the brothers from trying to connect with audiences on important issues.

What saved the studio was Harry Rapf's production of *Why Girls Leave Home* (1921), starring Anna Q. Nilsson and directed by William Nigh. Controversial films were Rapf's specialty; he also produced the racy *Ashamed of Parents* (1921) for Warner Bros., after a successful career producing vaudeville shows. *Why Girls Leave Home*, about the corrupting elements of city life, was a hit and made the studio nearly half a million dollars. The *Chicago Tribune* praised the film and opined, "if you don't like this picture it'll be because you're like a snail—all shell."[77] At the film's gala opening at the Warner Theater in Niles, Ohio, the night's program featured a photograph of Pearl Warner on one side with a caption reading, "The boss of them all."[78] The other side depicted Ben surrounded by his boys, including David. Unfortunately, David was suffering from an infectious disease called encephalitis lethargica, known as the sleeping disease, which reached epidemic proportions between 1915 and 1926. David would be unable to join his brothers in the film business and would live with Ben and Pearl until his death in 1939.

After a decade and a half, the Warners were finally getting some serious attention in the Hollywood trade press. In September 1922 they took out a three-page spread in *Motion Picture News* dedicated to the status and future of Warner productions. Each brother penned a short piece for the issue, featuring a headshot. Harry took issue with producers who oversold their films' quality through "smooth phrasing and ballyhooing" of inferior products.[79] He rightly understood that the result would be a loss of audience enthusiasm for the medium. Movies were just starting to see an increase in audience acceptance, and Harry was smart to attack the Barnum lites of the film business. The brothers were now seasoned veterans in exhibition; they understood the fragility of the business and never took viewer confidence for granted. Harry took truth in advertising seriously, and he always intended to deliver on his promises (going back to the days of shoes "repaired while you wait").

In 1922 the film industry was having image problems. Reports of drugs and debauchery in Tinseltown spread across the nation. When prominent comedian Fatty Arbuckle was accused of rape and murder after one of his wild parties, it only confirmed what some had feared about the film industry on the West Coast. Will Hays, the politically connected postmaster general for the Harding administration, was brought in to serve as commissioner to the movies. Hays stood in front of eighteen hundred members of the Motion Picture Directors Association at New York's Hotel Astor on March 16 and reassured his audience, "If the influence of the motion picture is limitless, and it is undeniable, then just so great is your opportunity, and just so great is your responsibility. That responsibility I accept for the motion picture industry RIGHT NOW!"[80] Hollywood was running the risk of federal intervention if the movie business could not get its act together. Just as baseball found its commissioner after the 1919 Black Sox scandal (a rigged World Series), movies found their czar. Hays chaired the organization that eventually became the Motion Picture Producers and Distributors of America (MPPDA) until 1945.

Harry Warner knew they could not succeed without the public's confidence. He wrote a column that appeared in *Exhibitors Herald* on October 30, 1922, explaining why he and his brothers stood behind Will Hays. "We believe Mr. Hays is performing a wonderful service to the industry," wrote Harry. "He is wielding a powerful weapon in developing the educational as well as the entertainment value and general usefulness of the motion picture in the eyes of the public."[81] Harry was increasingly passionate about using movies as a form of both entertainment and education. But it would be impossible to use motion pictures for the public good if the public lost faith in the medium.

The Warners worked to earn and maintain the public's confidence in multiple ways. Harry stated that the Warner studio was happy to work with Hays to communicate "the great scope of this wonderful medium for the transmission of clean, wholesome and instructive ideas."[82] Harry extolled the power of movies to both educate and entertain, setting up a future Warner Bros. slogan. More than any of the brothers, Harry was acutely aware of the power wielded by cinema, and in the coming decades, he would regularly refer to film as a powerful communication tool. One publicity stunt involved a float that traveled across the country advertising popular books by authors such as Sinclair Lewis and F. Scott Fitzgerald that would become Warner film adaptations. Producer Harry Rapf explained that Warner filmmakers were working toward the goal of "good stories well directed."[83] The advertising campaign reminded audiences that the Warners had their finger on the pulse of America. The Warner float stopped in every major city on its way west, delivering a letter from Will Hays to governors and city officials. *Motion Picture News* estimated that twenty-five million people saw the Warner float during its journey, which covered the top half of the country on its way to Los Angeles and made the return trip through the southern states.[84] The Warners' bid to restore the public's confidence in cinema was under way.

At the end of 1922 the Warners filed for a new trademark: "Warner Brothers' Classics of the Screen." Harry said the trademark was meant to set the brothers apart from other film production companies, which were too numerous to count. Harry assured audiences that Warner films were "distinctly individual in production and story value, and in excellence of screen players."[85] Sam and Jack, who oversaw day-to-day activities on the lot, elaborated the importance of reliable producers. It was up to them to provide a quality product for Harry and Albert to sell to exhibitors. Sam and Jack compared their dedication to quality to that of stage producer David Belasco, who had recently brought Avery Hopwood's *The Gold Diggers* to Broadway. Audiences knew that a Belasco production meant quality, and Warner Bros. hoped to achieve the same kind of name recognition.

Jack Jr. considered his father's early days in the film business as the best years of his life. The two often walked to the studio, and according to Jack Jr., on some days his dad danced the whole way there. Jack Sr. was interested in every detail of production, which included getting behind the camera to direct when necessary. There is even photographic proof that Jack spent some time in the director's chair for *Miracles of the Jungle* (1922). "If he needed a crowd, the extras would be friends and family," said Jack Jr., who was often one of those extras. The extras were paid with lunch. He remembered watching Jack and Sam set up a production somewhere on "Sunset Boulevard or on the beach or in the hills where Dodger stadium is now, and they'd stage

Jack Warner directing.

chase scenes."[86] Once filming was complete, the brothers would expect the crew to make a film out of the sometimes randomly shot footage.

Cinematographer Byron Haskin recalled his time with the Warners in the early 1920s. "I remember many times that word would come out onto the stage, 'Get ready, the stockholders are coming. H. M. [Harry M. Warner] is bringing a group of potential investors out.' We would get every camera out of the vaults, set it up on a phony set, and grab a few of the extra people around." Haskin continued, "Anybody was the director, anybody was the cameraman. . . . Nothing was actually happening; no film in the cameras or anything. Then H. M. would take them walking through and Jack would tell them, 'Well, there's Monte Blue, and here's Marie Prevost,' and they'd shake hands and so forth. Then they'd go through the laboratories."[87] The brothers were confident in their future potential, but they needed to make it appear that they had already arrived. By the early 1920s, the Warner name had been around long enough that investors believed in the brothers' staying power and their ability to weather financial storms in an uncertain industry. Harry knew how to talk the talk, but he also knew how to put his money where his mouth was.

2

Incorporation, Innovation, Triumph, and Tragedy

1923–1929

"Hollywood, California, [was] a land of gold, golden sunshine, ripe orang-
es and stately palm trees," remembered Johnny O'Steen, longtime Warner
Bros. story librarian. "A person could get rich there in no time at all while
enjoying all of the benefits of such a fine climate where it seldom rained and
almost never snowed." O'Steen, who got his start during Hollywood's salad
days, observed, "In some ways it was sort of paradise in the 1920s. Times
were good, there were jobs for those who wanted them. And there was no
denying that the climate made it a great place to live and work." However,
O'Steen had a more realistic perspective too: "What those far away film fans
didn't know was that film studios were a far cry from what they imagined.
Those studios were factories, with office buildings, and were in business to
make profits. A lot of hard work went into those efforts."[1] Warner Bros. was
like a well-oiled assembly line, humming for long hours over many decades
to create innumerable classic films.

The Warner family had a banner year in 1923. *Film Daily* reported that
on April 4, Warner Bros. was officially incorporated in the state of Delaware
as a $50 million highly capitalized corporation. The Warners actually cre-
ated three corporations and issued five hundred shares of stock. A second
corporation was "organized under California laws as a holding company
for various studio properties and other real estate," with assets controlled by
Sam and Jack; a third entity was created to hold the New York offices, where
Harry primarily worked; and all the Warner companies operated under the
umbrella of the Delaware corporation.[2] The Warners reserved $4 million
for film production, and eighteen motion pictures were planned, including
adaptations of four David Belasco plays: *Deburau, Daddies, Tiger Rose,* and

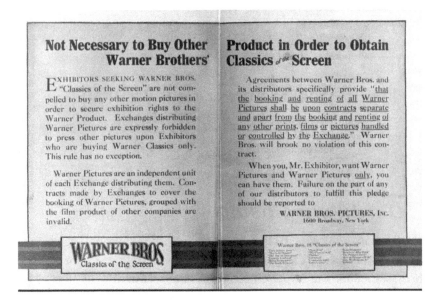

Not Necessary to Buy Other Warner Brothers' Product in Order to Obtain Classics *of the* Screen

EXHIBITORS SEEKING WARNER BROS. "Classics of the Screen" are not compelled to buy any other motion pictures in order to secure exhibition rights to the Warner Product. Exchanges distributing Warner Pictures are expressly forbidden to press other pictures upon Exhibitors who are buying Warner Classics only. This rule has no exception.

Warner Pictures are an independent unit of each Exchange distributing them. Contracts made by Exchanges to cover the booking of Warner Pictures, grouped with the film product of other companies are invalid.

Agreements between Warner Bros. and its distributors specifically provide "that the booking and renting of all Warner Pictures shall be upon contracts separate and apart from the booking and renting of any other prints, films or pictures handled or controlled by the Exchange." Warner Bros. will brook no violation of this contract.

When you, Mr. Exhibitor, want Warner Pictures and Warner Pictures only, you can have them. Failure on the part of any of our distributors to fulfill this pledge should be reported to

WARNER BROS. PICTURES, Inc.
1600 Broadway, New York

WARNER BROS
Classics of the Screen

Warner Bros. Classics of the Screen advertisement, 1923.

The Gold Diggers. Nearly $2 million was set aside to make these prestige productions.

Exhibitors Trade Review carried an advertisement listing the Warners' terms for rental of their "Classics of the Screen" brand. With the advent of block booking (which forced exhibitors to rent a studio's weakest titles to get the more prestigious star vehicles) well under way, Warner Bros. promised exhibitors that they would not be subject to strict contracts and that each film rental would be a separate transaction. The advertisement reprinted the studio's clause O in full.[3] The brothers believed in their product and did not need to rely on fine print to make a buck. Warner Bros. continued to advertise that same promise for the remainder of the year, and it asked that any distributor violating those terms be reported to the studio's New York offices.[4] The advertisement featured a list of the eighteen "Classics of the Screen" produced by Warner Bros. in 1923. By July, at least three films, including the adaptation of Sinclair Lewis's *Main Street*, had played for three weeks straight, solidifying Warner Bros. as a contender in Hollywood.[5]

Noting audiences' desire for high-quality films, Harry told exhibitors in August to "keep open play dates for the big ones that are coming, and don't clutter up your schedule with a lot of junk pictures." Warner Bros. films, he assured exhibitors, were "without question attractions of the highest order ever produced by a single organization." Boasting about Warner's upcoming slate, he said, "There are plenty of good pictures in the independent field, and the Warner Brothers are helping to fill the demand for big pictures by bringing forth eighteen great plays and novels," at a cost of $5.5 million for production and advertising. Harry made sure to name some of the prominent stars currently on the Warner lot, including Monte Blue, Marie Prevost, John Barrymore, and Mae Marsh, among others.[6]

In September Abe told the trade press that raising the standards of showmanship in motion pictures was the key to success for any major film company. He noted that the cost per production had been between $50,000 and $100,000 in 1921; by 1923, it had increased to $150,000 to $400,000. Part of that cost was higher advertising expenses, as well as bigger budgets to hire major stars. Abe assured exhibitors that Warner's films "have persistently worked for a faithful adherence to theme and plot of books and plays," exemplifying the studio's desire to cater to public interest.[7] Of course, part of the public relations plan was to show allegiance to the newly formed Motion Picture Producers and Distributors of America (MPPDA) by stating that "Warner Brothers have done their utmost to conform and raise the standard of showmanship."[8] The last thing any studio wanted after the inception of the MPPDA was to stray from the line of decency drawn and maintained by Will Hays.

Nobody knew that the next big star at Warner Bros. was going to be a canine. Harry Rapf first brought the idea of a Rin Tin Tin film to Jack Warner.[9] It became Hal Wallis's job to market the pooch. Wallis was first hired by Sam Warner as an assistant publicity director. Wallis had a deep appreciation for Sam, whom he called "the most brilliant of the brothers."[10] According to Wallis, Sam was the "nice, soft-spoken, underplayed character of the group."[11] Harry Warner later fired Wallis for taking outside accounts, even though the side jobs had been approved by Jack. When the studio's next publicity director left, Jack rehired Wallis at double his previous salary. Wallis made press books and arranged interviews; he took "well-known journalists to stars' homes for photographs and light conversation . . . reporters were not vicious then but were thrilled to meet the stars."[12] Similarly, he recalled that the stars were ordinary people, unpretentious and easy to relate to. Those were the days when one could still ride a horse through Beverly Hills, and Sunset Boulevard still had a bridle path.

Left to right: Darryl Zanuck, Jack Warner, Rin Tin Tin, and the pup's owner Lee Duncan. (Author's personal collection)

Wallis did not see Harry or Albert often, as they were mostly in New York, where Harry worked on payroll and Abe on sales. Wallis's office at the studio was near Jack's, just left of the main entrance, and the two spoke frequently. "He telephoned me every morning from the toilet," said Wallis. "When I heard him ask 'what's doing?' in that familiar brisk, hard-bitten voice, I knew he was on the Throne." Their conversations often ended with a flush. Whenever a film got a bad review, Jack brushed it off by saying, "Don't worry about it: today's newspaper is tomorrow's toilet paper." Wallis described Jack as a natty dresser; he often wore "yachting blazers with highly polished patent leather shoes, he always sported a big smile, he had a remarkable set of flashing white teeth." Jack was always looking to get in on the studio publicity, often making unattainable, grandiose suggestions. "He liked telling very bad jokes in a loud voice," Wallis remembered. "I did my best to be a good audience."[13]

Wallis claimed that Rin Tin Tin was "almost human," and he took the dog on a tour around the country to increase his celebrity. Rinty, as he was called, had been in some films and had been featured in the *Los Angeles Times* following a dog show at the Ambassador Hotel. Rinty could pick up change with his nose, jump up and land on a stool, count with his paws, and bark in ragtime. The dog was owned by Lee Duncan, a World War I veteran who had found him on the western front, left behind by German soldiers. Rin Tin Tin was the nickname soldiers gave to yarn dolls they kept as good-luck charms. The pup certainly brought good fortune to Warner Bros., starring in his first smash hit in 1923, *Where the North Begins*. When Jack Warner needed a follow-up film featuring his canine star, he offered the project to silent film actor Malcolm St. Clair, who recommended his friend Darryl F. Zanuck. It was Zanuck who boosted the dog's image as a star, to the great benefit of the studio.

Later, in an interview with the *Los Angeles Examiner,* Jack confessed a secret: "I guess there is no harm now in revealing what was secret information for so many years around the lot. It had occurred to us, when we realized Rinty's earning capacity, that our investment would be lost if anything happened to him." Warner claimed (although Duncan contested the story), "with Duncan's consent, we agreed to breed and train a kennel full of doubles that could be used if our hero were ill or injured or even killed in some of the dangerous stunts we planned."[14] The truth is that there were multiple Rintys because each dog had its own unique skill.

Zanuck was determined to be a writer, having traveled the country writing stories, with minimal success. After arriving in Hollywood, he sold some of his stories to studios and worked as a gag writer for Mack Sennett, Harold Lloyd, and Charlie Chaplin.[15] Legend has it that St. Clair brought Zanuck along when he pitched a story called "Find Your Man" to Jack Warner as the next vehicle for Rin Tin Tin. The story was about a dog that witnesses a murder and, when his owner is accused of the crime, works tirelessly to get justice for his human friend. The tall, thin Zanuck got down on all fours and barked along as St. Clair detailed the story, and his antics sold the picture. The film was so popular that, according to Wallis, the dog received twelve thousand fan letters every week.[16]

When Harry Rapf left and took a job with MGM, Zanuck replaced him as producer. Zanuck became so important to Warner Bros. that he made $5,000 per week as production manager, "the highest post possible without

Main entrance to the Warners' first Los Angeles studio.

being a Warner brother."[17] Alma Young, who was a script girl at Warner Bros. from 1923 to 1960, remembered that when Zanuck first arrived at the lot, "he got past the guy at the desk and walked into Jack Warner's office, and Jack Warner called the guy and [had Zanuck] . . . taken by the nape of the neck and thrown out." Young claimed that Zanuck eventually won Jack's respect with his tenacity. Their mutual interest in playing poker did not hurt either. She recalled that in those early days, Jack was transfixed as he watched the actors during film shoots, Sam was more interested in the film equipment, and Harry quickly passed through the sets, always focused on issues beyond the lot.[18]

Zanuck spent about a decade at the studio—long enough to form some opinions about the brothers. "Harry, being president, was prone to jump on Jack for any film that did not come out well," said Zanuck. "Sam was the bridge between them. . . . Jack played a role like Louis B. Mayer [who ran MGM but reported to bosses in New York] to a certain extent. It was a gentleman's role. He could captivate you." Jack's antics were well known at the studio, which is why one biographer referred to him as the "Clown Prince of Hollywood." Zanuck saw Harry and Jack as opposites. "Anyone who got over two thousand dollars a week [Harry] hated instantly even if he never met him. In Harry's mind, everybody was a thief, including Jack for condoning extravagances. What a boring guy Harry was. Jack was unreliable, but never boring."[19] Zanuck's views are predictable, given that he was similar to Jack in many ways.

Probably the most ill-suited person to join Warner Bros. during the 1920s was Jewish German auteur Ernst Lubitsch. The director was brought to America by Mary Pickford and landed a six-film contract with Warner Bros. in August 1923. Alma Young worked with Lubitsch, translating his scripts into English. Lubitsch's manager translated the script from German to French, and Alma translated it from French into English. Lubitsch directed five social satires for Warner: *The Marriage Circle* (1924), *Three Women* (1924), *Kiss Me Again* (1925), *Lady Windermere's Fan* (1925), and *So This Is Paris* (1926). While Lubitsch gave the studio the prestige and critical acclaim it desired, the director was not happy on the lot. He pushed for more control, which did not sit well with Jack and Harry. When Lubitsch requested story control, Harry reminded him that their contract allowed Warner Bros. to choose all story options. Lubitsch could pick from an approved list and had to give six weeks' notice before starting his next film.[20] Harry thought Lubitsch's films were too subtle. "The world wants thrill and excitement," the studio president said. "We want you to make bigger pictures hereafter but you should listen to what the world wants."[21] Lubitsch eventually left the studio, claiming that Warner Bros. had stalled his career. Paramount and MGM bought out the remainder of his contract. Harry Warner said of Lubitsch's departure, "It is a lucky star that this is off our hands, because I think [Lubitsch] is the worst lemon . . . , so thank the Lord this is over."[22]

Warner Bros. Experiments with Sound

Warner Bros. had come a long way in a few years. Gone were the days of hopping between rented spaces to make films. The brothers maintained a booming lot on Sunset Boulevard, bankable stars such as John Barrymore and Rin Tin Tin were identified with the studio, and new and inventive producers like Wallis and Zanuck were arriving, but the brothers did not yet have a major Hollywood studio. Their largest competitors owned national and international distribution networks, making the Warners look as if they were stuck on the "up-and-coming" treadmill. Being a shrewd and brilliant businessman, Harry was always eyeing expansion. His days managing grocery stores and shoe repair shops taught him that if you did not keep moving and growing, the world would leave you behind. Waddill Catchings, Harry's friend from Goldman Sachs, helped finance Woolworth's and Sears Roebuck's growth into national chains. Catchings had confidence in Harry's unflinching drive, but he also understood that "the consumer-oriented 1920s economy provided a fertile atmosphere for boundless growth in the movie field."[23] Harry brought Catchings onto the Warner Bros. board of directors and appointed him chairman of the finance committee. Catchings, in return, set up a $3 million credit line that gave Warner Bros. the backing to produce the films necessary to compete with major studios.

Around the same time Harry was brokering the deal with Catchings, the technologically savvy Sam was setting up a radio station in the new building at 6433 Sunset Boulevard (which would become the Warner Hollywood Theater). KFWB, the Warners' new radio station, featured the studio's contract stars on the air beginning in March 1925. The master of ceremonies was Jack Warner, and the first performer was Leon Zuardo—an embarrassingly out-of-tune singer who was actually Jack. When the song was over, Wallis recalled, it was followed by thunderous applause "from members of the Warner staff who valued their jobs."[24]

The studio hired Western Electric engineer Nathan Levinson to help Sam set up the radio station. Shortly thereafter Sam tapped Levison to test different processes for sound film. As Wallis recalled, their first test film featured a man saying "good evening" and then singing along with a piano and a violin.[25] Sam then approached Harry to discuss moving the studio into synchronized sound production.[26] Western Electric had developed sound-on-disk technology, but it had been rejected by every studio it approached.

Alma Young recalled Sam struggling to get money to create Vitaphone, the company that could bring Warner Bros. into the sound era.[27] Sam was working closely with Frank Murphy, the head electrician at the Sunset studio. Electricity was an interesting topic of conversation at Warner Bros. Jack always complained about how much they had to pay for electricity in the early years. Studio employees remembered Jack's eccentric behavior. "He would walk into an office, turn off the lights, and say 'what are you trying to do, compete with daylight?'"[28] Cinematographer Byron Haskin shared similar memories of Jack's penny-pinching. In addition to his obsession with the lights, Haskin recalled Jack making a stink about the nails that fell to the ground as carpenters built the sets. He would say, "Why don't they put the nails in the board, instead of throwing them in the air?" The studio spent

$11,500 for a "magnet machine that would go around the lot and pick up all these vagrant nails," said Haskin. "I kid you not."[29]

Harry, meanwhile, was in the process of negotiating the purchase of Vitagraph, his primary interest in the Brooklyn-based studio being its international network of film exchanges. Vitagraph was already a storied company, founded in 1897 by J. Stuart Blackton and Albert E. Smith. The two men had gained experience as showmen onstage. Smith's particular skill was shadowgraphy, using "projectors with a self-contained gas light source designed to cast still images from a glass slide through a lens and onto a screen."[30] William "Pop" Rock, a third partner, was brought in to help with distribution. According to Smith, Vitagraph newsreel cameras were on the scene during the Spanish-American War and the Boer War around the turn of the century. However, there are no documents to support Smith's stories of meeting Teddy Roosevelt and his Rough Riders in Cuba.[31] Although Vitagraph cameramen did shoot footage for Roosevelt, it is doubtful that Smith was there. Blackton and Smith were always reconstructing their narrative, which in the early twentieth century often meant reorganizing their company to avoid patent lawsuits from Thomas Edison. The famed inventor hurled numerous lawsuits at Vitagraph over the years, while simultaneously stealing its technology and films and selling them as his own.[32]

Vitagraph had an interesting relationship with Edison, beginning when Blackton met the inventor while working as a reporter for the *Evening World*. There are multiple accounts of why Blackton got the assignment to interview Edison, but Blackton's biographer posits that if he was not acting "as a spy or full-dress rival," he was undoubtedly acting "as someone with a direct business interest in the research being carried out by the technicians working under Edison."[33] Vitagraph eventually became part of Edison's Motion Picture Patents Corporation. Smith claimed that Edison lifted one of his patents, but contrary to popular belief, Edison "was not an ogre among saints. There were no principal ogres; wars were declared by all camps. It was a day of dark doings—plots and counterplots, conspiracy, poaching, privateering."[34] Certainly, there might have been an element of sweet revenge when Warner Bros. purchased Vitagraph, a former beneficiary of the Edison Trust. After being one of the companies shut down and sidelined by Edison, Warner Bros. had achieved a status that allowed it to buy one of the companies that was responsible, in part, for keeping new film businesses out of the competition.

Vitagraph produced the first film adaptation of *Les Miserables*. It was also home to some of the first major movie stars, including Florence Turner, Maurice Costello, Dolores Costello, Norma Talmadge, and Helen Hayes, the "first lady of the American theater." One of the reasons Vitagraph's players became major stars was Blackton's role in cocreating a publicity machine through *Motion Picture Story Magazine*. The publication "began in 1911 with a circulation of 50,000, rose in 1912 to 110,000, and by 1914 was 250,000."[35] Along with *Photoplay* and *Picture Play*, *Motion Picture Story Magazine* (which changed its name to *Motion Picture Magazine* by 1914) helped make both movies and their onscreen talent famous. During the early twentieth century, studios hired people to perform many tasks. Even the actors built sets or answered phones when not in front of the camera. Maurice Costello would play a role in changing that policy at Vitagraph, which helped onscreen talent fine-tune their performance while offscreen.

Even though Vitagraph was in financial trouble, Harry saw its holdings as an opportunity to expand the Warner Bros. network. One of its lucrative holdings was the distribution network V-L-S-E Incorporated, an agreement among Vitagraph, Lubin, Selig, and Essanay. The distribution network had almost merged with Paramount, but Vitagraph purchased the remaining controlling interest. Harry closed the deal to buy Vitagraph in April 1925. Smith remembered that final handshake: Harry Warner "walked out and there was a terrible silence in the room, as if every living hope had gone with him and I was left in a vast empty amphitheater swept clean of memories near and dear."[36] Smith may have been a bit melodramatic, but by this time, Blackton had left the company and longtime partner Rock had died, although his son was still involved in the business. The company had a million dollars in debt, and it was time for Smith to move on.

After buying the controlling interest in Vitagraph, Harry Warner issued a statement to the press. "We are taking over Vitagraph to distribute our future product over the world through its offices," which included twenty-nine film exchanges in North America, ten in England, and another ten throughout the rest of Europe.[37] The Vitagraph offices in Paris serviced Europe as well as a large chunk of Latin America. Reporting on the purchase, *Exhibitors Herald* noted, "Vitagraph was probably the largest realty holder in the matter of ownership and exchanges in the industry."[38] Harry promised to finish the productions already in progress at the studio, although the Vitagraph sound laboratory team would soon move to Warner Bros. on the West Coast.

Warner Bros. also purchased theaters in key areas, including the Orpheum in Chicago and the Piccadilly (soon to be renamed the Warner Theater) in New York, which served as the studio's flagship.[39] The manager of the Piccadilly, Lee Ochs, "was so impressed by the Warner product that he determined to give his patrons no other."[40] Warner Bros. announced the "Warner Forty," a list of new releases contained in a feature article in *Moving Picture World*. The films included four Rin Tin Tin stories, Lubitsch's *Lady Windermere's Fan*, and another yet-to-be-produced film from the director prior to his departure. *The Sea Beast*, featuring silent megastar John Barrymore, would be one of the studio's most successful films of 1926, along with *Don Juan*. Darryl Zanuck cowrote two films, including the adventure romance *Across the Pacific* (1926). Monte Blue, who got his start as an extra and stuntman for D. W. Griffith, became a mainstay at Warner Bros., starring in the Lubitsch comedy *So This Is Paris* (1926).

The notion of synchronized sound film became something of an entrepreneurial contagion, as even the influential Thomas Edison could not sell his phonograph sound technology. The phonograph "emitted a harsh, metallic sound, and its volume was never sufficient to fill a large vaudeville theater."[41] The idea of sound movies was considered dead by 1915, and any further investment in the technology was deemed questionable. In 1924 Western Electric experimented with sound and demonstrated its findings to potential investors. These demonstrations were conducted by Walter J. Rich, who took the technology all over Hollywood and around the country. Adolph Zukor of Paramount (formerly Famous Players–Lasky) was unmoved. Rich connected with Warner Bros. in 1925, which had become more interested since the Vitagraph acquisition.

Harry wanted to be in competition with the big three—First National, Paramount, and MGM—before making any risky moves. During a convention for the Motion Picture Theater Owners of America in Milwaukee in May 1925, Harry challenged Marcus Loew (MGM), Adolph Zukor (Paramount), and Al Rockett (First National) to "lay all the cards on the table."[42] Smaller companies such as Warner Bros., United Artists, and Universal were concerned that the major studios were working together to keep other production companies out of their exhibition networks. Interestingly, similar charges of monopolistic practices reared up in later decades, and Warner Bros. was accused of being one of the culprits. In the 1920s, however, the not yet vertically integrated companies were worried that collusion was keeping them out of the competition. One problem was the lack of reliable information floating around the conference of theater owners, including a rumor that Warner Bros. was going to merge with MGM—a rumor the brothers quickly denied.

Rockett and MGM's Irving Thalberg reassured the concerned parties that they were not keeping anyone out of the competition. "If there is a war going on, we don't know about it," countered Thalberg. "Pictures worth a first run will always get it, no matter who the producing organization is."[43] For Thalberg, owning key theaters in big cities did not entitle exhibitors to force inferior products on the public. Rockett responded by opposing any monopoly in the film industry. Harry was concerned that Rockett and Thalberg might have been unaware of the maneuvering going on at the corporate level. The ultimate plan among the independent owners convened in Milwaukee was to combine their funds and invest $500,000 in a press campaign to boost the independent companies, in the hope of balancing out the competition. Universal's Carl Laemmle contributed $50,000. After $400,000 was raised, $100,000 was earmarked for "the fighting fund against the combine."[44]

The fighting words from Milwaukee were covered at length in *Moving Picture World*. In an essay titled "The Significance of Milwaukee," conference organizer Sydney S. Cohen called the meeting a success because it brought "unity to theater owners to a degree never before dreamed of."[45] No longer did smaller companies have to buy product in May that would not be available until later in the year. Sam Warner wrote that the most important part of the convention was "getting acquainted firsthand with our product and other independent product." He noted, "Before the convention no exhibitor booking in the independent field knew exactly just what product could be obtained for their playdates." The Milwaukee convention brought to light that eight hundred films were ready for circulation throughout the independent networks. Warner Bros. had forty films, according to Sam, adding that "product for 1925–26 remains unsold and is open to anyone who wants it."[46]

With a better understanding of their place in the industry, Sam and Levinson convinced Harry to listen to a twelve-piece orchestra performing at the Bell Telephone Laboratories in New York. What Harry did not know was that he was actually listening to a recording being played to accompany moving images on a screen. When he found out, he was so stunned that he looked behind the screen to make sure there were no musicians playing real instruments. Harry was finally convinced, recalling later that if Sam and Levinson "had said talking picture I never would have gone, because [talking pictures] had been made up to that point several times, and each was a failure."[47] Harry's plan was to start recording all the greatest musical acts. The studio's newly acquired theaters would be outfitted for sound, positioning Warner Bros. on the cutting edge of production and exhibition. Now the challenge was to convince audiences, who were also familiar with the long, failed history of talking pictures, to open their minds to this new technology.

Walter Rich, Waddill Catchings, and Harry Warner met with executives at Western Electric and inked a deal for a one-year contract under which Sam and his team would turn their experiments into a system that could be reproduced. Owing to Harry's insistence, Western Electric agreed to quit using the term "talking picture" and to focus completely on synchronizing music. Harry contracted with the most prominent musical talent to record for Vitaphone, the Warners' new subsidiary. This was a smart move, as it drew on a built-in fan base and exposed them to this new technology. By December 1925, Warner Bros. was negotiating an exclusive contract with Western Electric to develop sound films. In early 1926 a new representative from Western Electric, John Otterson, tried to rein in the deal by asserting more control over the pricing of equipment and services. Otterson was unsuccessful, as Harry's clout with Goldman Sachs held sway. Western Electric signed an agreement with Vitaphone in April 1926 for all sound film production and distribution.

Albert and Sam both celebrated weddings in 1925, in April and July, respectively. Albert's first wife, Bessie Krieger, had died in 1923 due to complications of influenza. Albert subsequently became close with Bessie Siegal, the widow of his friend Jonas Siegal, and the two were married shortly thereafter. Albert and Bessie traveled to Europe that summer, and always with a mind on the family business, Albert collected information about theaters abroad. The couple had two children and remained married until Albert's death.

Despite Sam's work-centered lifestyle, he too managed to find love. Lina Basquette was born in 1907, after the Warners had already ventured into the film business. Lina had started acting in films as a child, appearing in Lois Weber's *Shoes* (1916). The experience was not fun for Lina, who did not like Weber because she resembled Lina's overbearing stage mother, Gladys. During the production, Lina's father committed suicide, which Lina blamed on her "mother's hunger for money."[48] In 1925 Sam saw Lina perform in a stage production of *Louie the 14th* and fell in love. She remembered that he "sent backstage an orchid corsage with an invitation to dinner for both me and my mother, who was guarding me like the Holy Grail."[49] Gladys was closer to Sam's age than her daughter was, and according to Lina, he "was bargaining [for Lina] through the one source who held the key to the merchandise . . . Mama!"[50] Lina did not want to marry Sam, a much older man, but her mother pushed for the arrangement, "having fallen for [Sam's] dazzling self-promotion, and imagining he was as rich as other Hollywood producers."[51] Of course, although Warner Bros. was growing fast, major profits were yet to come. Looking back, Lina said she "always suspected he had an affair with my mother during the two months he took us out to 'dinner.'"[52] One issue that mattered more to Sam's family than Lina's was faith: she was Catholic. "To my mother," recalled Lina, "Sam had one major virtue—he was a motion picture producer." Besides, according to Gladys, "he doesn't [even] look Jewish!"[53]

Another problem was that Lina was still hung up on an old flame, MGM director Jack Conway. "But I couldn't help liking Sam," Lina wrote in her autobiography. "He had an amiable, outgoing personality, and while he seemed 'old,' he was not unattractive. He was stocky, blondish with a broad friendly smile." Lina was terrified to admit to anyone that she still loved Conway. When she tried to tell Sam how she really felt, he interrupted and said, "Sure I know. How can a lil' innocent kid like you know about love. It's jake wid me dat you LIKE me. De rest'll come later."[54] Sam is quoted throughout Lina's autobiography in a similar manner, mocking his unrefined speech. Lina pleaded with her mother to call off the marriage, but Gladys's gold-digging knew no bounds. "Too late, Lina," she said. "It'll be a disgrace to us all if you back out now. All that stuff Sam has given us, it would have to go back."[55] Lina would have been willing to return everything.

Gladys picked out Lina's wedding ring, and the couple wed on July 4, 1925. The ceremony was performed at the apartment of Rabbi Nathan Krass. Lina's maid of honor was Pauline Mason, and Sam's best man was banker Motley Flint. None of Sam's family was present (Albert was in Europe; Jack, Ben, and Pearl were in Los Angeles; and Harry was either out of state or refused to attend the wedding on religious grounds). Immediately after the ceremony, Lina felt ill and ran to the bathroom; actress Constance Bennett followed and tried to comfort her. Lina did not want to admit her dismay at marrying Sam, but Bennett could read her like a book. "Take it easy, Lina," she said. "You'll make it—as long as you have a sense of humor. Sam's not a bad guy—as men go."[56] The reception was held at the Hotel Biltmore, and the newlyweds spent the night at the Congress Hotel. Despite Lina's worry about her lack of feelings for Sam, she colorfully described the wedding night and how it helped her fall in love with her husband.

Lina was soon steeped in both the family and the business, which were often one and the same. Sam gave his new wife the lowdown on the Warner family. He explained that although the brothers did not show great warmth toward one another, they remained incredibly loyal. Sam said he was close to Abe, did not care much for Harry's wife, and joked that Jack thought he was "the biggest swordsman in Hollywood."[57] Jack's skirt chasing was a major reason for the breakup of his marriage to Irma. Sam spoke warmly of his sister Anna but was not so gracious about her husband, who remained on the studio payroll as a favor to their sister. Ben and Pearl received the usual praise, but Sam warned Lina that Pearl was known to have difficulty warming up to her sons' wives. Sam also described his brother Dave as loony, not fully understanding his brother's illness (encephalitis lethargica).

Back in Hollywood, Mr. and Mrs. Sam Warner were welcomed to the studio by a KFWB jazz band. Lina colorfully described the Sunset lot as "a postage stamp dictatorship nestled between bigger and more powerful kingdoms, trying to emulate the established monarchies of movieland."[58] Lina described Sam as being the most well-liked brother. He had "sandy hair with flecks of gray and was tall . . . he always wore a three-piece suit," and before their marriage, he had apparently been "quite a guy with the gals."[59] Lina saw Jack as a less likable version of Sam, with a deep roster of yes-men. Bess Meredyth, matron of the lot, worked in the scenario department and, according to Sam, "keeps track of where de bodies are buried."[60] It was Meredyth who urged Jack to bring director Michael Curtiz to Warner Bros. in 1926. In addition to landing one of the studio's most reliable directors, Jack may have been unaware that he was also playing matchmaker: Curtiz and Meredyth wed in 1929.

Lina described Hollywood of the mid-1920s as surprisingly exclusive, in the sense that many parties around town were restricted (no Jews allowed). Marion Davies and publishing magnate William Randolph Hearst once hosted a party for Lina and Sam, but the other brothers were not invited. Presumably, because Sam had married a Catholic, he was now more acceptable in certain anti-Semitic circles. The couple encountered Jack Conway at some of these parties, leading only to friendly chitchat and shop talk. Sam

Sam Warner, Lina Basquette
Warner, Herman Heller
(Warner Bros. musical
director), and a Charlie
Chaplin imitator.

was soon needed back in New York to continue his work on Vitaphone. He
was suffering from regular sinus infections, which left him weak, but always
the workaholic, he pushed forward. Sam and Lina leased a home on Long
Island, once again getting past the gates in a restricted neighborhood because
of Lina's crucifix. And they were expecting their first child. Lina recalled
getting in hot water with the extended Warner family during a dinner she
hosted at their Long Island home: she forgot the orthodox kashruth rule
against shellfish. It was not entirely Lina's fault. Sam, who described himself
as the rebel outsider of the family, considered shirking the rules no big deal.

The Warner brothers continued to improve their stature with a lengthy
feature in *Moving Picture World* in August 1925. They were "about to launch
what they believe will prove the most gigantic and comprehensive national
advertising campaign in motion picture history."[61] The goal was to reach
eleven hundred newspapers and provide information on both the Warner
product and the venues that showcased the films. These advertisements built
brand recognition by highlighting stars like John Barrymore and directors like
Ernst Lubitsch, and the studio logo was prominently displayed. The serialized
stories used as source material for new films would also be published across
the nation. "The very essence of motion picture fandom will be reached

through page advertising to be run through a year in five of the leading fan magazines of the country."[62] The campaign emphasized the studio's impressive stock company of onscreen talent, including Lowell Sherman, Syd Chaplin, Irene Rich, Monte Blue, Marie Prevost, Helene Costello, Dolores Costello, Myrna Loy, and, of course, Rin Tin Tin. Harry Warner also worked out a deal to purchase First National studios, including their network of theaters. Warner Bros. now had the firepower to be a real contender in Hollywood.

According to Lina, Sam was offered a job as executive producer at Paramount, and she was smitten with the idea of her husband working for Zukor and a company as prestigious as Paramount. Lina saw Warner Bros. as a "third rate celluloid junkyard," citing Sam's own fear of what would happen to the studio if Vitaphone did not take off. The only problem was that his brothers, especially Harry, had warmed to the idea of venturing into synchronized sound, and they needed something to catapult Warner Bros. ahead of the others. It was a gamble, to be sure, but that was what the brothers did best. Sam was also hesitant to leave the family business—a move that would have destroyed his parents. It is unclear how serious the Paramount offer was, although the studio was in the process of merging Famous Players–Lasky with Balaban and Katz, both operating under the Paramount banner. Lina maintained that Paramount wanted both Sam and Vitaphone, but there is little evidence to support her claim. With the skepticism surrounding talking pictures at the time, it is difficult to know whether Zukor's offer was real. In her autobiography, Lina claims that Sam had decided to leave his brothers and had presented them with a well-rehearsed resignation. But the brothers convinced Sam to stay, showing once again that the Warners' blood bond could not be broken. Lina was devastated, as this move would have given her some distance from the Warner family.

It is difficult to believe that Sam would even consider leaving his brothers. Vitaphone was his brainchild, and he was confident of the technology's success. Lina and her money-hungry mother were likely impressed by the riches starting to befall the Warners. In 1923 Harry had architect Burnside Sturges build him a seven-bedroom, six-bath Georgian Colonial home in Hancock Park at 501 South Rossmore Avenue. The sprawling, 30,000-square-foot estate was complete with tennis courts, pool, and guesthouse. Jack had a somewhat less sprawling but equally beautiful home at 250 Plymouth Place in Los Angeles.

"More Good for Humanity than Anything Else Ever Invented"

Harry knew the importance of believing in any product one sold, and Sam was determined to work out any technological kinks before any Vitaphone shows were booked. One major issue was the hissing sound coming from arc lights on the set. Another problem was the trains that ran within earshot of the Vitagraph studio. In addition, much of the Vitagraph location was falling into disrepair. As Alma Young recalled in 1977, "The Vitagraph studio needed too many repairs honey. You could walk across a spot and the floor would go under your foot. It didn't pay. The only good thing they had at Vitagraph that they could use and did use was the theatre set."[63]

In May 1926 Sam leased Oscar Hammerstein's old opera house in Manhattan and turned it into a studio and laboratory. Hal Wallis described the scene: "the slightest sound—pigeons fluttering on the roof, the rumble of the subway, the sound of distant traffic—jolted the equipment and necessitated a complete revision of the work."[64] Another issue was the new subway being built nearby, leading to constant rock blasting during the day. Sam was so focused on the minute details of production it did not immediately occur to him that working at night would alleviate many issues—but eventually, that is what he did. The opera house was just a temporary location, and in July 1927 the entire production moved to Hollywood.[65]

Sam's initial purpose in synchronizing sound film was for music, sound effects, and adapting short plays for the screen (which would eventually become a voluminous catalog of Vitaphone shorts). Each act could last only eight to ten minutes, which was the maximum amount that would fit on each side of the Vitaphone disk. Sam hired actor and producer DeWolf Hopper (Hedda Hopper's former husband), who had made sound films for Lee De Forest's Phonofilm project, to record Vitaphone shorts. Harry signed "a great number of the popular musical artists monopolized by the Victor Phonograph Company, negotiated contracts with the stars of the Metropolitan Opera, and secured the New York Philharmonic to record orchestral accompaniments for feature films."[66] Harry was excited to see what Vitaphone could do with music, but when Sam floated the idea of synchronized dialogue, Harry acerbically responded, "Who the hell wants to hear actors talk?"[67]

Meanwhile, the brothers focused on adding sound to John Barrymore's adventure film *Don Juan*. The film premiered in New York at the Warner Theater on August 6, 1926, with a Vitaphone prelude of short subjects and an introduction by MPPDA president Will Hays (the only spoken words onscreen that evening) congratulating Warner Bros. and Western Electric on their presentation. Hays's first words were, "My friends: no story ever written for the screen is as dramatic as the story of the screen itself. Tonight, we write another chapter in that story." Like the Warners, Hays knew that film could have an "immeasurable influence as a living, breathing thing on the ideas and ideals, the customs and costumes, the hopes and ambitions of countless men, women, and children." Much of that impact would be due to the diligent efforts of Harry, Sam, Jack, and Albert Warner. "To the Warner Brothers," Hays concluded, "to whom is due credit for this, the beginning of a new era in music and motion pictures, I offer my felicitations and sincerest appreciation."[68]

The prelude included musical performances by the New York Phil-harmonic and by members of the Metropolitan Opera. In attendance were many notable figures, including cofounder of Paramount Pictures Adolph Zukor, banker Otto Kahn, Samuel Sachs of Goldman Sachs, heavyweight boxer Jack Dempsey, William Morris, *Forbes* magazine founder B. C. Forbes, Fox Studios founder William Fox, theatrical entrepreneur Samuel Rothafel, Hollywood studio investor Joseph Kennedy, and inventor and "father of radio" Lee De Forest. De Forest penned a feature for *Motion Picture News* discussing why sound on film was the future and congratulating the brothers, "who deserve credit for having the necessary imagination and courage to awaken the industry to these possibilities."[69] Photographing sound waves with film would fix the problem of skipping needles and synchronization issues and would ultimately become the preferred technology. Of course, as De Forest knew, that would never happen unless someone like the Warner brothers took a crack at commercial exhibition. August 6, 1926, marked the first commercially successful showcase of talking pictures. *Don Juan* was playing in Los Angeles as a silent film at the time, and its sound version premiered in October to great fanfare at Grauman's Chinese Theater on Hollywood Boulevard.

Moving Picture World mused that "Don Juan Barrymore" was the "finest contribution John Barrymore has made to the screen." "The greatest line of all," it stated, was "the waiting line. And Warner Bros. have coined the line anew with the Vitaphone—which is packing them in and standing them up outside [the] *Don Juan* program at the Warner's Theatre."[70] *Exhibitors Herald* lauded the presentation, stating that the synchronization was so on point

Don Juan advertisement on a historic date.

that it created "the illusion that human beings are being actually visualized instead of figures on a screen."[71]

Variety's headline read "Vitaphone Bow Is Hailed as Marvel," and the praise continued: "the Vitaphone has come and has amazed Broadway."[72] The entire program was not a marvel, however, as some of the opening shorts featured underwhelming sound. String, reed, and percussion instruments sounded great, but brass instruments did not translate well with the sound-on-disk technology. Despite the imperfections, audiences applauded passionately after each screening. The standout performance was by Metropolitan Opera tenor Giovanni Martinelli, who received a standing ovation. The response to Martinelli's performance might not have been great news for the Barrymore film, but it was good enough to solidify Vitaphone's success.

Hollywood insider and journalist Terry Ramsaye called the triumph of Warner Bros. "both a typical story of success in the American way and a romance of changing lights playing across the path of persistent ambition."[73] Still, the sound-on-disk technology was clunky and sensitive. The slightest rumble from a car or train or even a slammed door could make the needle jump from the disk. Western Electric engineer Stanley Watkins, who ran the *Don Juan* program many times, recalled, "One night, when we had been running for a couple of weeks, Will Hays opened his mouth and out came the tones of a banjo. After that I stayed close to the theater for quite a while . . . we were very particular about the level of sound."[74]

On Vitaphone's twentieth anniversary, Harry Warner sought to spread the credit around, saying, "The talking picture, like other revolutionary technological achievements, was the product of invention and research by many different scientists over a long period of years." He continued, "We intend to make this anniversary the occasion for honoring all of those far-seeing pioneers who contributed so much in the scientific research that made the talking picture possible." Harry was most proud of how sound had transformed the way film carried messages around the globe. "We also want to recognize the part that the talking picture played in bringing information, education, culture, and entertainment to people all over the world."[75]

Ben and Pearl Warner were incredibly proud of their boys. The parents wrote to Jack, "We never dreamed that we would live to see such a performance, and above all that we would be the parents of such wonderful boys . . . when four marvelous boys like you stick together through thick and thin, there is no question but that you will attain all the success you hope for."[76]

Sam Warner flanked by parents, Ben and Pearl, 1925.

Jack had missed the August 6 Vitaphone program, as he had been back in Los Angeles with Sid Grauman getting ready for the West Coast premiere of *Don Juan.*

Meanwhile, Sam and Lina welcomed a baby girl, Lita, into the world on October 10, 1926. When their lease was up on the Long Island house, Sam moved the family back to Manhattan so he could be closer to his Vitaphone work. Soon, however, they packed up and headed to Hollywood, where production began on *The Jazz Singer.* The Sam Warners, as Lina referred to her family, moved into the expensive Hotel Ambassador. The couple quarreled over the cost, given that Sam had recently purchased a new car and frequently mentioned that Vitaphone needed to take off if they hoped to clear their major debt. According to Lina, Sam also tried to get rid of the family's dogs. One story featured their dog Fritz, who apparently attacked one of Jack's horses, so Jack had the dog shot. It was impossible to corroborate, but it illustrates Lina's zeal for the dramatic.

Jack recalled the 1920s as a tumultuous time in Hollywood, especially for silent actors, whom he referred to as an "unstable commodity." Jack wrote about "men and women whose names around the world would disappear as suddenly as though they had been lost at sea."[77] And many of them were lost during that decade. Magician Harry Houdini died in 1926 after being punched as part of a stunt—a blow he thought he could take. Actress

Virginia Rappe died of a ruptured appendix in 1921, which sparked debate over her possible sexual assault by comedian Fatty Arbuckle. Director and producer William Desmond Taylor was murdered in his home in 1922, a case that remains unsolved to this day. Producer Thomas Ince died in 1924, amid rumors of foul play on a yacht owned by publishing magnate William Randolph Hearst. International sex symbol and "Latin lover" Rudolph Valentino died due to complications of peritonitis at age thirty-one in 1926. Moral crusaders branded Hollywood the Babylonia of the West Coast. The questionable nature of many of these deaths, along with stories of drugs and debauchery, was the main reason the film industry brought Will Hays in to head the MPPDA. It was the beginning of the industry's self-censorship, but it would not be fully enforced until the 1930s.

As Vitaphone equipment was being shipped out west, Jack received some mysterious threats at the studio, all of which he wrote off as coming from harmless attention seekers or perhaps from nervous actors fearing they would be let go if they could not speak coherently (which was true). One specific tip that did worry Jack was that some "hotheads were planning to wreck our Vitaphone equipment when it reached the freight yards from New York." Just to be safe, he had studio police chief Bill Guthrie and one of his cop buddies, armed with shotguns, patrol the grounds while Jack and a couple of others loaded the equipment onto a truck. Fortunately, Warner wrote, "There were no disgruntled actors or skulking hoodlums at the yard."[78] That particular threat may not have been credible, but the public relations–savvy Jack snapped photographs of the loaded truck being watched by armed guards.

Vitaphone was taking the industry by storm, and Hollywood movies were capturing the imagination of audiences everywhere. Harvard Business School took note when one of its prestigious alumni, Joseph P. Kennedy, organized a lecture series around the growing industry. Kennedy had a financial interest in the movie business, owning Film Booking Offices of America (FBO) and Keith-Albee-Orpheum Theaters (KAO). To acknowledge the school's support of the series, Kennedy donated $30,000 to Harvard's Fine Arts Department to fund research on Hollywood and the film industry. Kennedy wrote that Harvard's support meant "a recognition of [Hollywood's] artistic work by the oldest university in the United States [and] by a department that is second to none in the world."[79] The lecture series connected American films with elites on an Ivy League campus. Kennedy would edit and publish the lectures to ensure that the event would not be lost to history.

The lecture series featured detailed talks, three times per week, on each phase of filmmaking. Speakers included Will Hays, Adolph Zukor, William Fox, Marcus Loew, Jesse Lasky, Cecil B. DeMille, Samuel Katz, and Harry Warner, among others. The film industry was one of the top businesses in the country, and its global distribution network was helping other American exports. During his introduction to Harry's lecture, Kennedy described the mogul's bravery and said, "A man having . . . the courage to back up his faith, as he has, deserves well of the industry and may prove to be one of its very greatest figures."[80]

Despite the success and positive press of Vitaphone, some remained skeptical. The most important cynic was Thomas Edison, who claimed that sound films and talking pictures would never work in the United States. Edison explained that he had run his own experiments fifteen years ago, so naturally, if he could not make it work, the idea must be dead. It is important to remember that Edison's Motion Picture Patents Corporation had lost its stranglehold on film technology, so it is no surprise that the inventor would not be thrilled about another production company's success. Harry responded in *Motion Picture News,* explaining that Edison was "undoubtedly unfamiliar with exactly what the latest device for synchronizing sound and action has accomplished." Edison dismissed sound film by arguing that "there are many things needed more than the moving picture." Harry countered by asking how anything can "be relegated to insignificance when it is endowed with such tremendous educational possibilities?" For example, Harry mused, what if we could revisit Lincoln's Gettysburg Address? The Warner Bros. president concluded by quoting William C. Durant, who had been instrumental in the founding of General Motors, Chevrolet, and Frigidaire. Durant had told *Forbes,* "The thing that has the biggest possibilities of anything and everything I have come across in the last forty years is the Vitaphone."[81] Later that same year, Edison saw and heard himself on film and was still underwhelmed. He did, however, concede one of Harry's arguments. As the inventor told a crowd in West Orange, New Jersey, "the synchronization of voice and picture may be valuable in educational work."[82]

On March 30, 1927, Harry spoke to the Harvard class about future developments in the motion picture industry. He opened by telling the story about borrowing chairs from a funeral parlor for patrons in their small Newcastle theater. Harry also chided himself for not believing in sound film. "If I myself would not have gone across the street to see or hear a talking picture, I surely could not expect the public to do it. But music! That is another story." The mogul took the students on a journey through the Warners' experimentation and exhibition, as well as the challenges they faced while developing Vitaphone. Trials persisted, as actors at Keith-Albee (not yet merged into RKO) were forbidden to work with Vitaphone. But Harry was confident that once Vitaphone was playing in 140 theaters by August 1, the technology would literally and figuratively speak for itself.

One problem facing Vitaphone was Edison's recent comments that sound film was a failure. Harry responded, "It is not so comfortable to have your life's wealth invested in a thing which such a great authority as Edison says cannot succeed." Harry argued for the importance of visualization by predicting what both audiences and theater managers wanted from film studios. "We are confident people will go to hear the Vitaphone," Harry said, "but we know the proper kind of entertainment must be supplied, if it is going to be a great success." The first in a series of new films featuring synchronized dialogue would be *The Jazz Singer,* about a Jewish cantor's son who leaves home to sing on Broadway, starring stage actor Al Jolson.

A major concern for theater managers, in Harry's experience, was that they had orchestras play during some shows but not others, creating an inconsistent exhibition standard. A Strand Theater manager was worried because his competitor, the Roxy, had installed a Vitaphone. Harry shared his response: "You should put in a Vitaphone, too. You give six shows a day, but your orchestra only plays one and a half shows. In other words, when customers go into your house, they see one and a half complete shows. Now let your orchestra come in six times a day and play their overture and let the Vitaphone do the rest. You will not be eliminating your orchestra and you will give six perfect shows a day." Harry confirmed that the Strand was installing a Vitaphone and would be operating the new technology on April 23.

During the question-and-answer period, Harry addressed the particulars of the business, such as installation costs and lease pricing for Vitaphone parts, as well as questions about the New York premiere of Vitaphone. One person inquired how Vitaphone differed from Fox's Movietone, which was a sound-on-film application. Harry ducked the expediency of Movietone by launching into an explanation of why Vitaphone sounds better because the recording is happening in a room separate from the filming location (as it had been done in New York). Also, Movietone had amplification issues, and Vitaphone was able to use Western Electric's telephone amplification applications.

Harry also pointed out that his studio was engineering Vitaphone so theaters that installed the technology would still be able to exhibit Movietone films. It was clear that Harry wanted the entire industry to move forward, not just his own company. "The time is not far distant when you will be able to see and hear the inauguration of the next President," Harry predicted.

Harry concluded his lecture with what he saw as the larger impact of talking pictures. "We honestly believe the Vitaphone is going to do more good for humanity than anything else ever invented." Growing up poor and having to work hard his whole life, Harry believed that spreading knowledge through talking pictures would be a great way to educate the masses who had neither the time nor the money to read lengthy texts. "If we have a message of friendship or enlightenment that can be broadcast throughout the world," Harry said, "maybe the nations will be led to understand one another better."[83] Some of this may sound hyperbolic, but Harry truly believed these words. He was always a cautious optimist, never afraid to put in the work if it might result in a better world.

By the end of May 1927, Edwin Schallert of the *Los Angeles Times* reported on *The Jazz Singer*'s synchronized dialogue and music. Based on the 1925 play by Samson Raphaelson, the movie's dialogue would presumably be sparse, but it promised to be an important experiment for the brothers and the industry at large. Schallert noted that Sam Warner had made the trip to Hollywood from the East Coast to supervise the production of *The Jazz Singer*. As experimentation proceeded to production, a plant was built on the Warner lot to film and record sound. The most notable difference between the New York and Los Angeles operations, noted Schallert, "is the coordination achieved right on the set in the filming and recording of the scene."[84] Back in New York, microphone wires were fed to another room, often on a different floor, where the sound was recorded on a disk.

Schallert visited the Warner Sunset studio in July to watch the Vitaphone production. Two stages had been wired for sound, and two more were on the way. *The Jazz Singer* utilized dialogue from the song "Kol Nidre," significant for Yom Kippur, the Jewish Day of Atonement. Schallert noted the innovative use of incandescent lighting instead of carbon lighting. As Harry had explained in his Harvard address, using a string of incandescent lights minimized the number of electricians needed on the set. Schallert spent an entire day on the Warner lot and was impressed with the seamless production of Vitaphone. One major advantage over Movietone was that Vitaphone allowed the audio to be played back immediately, whereas Movietone needed to process the film before playback was possible (which could take a day or so). Sam told Schallert that Vitaphone had been installed in 135 locations. The Warners "are into the game with a vengeance," the reporter concluded, "and have already made very striking headway in a field in which they primarily are pioneering."[85] *The Jazz Singer* was scheduled to premiere in October, but a family tragedy would strike just before the next Vitaphone sensation reached the eyes and ears of audiences in New York.

Sam's work ethic was well known, but his long days were affecting his health. That September, Sam and Jack were in Los Angeles, preparing for the New York premiere of *The Jazz Singer*. Jack was used to seeing Sam worn out, but now he was looking especially "wan and listless."[86] Jack had always known Sam to be the type of person who could work himself into the ground, only to come back stronger. "Towards the end of September," Jack remembered, "he showed a certain unsteadiness on his feet around the studio." At thirty-nine years old, Sam was a tall, strong, relatively young man who had been burning the candle at both ends. He had been getting intense headaches, and it was a sign of trouble ahead when he considered sitting out the New York premiere. When Sam was advised to go to California Lutheran Hospital to get checked out, he "surrendered almost too willingly." Sam assured his brothers that all he needed was rest, so Jack left to meet the others in New York.

While Sam was hospitalized in Los Angeles, his wife and daughter were at his bedside. Lina, who was working on a film at Paramount, was allowed to stay in the room next to Sam's. Sam reassured his family that everything would be back to normal in a few days, but his high fever told another story. Sam had an acute mastoid infection (this was before the advent of penicillin) and underwent a couple of operations that did not help his condition. The stress of the surgery and the anesthesia left him in even worse shape. On October 4 the *New York Times* reported that Harry and Abe had boarded a train for Los Angeles accompanied by two physicians from New York, Dr. Jonas J. Ungar and Dr. Harold Hayes.[87] The following day the *Los Angeles Times* informed readers of Sam's condition, reporting that "physicians attending Warner were grave in all statements" and that Sam "had been seriously ill for about ten days."[88] Harry remembered that, during the long trip across the country, it felt like the train was traveling at a snail's pace. While crossing Arizona, Harry received a telegram informing him that Sam's condition was now terminal. The eldest brother struggled to find an airplane, desperate to reach Sam before it was too late. Harry managed to find another train that would get them to Los Angeles faster than their current route.

It is difficult to determine where the various family members were when Sam died. One version of the story has Jack passing through Chicago on October 5 when he got word that Sam had died. But Hal Wallis told an interviewer that he was at the hospital with Jack when Sam passed. Lina and Pearl were likely at the hospital, as they were in Los Angeles at the time. Harry and the New York doctors were just hours away from Los Angeles. Based on some accounts, Abe was on the train with Harry, while others claim he had taken an earlier train to Los Angeles. In any case, losing Sam was a serious blow to the whole family, but it took the biggest toll on Jack. "Throughout his life, Jack had been warmed by Sam's shiny optimism, his thirst for excitement, his inventive mind, his gambling nature," wrote biographer Bob Thomas. "Sam had always served as a cushion between the sternness of Harry and the jocularity of Jack. Now Jack would have to face his oldest brother alone."[89] According to Lina, Abe and Jack called her the following morning and asked her to return to the hospital and attend to some insurance details. "I'll be at Paramount, I have to report to work," she replied. Jack shot back angrily, "SCREW PARAMOUNT! Your husband is dead. You bitch!"[90] The death of the family's most reliable member, its voice of reason, left a permanent void in the Warner family.

News of Sam's death spread rapidly across the nation. The *Los Angeles Times* carried the story on page one. Meanwhile, the much-anticipated premiere of *The Jazz Singer* was happening in New York. Warner Bros. shut down for five days following Sam's death. At the height of the studio's popularity, one can imagine how difficult it was to move on without the creative genius behind its most successful innovations. In some of the worst luck in Hollywood history, the man most responsible for the first feature film exhibited with synchronized dialogue would die hours before his creation came to life. "It was an empty victory for us," said Jack, "something wonderful went out of our lives." Writing about the influence of his brother's work on sound pictures, Jack wrote, "Sam brought it into the world, and gave his own life in exchange."[91] Reminiscing about the years spent building the Vitaphone brand, Abe fittingly credited Sam for bringing the other brothers on board to develop sound film. "We've made millions," said Abe, "but that doesn't bring Sam back."[92]

There were many pioneers of sound cinema. Brilliant technicians and inventions such as Emile Berliner's early sound-on-disk gramophone, Leon Gaumont's Chronophone, Ernst Ruhmer's photographophone (an update of Alexander Graham Bell's Photophone), Thomas Edison's Kinetophone, Lee De Forest's phonofilm, and Theodore Case's sound-on-film innovations all played a role in advancing synchronized sound film. However, not a single one of these important figures had both the vision and the creativity to exhibit this technology on a mass scale. None of these men could connect their inventions to the larger public interest. None of them were successful in bringing their sound film products to market. Only one person saw the future and found a way to make it a reality: Sam Warner.

On the day of Sam's funeral, Harry, Abe, and Warner Bros. legal counsel Abel Thomas came to Lina's room and presented her with some papers to sign. She was encouraged not to read them but just sign her name. Lina recalled Sam's reluctance to trust some of the legal experts his brothers had drummed up, but, exhausted from watching her husband's rapidly deteriorating health, she reluctantly signed the papers. She knew something was up but "just wanted to be rid of these vultures." When Lina told her mother, Gladys was furious. "Those damn, conniving KIKES!" she screamed. She advised Lina, "Stop going to church and tell those damned Warners about the Jewish blood in your veins . . . if you play your cards right with these Yids, you can end up with millions!"[93]

The funeral was held the Sunday after Sam's death, at Bresee Brothers Undertaking Parlors on Figueroa Street in Los Angeles. Rabbi Magnin presided over the family-only service that preceded Sam's burial in the family plot at the Home of Peace Cemetery on Whittier Boulevard. Magnin praised Sam's "worthy family life and his kindness towards parents and friends as well as his success in the business world."[94] In attendance were Lina; Sam's parents Ben and Pearl; brothers Jack, Abe, Harry, and Dave; and sisters Sadie, Anna, and Rose. Lina remembered that a line of "professional mourners" showed up, including one unnamed woman who made a scene weeping at Sam's casket—someone with a peripheral connection to the family looking for attention, reasoned Lina.

A second service was held on Stage 2 at the Sunset studio, conducted by the Reverend Neal Dodd. Pallbearers were Frank Murphy, Monte Blue, and Leon Schlesinger, among others. A long list of honorary pallbearers included Harry Rapf, Joe Marks, Darryl F. Zanuck, Bryan Foy, B. P. Schulberg, Hal

Wallis, Sol Wurtzel, Cecil B. DeMille, Harry Cohn, Adolphe Menjou, Ernst Lubitsch, Douglas Fairbanks, Colonel Jason Joy (of the MPPDA), Sid Grauman, Archie Mayo, Hal Roach, and Al Jolson.[95] Sam's friend Edward Davis spoke at the studio funeral, and Al Jolson sang two Jewish hymns. Fittingly, Jolson's rendition of "Kol Nidre" was presented via Vitaphone. Another memorial service was held at the Breakfast Club, where Dr. Bruce Baxter gave a eulogy; afterward, Sam's favorite racehorse was walked out during a rendition of taps.

Sam's final years taught the brothers a valuable business lesson: Don't wait to find out what the audience wants. Don't be afraid to show them the possibilities of the future. Abe was confident his brothers would prevail, despite the loss of Sam. "The three of us who are left will carry on," said Abe, "and I believe we will always accomplish more work in one day than any other trio of men will in three, not because we are smarter, but because we trust each other implicitly and don't have to waste time with petty executive jealousies."[96] The Warner work ethic was well established. Although Ben and Pearl were given a home in Los Angeles where they could retire, the two continued to drive to the studio to keep an eye on things.

Abe hoped to see film take a larger role in education. Harry had already advanced the notion of film as an educational tool back at Harvard. "As I look back, if I have any regrets," said Abe, it "is that we brothers didn't get more education. Most of us stopped in grammar school. I had one year of high school because I played football. But often when I have to get up to address conferences, employees' organizations, and the like, I wish I had the gift of eloquence and the training that comes from a university education."[97] Of course, Harry had become a strong and articulate speaker, but for some, more training and practice were necessary. Movies could introduce people to new cultures and new ideas, which might lead to greater interest in education. By the 1920s, 20 percent of college-age adults were attending a university, and the brothers saw Vitaphone as a way to get on board that trend.

The Jazz Singer ran for many weeks, but its massive historical impact was not realized immediately. Although it was largely silent, it was the most successful experimental sound film to date. Other studios were still making major silent films, such as Paramount's World War I epic *Wings* (1927) and Fox's Movietone feature *Sunrise: A Song of Two Humans* (1927). As long as silent films were making money, there was a chance that sound films would remain a novelty. *Variety* called *The Jazz Singer* "a credit to everybody concerned," with "songs that hold good for any town or street."[98] Major power brokers requested private screenings to see whether the Vitaphone technology was as good as advertised. Even for people who had already heard Vitaphone voices, Jolson's singing was magical. Future Warner Bros. star Edward G. Robinson remembered seeing the film in New York with his wife, Gladys. Dedicated to theater and unimpressed with Warner's sound shorts, Robinson wrote that watching *The Jazz Singer* convinced him that "talking pictures were about to become a reality."[99]

Critics loved the musical scenes but were lukewarm about the synchronized speaking. Writing in the *New York Times,* Mordaunt Hall opined, "in the expression of song the Vitaphone vitalizes the production enormously"; however, "the dialogue is not so effective, for it does not always catch the nuances of speech or inflections of the voice."[100] Although the musical numbers had been perfected, much work remained to be done on the dialogue. In the *Los Angeles Times,* Norbert Lusk called the story in *The Jazz Singer* "negligible" but wrote that "the Vitaphone and Al Jolson put it over."[101] Lusk praised synchronized sound but thought the new technology only highlighted the rest of the film's shortcomings. Direction, photography, and lighting were all criticized.

While *The Jazz Singer* is undoubtedly a significant film, it remains historically problematic, marred by its blackface performances. That insensitive aesthetic was a carryover from vaudeville, which focused on a range of exaggerated stereotypes. Film historian Donald Bogle observes that while *The Jazz Singer* was a massive achievement, "Jolson's ever-crooning-swooning darky jester was a classic example of the minstrel tradition at its sentimentalized, corrupt best."[102] It is important to note that although none of the vaudeville stereotypes aged well, their intention was to be an ingenious leveler. Other comic archetypes in vaudeville included the dumb Irish cop, the stingy German, and the Italian lover—characters that everyone, at the time, could laugh at.

The Jazz Singer's story was chosen because of its success on Broadway, and its star, George Jessel, was offered the film lead. Jessel was too expensive, so the Warners cast another prominent Broadway star, Al Jolson. Most important for the Warners, the story of a Jewish cantor's immigrant son seeking approval in the United States spoke to them (and many other Hollywood moguls and performers). *The Jazz Singer* unquestionably helped pave the way for the sound era.

By 1931, sound-on-disk was scrapped for the superior sound-on-film technology. However, without Sam Warner's innovative zeal, it would have been many more years before sound film gained national prominence. Hollywood began to work to standardize film sound because, without a standard exhibition practice, studios' films could be played only in theaters set up with their own systems. The five-cornered agreement, as it was called, came after MGM, First National, Famous Players–Lasky (on the verge of becoming Paramount), Universal, and Producers Distributing Company pushed for a fast and permanent solution to prevent studios from adopting incompatible systems. The deliberations were difficult because the installers of both Warner's Vitaphone and Fox's Movietone were unable to keep up with demand. Photophone technology was also in the running. Warner Bros. continued to puff its system for its superior sound quality. Although sound-on-film technology had some quality issues, the process was much more convenient, and the sound did not get bumped out of sync if someone brushed against the machine.[103]

Now that Sam was gone, the question remained what to do about his daughter and the "curious agreement" with his widow, Lina.[104] When Lina was pregnant, she and Sam had agreed that if it was a boy, he would be raised Jewish, and if it was a girl, she would be raised Catholic. The potential problems of bringing a Catholic child into a staunchly Jewish family were obvious, but Sam—always the one to build bridges and keep the peace—would have been up to the task. Once Sam died, the family turned against Lina and tried to take custody of Lita. Lina refused cash offers to give up the child. Harry proposed taking Lita and raising her with his own children, and Lina finally agreed when Harry increased Lita's trust fund to $300,000. "I didn't sell my baby girl," Lina later said in her own defense. "I only tried to make her future secure." Lina told Kevin Brownlow that she fought to regain custody and blamed her failure on "crooked lawyers who wound up on the legal staff of Warner Bros."[105]

Lita did not see her mother again for decades, but she harbored no hard feelings. She understood that her mother had been very young when Sam died. Looking back, Lita said, "One of the beautiful things about Harry was that he wanted to take care of the whole family."[106] Lita fondly remembered Harry sharing his enthusiasm for horses with her, a love she retained throughout her life. One can interpret Harry and Rea's determination to care for Lita as more about protecting the Warner family than about taking a child away from a purportedly unfit mother. Raising Lita was also a way for the Warners to stay connected to Sam and create some distance from Lina's racist, gold-digging mother.

In addition to Lita, Sam lived on in the studio's sound films. The massively successful *Show of Shows* (1928) starred Al Jolson and other top musical talent (it was the most popular film until being unseated by *Gone with the Wind* in 1939). The Zanuck-produced gangster yarn *Lights of New York* (1928) would be the first completely sound-synchronized feature-length film. Both films solidified what the brothers had been working toward in the area of sound. Their other goal, which became more central in the coming years, was to make relevant films that enlightened viewers. This was part of Harry's drive to solidify film as an educational tool.

Lights of New York—the first full talkie, despite the use of intertitles—opens with a nod to the studio's developing headline-driven style: "This is a story of Main Street and Broadway—a story that might have been torn out of last night's newspaper." William Wellman, who directed some of the studio's most important gangster films, said that Zanuck "could take a headline in a paper and make a picture faster than anybody in the business."[107] This ripped-from-the-headlines production style would define Warner Bros. in the following decade, and Zanuck played a major role in its edgy filmmaking approach.[108] *Lights of New York* depicts all the details of the Roaring Twenties—bootlegging, speakeasies, murder, and gangland tough guys. This detailed depiction of crime landed the studio in hot water with the censors. According to Alma Young, *Lights of New York* director Bryan Foy "must have gone to various jails and just picked up people. He had so many criminals working for him. I'm not kidding. I'm serious. Sometimes it was a little embarrassing."[109] Warner Bros. would employ a criminal on the run for its production of *I Am a Fugitive from a Chain Gang* (1932).

Warner Bros. also took risks with the lavishly produced *The Sea Beast* (1926), an adaptation of *Moby Dick,* and the biblical spectacle *Noah's Ark* (1928), directed by Michael Curtiz. Biblical epics had been making the rounds in Hollywood, including Cecil B. DeMille's *The Ten Commandments* (1923) at Paramount and Fred Niblo's *Ben-Hur: A Tale of the Christ* (1925) at MGM. Jack Warner signed off on the project, even though Curtiz's last film had been a critical bomb. Jack knew Curtiz could handle the difficult effects-laden blockbuster. According to Curtiz biographer Alan K. Rode, the film began as a discussion between Harry and Curtiz in Europe.[110]

Picture-Play Magazine reported that the idea for the story came to Harry while looking out his office window during a New York City downpour that had pedestrians rushing for shelter. Musing at the sight, Harry wondered: if New Yorkers were annoyed by two hours of rain, "what must have been the sensation experienced by all creatures of the world, for forty days and forty nights, 'the windows of heaven were opened,' and water descended in torrents, in cascades, and cataracts, until every living substance was destroyed? What a picture it would make!"[111]

Noah's Ark quickly became legendary, as reports (or rumors) of deaths on the set surfaced. It took 139 technicians to construct three tanks that each held about one million gallons of water to create the deluge pouring down on unprotected actors and extras. The water flowed through multiple avenues of the old Vitagraph studios at the intersection of Prospect and Talmadge. Curtiz's biographer posits, "Though it is possible that the eyewitness accounts might have been unintentionally embellished over the years, there is little doubt that a number of people were severely injured in what was clearly a case of gross negligence."[112] The lack of detail in news reports about the filming of this scene indicates that the studio might have muzzled employees to cover up any tragedy. Workplace safety was not a major concern in early Hollywood, and *Noah's Ark* is a good example of the dangers of filming large-scale action scenes, as well as the carelessness of studio bosses and producers.

One hundred and fifty-seven theaters were wired for sound in 1927. By 1929, eight thousand theaters were ready for sound film exhibition; that number would reach fourteen thousand by 1931. Some studios that bought into the five-cornered agreement pushed against Vitaphone, but it was too popular. With the rush of success, Harry Warner "cannily exploited the film industry's disarray by launching a two-year spending spree that confused and confounded his competitors. Not even the stock market crash deterred him."[113] Harry continued to acquire prominent music publishers and placed his young son Lewis in charge of Warner Bros. Music. The studio purchased the Stanley Corporation of America, which held 250 theaters in seventy-five cities and seven states, along with First National and its theaters and studio lot in Burbank. The most prestigious acquisition during this spending spree was the Strand Theater in New York. It was essential to have key theaters in major cities. As the value of Warner Bros. shares skyrocketed (from $28 to $130 a share), the company paid off all its debt by the end of 1928 and saw a net profit of $2,044,841.

By the end of 1929, despite the stock market crash that heralded the beginning of the Great Depression, Warner Bros. was a major studio with a national distribution network. O'Steen remembered how fast both the company and the industry grew. Back in 1925, the First National lot in Burbank had still been a hog ranch; now it was being expanded into a major studio lot. O'Steen described the "102-acre portion of what was at one time the huge Rancho El Providencia. . . . Backed up against the brush and willow choked Los Angeles River behind and reaching to the pave[d] strip Olive Avenue in front. Otherwise surrounded by peach and apricot orchards and weed-filled acreage."[114] Warner Bros. transitioned its primary production units to the First National lot in Burbank. First National became a trade name under which Warner Bros. released films until it eventually transitioned to using Warner Bros. exclusively. Eighty-six feature films were produced by Warner Bros. in 1929, and forty-five of those titles were released under the First National banner.

The films ran the gamut of genres, including many that prefigured the iconic Warner Bros. films of the 1930s. *On with the Show* (1929) was a backstage musical based on a play by Humphrey Pearson and starring Betty Compson, Ethel Waters, and Joe E. Brown, making his Warner Bros. debut. Backstage musicals, where the characters are performers in an upcoming musical play, would become a Warner Bros. staple in the 1930s. The film utilized two-strip Technicolor and synchronized sound throughout, making it the first full sound and color feature film. Two of the film's musical numbers were performed by African American Ethel Waters, later known for her many iconic songs, including "Stormy Weather." Two-strip Technicolor was filmed on two reels, one red and one green. The two strips were combined when printing the final product, creating layers of color. The process was expensive, costing an extra $250,000. The film's director, Alan Crosland, was no stranger to employing new technology, having previously directed *The Jazz Singer*.

Other Warner Bros. films rounding out the decade included a string of Ken Maynard westerns and historical dramas. The lost film *In the Headlines* highlighted the studio's ripped-from-the-headlines reputation. Showing the breadth of Warner Bros. output were *The Forward Pass*, a college caper starring Douglas Fairbanks Jr. and Loretta Young, and *Little Johnny Jones*, adapted from a George M. Cohan musical play. Warner Bros. would also remake *The Gold Diggers* (1923) as *The Gold Diggers of Broadway* (1929), continuing a series of films that would be vaulted by Busby Berkeley's choreography.

As the studio became more successful, the brothers remained dedicated to philanthropy. Speaking in front of fifteen hundred people (including Warner sisters Anna and Rose and father Ben) at the Hebrew Orphan Asylum, Harry donated $125,000 for the Warner memorial gymnasium. The venue, on the corner of 137th and Amsterdam in New York, was a tribute to the late Milton Warner. In return, Harry was offered a seat on the institution's board of trustees. Prominent members of the community praised the Warners for their generosity. "Judge Samuel D. Levy of the Children's Court declared that 95 percent of the delinquency among the city's children was caused by the lack of gymnasiums and playground centers."[115] Additional praise came from Sol M. Strook, president of the Federation of the Support of Jewish Philanthropic Societies, and Dr. Nathan Krass, rabbi of the Temple Emanu-El.

After making it big with *The Jazz Singer,* Jack purchased an open lot next to the home of comedian Harold Lloyd, who would become a good friend. Jack Jr. described the home his father built there as an "oppressive Spanish house," or "what we used to call a Spanish clunker—but a gorgeous one."[116] An architect designed and built the house, but the interior was completely decorated by studio employees. Most of the Spanish furniture came from the studio warehouses. "It was like living in a museum," said Jack Jr., "with magnificent pieces of furniture, that should be in a gallery somewhere. Or over in the prop department, which is probably where they came from."[117] The grounds featured a nine-hole golf course, which was rarely used. There was also a bridge over the wall between the lots, providing easy access to Lloyd's yard. "My father was married to my mother [Irma] for twenty years. In the early years of their marriage, when he was struggling to move up in the movie industry and his big job was to get those actors out in the morning and to make sure the cameraman wasn't drunk, my father was a happy guy." Back then, "the brothers were not yet such wealthy men, and many of their later problems hadn't developed." Had Sam lived, mused Jack Jr., "I think so much history would have been different."[118]

3

Battling the Depression, Censors, and Stars

1930-1936

Warner Bros. stared down the Great Depression with an intensity unparalleled by anyone else in Hollywood. During the early 1930s, the studio gained a reputation for lightning-fast production of snappy, pertinent films. The studio's output is best described by historian Thomas Doherty: "The very speed of the production machine at Warner Brothers allowed the historical moment to leave a fresh imprint, unmediated and unpremeditated, like snapshots taken before the models could assume an artificial pose."[1] The studio's headline-driven mode of production hummed along with no signs of deceleration. Warner Bros. solidified a long trend of films ripped from the headlines, starting with *Doorway to Hell* (1930), a tough gangster picture that landed an Oscar nomination for Best Original Story. The biographical film *Disraeli* (1930) received a Best Picture nod but lost to Universal's *All Quiet on the Western Front* (1930). The aviation war drama *The Dawn Patrol* (1930) served as a powerful antiwar tale, though its depiction of alcohol use irked the censors. A young John Wayne found himself on the lot for a series of short westerns produced by Leon Schlesinger. Numerous female melodramas featured tough, independent women such as Barbara Stanwyck in *Night Nurse* (1931). Warner Bros. would have no shortage of punchy, topical films to entertain Depression-era audiences. Over the next decade, the studio would purchase the rights to more than fifteen hundred books, plays, and short stories. Though Warner Bros. was often known for its hard-hitting gangster, crime, and Depression narratives, the studio also offered prestige films such as the adventure movie *Captain Blood* (1935), the male melodrama *Anthony Adverse* (1936), and the biographical dramas *The Life of Emile Zola*

(1937), *The Story of Louis Pasteur* (1937), and *The Private Lives of Elizabeth and Essex* (1939).

The economic turmoil of the Depression created seemingly insurmountable chaos for many, including one of the Warners' first major backers. Motley Flint, who helped the brothers establish significant lines of credit for their operations in Los Angeles, spent the end of the Roaring Twenties tied up in the fallout from a Ponzi scheme known as the Julian Petroleum scandal. Julian Petroleum had issued an excessive amount of illegal stock and inflated its stock prices for potential investors. For his part in this plan, Flint was charged with five counts of usury. On July 14, 1930, Flint was testifying in downtown Los Angeles at a trial involving producer David O. Selznick and First National. Frank Keaton, one of the investors who had lost his life savings when First National stock crashed, was in attendance. When Flint was dismissed from the witness stand, Keaton stood up, fired three shots at him from a pistol at close range, and then threw his gun at the banker. Judge Collier stepped down from the bench to secure Keaton, who held his head in his hands as he uttered, "He ruined me!"[2] In that moment, the Warner brothers lost one of their most essential allies.

At a time when anti-Semitism was standard in the banking industry, there simply would not have been a Warner Bros. without Flint's assistance. Flint became a close friend of the Warners, especially Jack and Sam. Speaking to the *Los Angeles Times,* Jack expressed deep sorrow over the loss: "Mr. Flint was always the friend and advisor and always ready to help and did help those in the picture industry with finance and guidance just as he helped others in all walks of life. We have, indeed, lost a real friend and benefactor."[3] Though there were many pivotal moments that saved the brothers during the early years, the Warners always saw Flint as the man who made the studio's growth toward immortality possible. Flint's funeral was held on July 16 at the Forest Lawn Memorial Park mausoleum. Only days earlier, Flint had been there paying his last respects to his own mother. Jack Warner served as a pallbearer at Flint's funeral, and the family sent a massive array of flowers. Keaton was sentenced to death by hanging for Flint's murder, but in 1940 California governor Culbert Olson would commute the sentence to life in prison.

Harry Warner began the 1930s speaking about Hollywood's social responsibility. With the rising number of moviegoers, he said, "this steadily increasing influence over recreational hours of millions has grown a corresponding responsibility, and we have not shirked it."[4] Harry's daughter, Betty,

Motley Flint with the Warners during groundbreaking for the Warner Hollywood Theatre.

said her father "spent a lot of time thinking about issues and meeting as many people as he could to discuss them. He felt people should be part of politics and always encouraged others to get involved. Harry met with many political leaders not only for business reasons but also personal."[5] Harry's political interests were entirely genuine, which set him apart from other Hollywood moguls, who were only interested in how civics impacted their bottom line. Harry was always aware of how his position as studio president could be a conduit for social good.

The Warners fared better than most as the Great Depression engulfed the country. In fact, Harry purchased the remaining shares of First National a week after Black Thursday. Construction continued in Burbank, which can be seen in the background of *Showgirl in Hollywood* (1930). On May 29 representatives of Warner Bros., First National, and Vitaphone met at the Ambassador Hotel in Atlantic City, New Jersey. Jack provided details about the new Technicolor Vitaphone shorts, and Harry's son, Lewis, gave an impressive address on the company's future. Lewis had been rising through the ranks and quickly found himself managing the studio's music division.

Harry's long-term plan was to have Lewis eventually take over as president of Warner Bros., which undoubtedly irked Jack. However, Jack was a solid performer in his Hollywood role. His curt and colorful personality was put to better use on the studio's back lot than in shareholders' meetings.

Numerous accounts of the Atlantic City meeting cited Harry's controversial claim that there was space for only three major production, distribution, and exhibition companies in the film industry. No doubt he was remembering how often his family business had been run off the road by more powerful companies. *Harrison's Reports* called this "Harry Warner's Astounding Statement" and then continued the hyperbole, claiming that "the independent producers, the independent exhibitors, all, in fact, who do not fit in the Harry Warner's scheme of things, have no right to live and if he had his way about it, he would no doubt shoot them, to decrease the business population." The author concluded by asserting that "Harry Warner will go down in history as the man who tried to out-Scrooge Charles Dickens' Scrooge."[6] Perhaps some saw Harry as an easy target because he was unlike the other hot-tempered studio moguls. There would be multiple attempts to attack Harry's business practices, including antitrust and receivership lawsuits, in the coming years.[7] But the charges didn't stick, and Harry's practice of defending his studio and the film industry would become increasingly useful.

Other accounts from Atlantic City, those that cited Warner's own words, were a bit kinder. The *New York Times* reported that the nature of the competition among theater chains kept the business limited. Warner argued that if theater ownership was a criterion for success, soon every venue would be owned by a small number of companies. He asserted that in any town where Warner Bros. could not run a film, it would build a theater to show its pictures. The studio was also going to increase its investment in stage plays, something it had toyed with in the past (most significantly with *The Jazz Singer*). There was also mention of television; it was still nowhere near market ready, but Warner saw it as a useful supplement to motion pictures by adding to the desire for entertainment. What was most important to Harry, however, was the growing intellect of movie audiences. He observed that predicting which films would be popular had become increasingly difficult, "due largely to the intellectual advancement of the people themselves, which has been largely brought about by the screen. The screen has educated people to think for themselves." Warner continued, "in looking to the future we must ascertain just what will do good as well as amuse."[8]

Warner's Twenty-Fifth Anniversary

By the end of 1930, Warner Bros. held 51 companies, 93 film exchanges, and 525 theaters in 188 American cities, in addition to the studio lots. The company's stock was valued at over $200 million, and it employed a total of 18,500 people.[9] Johnny O'Steen spoke warmly of Harry during these years: "Without his genius for getting loans, there never would have been a Warner Bros. He was the wise head, the restraining hand, the money getter, and the social[ly] conscious Warner who made the machine go."[10] Harry led the company on many fronts. He had always been a shrewd businessman—that came naturally to him—but over the last few years, Harry hit his stride, lobbying for both the future and the social importance of the cinema. To celebrate the continued success of the company, Warner Bros. was given a hundred-page twenty-fifth-anniversary spread in *Variety* on June 25, 1930. The Warners were billed as the "pacemakers of the amusement world" for their leadership in trendsetting motion pictures.[11] Warner Bros. made a splash by pushing the industry into the sound era, and it was about to solidify its role in the 1930s with its gritty house style.

Twenty-one-year-old Lewis Warner penned an essay projecting a positive future and a mutually beneficial relationship between stage and screen. Speaking like a man who was planning to run the company one day, he wrote, "The legitimate stage and talking pictures are now going after the same type of audience." Although there was a certain "kind of theatergoer whose nose tilted high at the mention of movies," Warner argued that "the presence of class players like John Barrymore, George Arliss, and Al Jolson . . . has helped right this prejudice against screen entertainment." Simply put, talkies started to change the perception of movies. What could be accomplished onstage could be duplicated on film with fewer limitations. Movies took popular stage plays and projected their adaptations across the world's screens. Warner concluded, "The fine thing is that talking pictures refuse to conform to a set pattern. They won't stay put."[12] Lewis had his father's confidence in the studio's role in shaping the future of motion pictures. The movies, like the Warner brothers, were forced to duck and weave cultural and economic blows to survive. The movies always prevailed. For the Warners, it was their increasing use of headline-driven entertainment that set them apart.

Harry took a small column next to his son's article titled "Warners—Past and Future." Harry used the space to acknowledge Sam's dedication to sound film, writing, "Today we are gathering the rewards of success, a success shadowed only by the absence of our brother, Sam, who brought Vitaphone to us when it was only a vague idea, and inspired to make it a reality." Being the astute businessman he was, Harry reminded the 16,250 stockholders of his commitment to their investment, as well as his commitment to the public. He summarized his view of the studio's role in the world by noting, "The measure of reward received by any of us is governed by the measure of service rendered."[13] Harry always believed in serving the public good while making solid business decisions.

Albert's essay in the *Variety* spread, titled "Warners and Finances," described the studio not only as providing good entertainment but also as "rank[ing] with the largest and most progressive in America."[14] Like Harry, Albert puffed their theater revenue and attendance numbers, both of which would impress the stockholders. Being the financial guru, Albert argued that "nothing proves so conclusively the stability of Warner Bros. pictures as the valuation of its bond and stock issues." Albert was most interested in the studio's growth—not just its profits but also its physical presence. The studio owned theaters in key areas of New York and Los Angeles. For Albert, the main point of pride in the success of Warner Bros. was its impact on the financial world.

By 1930, Jack was, in effect, running two studios: Warner Bros. and First National. Jack was studio boss, of course; Darryl Zanuck was second in charge, with Hal Wallis and G. Graham Baker sharing co-executive roles. Jack's essay in *Variety*, titled "But a Few Short Years," reflected on the time since the studio led the industry into the era of synchronized sound. Running early sound films was a tricky business. Warner noted that setting up a talking picture was akin to a stage manager organizing actors and props: "You just cannot run a picture and set the fader at 8 and say goodbye." There were additional considerations, such as managing a theater's acoustics, which Warner rightly saw as pivotal to proper sound exhibition. He discussed how studio operations required 250 electrical engineers, 100 writers, and 50 directors working across four lots. Echoing Harry, Jack described the film industry as "a business of intelligence," "better understanding," and "of the better thinking person."[15] This claim was no doubt a carryover from the early years, when moguls worked hard to justify the film business as being inhabited by more than just lowlifes, cheats, and scoundrels.

Three Musketeers of Hollywood: Harry, Albert, and Jack.

Other essays expounded on the grandiosity of the Warners' studio operations, such as managing one hundred trucks and two hundred touring cars of all makes and models, along with running a lumberyard that used about twenty million feet of lumber per year. Employees in the studio's animation unit, to which the brothers gave minimal attention, wrote about the unit's history and technical operations. The department was headed by Leon Schlesinger, who would shepherd Warner Bros. animation before going on to make the influential Superman cartoons in the 1940s. The animators were starting to transition to celluloid film, which allowed them to reuse drawings and save on labor. The first Looney Tunes Vitaphone cartoon was "Sinkin' in the Bathtub," inspired by the Warner film *Show of Shows* (1929). Brunswick, a Warner Bros. subsidiary, manufactured Vitaphone disks. Theater owners Spyros and George Skouras sold their properties to Warner Bros. and later worked for the company. Spyros wrote, "We conduct Warner Bros. theatres as though they were our own personal property."[16] George noted that the studio's profits had much to do with how "Warner Bros. has always been synonymous with clean entertainment."[17] Anyone familiar with the studio's output in the 1930s knows that this reputation would not hold for long, as

Warner's became known for its edgy, Production Code–defying films about crime, desperation, and debauchery.

The *Variety* anniversary issue also featured a piece by Zanuck, who wrote, "On Warner Brothers' pictures, special care is given to the editing. Weeks and very often months are spent in cutting and recutting and juggling to the best advantage sequences or episodes of the finished pictures." The proof is in the product, and the 1930s saw a long line of tight, punchy films from the studio, including gangster movies, Depression yarns, musicals, and anti-Nazi films by the end of the decade. Zanuck revealed that the studio cut each film to its essential pieces, something that saved money but also improved continuity. There was no room for filler in a Warner Bros. film. Zanuck concluded, "New Warner Brothers' pictures are recognized for their tempo, speed, and direct continuity of thought and action."[18] Hal Wallis echoed Zanuck in his column, noting that First National's system of production consisted of "complete harmony" between efficient and detail-oriented departments.[19] The Warner lots certainly embodied the genius of the production system in the early 1930s and featured a range of films, such as the gangsters of *The Public Enemy* (1931) and the tough female lead in *Night Nurse* (1931), Michael Curtiz's two-strip Technicolor horror films *Doctor X* (1932) and *Mystery of the Wax Museum* (1933), and a variety of social problem films such as *Five Star Final* (1931) and *Heroes for Sale* (1933). Many of the studio's films probed the nation's headlines, engaging audiences in familiar and relatable stories (even *Mystery of the Wax Museum*'s protagonist is a journalist investigating a crime).

Nobody on the Warner lot was more familiar with the studio's style than story editor Jacob Wilk, who wrote, "It is not only the active reaching out and search for material, which is the function of the story department, which is conducted like a newspaper office in a large city. The executive in charge must keep his finger on the public pulse all of the time."[20] The brothers had long been drawing on prominent stories, often found in newspapers or popular books, and in the 1930s the studio hit its stride with innumerable classic films based on famous or infamous tales. Warner Bros. films were rarely fantastic; in the early 1930s the studio solidified a house style to "reflect the cultural tensions of newspaper headlines, taking the dross of the daily grind and transforming it into entertainment gold."[21] A. P. Waxman, head of Warner publicity, knew how to sell an image and wrote warmly of the brothers. "They are democratic, with an open door to all," he noted. "That is the way they run their business." Waxman told of the brothers' dedication to charity and predicted that "when the final story is written about them, it can be summed up in four words: Warner Bros.—regular fellows."[22] The brothers were consistently generous, donating to various charities, both social and political, for their entire lives.

Warner's Gangsters

Warner Bros. continued to produce headline-driven material, which was often controversial and regularly caught the attention of censors and moral crusaders. A July issue of the *Houston Chronicle* argued that "Mr. Hays had sufficient opportunity to wash Hollywood's face. He had pleaded for a chance to improve the movies from the inside. He has had his chance. And if the sort of stuff Warner Brothers are placating on the pages of *Variety* be any criterion of his work, he has failed."[23] In August 1930 Will Hays wrote to Harry, Albert, and Jack to complain about the studio's indifference to the Production Code and its advertising rules.[24] Jack would reportedly get the censors' approval of a script and then let the director do whatever he wanted with the film. By the early 1930s, it was widely known that Warner Bros. "never observed the Code."[25] The frequent infractions had much to do with the type of material the studio pursued. Gangster stories and tales of fallen women, full of crime and sexuality, made up a great deal of the studio's output in the 1930s and kept the conservative censors busy. Even the studio's musicals and occasional horror films pushed social boundaries in true Warner Bros. fashion.

Director Mervyn LeRoy described the day Jack Warner approached him with galley proofs of a new book called *Little Caesar* by W. R. Burnett. LeRoy took the proofs home and became enthralled with the tale of gangster Rico Bandello. "I read straight through the night, my excitement heightening with every page," wrote LeRoy. The next morning, the director went right to Warner's office, where he found Jack sitting with Zanuck and Wallis. Fortunately, Warner was not constrained by formalities and allowed LeRoy to barge in. "This is what I've been looking for, Jack," LeRoy enthused. "This guy Burnett must have written this for me to do." Warner was somewhat skeptical because he was not sure the public would be interested in such a dark story just as the Depression was setting in. LeRoy remembered that all the moguls were leery of dark film fare in the early years of the Great Depression. After LeRoy pressured Warner for an hour, Jack finally gave in and gave the director the go-ahead to make *Little Caesar* (1930). LeRoy had confidence in the film because it reflected real-world brutality. As evidenced in the daily press, "There really were people like Bandello."[26] Mobsters like Al Capone were all over the headlines, and the St. Valentine's Day massacre was a recent memory. Warner knew the studio had done well with other films drawn from the headlines, so *Little Caesar* got the green light, even if it was yet another sordid tale from the streets.

Much of the film's power comes from Edward G. Robinson's performance as Rico. After dabbling in silent films in the 1920s, Robinson left a Broadway career for Warner Bros. He and his wife, Gladys, moved across the country because the money was too good to turn down. Growing up and living in New York City, Robinson had never needed a car because all the boroughs were easily accessible by train. But he soon got tired of riding around Los Angeles in taxis, so Robinson purchased a Ford. He quickly learned that the Warners frowned on Ford automobiles, likely because of Henry Ford's anti-Semitic views. The automaker was a financial supporter of Hitler and proudly had a photograph of the dictator hanging in his office. Ford's *Dearborn Independent* articles were translated into German and distributed by the Nazis. Although the *Dearborn Independent* ceased publication in 1927, the stench of Ford's anti-Semitism remained for many years. The studio purchased a LaSalle for Robinson to replace the Ford. The actor was initially assigned a small role in *Little Caesar,* but he pressed producer Hal Wallis for the lead. Wallis took the issue to Jack Warner, and "within a matter of hours I was cast as Little Caesar," Robinson wrote.[27] In his autobiography, Jack took credit for giving Robinson the role. Part of his story includes LeRoy's desire to give Clark Gable the title role, but Jack objected because of the actor's big ears. According to LeRoy, it was Zanuck who objected to Gable's ears. Casting Robinson as Rico would bear fruit for both the studio and its star. *Photoplay* soon declared Robinson the "First Gangster of Filmland."[28]

The studio's association with gangster films was permanently solidified when James Cagney's notorious mobster Tom Powers hit the screen in *The Public Enemy* (1931). Cagney landed the lead role after overshadowing Lew Ayres in *Doorway to Hell* (1930). The actor's hard-hitting demeanor led to his unshakable reputation as a tough guy. The film was directed by William "Wild Bill" Wellman, then best known for his aviation epic *Wings* (1927). When Zanuck questioned the advisability of doing another gangster film so soon after *Little Caesar,* Wellman shot back, "I'll make the roughest, toughest, goddamn one of them all!"[29] Wellman delivered a sucker punch of a film, but he may have gone too far for Jack Warner and studio director Michael Curtiz. The biggest problem was the gruesome ending: a lifeless Tom is leaned up against his mother's door and falls at her feet when she opens it. "It'll make everybody sick," complained Jack. Wellman vividly recalled that when Curtiz spoke up and agreed with Jack, Zanuck "hauled off, knocked the cigar right down his [Curtiz's] throat. I'm not kidding. That's what made pictures in those days."[30] The corpse scene stayed but would ultimately be overshadowed by another jarring scene in which Cagney shoves a grapefruit into Mae Clarke's face. In his autobiography, Jack noted that "this brutal bit of business achieved a kind of grisly immortality, aroused endless resentment among militant feminists and made 'Czar' Will Hays stew in his office where he was being paid a huge salary to protect the movies from that sort of attack."[31] As the studio found success in boundary-pushing films, Warner Bros. kept Hays busy for years to come.

The Warners' approach to challenging films is best illustrated by a *Photoplay* advertisement for their 1931–1932 feature films. It pictured two clenched fists, and the copy read: "Put up or shut up! There's only ONE answer to this challenge, Warner Bros. say it with pictures."[32] The studio continued to push the limits of decency in the coming years with a steady output of films about crime, sex, and surviving during the Great Depression. Jack Warner fondly remembered these years as the time the studio cemented "the Warner stock company," which ultimately consisted of Cagney and Robinson, of course, as well as "Bette Davis, Paul Muni, Errol Flynn, Olivia de Havilland, Ann Sheridan, Barbara Stanwyck, Jane Wyman, Ronald Reagan, Wayne Morris, Humphrey Bogart, John Garfield, Joe E. Brown, George Brent, Kay Francis, and Alan Hale." Warner was happy to counter MGM's claim that it had more stars than there are in heaven, noting, "These people made up the brightest constellation of stars in the sky." The proof could be found in the Warner Bros. trophy room, where there were so many Oscars "it looks like the assembly line in the factory where they are made."[33] Warner had good reason to be proud of his studio's talent, as they undeniably elevated cinema during the Depression years using their own brand of gloomily engaging entertainment.

Five Star Final, a newspaper drama starring Edward G. Robinson as an editor whose decisions lead to tragedy, caused problems with publisher William Randolph Hearst. Warner Bros. was not the only studio to make films about newspapers, and they covered the profession with the same brand of sharp observation used by many top journalists of the day. Hearst complained to Jack Warner that such films tried "the patience of newspaper people," mostly because of the "constant attacks on the newspaper fraternity in films which portray reporters as drunkards and editors as unscrupulous rascals."[34] Hearst tried to convince Warner that depicting reporters in a negative light would not lead to positive newspaper coverage of the studio and its films. Hollywood columnist Louella Parsons told Hearst she would try to convince Warner that *Five Star Final* could hamper the possibility of Marion Davies, Hearst's mistress, signing with Warner Bros. Jack Warner released the film anyway, and Hearst initiated a campaign to ban the film in key cities; he was successful in Boston. Hearst and Davies ultimately moved their production company, Cosmopolitan Pictures, to Warner Bros. anyway.

Heartbreak: Lewis Warner

Tragedy struck the Warner family while the studio was enduring the Depression and solidifying its future stars. Harry's only son and likely heir to the throne, Lewis, began to have serious health issues. Betty Warner, Lewis's sister, recalled that when her brother became infatuated with an actress, her father "had the same feeling he had upon learning of Jack's affair with Marilyn Miller. Sex and business didn't mix."[35] Harry suggested that Lewis take some time off before moving to Hollywood, so Lewis took a trip to Cuba, defying his doctor's orders to stay in New York until an infected wisdom tooth extraction could heal. While in Havana, his condition worsened. Lewis saw a dentist in Cuba, but it did not help. The *New York Times* received a cable on February 27 confirming that Lewis was at the Anglo-American Hospital in Cuba suffering from an infection after having a tooth removed in New York. The prognosis was good and there was no reason to worry, the first reports stated. Lewis would be back in shape in a couple of days. Even so, Harry, Rea, and Albert flew to Cuba to make sure everything was okay.

Little did anyone realize that the infection had found its way into Lewis's bloodstream, creating an extremely dangerous situation. The *New York Times* received another cable the following day that deceptively read, "Lewis Warner Improves." Lewis was, in fact, "critically ill with blood poisoning. At noon today, his recovery was considered problematical."[36] As his condition worsened, Harry and Rea chartered a plane on March 4 to fly Lewis to Miami, followed by a train ride back to New York. By this time, Lewis had also developed double pneumonia, making his condition increasingly dire.

Betty recalled seeing her brother in the hospital shortly before his passing: "I couldn't stand the idea of my beloved brother, my special, dynamic brother, swathed in bandages." At her mother's insistence, Betty visited Lewis. "Even with all the bandages on he joked with me," she remembered; he "tried to make *me* feel better. I left in tears."[37] Sadly, Lewis died on April 4, at the age of only twenty-two. His obituary appeared in the *New York Times* on April 6, along with condolences from myriad organizations. The funeral was held at 11:00 a.m. on April 7 at Temple Emanuel in New York City. Lewis was interred at Salem Fields Cemetery. Harry donated $250,000 to the Worcester Academy in his son's name. Lewis was a 1928 Worcester graduate.

Sam's daughter Lita had been living with Harry and Rea for only a short time when Lewis passed. Although the two shared a birthday, he was much older, so there was no sibling-type bonding. Lewis's sister Doris was very close to him, so his death hit her hard. His mother mourned for two decades and was often seen openly crying. Betty recalled that her mother "wouldn't allow music in the house because when Lewis was alive each room was filled with laughter, friends, and music. I was still allowed to have friends over, but her grief permeated the house."[38] His cousin Jack Jr. was also devastated. Lewis and Jack Jr. were supposed to be the next Warners to rise to the top of Hollywood.

Lita believed that losing a son was one of the worst things that could happen to a man like Harry, who was dedicated to his family, his faith, and his business. After Lewis died, Harry "lost interest in a dynasty." Even so, Harry tried to convince daughter Doris to join the family brand, but she was always lukewarm to the idea.[39] For a time, Harry took an interest in real estate and horse racing. Lita spent a lot of time with Harry, riding horses at the ranch he owned in Calabasas. She also accompanied Harry to the Santa Anita track, where Harry was a stockholder, and at the Del-Mar track, a horse racing facility founded by Bing Crosby in 1936. In her view, Harry was on autopilot in terms of the film business. Jack wrote warmly of his nephew, Harry's "fond young son," who "had a remarkable grasp of the picture business, and who was being trained to take his father's place in later years."[40] It is thought provoking to consider how history could have been different if Lewis (and Sam) had survived.

Jack certainly mourned the loss of Lewis, but his views on family were quite different from that of his brothers. When Albert Einstein visited the studio in 1931, Jack famously quipped, "Doctor, you have a theory of relativity

Left to right: Lewis Warner, Jack L. Warner, Bobby Jones, Harry M. Warner, and Albert Warner.

and I have mine. Never hire a relative." Jack Jr., who was written out of his father's autobiography, always asked, "Where would you be, pop, if your brothers hadn't hired you?"[41] By this time, Jack's marriage to Irma was on the rocks. Jack Jr. felt that coming from a large family and being the youngest and most vulnerable made Jack Sr. incapable of fatherhood. He also maintained that success changed his father for the worse and made it hard for him to carry on a relationship with anyone. Put simply, according to Jack Jr., "Success ruined my father."[42] Jack's best relationships were always with the people he worked with. Certainly, he sparred with some of his employees, but many admired him. Any knock-down, drag-out fights would eventually be laughed off, allowing Jack's quirky personality to take center stage.

Confronting the Depression and Family Quarrels

The novelty of sound films had kept the industry afloat for about a year, delaying the impact of the Depression. Harry continued the studio's rapid expansion, earning $17 million in profits in 1929. The studio also managed to turn a profit in 1930, but only $7 million. By 1931, Warner Bros. experienced a loss of about $8 million.[43] At the end of 1931, after facing a brief investigation into possible stock market malfeasance, the Warner Bros. board of directors received a vote of confidence, and all the officers kept their posts, including board president Harry Warner.

While on a Florida vacation with his family in early 1932, Harry was interviewed by a reporter from the *Miami Daily News*. When asked about the future of the movies, Harry's candid answer was that new developments were always needed. Regarding the studio's gamble on sound film, Harry modestly responded that it had involved "no more risk than that which every auto manufacturer takes when he brings out a new model." Purchasing Vitagraph had been a major risk, but a calculated one, thanks to Harry's cool leadership and Sam's dedicated vision. The mogul did not spend much time talking to the press, making sure to prioritize family time while on vacation. The interviewer described the scene: "And modestly dismissing with these few words the greatest pioneering feat launched on an amazed world by screenland, he snatched up his youngest daughter [actually, niece], Lita, and dashed into the surf."[44] With so many stories about Harry's coldness as a leader, it is fortunate that this journalist was able to see the stoic studio boss playing with his children at the beach. Not everyone in Hollywood is the caricature they are made out to be.

The film industry's future was up in the air, with many studios struggling to stay afloat. Harry was confident that movies would prevail; they always had. Warner had weathered nearly three decades of storms to earn his current post as president of Warner Bros. His indefatigable composure would lead the studio through many more challenges following the Depression years.

The *Boston Globe* caught up with Harry in 1932, when he was in town to play golf with Mayor James M. Curley as part of a public endorsement. Warner spoke about the development of color film and bemoaned the increase in talent agents. At the time, James Cagney was in the middle of one of his many battles with the studio over his salary. As Cagney's status had turned from new kid on the block to major star, his $400 per week had been raised to $1,400. Warner was holding firm at that salary and asked, "Now does a man need more than $1,400 a week to live?" Harry also quickly dismissed criticism from those who feared that crime narratives turned youths into savages. "If there were no pictures in the world," Warner observed, "the same boys would be bad boys and something else would be to blame."[45] Movies continued to be the target of both social crusaders and political attacks for decades to come. Harry remained a staunch defender of the medium for the rest of his life.

Gangsters sparked interest across Hollywood, and gangster films led to protests around the country from social conservatives. Howard Hughes's production of *The Racket* (1928), a film about Al Capone, led to death threats, and *Scarface* (1932), a Hughes-produced independent film released by United Artists, endured a lengthy censorship battle. The Payne Fund studies, which sought to connect movies with delinquency, were in full swing. Harry jumped in front of the expected controversy, arguing that movies were not responsible for social ills. Pressure continued to mount against Warner Bros. and the other Hollywood studios as they developed projects that did not adhere to Production Code standards. Always calm, collected, and confident, Harry radiated the aura of a seasoned businessman. A 1932 issue of *Screenland* described him as having "a touch of the Wall Street broker about his alert personality that expresses a new type in the amusement and commercial world: an international showman, a sort of three-in-one combination: showman-realtor-banker." He knew the business inside and out and continued to venerate the cultural importance of film. According to *Screenland,* Harry viewed "money somewhat as an engineer regards electricity. It is power, and useless until it is turned on to keep the wheels moving."[46] The proof was in his actions. Harry was known to advocate for business plans that benefited the largest number of his many thousands of employees. He was also a well-known philanthropist, always generous with his money.

The studio continued to engage audiences in topical, provocative, socially conscious narratives, and none was more powerful than *I Am a Fugitive from a Chain Gang* (1932), directed by Mervyn LeRoy. The film's subject was real-life fugitive Robert E. Burns, who had escaped from a Georgia chain gang. LeRoy had read Burns's serialized tale in *True Detective Mysteries Magazine,* and Jack Warner quickly purchased the story rights. Burns had been sentenced to hard labor in 1922 for a petty crime and had been on the run for some time when Warner Bros. picked up the project. He had even made the national news, such as a *New York Times* headline that read, "R. E. Burns Escapes Georgia Chain Gang: Chicago Ex-Publisher, Serving Term for $4 Hold-up, Flees for Second Time."[47] This film was a perfect example of the studio's ripped-from-the-headlines style. The picture also served

Harry's interest in using cinema to keep the public engaged in important social issues.

Burns traveled under an alias, Richard M. Crane, to avoid attracting attention while he was on the move.[48] LeRoy and Wallis located him in New Jersey, where there were no extradition laws. An agreement signed by Burns and Jack Warner on February 25, 1932, indicates that Burns was assisting with the film, but studio lawyers were careful to make the contract look like the majority of his pay was for book rights (to avoid the appearance of employing a fugitive from the law).[49] Both LeRoy's autobiography and interviews with Wallis confirm that the studio attempted to minimize the paper trail while Burns was on the run. The director also remembered that Burns was an important resource during filming. He was consulted regularly and had been set up in a secret location on the Warner Bros. lot. Story editor Wilk told producer Zanuck, "You may find Burns a little erratic, but you are used to all kinds of people so I am sure you will handle him and get the best out of him."[50] The film generated so much fanfare that it led the state of Georgia to amend its chain gang system. As a result, Jack Warner and LeRoy received numerous letters making it clear that they were not welcome in Georgia. But when LeRoy returned to the state in 1968 to assist John Wayne with *The Green Berets*, "there wasn't a lynch rope in sight."[51]

Meanwhile, the relationship between the Warners and Lina Basquette did not improve. Harry and Rea Warner won custody of Lita on March 19, 1930, after Lina finally caved, reluctantly, for "a $40,000 insurance policy, [Sam's] Minerva car, complete with chauffeur who doubled as a Warner spy, a $100,000 trust fund, and a $300,000 trust for the little girl."[52] In addition, Lina had married Cecil B. DeMille's cinematographer Peverell "Pev" Marley, who did not like children and wanted Lina to give up her custody battle with the Warners. "I'm getting damned sick and tired of all this bullshit about the kid," snapped Pev after one of Lina's shows in Chicago.[53] Back in Hollywood, even Louis B. Mayer implored Lina to go along with the Warners, insinuating that she had only married Sam for the money. Lina snapped back, telling Mayer that he should have "more important things to do than join a conspiracy to steal a baby from her flesh-and-blood mother." When Lina refused to apologize, Mayer stood up and shouted, "Young woman, you have a lot to learn. You are nothing but a stupid nobody. From now on, Harry and Jack Warner will see to it that in this industry you won't be able to get a job in a brothel!"[54] Hollywood would not see Lina in a film for nearly a decade.

Lina's marriage to Pev didn't last the year. No doubt his constant siding with the Warners didn't help. Lita was taken to live with Harry and Rea in Mount Vernon and would not see Lina more than a couple of times in the coming decades. Rea made it clear that it was her intent to keep the child away from her mother until Lita turned twenty-one. Despite her animosity toward the rest of the Warners, Lina spoke fondly of Sam throughout her life—a life that took many interesting turns, including a relationship with notorious gangster Johnny Roselli and an encounter with Nazi filmmaker Leni Riefenstahl (as well as other detestable Nazi notables). According to Lina, Riefenstahl mentioned meeting Sam when he was in Germany selling a Rin Tin Tin film. "I found him a delightfully attractive man," said Riefenstahl, and "almost fell in love with him. He offered me a contract which I was about to accept when I was painfully disillusioned and shocked when he admitted he was a Jew." Lina confidently replied, "My husband, Sam Warner, was one of God's finest contributions to the human race."[55]

Lita had a happy life with the Warners, being raised by Harry and Rea at the Mount Vernon farm.[56] She felt like an only child of sorts, as the older Warner siblings were off doing other things. She remembered Harry being gone quite often. The family eventually moved to Santa Monica, where Lita watched the parties thrown by Louis B. Mayer off in the distance. The conservative Warners never let her get anywhere near the debauchery occurring at the Mayer residence. On one occasion, Columbia mogul Harry Cohn brought his mistress to the Warners' house. Lita was quickly told to go upstairs so as not to be exposed to this indiscretion. Harry Warner was a staunch social conservative and, according to Lita, did not care much for actors or actresses. Perhaps that explains why Harry was such an oddity in Hollywood—a man who was unfailingly faithful to his wife and family. Lita saw Harry as a very "sentimental and sweet man," as well as "very generous." He was firm but fair and never abusive. Lita looked back fondly at her life with the Warners, knowing that her mother's tumultuous lifestyle would have been wrong for a child.

A 1932 profile by Louis Nizer in the *Exhibitor* described Harry as having a "shrewd, owlish, quizzical face whose good nature expresses a condescension towards life." Nizer emphasized Harry's "good humor," which was "written across his features. It is not unsophisticated kindliness. It is the tolerant friendliness which only the bitterest struggle through life can leave."[57] The Warners' journey from poverty and prejudice to success in the United States unquestionably benefited from Harry's cool, calm confidence and self-assuredness. As the Depression reached its greatest depths in 1933, homeless camps called "Hoovervilles" sprang up. The name was a dig at the sitting president, whom many felt could have mitigated the economic disaster more effectively. Harry was increasingly passionate about helping the nation's struggling citizens reconstruct their lives.

The New Deal Studio

When Franklin D. Roosevelt ran for president, it signaled a major shift in the political winds for Harry, a longtime Republican. That political shift was evidence of Harry's practical nature and his belief that he owed blind allegiance to no particular ideology. In contrast, Jack and Albert were latecomers to the Democratic bandwagon. Jack was not sure FDR had the following to win a national election, although he may have underestimated the extent to which Hoover had fallen out of favor. John Steel, who grew up listening to Albert's stories, recalled that Abe was not overly impressed with FDR and thought Roosevelt did not do enough to protect Jews from the bigotry they faced in the United States at the time. Ultimately, however, all the brothers supported Roosevelt. As the effects of the Depression and fear for the future grew, the Warners realized that FDR had a good opportunity to regain the nation's trust and stabilize a faltering economy.

As FDR's recovery plans increased in popularity, Warner Bros. became known as "the studio that most explicitly upheld the New Deal in its production."[58] The studio had been showcasing relevant dramas such as *Three on a Match* (1932), a lightning rod of a story about three women struggling to oust themselves from life in the slums; *The Crash* (1932), which featured a man's plight following the Wall Street crash; *Taxi* (1932), which dealt with struggling cab drivers in New York; and, of course, *I Am a Fugitive from a Chain Gang*. The studio's gangster films also resonated with desperate Depression audiences. This may be why some of the more socially conservative members of the public feared the genre would erode society's moral fabric. Of course, there was no proof that movies created criminals, and audiences were smart enough to empathize with a character's struggle while understanding that bootlegging and racketeering were not stable lines of employment. Warner Bros. continued to have its finger on the pulse of American culture.

When Roosevelt was elected in November 1932, his support from the Warners did not go unnoticed. Jack Warner was delighted to learn that his whole family had been invited to the inauguration and, being a shrewd businessman, found a way to both celebrate FDR's victory and advertise the studio's blockbuster musical *42nd Street* (1933). Directed by Lloyd Bacon and featuring kaleidoscopic dance sequences by choreographer Busby Berkeley, *42nd Street* not only was a success for Warner Bros. but also helped revive the musical genre in the sound era. Berkeley became known for his ability to combine the strengths of stage and film to create a unique perspective for cinema audiences. With the addition of sex appeal—such as the scene in which the camera takes viewers through women's legs to ultimately meet a smiling Ruby Keeler and Dick Powell—the studio knew the film would be a hit.

It is worth noting that Warner Bros. musicals such as *42nd Street* and *Gold Diggers of 1933* evoked social problems that were absent from other popular musicals of the era, such as RKO's run of whimsical Fred Astaire and Ginger Rogers tap-dancing numbers. References to bread lines and the forgotten men of World War I were peppered throughout Warner Bros. musicals, giving them a distinct feel. These musicals were not escapist. Even though Berkeley's choreography was enchanting, the films were grounded in the reality of the Great Depression.

Recalling the Warners' nationwide book tour from years ago, Jack worked with General Electric to develop a cross-country promotional tour with a train named the 42nd Street Special. The train was fully covered with film advertisements and bright lightbulbs, and it glowed its way from coast to coast. The journey began in Los Angeles and included many stops, including the GE convention in St. Louis. The itinerary for the trip made front-page news in *Film Daily*, which described the train's cargo as "a batch of stars and a bevy of beauties," including *42nd Street* cast members as well as James Cagney, Joe E. Brown, and Bebe Daniels.[59] As the inauguration drew close, the studio puffed its 1933 slate of films as "inaugurating a NEW DEAL in ENTERTAIN-MENT."[60] *Film Daily* also featured a full-page advertisement from Warner Bros. touting the new president, which read "OFF WITH THE OLD LEADERS. ON WITH THE NEW! WARNER BROS. PICTURES, THE PEOPLE'S CHOICE."[61]

Jack Warner quickly moved to produce two more musicals that could benefit from Berkeley's sense of style and staging. *Gold Diggers of 1933*, directed by LeRoy, reunited much of the *42nd Street* cast and included memorable musical sequences from Berkeley. The film's finale directly addressed the "forgotten man," the World War I veterans hit hardest by the Depression.

OFF WITH THE OLD LEADERS.

ON WITH THE NEW!

WARNER BROS. PICTURES
The People's Choice

"42ND STREET"—THE MIRACLE SHOW OF 1933"	"FAIRBANKS JR., LORETTA YOUNG —"JIMMY DOLAN"
"GRAND SLAM"— PAUL LUKAS, LORETTA YOUNG"	"CAGNEY —"PICTURE SNATCHER"— ALICE WHITE"
"THE KEYHOLE"— KAY FRANCIS, GEORGE BRENT"	"JOE E. BROWN — — "ELMER THE GREAT"
"WARREN WILLIAM — — "THE MIND READER"	"ARLISS — THE ADOPTED FATHER" —BETTE DAVIS"
"BETTE DAVIS —"EX-LADY"— ALL-STAR CAST"	"BARBARA STANWYCK—"BABY FACE"—GEO. BRENT"
"RICHARD BARTHELMESS —"CENTRAL AIRPORT"	"EDWARD G. ROBINSON— THE LITTLE GIANT"

FDR and Warner Bros.

The 42nd Street Special.

One of the most famous scenes, the "Shadow Waltz," featured dancers on elevated stairs playing violins wired with electric light. During filming, a massive earthquake shook Southern California, and people recalled the water tower swaying from side to side, sloshing its contents. None of the dancers were injured, but some of the lighted wardrobes short-circuited. Berkeley nearly fell from the camera boom from which he was directing.

The talented choreographer also oversaw musical sequences for *Footlight Parade,* directed by Bacon. Berkeley outdid himself again using hundreds of choreographed swimmers in his "By the Waterfall" number. These mesmerizing sequences added flair to the studio's established gritty presence. James Wingate of the censor's office wrote numerous letters to Jack Warner, asking for deletions. One of the film's hottest lines—when Nan (Joan Blondell) tells a woman, "As long as there's sidewalks, you've got a job"—was suggested for deletion but ultimately remained in the film.

The 1933 lineup was not limited to musicals; it included an impressive number of powerful films. An important woman's film, *Baby Face,* dealt with a sexually abused woman who grew up to use sex to her advantage. This film became notorious with the censors and led to conversations about imposing stricter censorship standards. Prominent censor boards in Ohio and Chicago banned the film, although *Baby Face* would eventually be okayed in Chicago after minor cuts. William Wellman's *Heroes for Sale* (1933), about a struggling World War I veteran who becomes a drug addict, was released in June, nearing the lowest point of the Great Depression. Wellman's son described *Heroes for Sale* as "Warner Bros. at its best, taking real-life stories and events from the day's newspapers about ordinary people struggling to survive."[62]

Another film directed by Wellman, *Wild Boys for the Road,* is a heartbreaking tale of children who go out on their own to help save their families from the Depression. The censors were deeply nervous about the gruesomeness of this film, especially one scene in which a boy loses a leg. Wingate once again wrote to Jack Warner, asking that the film be toned down. Warner stood by Wellman's final product, except for the final scene, where the boys are hauled off to jail. Instead, Warner insisted that the film include the potential for redemption, with a judge showing mercy on the boys for their misdeeds during such a desperate time.

The Warners hit a snag when Darryl Zanuck resigned in April 1933. He was an essential figure at the studio, which was humming with powerful films. Zanuck had both the insight and the talent to run a studio, but he knew Jack Warner would never give up his post. Milton Sperling, who was Zanuck's assistant, remembered his first sighting of the producer: "He was carrying his polo mallet and was followed by his retinue of stooges. Suddenly he stopped, walked over to the stage wall, and peed on it, all the while talking over his shoulder to the people he was with."[63] One version of the final dustup between Zanuck and the studio is that it took place during a dinner at the Brown Derby, where a few producers were discussing the studio's latest features. Harry Warner opened the door, looking to have a word with Zanuck outside. According to Wallis, Zanuck gave him a "this is trouble look." Wallis and the other producers could hear the two men shouting outside. Zanuck came back into the restaurant looking "flushed and irritable," sat down, and ordered another drink. "I'm leaving Warners," said Zanuck, "and I'm not coming back."[64]

"Zanuck Resigns from Warners" read an April 15 headline in the *Los Angeles Times.*[65] Both Zanuck and the Warners claimed the split was over a contract dispute. A central point of contention was the industry's furloughs, which were scheduled to be restored. When Warner Bros. was slow to comply, Zanuck sent Jack a resignation letter. Harry knew Zanuck's talent would be in demand elsewhere, so he wired Hays about a possible arbitration violation: "If at any time within six months after the termination of an individual's employment, another company would not employ him until all of the terms of the proposed employment were communicated to the company that had employed him previously, giving the prior employer the right to meet the terms offered by the prospective new employer."[66]

Zanuck was interested in teaming up with Joseph Schenck at Twentieth Century (which would soon merge with Fox), where the talent had access to profit sharing. One problem for the Warners was that several employees followed Zanuck out the door.[67] Schenck wrote to Hays, clearing Zanuck of any wrongdoing. The memo revealed that after Zanuck's resignation, the Warners instigated a conflict with Schenck, accusing him of luring Zanuck away from Warner Bros. Schenck declared, "Mr. Zanuck informs me that he had no thought or intention of leaving Warner Bros. and that he never would have considered doing so had it not been for a situation which developed during the fifty percent wage cut in March of this year." Schenck also believed the Warners were spying on Fox:

> Not only were detectives engaged by certain employees of Warner
> Bros. to check the activities of Twentieth Century in and about
> the studio, and the information obtained by such detectives used
> by Warner Bros. in an effort to intimidate prospective employees
> of Twentieth Century, but a deliberate effort was made to induce
> a stenographer working in the executive office of Twentieth
> Century to divulge to employees of Warner Bros. all information
> of value concerning the company's business and to deliver them
> topics of telegrams and correspondence in order that they might
> be advised as to pending deals and activities, particularly with ref-
> erence to engaging of talent and the purchasing of stories.[68]

Schenck believed the stenographer had been offered a better job at Warner Bros. in the event she lost her position at Twentieth Century. He claimed to have a letter given to the stenographer by a Warner Bros. employee, along with a $50 bribe. The accusations were never proved, and Warner Bros. restored full pay on the lot.[69] In all likelihood, Zanuck left Warner Bros. to pursue an opportunity to run a studio. Any skirmish over pay was a convenient excuse, even if Zanuck's concern was justified. After all, Harry Warner was so supportive of Roosevelt's National Industrial Recovery Act of 1933 (NIRA) that *Variety* billed him as a "NIRA propagandist."[70] Warner worked with New

Deal architect Hugh S. Johnson to develop film trailers in support of NIRA and would get approval to use the National Recovery Administration logo in multiple Warner Bros. films.

There is no question that Warner Bros. was the Roosevelt studio. Harry Warner continued to see the medium and the industry as culturally important. FDR's inaugural message of fearlessly moving forward could not have been better connected to Harry's determination to ensure a future that looked better for everyone. Warner continued to press Hollywood filmmakers, who, he said, had a "gigantic obligation, honorable but frightening." For Warner, studios "must have the courage and wisdom to make pictures that are forthright, revealing, and entertaining, pertinent to the hour and the unpredictable future."[71] The Warners, of course, had been leading such a charge by making topical films about crime and struggle, but 1934 would be a transitional year for the studio and its boundary-pushing content.

The Production Code

On June 23, 1934, *Film Daily* reported "Producers Move to Tighten Production Code" in response to growing religious outrage at "so-called immoral pictures."[72] Moral crusaders had been ramping up protests against Hollywood for years. The Catholic Legion of Decency drew a substantial following overflowing with anti-Hollywood sentiment. Women's groups were particularly peeved at Hollywood. The two movements were connected, often by faith. The *Chicago Daily Tribune* reported that "the church campaign [is] rolling up like a snowball over Hollywood."[73] The General Federation of Women's Clubs stated that both MGM and Warner Bros. had the wrong attitude and "still believe that the type of pictures they turn out is satisfactory and no new policy is necessary."[74] Both Jack Warner and MGM chief Louis B. Mayer refused to comment on the issue. Members of the Legion of Decency, which often allied with Protestant groups, urged their congregations to pledge against Hollywood. The Legion Pledge was regularly read aloud from the pews, and adherents promised to condemn all immoral films and related advertising and to view only films that did not conflict with Christian principles. Other Christian leaders pushed followers to avoid movies altogether.

Roosevelt made the mistake of appointing Dr. A. Lawrence Lowell to the National Recovery Administration (NRA) Code Authority to assess and regulate Hollywood. Lowell had been president of Harvard University, where

he worked to limit the admission of Jews and purge the campus of homo-
sexuals. It is unclear how Lowell's history of prejudice went unnoticed by
Roosevelt. Lowell had been president of the Motion Picture Research Council,
which oversaw the Payne Fund studies that investigated the impact of movies
on youth. The *Motion Picture Herald* went so far as to describe the Payne
Fund studies as "propaganda directed against the freedom of speech."[75] Upon
Lowell's appointment, the *Los Angeles Times* reported that "unconcealed
resentment was displayed in regard to the naming of Dr. Lowell, who recently
confessed to having seen only three movies in the past two years."[76] Harry
Warner, along with a number of other studio bosses, lined up to openly
debate Lowell's grounds for censoring Hollywood films. The NRA Code
represented the latest threat of government censorship. Under pressure once
again, Hollywood made the difficult decision to increase self-censorship to
keep the moral crusaders at bay.

By 1933, as the Great Depression reached its lowest ebb, Jack Warner
wondered whether audiences might prefer lighter fare. A *Film Daily* headline
touted in early 1934, "Jack Warner Says Public Demands More Gayety in
Pictures."[77] The 1934 slate of Warner Bros. films contained much less doom
and gloom and more humor. Musicals such as *Flirtation Walk* and the Lloyd
Bacon–directed, Busby Berkeley–choreographed *Wonder Bar* gave audiences
more escapist fare. James Cagney also brought some of his comedic charisma
to *Here Comes the Navy*. Warner Bros. began a series of shyster satires with the
Edward G. Robinson vehicle *The Little Giant* (1933) and *Lady Killer* (1933)
with Cagney. Robinson reprised the comedic gangster role in *A Slight Case
of Murder* (1938) and *Larceny, Inc.* (1942). Berkeley received solo directing
credit for the comedy *She Had to Say Yes* (1933), although he was assisted
by George Amy at Jack Warner's insistence. Joe E. Brown continued to carry
Warner's talking clown comedies, the latest of which was *Son of a Sailor* (1933)
with Loretta Young and Thelma Todd. Brown was one of the most popular
comedians in the United States, and his films should not go unnoticed for
their cheerful appeal during the Depression. Aligning with Warner's civic
interests, Brown became a major Hollywood supporter of Jewish immigration
in the coming years, with World War II on the horizon.

Another problem for the industry was self-censorship, which had been
easy to duck since 1922 but was now up against a new sheriff. Joseph Breen
had risen through the Catholic ranks after serving as publicity director for the
Twenty-Eighth International Eucharistic Congress in 1926. By 1931, Breen

had worked his way into the Hays office, and by 1934, he was a Hollywood insider who had the ear of the Legion of Decency and the weapons to push back against the powerful studio bosses. Breen was particularly annoyed with Warner Bros. He once said, "Warners makes cheap low-tone pictures with a lot of double meaning, wise-cracks, and no little filth which they think is funny," branding the studio "the lowest bunch we have."[78] Harry Warner, who fully understood the repercussions of failing to self-censor, reluctantly told his studio, "If Joe Breen tells you to change a picture, you do what he tells you. If anyone fails to do this—and this goes for my brother—he's fired."[79] Harry understood that federal censorship was something to be avoided at all costs.

Family Affairs

Wedding bells were ringing for Harry's daughter Doris and Jack's friend Mervyn LeRoy. After Lewis died, Harry was adamant that his daughter take a greater interest in the family business, so she had made a few trips to Los Angeles. Doris and Mervyn met on the lot one day and had lunch together (although they had first met in San Francisco, when Doris was just a child). When Doris went back to New York, the two kept up a constant correspondence. They also made regular trips across the country to see each other. Love was in the air when Mervyn asked Jack about proposing to Doris. Jack didn't think the two were right for each other, but that didn't matter. "Love listens to no advice," remembered LeRoy, "I was in love . . . I proposed. She accepted."[80] They wed in the first week of 1934. Jack Warner did not disappoint as best man. Betty Warner served as flower girl, Lita Warner was ring bearer, and Doris's friend Gwen Heller was maid of honor.

The wedding was held at New York's Waldorf-Astoria Hotel. The ceremony, officiated by Rabbi Israel Fineberg, was conducted under a pergola, flanked by cedars and calla lilies. What made this a true Warner Bros. wedding was the heat and hum of arc lamps highlighting the scene for the cameras. Harry wanted to record the wedding as a gift to the couple, and the *New York Times* reported, "Warner Marriage Filmed as Talkie."[81] Guests included Harry and Rea Warner, Albert Warner, Will Hays, Paul Muni, Eddie Cantor, Adolph Zukor, Leon Schlesinger, and Shirley Warner. Benjamin and Pearl Warner, unable to make the trip east, listened over the radio. Mervyn's best man, Jack Warner, showed up fashionably late. Running into the venue, Jack found the groom and said, "Hey, Mervyn, we're on!" "You're not on, I'm on," he replied. Jack, always the performer, did a quick "Shuffle off to Buffalo" and quipped, "Okay, let's go."[82] Mervyn and Doris spent their honeymoon traveling the world on the SS *Empress* of Britain. Back in Los Angeles, Hal Wallis threw a star-studded party for the newlyweds.

Despite Harry's efforts to bring Doris into the family business, she quickly embraced her socialite status. Although she still dabbled in studio affairs (she pitched *Gone with the Wind* to Jack, but he turned it down, and the rest is David O. Selznick and MGM history), Doris understandably did not want to wage the uphill battle of being a female executive in the 1930s. Harry had no qualms about breaking the sexist cultural norm and allowing his daughter to ascend the studio ranks. But perhaps Doris was not cut out for the role; as her sister Betty remembered, Doris was the princess of the family. She had been raised to marry well, which she did. Betty thought Doris was more interested in hosting swanky parties, which was much more fun than spending long hours at the studio. Mervyn always spoke highly of Doris, even long after their divorce.

The brothers faced their most difficult struggle in 1934 with the passing of their beloved mother, Pearl. Her obituary ran in the trade press as well as in the *New York Herald Tribune* and *Los Angeles Times*.[83] Jack and Sadie were at Pearl's side when she passed. Harry, Albert, David, Rose, and Anna chartered a plane from New York as soon as they learned of their mother's deteriorating condition, but Pearl's fatal cerebral hemorrhage struck while they were in flight. Having spent her last ten years in Beverly Hills, Pearl dedicated most of her time to charity work, including at the Los Angeles Sanitorium. The funeral was held at B'Nai Brith Temple, and another service took place at Warner's New York office. Pearl was interred at the Home of Peace Cemetery, alongside her son Sam. Pearl, seventy-six, had been married to Ben for fifty-eight years.

Such dedication to family had certainly been instilled in Harry, who remained faithful to his wife, but Jack, always the outlier, was another story. Harry learned of his brother's infidelity with the young Ann Page one evening when Jack failed to return home as expected. He needed to be at the studio early to finalize a film shipment, and Irma phoned Harry, worried sick about her husband's whereabouts. She knew about Jack's affair with Marilyn Miller but thought his indiscretions were in the past. Harry's suspicions proved correct when he called the studio police, and they knew exactly where Jack was. Harry phoned Ann's number and reamed Jack: "You no-good-son-of-a-bitch!

Harry and Rea. (Author's personal collection)

Irma's worried to death, thinking you're dead in the ditch somewhere. For all I care, that's where you should be. Not with some whore." "I do what I want," Jack fired back.[84] Harry never understood why Jack refused to be happy with his wife and family and always succumbed to temptation. Irma would have done anything to keep Jack, whom she truly loved. Jack and Ann would have a daughter, Barbara, while Jack was still married to Irma. After years of struggle, Irma and Jack divorced, and he wed Ann in 1936. Irma retained custody of their son, Jack Jr., whose relationship with his father would suffer as the years went on.

As Jack was working his way out of one marriage and into another, Ben Warner died unexpectedly in 1935 while visiting Anna and her husband in Youngstown. Harry and Rea, Albert and Bessie, Anna and David, and Doris flew to Ohio to accompany the body back to Los Angeles. Harry made the funeral arrangements. Although the family asked for a small, simple service, about seven hundred people attended. The service was conducted by Rabbi S. M. Neeches at B'Nai Brith, and Ben was buried alongside his wife in the Home of Peace Cemetery. Ben's will gifted his property to the Warner girls—Anna, Sadie, and Rose—with Albert serving as executor of the estate. For the Warner family, losing Sam, Lewis, Pearl, and Ben in less than a decade was a series of serious blows. The Great Depression caused turmoil across the country, but nothing hurt the Warners more than losing family members.

Nazis and Union Thugs

In addition to battling the Depression and censorship and losing their parents, the brothers were acutely aware of the increasing instability in Europe in the mid-1930s. Warner Bros. was the first film company to put decency ahead of profits by pulling its products out of Germany in 1933. Universal followed suit, but the other studios stayed put, unwilling to cut off the lucrative German market as they dug out of the Depression. Warner's reasons behind the move are not clear. One problem is Jack Warner, who used his mythmaking skills to weave a tall tale in his autobiography. Writing about a trip to Austria with Ann (while he was still married to Irma), Warner claimed it was "there I got the sickening news of Joe Kauffman, our Warner Brothers man in Germany, had been murdered by Nazi killers in Berlin. Like many another outnumbered Jew, he was trapped in an alley. They hit him with fists and clubs, and kicked the life out of him with their boots, and left him lying there."[85] According to Jack, this was the reason the studio stopped operating and distributing in Germany. This story lived on for decades, with Warner as the only source. Skeptical historians have been unable to figure out who Joe Kauffman was or whether he was murdered by Nazis.

Here is what we do know. On April 11, 1933, *Variety* reported several rumors out of Germany, including that a man named Phil Kauffman, Warner Bros. general manager in Germany, was "scramming to Paris for safety."[86] The studio was relocating its employees as anti-Jewish activity was spreading, so this may have accounted for part of what Warner remembered. On April 25 *Variety* reported that Kauffman had "his automobile stolen by Nazis, his house ransacked and himself beaten, despite the fact he's British. The Nazis later apologized to him, explaining it was only a mistake. They thought he was two other fellows."[87] Kauffman did not die at the hands of the Nazis, but he collapsed shortly thereafter while on business in Stockholm, suggesting that Jack "took dramatic license to spin a more colorful tale."[88] Strange as this story is, it was time for Warner Bros. to lead the industry again, this time by pulling its exhibitions out of Germany.

In spring 1934 attorney Leon Lewis began looking for support to create an underground anti-Nazi spy operation. Through MGM attorney Mendel Silberberg, Lewis was able to arrange a meeting of the minds at the Hillcrest Country Club in Beverly Hills. The Hillcrest had opened in 1920 as a Jewish country club, at a time when most clubs did not allows Jews. It was the perfect place to inform Hollywood moguls and other powerful personalities, including Louis B. Mayer, Irving Thalberg, Harry Cohn, Ernst Lubitsch, and Jack Warner, about local fascist activity. Lewis had a private room set up with copies of publications from the Silver Shirts, a local Nazi organization. As the attendees read a series of anti-Semitic essays about Hollywood Jews, Lewis regaled the group with stories of his activities. As historian Steven J. Ross tells it, "Over the past seven months his [Lewis's] spies had infiltrated the Friends of New Germany (FNG) and uncovered evidence of espionage, sabotage and rebellion, findings that had been well documented by the local press during the recent German-American Alliance trial."[89] The moguls, who were certainly familiar with US anti-Semitism and the increasing violence in Europe, were surprised to see such blatant Nazi activity in their own backyard.

Lewis sought funding from other local leaders, and while money was pledged, collecting it was another story. Silberberg and Lewis arranged for a committee of Hollywood power players to solicit funding for the spy operation. Chaired by Silberberg, who had the eyes and ears of Hollywood, the nondescriptly named Community Committee found its way into the offices of industry leaders. MGM's Irving Thalberg took particular interest, giving a boost to fund-raising efforts. After Jack Warner and other moguls pledged $5,000 each, Warner convinced thirty of his employees to collectively donate another $2,600. Lewis's operation would thwart assassination and sabotage plots, including one to kill many Hollywood figures. Nazi groups would never achieve success in prewar Los Angeles, thanks to Lewis and his spies, who were funded in part by the Warners and their employees.

The FNG disbanded in 1936 and became the deceptively collegial sounding German-American Bund. The Hollywood Anti-Nazi League (HANL), a communist front group cofounded by Russian spy Otto Katz, kept tabs on the bund and others of its ilk, in addition to holding public rallies in opposition to Hitler. The HANL was launched during a fund-raising dinner at the Wilshire Ebell theater in June. In attendance were Jewish moguls Jack Warner,

Carl Laemmle, Irving Thalberg, and independent producer Walter Wanger. Irish Catholics were represented by director John Ford, actors James Cagney and Pat O'Brien, and Los Angeles bishop John J. Cantwell. The event was organized by Hollywood leftists Dorothy Parker and Donald Ogden Stewart. Other attendees included screenwriter and author Rupert Hughes, actor Paul Muni, and actress Gloria Stuart. The dinner featured a lecture from Prince Hubertus zu Lowenstein, who spoke about Hitler's plan to take over the civilized world. The HANL would grow into a unique mix of Popular Front politicos ranging from card-carrying communists to staunch conservatives, all of them united against Hitler.

In October the HANL held a rally that filled the Shrine Auditorium in Los Angeles. Irving Berlin and Dorothy Parker headlined. High-profile attendees included Fritz Lang, Mervyn LeRoy, Gloria Stuart, and Walter Wanger. Another, more exclusive gathering was held at the home of Warner Bros. star Edward G. Robinson. Among the honored guests were Bette Davis, Ginger Rogers, Paul Muni, Miriam Hopkins, Robert Montgomery, John Ford, Anatole Litvak, Jack Warner, Walter Wanger (presumably spending time at both events), and Carl Laemmle. Warner's KFWB radio station broadcast the HANL's anti-Nazi news across Southern California. Starting in early 1937, KFWB aired anti-Nazi news on Saturdays from 7:00 to 8:00 p.m., often centered around Donald Ogden Stewart's dramatic monologues. On Thursdays, screenwriter Hy Kraft criticized the Nazis during the 9:15 news break. The HANL's radio programming, coupled with its publications *Hollywood Anti-Nazi News* and *Hollywood Now,* ruffled the feathers of fascist sympathizers, and in April 1937 HANL headquarters was vandalized and burglarized. In the coming years, Warner Bros. would be the first studio to outwardly attack Hitler and the Nazis, but for the time being, the Production Code did not allow content critical of other nations. Nevertheless, the studio found clever ways to work around these strictures and produce narratives with antiauthoritarian messages.

Another problem for studio bosses was the mobbed-up trade union known as the International Alliance of Theatrical Stage Employees (IATSE), made up mostly of projectionists. In the mid-1930s struggling labor leaders Willie Bioff and George Brown violently took over the IATSE, carrying out a string of murders around the country and targeting anyone who tried to organize an independent union. Projectionist Herbert Green was supposedly beaten to death by Bioff himself. Louis Altrie was murdered when he attempted to set up a union for theater janitors. While walking home with his wife in Chicago, would-be union organizer Clyde Osterberg was killed when a gunman drove up alongside the couple and opened fire. Once Osterberg was on the ground, the shooter got out and fired two more bullets into his victim's head. Osterberg's wife witnessed the entire ordeal and was left unharmed. Riddled with fear, she clammed up when questioned by the police. The grisly, coldhearted nature of the mob execution was detailed on the front page of the *Chicago Daily Tribune,* sending a message to the entertainment industry: this is what happens to the opposition.[90]

Warner Bros. was careful when it released Michael Curtiz's *Black Fury* (1935). The film's narrative centers on a coal miner (played by Paul Muni) and is based on a 1929 strike where one employee was beaten to death by the Coal and Iron Police, a private company hired to keep workers in line. When the project was in preproduction, the coal industry complained to Will Hays. Hal Wallis suggested to Jack Warner that the original title, *Black Hell,* be changed. The studio wanted to avoid backlash from the coal industry, especially as it was dealing with growing labor issues in its own industry, complete with threats of violence. Byron Haskin, the film's cinematographer, bemoaned *Black Fury*'s central stance: "So an unnamed agency gets all the blame. The unions, the workers, and the management all come off as real nice guys."[91] Curtiz biographer Alan Rode surmises that the film ultimately "strengthened the burgeoning reputation of Warner Bros. as a producer of socially significant pictures while allowing the studio to avoid publicly aligning with either management or labor."[92] The Warners were in a tough spot, as their usual fearless cultural criticism had to be muted until an understanding was reached with IATSE. And any conflict with the coal unions could certainly impact the future of labor in Hollywood.

Film historians have observed that Hollywood's studio bosses may have partnered with the mob and its money to survive the Great Depression. In short, if a studio supported a union on its lot, IATSE would collect dues, and the mobsters could kick back some cash to the studio, while the studio paid the mob to avoid labor strikes. It was a vicious circle that lured many moguls. Stories about standoffs with Bioff and studio brass can be found in myriad Hollywood histories, and the Warner brothers are no exception. Bioff visited Harry Warner at temple and at his ranch in the San Fernando valley. Bioff regularly met with Columbia's Harry Cohn and others. Nicholas Schenck maintained that his company, Loew's, received mob threats, including a bomb hidden in one of its larger theaters. One day, Harry got a call from a man who said, "Watch out! Within forty-eight hours we'll have both your daughters."[93] Harry knew this was likely just mob intimidation, but he added security to protect his family for six months.

Albert Warner feared for his life whenever Bioff exerted pressure. The gangster was eventually charged for his role in a million-dollar Hollywood extortion plot. During the investigation it was revealed that Warner Bros. had paid $50,000 in 1936 and another $30,000 in 1937 for Bioff to call off IATSE strikes at the Warner lot. Although the California governor was actively and aggressively going after racketeers, Albert "was afraid protection would come too late" if he spoke up. "I was afraid if I went to any of these agencies that I would never return to my office and that it would wreck my business." Chief defense counsel James D. C. Murray asked Albert if he thought going to the FBI might have resulted in his being killed by Bioff. "Possibly," Albert responded. "You, a major in the Army Reserve, were afraid of Bioff?" asked Murray. "Yes, I was plenty scared," Albert admitted. "Plenty of guys smarter than I would have been frightened." Murray fired back, "Do you really believe that a thing like Bioff could walk into your office and offer personal violence?" asked Murray. "Yes, sir," Albert affirmed.[94] Albert had first learned about Bioff in 1936 from Schenck. The Warners disbursed what they thought would be a one-time payoff, only to discover that Bioff considered this a new line of income in return for keeping strikes away from Warner Bros. The Warners learned the hard way when a picket line formed at the lot until the next payment was sent.

Remembrances of the Early 1930s

Studio bosses were known for many things beyond producing films. Many times, they had to play the role of fixer when one of their stars ran afoul of the law. Jack Warner found himself in this position many times in the 1930s, including in 1935, when star choreographer Busby Berkeley wrecked a car, killing three people and injuring others. Knowing the press would have a field day with the news, Warner yelled, "Get me Geisler!" Jerry Geisler was lawyer to the stars and the infamous alike, getting gangster Mickey Cohen out of lockup and actor Errol Flynn out of statutory rape charges (teeing up the phrase "in like Flynn" for someone who avoids consequences they shouldn't). Berkeley was so banged up that he came to court on a stretcher.

The choreographer's accident was so grisly and avoidable that he faced murder charges. A gas station attendant who had fixed Berkeley's tire just prior to the accident testified that he "talked thickly" and smelled of alcohol.[95] With Geisler's help, Berkeley got two hung juries and an acquittal on his third trial. Upon receiving news of the acquittal on Christmas Eve 1935, Jack Warner wired his congratulations: "Merry Christmas. Awfully sorry that you weren't completely exonerated . . . if there is anything I can do."[96] While Jack had no interest in being loyal to his family, he remained loyal to his talent whenever they were in a pinch.

Many Warner Bros. stars looked back at the 1930s as a time of ongoing battles. In March 1936 one *Motion Picture Herald* headline observed, "It's Open Season for Star-Studio Squabbles."[97] James Cagney, frustrated with his pay and tough-guy typecasting, sued the studio to get out of his contract. One of Cagney's first impressions of the casting process was that "it seemed as if the Warner boys were confusing their actors with their racehorses."[98] By this time, Harry Warner was a regular presence at the Santa Anita racetrack, along with his betting rival Louis B. Mayer. Cagney and another studio contract player, Ann Dvorak, sued on the grounds of being overworked (making four films per year and fearing the studio would push for more). Jack Warner maintained that there was no way the studio could make actors complete more than four films in their forty-week contract period. Pat O'Brien also pushed back when he was unhappy with a role in *Star Struck* (1936) and wrangled himself out of it.

Bette Davis was one of the studio's top stars as well as one of Jack Warner's most consistent headaches. Davis pushed back on her contract, wanting $100,000 per year and, after six years, more than double that amount. She was suspended without pay in early 1936, until she accepted the studio's current offer that had the actress receiving just over $182,000 per year after six years. Similar battles played out over the next decade, and every time, Davis claimed she would happily quit the movie business.

Other Warner stars, such as Joan Blondell and Loretta Young, did not see much use in fighting with Jack Warner. "Oh, Jack Warner, everybody fought him but me," recalled Blondell. "I just thought he must know something and I like to give people credit for knowing something." The actress was known for her sassy, brassy characters in films like *Blonde Crazy* (1931), where she was paired with James Cagney. The two had been hired by Warner Bros. to reprise their Broadway roles in *Sinner's Holiday* (1930). Blondell and Cagney

The many faces of James Cagney, who always kept Jack Warner on his toes.

were also part of the great ensemble cast in *Footlight Parade*, alongside Dick Powell and Ruby Keeler, but they had little patience for fighting on the lot. Despite her lack of combative instinct, Blondell remembered Cagney telling her, "Would you just beat it? Get out of there, just walk out, that's all you have to do. Then you'll get what you want and decent money."[99] Cagney was right. Once stars began to walk out on people like Jack Warner, better contracts became more common. Wilson Mizner, co-owner and manager of the Brown Derby and actor in *Heroes for Sale* (1933), had stern words for Jack Warner. Before his death in 1933, Mizner reportedly said, "Working for Warner Brothers is like fucking a porcupine: it's a hundred pricks against one."[100]

S. J. Baiano joined Warner Bros. as a talent scout in 1935 and worked for the company until 1970. He claimed that no words could fully capture the presence of Jack Warner, who was a brilliant producer. "I'll tell you," Baiano said, Warner Bros. was "the one studio where they never passed the buck. You get Jack Warner and that's it."[101] As a talent scout, Baiano remembered stage mothers bombarding him with letters or showing up at the studio. He described Warner Bros. as a close-knit studio where the vast majority of employees got along with one another. Sure, there were contract scuffles between powerful stars and Jack Warner, but Baiano's decades at the studio were full of wonderful memories, such as office Christmas parties that lasted well into the night, with crowds jumping from one office to another. "It was the most exciting era in the late thirties and the early forties," Baiano fondly recalled, "the most exciting era of them all."[102]

Baiano discovered many talents, including Dorothy Malone, Debbie Reynolds, and Lana Turner. Of course, Hollywood legend has it that Billy Wilkerson saw Turner at Schwab's Pharmacy and then introduced her to Baiano. However, Baiano claims he discovered her at a little store called Nancy's on Hollywood Boulevard. What we know for sure is that Baiano took Turner and her mother to Mervyn LeRoy, who cast her in a small role in *They Won't Forget* (1937).

Betty Warner, who was a teenager in the mid-1930s, vividly recalled spending quality time with her father, Harry. She described him as a "quiet man, stern man, with positive opinions and ideas . . . his real commitment and passion was motion pictures." He knew exactly what he expected of others, even if those expectations were unrealistic. Betty said Harry was a bit shy: "Social graces did not come easy, he was not a fast talker or storyteller, he was just a straight-talking honest person. No tricks, you always knew where you stood with him." Harry could be demanding, but those who knew him quickly learned that he was an honest man with high standards. Those who knew Harry the longest could attest that he was the same man both before and after acquiring a mountain of riches. "He was quite a marvelous person," Betty said. Harry was the social conscience of the Warner brothers. Betty recalled that during the Great Depression, Harry took his kids on a tour of New York City to show them how the economic turmoil hurt the masses. It would have been easy for a man in his position to wall up in a penthouse suite, but he did not. "[There] for the grace of God, go you," he often said, knowing just how fortunate he was.[103] Even though Harry was a tough boss, he was a caring leader. He always gave gifts or made donations whenever an employee got married, had a child, or lost a family member. This caretaker mentality stemmed from being the eldest of eleven siblings and having to step up at an early age to help the family. Harry knew how much even a small offering could mean to someone. Those closest to Harry always sought his approval, and all the Warner sisters made sure that Harry approved of their husbands.

Jack, in contrast, did not seek anything from his family. After the divorce from Irma was finalized, Jack wed Ann Page in January 1936. The wedding

Jack and Irma Warner with C. Graham Baker, a production executive at First National studio.

took place in New York at the residence of justice of the peace Julius A. Raven, and Rabbi Lawrence W. Schwartz conducted the ceremony. His colleagues at the studio were told that Jack and Ann's child, Barbara, was adopted, but everyone knew better. Ann redecorated and remodeled Jack's Beverly Hills estate, converting the old Spanish style into Greek revival. Jack Jr. did not get along with Ann, leading to an increasingly turbulent father-son relationship. Ann told Jack Jr. that his father had a tough time seeing his son because it reminded him of Irma. The Warner family did not see much of Ann because Jack feared their judgmental stares and comments. He knew full well that he had hung Irma out to dry, and he soon did the same to his son. Jack's only real dedication was to the studio and to his position as top man on the lot. Soon, however, the Warners would have to put their differences aside to focus on a foreign enemy gaining popularity in the United States.

4

Fighting Fascism, America Firsters, and the US Senate

1937–1941

Ann Sheridan, who would soon star in *Black Legion* (1937) and *Angels with Dirty Faces* (1938), described her experience at the studio: "I had to fight for everything at Warners. From the casting director up to Jack Warner. Of course, at Warners everybody seemed to have a fight. Cagney and Davis. That's the only way it was done. A knock-down, drag-out fight. You didn't always win, but it let them know you were alive." Sheridan told one story about Warner Bros. publicity that partially defined her forever. An influential columnist had described Sheridan as possessing an "umphy quality." Around this time, Jack Warner "had probably been sitting in his barbershop chair reading a paper and not finding his name in it, and told the publicity department to get the studio some space. That was how these things worked, darling." The studio put its own spin on "umph" by spelling it "oomph," hired famed Hollywood photographer George Hurrell to take some photos, and the rest is history. When the press inquired what "oomph" meant, Sheridan always irritated the studio by saying, "It reminded me of a fat man bending down to tie his shoelaces."[1]

Warner Bros. continued its cycle of prison films with *Alcatraz Island* (1937), *San Quentin* (1937), and *Each Dawn I Die* (1939). Busby Berkeley received critical acclaim for *The Varsity Show* (1937). Bette Davis won an Oscar for her role in the romantic melodrama *Jezebel* (1938). Byron Haskin, working as a director and special effects coordinator, earned Oscar nominations for *The Private Lives of Elizabeth Essex* (1939), *The Sea Hawk* (1940), *The Sea Wolf* (1941), and *Desperate Journey* (1942). Haskin spent a great deal of time on the lot in the 1930s and 1940s and remembered Jack regularly saying, "Show me a happy set and I'll show you a flop."[2] Both the biographical film

Juarez (1939), cowritten by future legendary director John Huston, and the Bette Davis melodrama *Dark Victory* (1939) would be critically successful.

Huston was a screenplay workhorse prior to getting his shot at directing. In addition to *Juarez*, he cowrote *The Amazing Dr. Clitterhouse* (1938), *Dr. Ehrlich's Magic Bullet* (1940), and *Sergeant York* (1941). Huston recalled that Warner Bros. "liked to regiment their troops." Writers were expected to be in the office from 9:30 a.m. to 5:30 p.m. Huston liked to write in the evenings, so after a late night he might not clock in until 10:00 or 11:00 in the morning. One day Huston received a note from Jack Warner on the boss's blue stationery. "What kind of racket do you think this is?" asked Warner. "I didn't know I was in a racket," Huston responded in person. "I don't associate with racketeers, but if such is the case, I prefer to terminate my contract here and now." Not amused, Warner assured Huston that Warner Bros. operated with the highest of standards. Huston never caught flak for coming in late again, and the two would eventually become good friends. Describing Jack, Huston wrote, "There was a funny, childlike candor to the man . . . he was anything but pretentious, and seemed to be constantly laughing at himself." Though Jack had the final say on green-lighting any project, Huston gave Hal Wallis credit for producing the studio's string of biographical dramas in the late 1930s.[3]

Another struggle for writers and producers was Jack Warner's practice of screening rough cuts of new films at his Beverly Hills home in the evening, often with his young daughter Barbara in attendance. Robert Buckner, who wrote the screenplays for *Dive Bomber* (1941) and *Yankee Doodle Dandy* (1942) and produced the ill-fated *Mission to Moscow* (1943), experienced this ritual early in his tenure at the studio. Jack would turn to his daughter during the film and ask her what she thought. Being only four or five years old at the time, Barbara had little to no interest in many of the films. At the end of each reel, she would inevitably tell her father, "It stinks." Buckner did not take kindly to a kid criticizing a film he had worked on for a year, so after a few rounds of Barbara's reviews, Buckner asked producer Henry Blanke for help. Blanke said, "I'll let you in on a little secret. Put a couple of packs of chewing gum in your pocket. Before the film starts rolling, slip Barbara one. Keep slipping them to her every three or four minutes." It was a brilliant solution. By the time Jack asked for feedback, Barbara was preoccupied by a mouthful of sweets. "By God, it worked," laughed Buckner. "Ten cents worth of chewing gum against a million-and-a-half dollars in the picture."[4]

After Darryl Zanuck left the studio, Hal Wallis took over as head of production, putting him in closer working proximity to Jack Warner. He was "a strange sort of Jekyll and Hyde character," Wallis said of Jack. "I got along very well with him, and I must say I owe him a debt of gratitude, because he brought me along in the organization." According to Wallis, the biggest difference between Zanuck and Warner was in the editing room. Zanuck knew every inch of film processed on the lot and had a great eye for editing. Warner, in contrast, had a knack for finding good stories but little impact on editing. When Wallis took the reins from Zanuck, he continued to press for tough, splashy fare, and Warner Bros. became known as "Murder Incorporated." Movies like the FBI-supported *G-Men,* the gritty gangster yarn *The Roaring Twenties,* and the courageously antifascist *Confessions of a Nazi Spy* "came off the front pages."[5]

Warner Bros. films often fought prejudice and pushed beyond the limits of the Production Code to make important films about real-world issues. German consul Georg Gyssling issued a warning to Universal, which had been on thin ice with Germany since the release of *All Quiet on the Western Front* (1930) and was now expressing anti-German sentiment in another World War I tale titled *The Road Back* (1937). *Box Office* reported that Gyssling "had inserted his head into a hornet's nest of almost solidly anti-Nazi Hollywood."[6] Gyssling backed down, but that did not stop the Hollywood Anti-Nazi League from demanding the consul's removal from his Los Angeles post. Warner Bros. was about to give the Nazi Party plenty to fret about with its upcoming series of antifascist films based on real stories, current and historical, dealing with the rise of fascism in the United States.

With its eye on the headlines, Warner Bros. found an easy target for its attack on domestic fascism. The Black Legion, a midwestern offshoot of the Ku Klux Klan (KKK), was attracting "men of violence" and "would-be politicians anxious for power."[7] In May 1936 a front-page headline in the *New York Herald Tribune* read, "Many Murders Laid to Detroit Black Legion," a "hooded vigilante organization" that was terrorizing Michigan residents.[8] Another article tagged the Black Legion as a "secret society of terrorism" that was hoping "to assume ultimate dictatorship over the United States" through its six million members.[9] The Black Legion struck fear throughout the Midwest, making headlines across the country. Many years later, civil rights activist Malcolm X revealed that his father had been killed by the Black Legion in Lansing in 1931. By the summer of 1936, newspapers were filled with stories about the murder of Charles A. Poole, an employee of the federal Works Progress Administration who had been taken from his home and shot on May 12. Twelve members of the Black Legion were charged with his murder. Black Legion member Dayton Dean admitted shooting Poole eight times with two revolvers.[10] Eleven of the twelve were found guilty and sentenced to life in prison. The story of the fall of a racist terrorist organization was tailor-made for Warner Bros.

The studio's press book for *Black Legion* (1937) included a wealth of information about both the film and the real-life group. One ad line declared, "The story the nation whispered now thunders from the screen!" The press book also suggested that theaters take newspaper stories about the Black Legion's terror, "blow them up for your lobby," and add the following: "It really happened. See what the 'Gazette' had to say about the Black Legion." Wanting to both wow and terrify audiences, the Warner Bros. publicity department presented the idea of making cardboard cutouts of hooded Black Legion members and standing them up with actual flaming torches. Aligning with Harry Warner's dedication to education, the studio's press agents suggested that screenings of the film be coupled with discussions and debates among community leaders and community members and editorials in local newspapers.

As *Black Legion* went into production, security at the lot was increased in case any of the group's millions of followers were tempted to try sabotage. The film perfectly represented the Warners' concerns about prejudice and the increase in domestic fascism. Michigan was a hotbed of racism and prejudice in the 1930s. Father Charles Coughlin, whose syndicated radio broadcast attracted millions of listeners, drifted from his traditional sermons and spewed anti–New Deal and anti-Semitic rhetoric. Like Henry Ford, who used his *Dearborn Independent* newspaper to attack Jews, Coughlin published *Social Justice,* where Jewish hatred and conspiracy theories were commonplace.

Black Legion focuses on a disgruntled factory worker, played by Humphrey Bogart, who is passed over for a promotion and then falls victim to Coughlinesque rhetoric on the radio, which leads him to join the Black Legion.[11] Red Kann of *Motion Picture Daily* described *Black Legion* as "celluloid dynamite" and noted that Harry Warner "spoke off the record about this picture and urged that it be seen the minute available."[12] The KKK filed a lawsuit against Warner Bros. for patent violation, related to the wardrobe

Clipping from Warner Bros. press packet for *Black Legion*.

used in *Black Legion*. The insignia on the uniforms was the same as or similar to the Klan's, which apparently owned a 1925 patent on the design. The KKK demanded a $250 royalty for every screening of the film, for a total of more than $113,000, in addition to another $100,000 in damages.[13] The case would be thrown out of court, and the judge would order the Klan to pay all legal fees.[14]

Harry's interest in Warner Bros. as a platform for antifascism resulted in a series of powerfully relevant motion pictures. *The Life of Emile Zola* (1937) stars Paul Muni as the title character, who took up the wrongful conviction of French captain Alfred Dreyfus for treason. When military secrets were leaked to the Germans, some French officials were quick to finger the Jewish Dreyfus. Zola would be integral in overturning the captain's life sentence.

Another film, *They Won't Forget* (1937), which starred Claude Rains and introduced Lana Turner to the world, was based on the 1913 trial and lynching of Leo Frank. When sixteen-year-old Mary Phagan was murdered after leaving her job at a Georgia factory, the Jewish Frank was quickly accused, tried, and sentenced to death. The unusually fast rush to judgment was noted in the *New York Times:* "Leo M. Frank, an innocent man, may suffer a disgraceful death for another's crime."[15] The *Chicago Daily Tribune* asked, "Will the state of Georgia hang an innocent man?"[16]

The novel on which the film was based, *Death in the Deep South,* written in 1936 by Ward Greene, was a striking indictment of anti-Semitism at a time when those sentiments were once again gaining traction. Jack Warner read the novel and suggested that Harry's son-in-law, Mervyn LeRoy, direct the film adaptation. Cowritten by Robert Rossen, the film was a hit with the critics. The *New York Times* described it as "an indictment of [the] intolerance and hatred juggernaut," and the *Los Angeles Times* called *They Won't Forget* a "masterpiece."[17] The *Wall Street Journal* wrote that *They Won't Forget* offered "a relentless searchlight to be turned on bigotry and prejudice underlying our public life."[18] Harry's drive to use movies to educate audiences brought numerous social issues to the forefront and tried to push back against the increasing hatred in America.

By December 1937, the Warners' reputation for pursuing trenchant tales got the attention of *Fortune* magazine. Jack and Albert were described as the manager and distributor of products from a factory line that kept the studio constantly humming. Jack was characterized as "a comedian of almost professional pretensions, with that sunny gift for slangy self-exposure that only show people very really master." Jack also ensured that all films came in on budget, which kept the company running smoothly and the stockholders happy. Loose-cannon producers and directors were not welcome on the Warner lot, nor were prima donna actors and actresses—all of whom were common at many other studios. *Fortune* noted that actors on the Warner lot "are not coached or argued with because their time is expensive, and they consequently have more freedom to act." The exception, of course, was James Cagney, who made a lot of noise to get a better contract. *Fortune* described Jack's leadership as a "bargain-counter dictatorship," but to be fair, that leadership "has produced some excellent pictures."[19]

Fortune queried why Warner Bros. was the only studio in the late 1930s without a genius producer serving as the face of production (apparently overlooking Hal Wallis). Of course, Darryl Zanuck had led the studio's gritty house style in the early sound era, but even with the brilliant Zanuck gone, *Fortune* argued that Warner Bros. films continued to improve. "The inexpensive topical stories Zanuck so successfully snitched from the day's headlines (*Doorway to Hell, The Public Enemy*) are still pouring from Burbank in a uniformly profitable stream (*G-Men, Black Legion, Marked Woman, China Clipper*)." *Fortune* noted the studio's willingness to produce grand films like those made at MGM, such as *A Midsummer Night's Dream, Green Pastures,* and *Anthony Adverse,* but Warner Bros. also had its own brand of adventure, such as Errol Flynn in *Captain Blood* (1935) and *The Adventures of Robin Hood* (1938). While applauding MGM's production of *Fury* (1936), a timely indictment of mob mentality, *Fortune* argued that Warner Bros. was "the only major studio that seems to know or care what is going on in America besides pearl-handled gunplay, sexual dalliance, and the giving of topcoats to comedy butlers."[20] Going further, the article surmised, "Warner pictures are hence as close to real life as Hollywood gets."[21] *They Won't Forget* was mentioned as one of the most realistic films in recent memory, serving as a testament to the studio's dedication to topical, punchy narratives.

The clear hero of *Fortune*'s exposé was Harry, whose career was described as "more entertaining than some of Jack's movies." What readers learned, if they hadn't been following the Warners, was that Harry's dedication to liberty and education was evident in many of the studio's most memorable films. Harry was credited with being the moral business leader of Warner Bros., and, echoing his previous defense of controversial content, the studio president told *Fortune*, "The motion picture presents right and wrong, as the Bible does. By showing both right and wrong we teach the right." The truth of Harry's words was evident in *Black Legion* and *They Won't Forget,* as well as the studio's history of producing crime and gangster films. *Fortune* continued, "If you see Harry's proselyting hand in a movie, it will be raised against the injustice that he has had to feel and hopes you will not have to." Harry's drive and passion rubbed off on the *Fortune* reporters, who wrote that he was "so violently anti-Nazi that his incalculable influence could be all too quickly enlisted in America if the democratic nations should go to war."[22] No better words could explain Harry's passion and presence, along with his undying confidence and determination to build a better future.

Harry pushed other film industry leaders to take a greater interest in creating a better future. In July 1938 Harry held a gathering at his Santa Monica home to discuss his concern about the growing prejudice both Stateside and in Europe.[23] Among those invited were spymaster Leon Lewis, independent producer David O. Selznick, director Mervyn LeRoy, actor Paul Muni, MGM producer Al Lichtman, writer-producer Jerry Wald, Warner Bros. producer Hal Wallis, MGM producer Harry Rapf, and exhibition executive

Sam Katz. Warner made it clear that this gathering was a discussion, not a fund-raiser, hoping he would attract a more open-minded crowd if they knew in advance that they could leave their checkbooks at home. The evening's topic was *Common Ground: A Plea for Intelligent Americanism* (1938) by Morris S. Lazaron.[24] Written by a World War I veteran and cofounder of the interfaith Military Chaplains Association, *Common Ground* argued that prejudice was not simply a Jewish problem. "A Jew or Catholic or Protestant citizen is an American," argued Lazaron, "and if he imports the hates of the Old World, he is lifting a banner other than the stars and stripes."[25] Like Warner, Lazaron traveled the country giving speeches about fighting intolerance. Gatherings like this one proved that Harry's patriotic passions were legitimate and not simply trotted out when they aligned with a Warner Bros. promotional opportunity.

Harry continued his public service by addressing the American Legion, an organization created in support of World War I veterans. Warner Bros. studio hosted a luncheon and open house in September 1938 for 150 legionnaires, including California governor Frank F. Merriam and Daniel Doherty, national commander of the American Legion. Jack Warner served as the toastmaster and introduced the illustrious guests, who included Senator David I. Walsh (D-MA) and prominent broadcasters Lewis Allen Weiss (Don Lee Broadcasting), Don I. Gilman (National Broadcasting Company), and Donald W. Thornburgh (Columbia Broadcasting System). The event served as a continuation of Harry's antifascist public relations tour. The mogul had recently traveled through Europe and personally witnessed the cultural and political unraveling led by the Nazis. *Kristallnacht,* the infamous "Night of Broken Glass," when Nazi brownshirts openly terrorized Jewish families and burned down their businesses, was still two months away. But Harry had long understood the consequences if the fascists were allowed to continue their hateful mission. According to one historian, Harry was so preoccupied by Nazism that it impacted his health. Jack told studio employees to stop discussing the subject with him.[26]

Harry was acutely aware of the increasing number of Nazi sympathizers in Los Angeles because Leon Lewis's operations were providing intel to the studio bosses (who were financing the espionage). Harry said, "In recent years, since various foreign governments have fallen into the bloody hands of dictators, autocrats and tyrants, other organizations have grown up within our own borders." "These groups," Harry continued, "are inspired, financed, and managed by foreign interests, which are supplying a never-ending stream of poisonous propaganda aimed, directly and indirectly, at the destruction of our national life." He made it clear that Americans had to work together to undermine intolerant groups "who ape the bigoted leaders of other troubled lands." The mogul, continuing his drive to make motion pictures both entertaining and educational, bragged that Warner Bros. added to the "welfare and peace of our country through the pictures we make here." Harry was clear that there was no room for any ism in Hollywood, whether fascism or communism. This was a direct reference to the Dies Committee, a precursor to the House Un-American Activities Committee (HUAC) that would target Hollywood in 1947. The Dies Committee (1938–1944) investigated communism in Hollywood after probing Nazi propaganda under its previous leadership.[27]

For Harry, no extremist was welcome in the United States. "Make America unsafe for those who seek to tear down what others have built up," he demanded. Harry witnessed the same seeds of intolerance in America that he had seen as a child in Poland. His family had escaped a culture of standardized prejudice, and he was not going to stand by while it blossomed in his new backyard. "Drive them from their secret meeting places," Warner sternly directed, "destroy their insidious propaganda machines, drive out their 'Bunds' and their leagues, their Klans and Black Legions, the Silver Shirts, the Black Shirts, and the Dirty Shirts. Help keep America for those who believe in America." Harry's speech "received uproarious applause," with particular acclaim from American Legion leader Doherty.[28] After his speech, Warner introduced four patriotic shorts, which the studio had been producing since 1936. This series of two-reel films allowed Warner Bros. to showcase both its patriotism and its talent.

The *Motion Picture Herald*'s Vance King found himself on the Warner Bros. lot one day in September 1938. Harry Warner got wind of the reporter's presence and hurried to ask him why he hadn't provided any coverage of the studio's patriotic shorts. When King replied that he had not seen any of them, a frustrated Warner brought the journalist into a projection room to view some of the films. Warner pointed out that, through this series of films, "Warner Brothers is materializing its obligation not only to exhibitors but to the country as well." The mogul highlighted the high marks received from audiences, who encouraged the studio to produce more of the same.

Harry and Jack Warner with Daniel Doherty, national commander of the American Legion.

Warner touted the series as "present[ing] historical facts in an interesting manner, aligning our stories with government records and at the same time keeping them in the field of screen entertainment." According to Warner, the shorts had been shown to one thousand top educators, who promptly suggested they be screened for ten thousand school superintendents at their upcoming conference. "In order to insure historical accuracy," continued Warner, "all our scripts are submitted to the government at Washington." Concluding his pitch, Warner spoke proudly of his studio's responsibility: "We are making more than a commercial product. We believe that we are rendering a service to the entire nation through the presentation of subjects that inspire greater patriotism."[29]

These patriotic shorts sustained Harry's dedication to educational film-making, best described by Jack Warner as "defensive Americanism."[30] In September 1938, when the studio brought those one thousand teachers to the Warner theater in Hollywood to screen some of the shorts, it provided them with programs detailing all the studio's patriotic shorts, including *Sons of Liberty, Lincoln in the White House, Monroe Doctrine, Old Hickory, Bill of Rights, Declaration of Independence, Give Me Liberty,* and *Under Southern Stars.* In addition, the program suggested that teachers use the short films in classroom settings. "It has been said that one photograph teaches more than a thousand words. Conforming to this vital principle of visual education, this folio will be welcomed by the teacher as a means of dramatizing and modernizing the study of American History," stated the program. It then provided a list of how the films could be used in the classroom: (1) illustrations in conjunction with study; (2) basis for historic research: (a) historic background, (b) costuming, (c) architecture, (d) speech; (3) material for scrapbooks; (4) subjects to be framed and hung in classrooms; (5) aids for historic, dramatic presentations; and (6) basis for history and English compositions.[31] *Sons of Liberty,* the most notable short, resembled an A production. Directed by Michael Curtiz and starring Claude Rains, the film celebrates Hyam Salomon, a Jewish financier of the colonists' efforts during the American Revolution.

Some of the most prolific short subjects went largely unnoticed by the Warners in the early days: animated films. Leon Schlesinger had rented space on a corner of the studio's Sunset lot beginning in 1933. The rotting bungalow was known as "Termite Terrace." Schlesinger's employees joked that the Warner brothers didn't even know they were there. Over the years, Schlesinger would hire voice actor Mel Blanc and artists Isadore "Friz" Freleng, Frank Tashlin, and Fred "Tex" Avery. Once overshadowed by those working with live-action motion pictures, Warner animators are now considered a who's who of early animation legends. The lack of notoriety allowed them a certain freedom in their early short films. For example, *She Was an Acrobat's Daughter* (1937) openly lampoons Jack Warner, showing a singing flea carrying a handbag with the initials "J.W." An MGM lion–type cat named Jack bites the acrobat's daughter, and there is a send-up of Warner's latest gangster film, *The Petrified Forest* (1936), as "The Petrified Florist." The opening title card reads "Warmer Bros." instead of Warner and "Vitamin Productions" instead of Vitaphone. Warner Bros. animation remained largely peripheral to the brothers, even though famous cartoon characters such as Bugs Bunny topped popularity polls in the 1940s. Despite the Warners' lack of interest, Merrie Melodies and Looney Tunes would become staples of twentieth-century animation.

Attacking Domestic Nazis

Continuing their support of defensive Americanism, the Warner brothers decided to ban the newsreel *Inside Nazi Germany* (1938) from the studio's programs. Shot by journalist Julien Bryan, the film became a unique example of simultaneous pro-Nazi and anti-Nazi propaganda. Footage displayed the anti-Semitism in Germany, along with the intimidating power showcased during Nazi rallies. One major problem was that before the footage left Germany, it was edited by German officials for "accuracy," thus serving pro-Nazi purposes. The Warners feared that although many would see the horrors of fascism apparent in the film, it could also be used to rile up fascist sympathies. Harry Warner's first impression was that *Inside Nazi Germany* was simply "pro-Nazi propaganda." He told the press, "We do not, therefore, intend to make our screens a medium for the dissemination of propaganda for Germany no matter how thinly veiled that purpose may be."[32] *Inside Nazi Germany* was subsequently banned at all 460 Warner theaters, a move that was appreciated by the Hollywood Anti-Nazi League and others in the media. Harry was concerned that the anti-Nazi voiceover was not strong enough to counteract the imposing onscreen images of Nazi force. *March of Time*'s Henry Luce responded, calling Warner's claim that *Inside Nazi Germany* was inadvertently pro-Nazi "ridiculous" and adding, "Fortunately, Mr. Warner does not control the entire motion picture industry."[33]

Back in March, researchers at Columbia's Institute for Propaganda Analysis had called on Hollywood to develop films with more "social significance" that provided a "realistic view of life." The institute faulted Hollywood for oversimplifying crime and its prevention; for making war look "thrilling, heroic, and glamorous"; for depicting luxurious living as the only evidence of a good life; and for stereotyping minorities as "comical," "dull-witted," or otherwise "inferior."[34] Warner Bros. was not immune to such criticism, as anyone who saw the studio's B western *Haunted Gold* (1932) could attest. The institute also complained that for every *All Quiet on the Western Front* that showed the horrors of war, there were a number of films depicting war as an exciting adventure. Examples from Warner Bros. included the musicals *Flirtation Walk* (1934) and *Shipmates Forever* (1935), along with the romantic comedy *Here Comes the Navy* (1934) and the aviation adventure *Devil Dogs of the Air* (1935). However, Jack Warner was not about to let the researchers at Columbia claim that his studio lacked social impact. Perhaps they had not seen *Black Legion* or *They Won't Forget,* but Warner's next foray into antifascism would be impossible to ignore.

The idea for *Confessions of a Nazi Spy* (1939) originated in 1938 when FBI director J. Edgar Hoover spoke about a team that had exposed and taken down a Nazi spy ring, several members of which were active in the German-American Bund. A total of eighteen Nazi spies were charged; most of them were able to escape to Germany, but four were convicted in the fall of 1938. *Variety* reported that Jack Warner sent writers Milton Krims and Casey Robinson to attend the trial and take notes for a screenplay.[35] FBI agent Leon Turrou had serialized his story in the *New York Post* and was hired as a consultant for the film. Warner Bros. star Edward G. Robinson got wind of the production and wired Hal Wallis, "I want to do that [film] for my people."[36] Other Hollywood studios became wary when they learned that Warner Bros. was going to launch an all-out attack on Nazi Germany. Those "Warner brothers had guts," remembered Joseph Mankiewicz. "They hated the Nazis more than they cared for the German grosses."[37] Jack Warner still believed that a studio employee had been murdered in Germany; he was also aware of Nazi activity in Los Angeles, thanks to the continued success of Leon Lewis's operation. When pressed to reconsider his anti-Nazi push, Jack told a rival studio boss, "The Silver Shirts and the Bundists and all the rest of these hoods are marching in Los Angeles right now. There are high school kids with swastikas on their sleeves a few blocks from our studio. Is that what you want in exchange for some crummy film royalties from Germany?"[38]

Confessions of a Nazi Spy, directed by Anatole Litvak, was produced quietly, complete with additional security, a closed set, and regular safety inspections. Rumors of threats and sabotage circulated in Hollywood. The working title was "Storm over America," and the script's cover page was deliberately left blank during the early stages of production. The only words printed on the cover were "Important! Return to Story Department!" The title was officially changed to *Confessions of a Nazi Spy* on the draft dated January 27, 1939.

Echoing his brother Harry, Jack Warner openly criticized radicalism: "There is no place in the organization of Warner Bros. or of any other patriotic American business for Nazi, Fascist, or Communist fellow-travelers or followers of any other 'ism.'"[39] Screenwriter John Wexley recalled Texas congressman Martin Dies coming to the Warner lot. Dies was running HUAC and investigating radicals on both the right and the left. The congressman attempted to convince Jack Warner to rewrite the script to include anticommunism in addition to anti-Nazism. After Dies left Warner's office, Wexley asked Jack, "Are you knuckling under to that pipsqueak congressman from Texas?" "Oh no," replied Warner, "but if you could work in something about the pinkos. . . ."⁴⁰ Wexley left the script as it was.

The censors, particularly the anti-Semitic Joseph Breen, tried to halt the film, citing the Production Code's strictures on deriding other nations. Karl Lischka of the Production Code Administration (PCA) pressed Jack, asking, "Are we ready to depart from the pleasant and profitable course of entertainment, to engage in propaganda, to produce screen portrayals arousing controversy, conflict, racial, religious and nationalistic antagonism and outright, horrible human hatred?"⁴¹ The answer was a resounding yes. Lischka saw any depiction of Hitler as a madman as patently unfair, but that argument would not stand with Jack Warner, who told the press that the film provided "dramatic entertainment" and "exposed conditions concerning which every American and every free man everywhere should be informed."⁴² As the film was in production, Motion Picture Producers and Distributors of America (MPPDA) president Will Hays called for more realism in motion pictures, noting that he hoped the medium could connect to real-world issues facing everyday citizens.⁴³

In May 1939 twelve thousand handbills were circulated in Los Angeles, urging people to boycott *Confessions of a Nazi Spy*. The headline read: "Suicide of the Hollywood Motion Picture Industry," followed by "JEWISH MONOPOLY of the motion picture industry, BRAZENLY DISCHARGES NON-JEWISH MEN AND WOMEN, and replaces them with refugee JEWS FROM EUROPE." The handbill perpetuated the fear that Jews in Hollywood were hampering the bottom line in foreign markets. In short, "real" Americans should be leery of Jews in the industry. Also appalling was the production overview of *Confessions of a Nazi Spy*, which highlighted the Jewish-heavy crew:

"CONFESSIONS OF A NAZI SPY"
Produced by **Jew** Jack Warner.
Story by **Jew** Milton Krims.
Acted by **Jew** Emannuel Goldenberg (Edward Robinson),
Communist supporter of Leon Trotsky.
Acted by **Jew** Francis Lederer, Communist "peace" advocate.

Ad copy for *Confessions of a Nazi Spy.*

Directed by **Jew** Anatole Litvak, sponsor of
Communist Hollywood Anti-Nazi League.
Technical Advisor **Jew** Rabbi Herman Lissauer,
founder of the Communist "Liberal Forum."
Historical Director **Jew** Leon Turrou,
former employee of Jacob Stern.[44]

It is easy to understand why these men were eager to take part in the film, given their Jewish heritage.

In a *Motion Picture Herald* advertisement for *Confessions of a Nazi Spy,* Jack Warner told distributors, "It was Warner's American duty to make it, it is your American duty to show it!"[45] The film premiered in Los Angeles to great fanfare, although it was rumored that other studios had asked their top talent to stay away, afraid that it would not be good press for them to be photographed at the premiere of such a controversial picture. MGM's Louis B. Mayer apparently held a party for John Barrymore on the same day and made attendance mandatory to ensure that his stars were not at the Warner Bros. premiere.[46] Edwin Schallert of the *Los Angeles Times* called *Confessions of a Nazi Spy* a "vigorous film document of Nazism."[47] At one point in the film, the *March of Time*–esque narrator declares the Nazi Party part of the "German concept of mass stupidity." *Confessions of a Nazi Spy* was a true watershed moment that inspired other studios to follow suit with productions such as *Four Sons* (20th Century–Fox), *The Great Dictator* (United Artists), and *The Mortal Storm* (MGM).

Predictably, *Confessions of a Nazi Spy* was banned in Germany and eighteen other countries where the Nazis' tentacles reached. The German embassy expressed its objections to the film to the State Department.[48] There were protests in some US cities; in Kansas City, the German vice consul strong-armed locals into boycotting the film.[49] Reminiscent of the KKK's reaction to *Black Legion,* Fritz Kuhn and the German-American Bund sued Warner Bros. for libel—and failed. Hitler's minister of propaganda Joseph Goebbels shut down the shipment of Nazi films to America, a victory for anti-Nazis in the United States.[50] Once Goebbels saw *Confessions of a Nazi Spy,* with its newsreel aesthetic, he knew his party was being mocked using its own fearmongering tactics. The film was a powerful mix of newsreel, courtroom drama, and spy thriller set to the current news cycle, as only Warner Bros. could deliver.[51]

Warner story librarian Johnny O'Steen remembered the pressure caused by *Confessions of a Nazi Spy.* He noted that Jack Warner "was lucky some Nazi fifth columnist in the USA didn't try to do him in. Hitler knew about the Warner film and tried to prevent its filming." O'Steen recalled that, in the prewar years, there were "very few communist sympathizers on the lot. There were some pseudo ones. There were a lot of fascist haters."[52] Maurice Kann, editor in chief of *Box Office,* commended the Warners in a "Salute to Courage" column. Kann applauded the studio for forcing the public to confront social ills. In closing, Kann wrote that *Confessions of a Nazi Spy* "does democracy well," and he "wish[ed] others in the industry displayed something resembling the Warner backbone."[53]

Jack issued a press release doubling down on the studio's commitment to "this revolutionary type of picture." He responded to the criticism circulated by pro-Nazi organizations that "do not have an understanding of the Warner type of determination or progressiveness." Citing *The Story of Louis Pasteur* and *The Life of Emile Zola*, among others, Jack explained how such films were "guiding us in our determination to stick to our policy of showing the public what exists in the world today. We firmly believe, as Zola did, that 'truth is on the march' and that nothing can stop it, and we hope to play a part in bringing these evident truths to all the people of all the world."[54]

Following the critical success of *Confessions of a Nazi Spy*, Jack Warner approved two more anti-Nazi productions. One was a biopic about Martin Niemoller, a Lutheran minister who was thrown into a concentration camp; it may have been abandoned due to Niemoller's initial support of Hitler. The other, *Underground*, was a harrowing B production about radio technicians informing the resistance via a secret mobile radio unit. *Underground* director Vincent Sherman compared the kind of "nitty-gritty pictures" Warner Bros. made with MGM's glossy "society pictures." In Sherman's view, Warner Bros. was the only studio down to earth enough to make that kind of film. According to Sherman (among others), there was also great camaraderie among the film crews at Warner Bros.[55]

Sherman was aware that although many anti-Nazi films were not commercial successes, they were culturally important. Films like *Confessions of a Nazi Spy* and *The Mortal Storm* "were downbeat, they left audiences feeling depressed and helpless," explained Sherman. In contrast, "*Underground* will give them hope."[56] Information about the anti-Nazi movement in Germany was nearly nonexistent, so a film like *Underground* could stir up a lot of useful curiosity and, perhaps, inspiration. The cast included many German refugees, adding a level of realism. Jack Warner was elated after screening *Underground*, and he invited Sherman to his home for breakfast. Warner praised Sherman's efforts, promoted him to work on A films, and would depend on the director for many years as one of the most frugal and reliable on the lot. Sherman was proud of the film, saying, "I relished every minute of it because I felt that I was helping alert the world to the menace of Hitler and the Nazis." The director also recalled the terrifying nature of the prewar years: "America was still in the throes of isolationism. The America Firsters

Betty Warner accepting the "Distinguished Americanism" award for Harry.

were dominating the thinking of the country, supported by Father Coughlin and Charles Lindbergh, who were favorably disposed towards the Nazis."[57] It would not be long before Lindbergh was speaking out against Hollywood at America First rallies.

Even though war was on the horizon for the United States, Harry Warner had reason to celebrate. At the end of 1938 he received an award for "Distinguished Americanism" from the American Legion and the Disabled Veterans of the World War. Because Harry was nursing a minor illness, his daughter Betty collected the award on his behalf in front of three thousand legionnaires at the Warner Hollywood Theater. Harry wrote a letter of acceptance, which Betty read. In early 1939 Betty, a nineteen-year-old UCLA student, got engaged to Milton Sperling, a writer at 20th Century–Fox. Hollywood gossip queen Louella Parsons described the couple's relationship as "one of Hollywood's sweetest romances."[58] The wedding took place at the Beverly-Wilshire Hotel in July 1939, with Doris serving as matron of honor and Lita as maid of honor and Rabbi Maxwell Dubin officiating. The marriage lasted until Sperling's death in 1988. Years later, Betty told her own daughter, Cass, that when the couple and other family members boarded a train for the honeymoon, Jack's wife Ann snuggled up to Milton and said, "You know, you made a terrible mistake. You shouldn't have married Betty, you should have married me."[59] Betty maintained that Ann had a few extramarital relationships of her own, which, if true, served Jack right for all the heartache he put Irma through.

"United We Survive, Divided We Fall"

Harry Warner's passionate Americanism undoubtedly trickled down through the studio ranks. Warner Bros.'s resident comedian Joe E. Brown testified

131

before the House Immigration Committee in 1939 in support of a bill that would allow twenty thousand German Jewish children into the United States. Brown adopted two refugee children of his own. Harry was proud of his positive work and influence and the studio's public stance against fascism. The studio was so well known for its pro-American filmmaking that in January 1939, prior to the release of *Confessions of a Nazi Spy*, the *Motion Picture Herald* ran an interview with Jack Warner under the banner "Americanism, Motion Pictures, and a Warner Creed." Although Jack and Harry rarely got along, they saw eye to eye on the studio's role in engaging audiences with intelligent and provocative content. Stories that "constitute American history afford perfect screen material," said Jack, and "the policy of the United States is at all times the policy of Warner Brothers."[60] He concluded by noting that a quality stage play might reach thousands, but a film can reach millions. The Warners were always aware of the power of the movies they helped enshrine in American popular culture.

On June 5, 1940, Harry Warner delivered one of his most memorable speeches to a crowd of nearly six thousand employees and their families on the Warner Bros. lot. Thousands of seats were arranged in the 130,000-square-foot carpenter mill shop, and hundreds of others stood. According to Johnny O'Steen, the crowd included "stars, directors, executives, mail boys and janitors and their families."[61] Harry and Jack were up front on a platform with US Air Force members, local politicians, and Arthur Cornelius Jr., head of the Los Angeles FBI. The event opened with "The Star-Spangled Banner" performed by the Metropolitan Opera. Harry's speech, titled "United We Survive, Divided We Fall," was a rousing call to action against the enemies at home. Harry feared that ideas such as the Nazis' *Rassenschande*, or race defilement, were taking root in the United States. The Nuremberg laws, put in place in 1935, forbade relations between Aryans and non-Aryans and effectively stripped Jews, Romanies, and Black people of their German citizenship.

Harry cared deeply about his employees and suggested that they see him as more of a colleague than a boss. He brought the Warner employees together out of a deep concern that too many people in the United States did not fully understand the threat of homegrown radicalism. Part of Harry's concern stemmed from his recent trips to Europe. In one instance, Warner met with the Danish prime minister in Copenhagen, who, when the issue of Nazism was raised, declared, "They wouldn't dare come near us."[62] Similarly, leaders in Oslo, Paris, and London refused to believe Harry when he suggested that enemies might already be active within their borders. This message about domestic fascism was particularly important in Los Angeles, which was teeming with Nazi sympathizers. Warner spoke directly of the gatherings at Hindenburg Park in Crescenta Valley, where the German-American Bund held pro-Nazi rallies. The park was named after Paul von Hindenburg, president of Germany from 1925 to 1934 and the man who appointed Hitler the country's chancellor.

Harry's main theme was unity of faith. Once again pulling inspiration from Lazaron's *Common Ground,* he emphasized ending the practice of defining people by their religion—as Catholic, Jewish, Protestant, and so on. "We must unite," he warned, "or we will fall the same as they did over there, because we are confronted with the greatest organized machine, subversive or otherwise, that the world has ever had." Warner spoke of the pamphlets flying around town that stoked the flames of racial prejudice. Harry wore his faith on this sleeve, but never to the point of condescending to others. Speaking of his parents, he said, "I am not ashamed that they were Jews and that I am of the same faith." For Harry, it was important to have faith—any faith that provided a vision. He saw the rise of the Nazi Party as a break from faith, elevating the party above all else.

Having grown up in nineteenth-century Poland, where persecution was commonplace, Warner knew firsthand what it was like to live in fear. Many of those born and raised in the United States "can't conceive what it is to live in constant danger," he continued. "We live in California with sunshine—thank the Lord we do—and we don't realize what's going on in this world." Warner had visited London days before the blitzkrieg began in September 1940, where he saw displaced families and buses full of children trying to get out of the city. Unfortunately, for many, it was too late. That was Warner's fear: the idea that "it can't happen here" was a deadly one. Though staunchly antiwar, Warner argued that the nation had to defend itself against saboteurs. He understood that the enemies of the free countries of Europe were the enemies of the entire free world. "God knows I want peace," Warner explained. "I long and pray for it but the only certain way of insuring our peace is to be so strong in arms and defense that we can command peace."

Looking to avoid party politics, Warner sternly stated, "We don't want anybody employed by our company who belongs to any Bunds! Communistic, fascistic or any other un-American organization." Warner's politics was always based on opposition to hatred and prejudice, regardless of where it originated.

Going further, he argued, "I would like to see a law passed that any and all members of un-American organizations, especially those sponsored and paid for by enemy foreign powers would have their citizenship revoked and be deported to their own native lands, or the land in whose hidden employ they are." This was strong language, but Harry meant every word. He was truly committed to eliminating hatred before it took over the ranks of power. Harry was not a politician looking to gain votes; he was speaking to many long-term employees (nearly three thousand of them had been with the company for many years) and hoping to spark conversations about the future of their community, their country, and the world. Harry concluded, "Oppressors have been destroyed in the past, they will be destroyed in the future. And I am sure we who have faith, whatever that faith may be, will in the long run survive in a great world hereafter." After the event, the attendees exited slowly, nearly everyone engaged in deep reflection and conversation about Warner's speech—a testament to their respect for him. Toward the end of 1940 Harry donated twenty-two ambulances to the British Red Cross in memory of his late son, Lewis. The fleet quickly went into service aiding victims of the Coventry blitz, when the German Luftwaffe sent 515 planes to bomb the industrial city. The Luftwaffe referred to this raid as the "Moonlight Sonata."

Warner Bros. always had a knack for reading audiences' desire for particular types of stories. With the bleak global outlook as the 1930s ended, Jack Warner green-lit a long line of crime films, including *They Drive by Night* (1940), starring George Raft and Humphrey Bogart and directed by Raoul Walsh. *The Letter* (1940), a female melodrama based on a W. Somerset Maugham play, was nominated for seven Oscars, including Best Actress (Bette Davis), Best Director (William Wyler), Best Original Score (Max Steiner), and Best Picture (Hal Wallis).

Jack Warner green-lit another Raoul Walsh–Humphrey Bogart collaboration, *High Sierra* (1940). The film also starred Ida Lupino and was based on the novel by W. R. Burnett, one of the studio's most trusted crime writers. Joseph Breen wrote a ten-page memo to Jack suggesting deletions and alterations; his concerns included references to illicit sexual relations, the use of a submachine gun, the depiction of crime details, and so on. George Raft turned down the role of the killer because he did not want to die at the end, which the censors demanded. Walsh suggested Bogart, who up to this point had been merely a supporting actor. "He's tough enough already, or thinks he is," Jack told Walsh. Bogart "goes around with a big chip on his shoulder, and lately he's been telling people I'm a fairy. But if you want to take a chance, go ahead."[63] Ultimately, Jack trusted his director's instincts. That film, along with the one that followed, would make Bogart a star.

Bogart solidified his position as the king of noir with John Huston's *The Maltese Falcon* (1941), based on the controversial Dashiell Hammett novel. *The Maltese Falcon* arguably introduced the prototypical private detective that would appear in scores of Hollywood films, perhaps most famously in Warner Bros.'s own *The Big Sleep* (1946). Jack Warner continued the studio's streak of biographical films with *A Dispatch from Reuters* (1940), starring Edward G. Robinson as Paul Reuter. The Warner Bros. romantic melodrama starring Bette Davis and Charles Boyer, *All This, and Heaven Too* (1940), was nominated for Best Picture, losing to Alfred Hitchcock's *Rebecca* (1940).

US Senate versus Hollywood

As conditions in Europe worsened, President Roosevelt signed the Lend-Lease Act in March 1941, which provided aid such as planes, ships, and weapons to Allied nations. This move irked American isolationists and members of subversive profascist groups, many of whom held positions in the US government. Two senators who stoked the flames of isolationism were Gerald P. Nye (R-ND) and Bennet Champ Clark (D-MO), the architects of Senate Resolution 152, which accused Hollywood of warmongering.[64] Nye referred to Hollywood and its anti-Nazi films as "gigantic engines of propaganda in existence to rouse the war fever in America and plunge this nation to her destruction," and he described Hollywood as a "raging volcano of war fever" because "the place swarms with refugees."[65] John T. Flynn, a journalist who helped create the America First Committee, worked closely with Nye to uncover dirt on Tinseltown.

The America First Committee was founded in 1940 as an isolationist pressure group, but it was quickly co-opted by fascist sympathizers, including members of the German-American Bund. One of the most prominent members of America First was famed aviator Charles Lindbergh, who had risen to celebrity status with his groundbreaking transatlantic flight in 1927. During an America First event in Des Moines, Iowa, Lindbergh called the Jews a major threat to the United States. "Their greatest danger to this country," he said, "lies in their large ownership and influence in our motion pictures, our press, and our radio and our government."[66]

An America First rally was held at the Hollywood Bowl in the summer of 1941. Studios asked their employees to boycott the event, which featured speakers Senator Burton Wheeler (D-MN) and Lindbergh. A competing event featured the popular dark-horse presidential candidate Wendell Willkie. In response to these two events, Harry Warner brazenly asserted, "We'd rather march to hear Willkie on National Unity than be marched to a concentration camp."[67] As isolationist pressure mounted on Hollywood, Will Hays defended film narratives highlighting the conflict in Europe. When the *Los Angeles Times* published a column critical of Hollywood that was praised by America First chairman William Hunt, Harry Warner and Louis B. Mayer complained to *Times* publisher Harry Chandler. The column was written by Hollywood gossip columnist and professional studio hater Jimmie Fidler, who became a key witness for the isolationist senators.

When Senate Resolution 152 became a reality, Hays hired Willkie to defend Hollywood. The hearings lasted from September 9 to 26, 1941. Those called to testify on the isolationists' behalf were Jimmie Fidler, John T. Flynn, Senator Clark, Senator Nye, and a few others whose testimony amounted to nothing more than distractions. During the inquiry, the senators received numerous letters of support from anti-Semitic fans, including one who thought the investigation was proving the Franklin prophecy, a conspiracy theory about Benjamin Franklin lobbying to get Jews written out of the US Constitution. That theory, which some still believe, originated as propaganda from the profascist Silver Shirts in the early 1930s. Willkie was muzzled during the hearings, but he unloaded to the press daily. Although the isolationist senators had some supporters in the press, most of the national newspapers lambasted the entire show. Even one of the senators on the committee, Ernest McFarland (D-AZ), played a role in unraveling the entire production.

Nye opened the hearings by attacking Hollywood and making a series of unfounded claims about the film industry's allegiance to foreign interests. Of course, this was coded language in the eyes of America First, which considered anything not 100 percent American to be foreign. Nye argued that studios making anti-Nazi films were in violation of the Sherman Act, which prohibited monopolization. The practice of claiming that Hollywood was a monopoly would be an ongoing deviation from the inquiry into warmongering in motion pictures. Nye listed a series of objectionable films, including *Convoy* (RKO), *Flight Command* (MGM), *Escape* (MGM), *I Married a Nazi*

(20th Century–Fox), *That Hamilton Woman* (United Artists), *Man Hunt* (20th Century–Fox), *The Great Dictator* (United Artists), and *Sergeant York* (Warner Bros.). The North Dakota senator was shaken when McFarland, admittedly not a regular movie patron, asked what, specifically, was propagandistic about these films. Nye could not answer, as it turned out that he had not actually seen any of the films, though he assured the room that he was working on good information from a trusted source (likely Flynn). Nye also responded to accusations of anti-Semitism by asserting that he could not be anti-Semitic because he had Jewish friends.

Clark followed the next day, echoing Nye and expressing his frustration that movies got more press attention than elected politicians. Clark fingered Warner Bros. as the studio that had "probably . . . made more of these hate-producing films than any other company in America." Continuing his attack on Warner Bros., Clark singled out *Confessions of a Nazi Spy, Dive Bomber,* and *Underground* as "extremely inflammatory."[68] Again, when McFarland asked for specifics, the senator could not deliver. The *Hollywood Reporter's* Jack Moffitt chided the isolationist senators, arguing that "Clark [is] as ignorant of [the] subject as Nye."[69] An op-ed in the *Los Angeles Times* mused that the "seething senator says the films are propagandizing us into war, [and] he probably thinks those United States ships [bombed while assisting the British in November 1940] were sunk by a director for Warner Bros."[70] When Flynn testified, he provided a list of problematic films, including several of the usual suspects from Warner Bros. McFarland quickly squelched Flynn by asserting that if Warner stockholders were upset with this line of filmmaking, they could have pushed back, but they did not. Fidler was largely discredited when it was revealed that he was actually a Warner Bros. stockholder. The constant ribbing of *Underground* led to a massive increase in interest in the film; profits grew from 132 percent prior to the investigation to 162 percent after it commenced.[71]

Other Hollywood leaders subpoenaed to testify before the Senate subcommittee were Nicholas Schenck (president of Loew's), Howard Dietz (MGM publicity), Darryl Zanuck (vice president of production at 20th Century–Fox), Barney Balaban (president of Paramount), and Harry Warner. The isolationist senators were clueless about Hollywood, which meant that Schenck, Dietz, and Zanuck spent most of their time explaining film studio operations. Zanuck went so far as to assure committee members that he was not Jewish and had been born in America, so they need not fear him.

Advertisement for *Underground*.

The press pummeled the senators daily, including a poll in *Film Daily* that revealed most national film critics opposed the investigation and perceived no warmongering by Hollywood.[72] The subcommittee asked each major Hollywood studio to submit a list of recent films with any type of war theme. Warner Bros. complied by providing an interesting mix of films.

Some of the expected films that appeared on the Warner Bros. list were *British Agent* (1934), an espionage film directed by Michael Curtiz about R. H. Bruce Lockhart, a member of the British Secret Service during the Russian Revolution; *The Dawn Patrol* (1938 version), a World War I aviation film directed by Edmund Goulding and starring Errol Flynn; *Confessions of a Nazi Spy* (1939), for obvious reasons; *Juarez* (1939), about the twenty-sixth president of Mexico, starring Paul Muni and Bette Davis and directed by William Dieterle; and *Sergeant Murphy* (1938), a film about a cavalry horse. Also included were a string of lighthearted romances with armed forces components such as *Here Comes the Navy* (1934), an upbeat film starring James Cagney, Pat O'Brien, and Gloria Stuart about a couple of rabble-rousers; *Son of a Sailor* (1933), a Joe E. Brown comedy about a sailor who sniffs out a few spies among the officers; *Devil Dogs of the Air* (1935), a Cagney and O'Brien male buddy film; *Submarine D-1* (1937), a romantic melodrama set on the high seas and directed by Lloyd Bacon; and the aviation-themed romance *Wings of the Navy* (1939), directed by Lloyd Bacon and starring Olivia de Havilland and John Payne.

The strangest submissions to the investigating committee were a trilogy of Warner Bros. musicals starring Dick Powell, two of which also starred Ruby Keeler: *Flirtation Walk* (1934), *Shipmates Forever* (1935), and *The Singing Marine* (1937). Notable omissions were *The Dawn Patrol* (1930) and *Underground*, both seemingly obvious choices for a discussion about warmongering. One wonders whether Warner Bros. submitted lighthearted and musical fare—its least propagandistic films—as a way to thumb its nose at the subcommittee (and one wonders whether committee members viewed any of the films at all).

Harry Warner's testimony came near the end of the hearings on September 25, 1941. The isolationist senators were on their heels, though they would never admit defeat. The gallery was overloaded with more than 250 Warner supporters. During previous sessions, the witnesses had started by reading statements, but they were quickly interrupted by questions, which turned into

Jack and Harry at a Warner Club event.

conversations. Warner began his testimony by demanding that he be allowed to finish his statement before fielding any questions. There was no doubt that Warner was in command of the room as he quickly dispelled rumors of war hysteria. He criticized the subcommittee members who had failed to watch any of the films in question before launching their attack against Hollywood. "The only sin of which Warner Bros. is guilty is that of accurately recording on the screen the world as it is or as it has been," he declared.[73]

Anyone familiar with the industry knew that Warner Bros. made its name on headline-driven narratives. With reports about fascism filling the newspapers, it was entirely predictable that the Warners would be drawn to stories about Nazis, just as they had been drawn to stories about gangsters in the early 1930s. Harry made it clear that the studio did not take orders from FDR, whom the isolationists feared was pushing the country toward war. The mogul explained his studio's recent record of historical and headline-driven films, including *I Am a Fugitive from a Chain Gang, British Agent, Black Fury, The Story of Louis Pasteur,* and *The Life of Emile Zola,* as well as the war- or Nazi-focused *Confessions of a Nazi Spy, Sergeant York, Underground,* and *International Squadron.* The unapologetic Warner said, "I, as president of the company, wish to assume the full responsibility for the pictures we produce. That is the responsibility that should be mine, and one from which I do not shirk."[74] Having watched previous testimony, Warner took it upon himself to educate the senators on the history of the film industry. He also detailed his family's immigration and difficult rise through the ranks of motion picture producers.

The investigation was already dead in the water, but Warner added insult to injury by presenting a 1939 telegram from Senator Nye expressing his opinion after watching *Confessions of a Nazi Spy:* "The picture is exceedingly good. The cast is exceptionally fine. The plot may or may not be exaggerated but is one that ought to be with every patriotic American." As Nye turned red, Warner continued to read: "I hope there may be more pictures of a kind dealing with propaganda emanating from all foreign lands. Anyone who truly appreciates the one great democracy upon this earth will appreciate this picture and feel a new allegiance to the democratic cause."[75] This embarrassing revelation unspooled the last thread of hope that Nye could pin anything on the film industry.

Not letting up, Warner went on to explain how insignificant the films in question were. In the last two and a half years, only 7 of the studio's 140 films had been accused of warmongering. The studio received 9,000 story ideas annually, out of which only 50 films were made. Warner explained that 70 percent of nonfiction books, 10 percent of novels, and a high percentage of newspaper and radio reporting covered Nazis and fascist causes. It was curious to see the Senate going after Hollywood for what newspapers and magazines had been guilty of since time immemorial.

Senator Worth Clark (D-ID) questioned Warner about *Underground* specifically, even though he had not seen the film. He asked whether it depicted Nazi brutalities and commented that he did not appreciate onscreen viciousness, to which Warner responded, "Yes, well, do you think we should have made a picture that showed the Nazis kissing them or in love with them, or what?" Clark argued that *Underground* was a hate film, and Warner shot back, "I think it is entirely wrong to produce pictures that produce hate against anybody. We are making pictures of facts," he stated, "that is the whole story in a nutshell." Clark showed his ignorance when he told Warner that the United States could not trust England, a country that had yet to repay its debts after World War I. Harry promptly responded, "I do not think it is the intention of England to destroy the rest of the world. . . . I am positive that is the intention of Hitler."[76] Warner's confident and intelligent defense resulted in numerous outbreaks of applause throughout the day.

The press ran circles around the senators following Warner's war on the ignorant isolationists, and a thick cloud of shame hung over the investigation. Jack Moffitt described Harry Warner as "a citizen [who] got loose among a bunch of United States Senators and talked them all down." Warner's engagement with the senators was so effective that, Moffitt argued, "unless a new method of attack is thought of, I believe this investigation will crawl up in some alley and die." Moffitt correctly predicted that historians would one day cite Warner's testimony as an admirable defense of free speech. He wrote, "Instead of backing the movies into a strait jacket, the committee may end up wearing one. If it does, Harry Warner is the guy that buckled it on."[77] The senators eventually agreed to a recess so that they could watch the films being discussed, but this would never occur. After the December 7, 1941, attack on Pearl Harbor and Hollywood's support for the new war effort, the subcommittee was dissolved. On December 8, 1941, Harry called a meeting of five hundred war veterans to discuss how to watch out for saboteurs. Since motion pictures were part of the war effort, film studios could become targets.

Immediately after Pearl Harbor, Harry continued to use his position as a studio mogul to pay it forward in the country's time of need. He did not like losing employees to military service, but he certainly understood why they would enlist and sympathized with their decisions. O'Steen remembered that Harry "set up organizations in the company to see that each man who entered the service was given a wrist watch, was guaranteed a job when he returned, that pretty girls on the lot wrote letters regularly to the boys, other girls sent candy, magazines, and cigarettes to the boys while they were in service."[78] When the Office of War Information set up the Bureau of Motion Pictures to enlist Hollywood in the global battle against fascism, Warner Bros. was first in line to do its patriotic duty. Jack Warner immortalized his employees who served in the war with a memorial that still stands on the lot. Names include Lloyd Bacon, Philip Epstein, Julius Epstein, John Forsythe, John Huston, Orry Kelly, John Payne, James Stewart, and, of course, Jack L. Warner.

The war impacted everyone differently. Curtis Bernhardt, a German Jew who fled the Third Reich in the 1930s and became a director at Warner Bros., got an interesting request from Jack. Bernhardt recalled, "Jack Warner called me in and said, 'Kurt, we are about to go to war with Germany. Kurt is a very German-sounding name. Can you do something about this?' I said I didn't give a damn what they did. So, I went to court and got my name legally changed to Curtis, but my family name remained the same."[79]

With the United States officially involved, Jack Warner was bombarded with questions from the press regarding the studio's role in the war effort. "We will cooperate in every way with the President of the United States and the government he heads" to meet the "increased and multiple needs for entertainment."[80] Of course, for Warner Bros., moviemaking was never about only entertainment. The studio did not back down on its commitment to make war films, but Jack recognized that the public needed and deserved lighthearted entertainment and straightforward amusement to counteract the constant stream of bleak news from Europe.

Harry, who had been serving on the Motion Picture Committee Cooperating for National Defense since July, demanded, "Now is the time for Hollywood to come forward again, ready to do its full duty and to fulfill all its many responsibilities to the nation it serves." He believed that Hollywood should be willing to defend the country that made the film industry possible by sharing the "burdens of liberty." He was proud that Warner Bros. had stood up against fascism when the other studios had been reluctant to risk financial loss by taking on the Nazis. Harry boasted, "We have always turned a deaf ear to the carping criticism of those who shouted 'propaganda' whenever we extolled the glories of our free country and the road it followed to get where it is." Warner Bros. had a consistent track record of working with US defense programs, such as producing training and recruitment films for free. Harry had no problem donating company time and resources to the country that had allowed his family to escape persecution in Poland.

Harry declared that the studio's cinematic offerings would be "liberally sprinkled with service and patriotic pictures, made for entertainment but also boasting [a] patriotic motif." He noted that *Captains of the Clouds* (1942), a war film starring James Cagney, directed by Michael Curtiz, and inspired by Winston Churchill's Dunkirk speech, highlighted the importance of the Lend-Lease Act and reminded audiences of Britain's need for assistance in the global fight for freedom. Another film continuing the studio's staunchly anti-Nazi fare was *Dangerously They Live* (1941), an espionage tale starring John Garfield and Nancy Coleman.

Following its success on Broadway, *Yankee Doodle Dandy* (1942) would become one of the most beloved Warner Bros. films of the 1940s. It starred James Cagney in a celebration of George M. Cohan's work. Like Jack, Harry acknowledged the need for escapist films. Examples include *The Man Who Came to Dinner* (1942), starring Bette Davis and written by the Epstein brothers, as well as *Arsenic and Old Lace* (1943), the Frank Capra–directed farce starring Cary Grant and Priscilla Lane. Harry believed that, after the tragedy of Pearl Harbor and the bleakness of entering into a world war, entertainment "is the one thing the nation craves most just now."

In December 1941 Blaney F. Matthews, director of plant protection and superintendent of personnel at Warner Bros., published a book titled *The Specter of Sabotage*. Matthews was a graduate of USC Law School and worked for the FBI before becoming chief investigator for Los Angeles district attorney Buron Fitts, where he learned how to be a fixer. When Jean Harlow's husband Paul Bern committed suicide, MGM allegedly called Fitts to cover up the details of Bern's death to protect the star's image. Fitts was also accused of meddling in the case against the person who raped Patricia Douglas in 1937 (the case resurfaced in the 2007 documentary *Girl 27*). Matthews eventually became the Warner Bros. version of Eddie Mannix and Howard Strickling at MGM. Formally, he was the studio's security chief, but he often took "a behind-the-scenes role in anything from fixing a speeding ticket to quashing a charge of statutory rape or vehicular homicide."[81]

Matthews dedicated *The Specter of Sabotage* to the Warner brothers: "To Harry M. Warner, Jack L. Warner, and Albert Warner, courageous and far-seeing Americans, who were among the first of the country's industrialists to recognize the menace of the Fifth Column, and to engage in a relentless fight against subversive elements."[82] In his book, Warner's top cop covered a series of concerns and provided guidelines on how to recognize an invisible army, prepare for sabotage, identify weak spots, and hire personnel, along with a number of other safeguarding techniques. "Sabotage! Destruction of Industrial Effort! Undermining of Civilian Morale! Despair and Defeat! These are the aims of the saboteur," wrote Matthews.[83] Over the next decade, Matthews would become a notorious figure on the Warner Bros. lot when labor strikes swept across the industry.

By the end of 1941, Warner Bros. was encouraging other studios to take the gloves off. Emotions had been running high prior to the attack on Pearl Harbor; now they were boiling over. An industry memo that reads as if it were written by Harry Warner stated, "Service pictures now can call a spade a spade, a German an enemy and a Japanese any name that a scenario writer can think up." The new wartime standard was to engage the enemy directly, as Warner Bros. had been doing for years. "Hollywood no longer needs to tread lightly on wartime subjects," the memo continued. "Studios are free, at long last, to 'give the devil his due' and they will proceed along that line, presumably, as long as America is at war." Warner Bros. commended other studios for getting on board and pushing back against the Production Code's rules against ridiculing other nations. MGM's *Escape,* 20th Century–Fox's *Man Hunt,* and Warner's *Underground* were considered films that "did not mince words or sentiments in giving their audiences their stories of inside Germany nor did they make any effort to hide the prejudice felt in America against those who are now openly for its enemies."[84] Following the example set by Warner Bros., Hollywood was now all in. *Desperate Journey* (1942), about a bomber crew escaping Nazi Germany, was in production by the end of the year. The war was on, and Warner Bros. was the entertainment industry's front line.

5

The War Years
1942–1945

The Warner brothers were ready for war. The studio had already initiated an emergency protection program prior to the attack on Pearl Harbor. Anti-sabotage plans, supervised by Blayney Matthews, included a modest survey of employees' activities, investigation of subversive goings-on in the vicinity of the studio, and a comprehensive examination of the studio's doors, boundary fences, and gates, adding more security where necessary. The lot was fitted with better lighting. Areas of the lot that were difficult to secure were restricted to essential employees only. Signs were placed around the studio reminding employees to refrain from discussing their work with strangers. Legend has it that Jack Warner had a sign installed on the roof of one building that read "Lockheed-that-a-way," with an arrow pointing toward the nearby Lockheed Martin aviation manufacturing plant. True or not, the concern was justified; from the air, it would be hard to distinguish a film studio from a munitions or aviation factory. Air-raid shelters were constructed with concrete- and steel-reinforced basements. Each had multiple entrances and exits, complete with gas curtains. Every shelter was equipped with candles, buckets, fire extinguishers, first-aid supplies, radios, shovels, and crowbars, as well as emergency food and drink rations. Mirroring the plans in place in most communities, the studio lot was broken into four zones, each with its own commander to lead an evacuation in the event of an emergency. Studio fire and police forces were equipped with additional resources such as steel helmets, gas masks, and sandbags for barricades. A listening post was set up to monitor for air-raid warnings on the radio. Nighttime blackouts were mandatory on the lot, as they were throughout the rest of Los Angeles.

Harry continued to work with the War Activities Committee (WAC) and its division for motion pictures, in addition to serving as president of the Association of Motion Picture Producers.[1] The WAC announced a fifty-two-week program involving more than fifteen thousand theaters that played one Victory Short per week. These short films, inspired by Warner's patriotic shorts, were produced and distributed without profit. Working in conjunction with the Office of War Information (OWI), Warner Bros. released several Victory Shorts, including *Any Bonds Today,* a two-minute Technicolor trailer for the Treasury Department; *Fighting the Fire Bomb,* a five-minute short detailing what the average civilian should know about handling and extinguishing incendiary bombs; *Ring of Steel,* a ten-minute short depicting the American soldier's contribution to preserving national ideals of democracy and liberty, featuring dialogue by Spencer Tracy; and *Winning Your Wings,* an eighteen-minute recruitment film for the Army Air Force, with dialogue from Lieutenant James Stewart, who explained the requirements for enlistment and the benefits of service.[2] General Hap Arnold credited the film with recruiting 100,000 pilots. Because Arnold had made Darryl Zanuck a colonel in his service, Jack Warner asked to be made a general. Arnold granted Jack the rank of lieutenant colonel, one level below Zanuck. As soon as he got back to the Warner lot, Jack had the wardrobe department fit him with a uniform that matched his newly authorized rank. The producer paraded around the lot in his uniform and asked employees to refer to him as Colonel Warner. These points of pride provided many opportunities to rib the mogul behind his back. Albert Warner received the rank of major for his service to the US government during the war and would regularly be referred to as Major Warner in the press.

The Warner radio station KFWB continued to play an essential role in wartime Southern California. In late 1941 or early 1942 Warner Bros. hosted a broadcast from Washington, DC, on behalf of the Treasury Department. Prepared patriotic copy was read on the air by a leading Warner Bros. employee (archival documents don't specify, but it was likely Jack or Harry Warner). Vincent F. Callahan, chief of the Treasury Department's radio and press operation, sent a memo to all affiliated stations about Warner's announcement. The on-air statement read: "We have been shocked by the stealthy attack made upon our soil by Axis tyrants. We need no rallying cry to compel us to gather around the flag of America. Every citizen is well aware of the task which confronts America. We will not be daunted in our determination to end forever the tyranny imposed on helpless people by the will of a few."[3] This was followed by encouragement to buy bonds and stamps each payday to support those fighting overseas.

The *Warner Club News* was the Warner brothers' way to connect with their employees. The Warner Club was created in 1938 and ran until 1962. To join, employees had to pay dues of 25 cents per month or $3 per year, which entitled them to the newsletter, invitations to events (parties, dances, picnics, golf tournaments), and monetary gifts when they got married or had a child. In January 1942 Jack and Harry had a specific message for studio employees, titled "Courage":

> Our country is at war. It is our war, our fight for freedom, our chance to prove our love of America and our determination to keep our precious freedoms.
> We have new duties and added responsibilities now. Production of all kinds is vital to the success of our country's effort to rid the world of a horrible danger.
> This applies, we believe, to the work of making and exhibiting motion pictures as it does to every vital industry in America. Ours is an important link in the chain America seeks to forge around the forces of evil.
> We are working now with a double purpose and it is necessary, we believe, that every loyal American employed by Warner Bros. recognize this and have a hand in building entertainment that will help keep up the courage of the workers at home as well as of the troops in the field.
> This is the time for every man and woman to consecrate themselves to the serious business ahead of us and give freely to his time and strength and courage to the victory we will at sometime celebrate.
> The word is COURAGE.[4]

In December Warner Bros. sent a lengthy memo to the *Hollywood Reporter*, puffing its upcoming films: "Warner Bros. has only one objective for 1943—victory." Once again sounding as if it were written by Harry Warner, it continued: "This is not a New Year's resolution. It is a timely reaffirmation of the policy which has governed Warner Bros.' every action, dictated every decision it has made since bombs fell on Pearl Harbor." The studio's employees had purchased war bonds at a rate of $25,000 per week, totaling over $2 million by the end of 1942. Warner Bros. saw "that opportunity lies

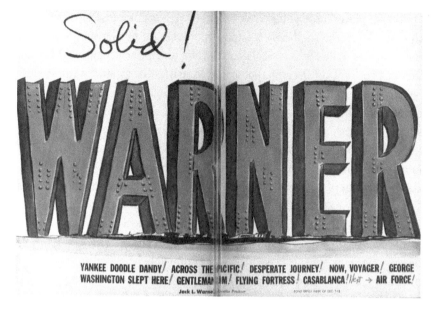

YANKEE DOODLE DANDY/ ACROSS THE PACIFIC/ DESPERATE JOURNEY/ NOW, VOYAGER/ GEORGE WASHINGTON SLEPT HERE/ GENTLEMAN JIM/ FLYING FORTRESS/ CASABLANCA/Next → AIR FORCE/

Warner's war films.

in the proper dissemination of information and in the effective bulwarking of public morale," and "Harry M. Warner believes, sincerely and strongly, that this is more than an opportunity. It is an obligation." Readers were reminded that this did not eliminate the need for "hours of wholesome relaxation, of temporary escape from the grim realities of a world plunged into horror by the ambitions of totalitarian lunatics," which could make a "considerable contribution to the morale of the ever-increasing army that fights on the production front." Warner Bros. continued its obligation to bring audiences the truth: "America can leave propaganda to the Axis. Goebbels and his Rome and Tokyo counterparts must deal in lies and fabrications. America need only tell the truth. And no more potent weapon has ever been forged for freedom's cause."[5]

Following *Confessions of a Nazi Spy* and *Underground,* Warner Bros. produced *Sergeant York* (1941), a biopic of Medal of Honor recipient Alvin York, and the war films *Wings for the Eagle* (1942) and *Captains of the Clouds* (1942). *Dangerously They Live,* which premiered at the end of 1941 and was released internationally in early 1942, stars John Garfield as a doctor who stumbles on a Nazi espionage plot. Directed by Vincent Sherman, *All through the Night*

(1942) is a clever farce-gangster hybrid about a Nazi plot to destroy a battle-ship in New York. The Nazis resemble members of the German-American Bund, adding to the film's topical flair. The film also bravely mentions Dachau, the Nazi concentration camp that would soon become infamous worldwide. Some critics saw through the war fervor of *Desperate Journey* (1942) and pinned the film as an overly simplistic adventure yarn, but it was popular with audiences eager for hoorah patriotism. *Across the Pacific* (1942) was directed by John Huston and completed by Vincent Sherman after Huston joined the army. The film stars Humphrey Bogart and Mary Astor in a story about passengers on a cruise ship who learn of a Japanese sabotage plot in Central America. After attending a preview of *Across the Pacific* in Washington, Jack Warner wired the studio to report that the audience reaction "convinces me beyond a shadow of a doubt that Humphrey Bogart is one of our biggest stars. In Bogart we have what I honestly consider the equivalent of Clark Gable." Bogart's biographers suggest that it was during this trip to Washington that Jack Warner first met with President Roosevelt about making the ill-fated *Mission to Moscow*.[6]

Bogart had been a workhorse at Warner Bros. for many years, acting in dozens of Warner films by the end of the 1930s, often taking the scraps left by James Cagney and Edward G. Robinson. Bogart described Jack Warner as having "an ability to read a screenplay and find its weakness, or to know from a one-page synopsis of a submitted property whether it would play or not." Although producers like Hal Wallis and Darryl Zanuck before him had a significant impact on many important films, every production began with what Jack thought or wanted to see or disapproved of. Jack Warner was many things, and his goofy public persona made it easy to underestimate him, but he was also "a natural editor who loved the cutting room and had a spectacular feel for the pacing of a film."[7]

Bogart had starred with Mary Astor in *The Maltese Falcon* (1941), directed by John Huston and based on Dashiell Hammett's hard-boiled novel. The film had an impressive supporting cast that became the bedrock of Warner's noir-style crime films during the war and postwar years. Huston eventually became good friends with Jack Warner, who had "a funny, childlike candor" and "was never guarded in anything he said; words seemed to escape from him unthinkingly." Warner had a reputation for saying the wrong thing at the wrong time, but some gave him the benefit of the doubt, believing that this was part of his charm. "He was anything but pretentious," added Huston, "and seemed to be constantly laughing at himself, but he was certainly a canny, astute individual when it came to his own interests."[8] For now, those interests included enlisting his studio directly in the war effort.

How Will This Picture Help Win the War?

In December 1942 Hollywood was notified that the Office of War Information was authorized to censor films. As they had with the Production Code Administration (PCA), studios would submit scripts for approval by the OWI. According to Lowell Mellett, chief of the OWI's Motion Picture Bureau, this step became necessary because previous films had hindered the US war message. Although some observed that the OWI intervention paralleled what was already being done in accordance with PCA rules, the major objection from studio brass was the production delays caused by having yet another office vet scripts. Mellett assured studios that the OWI's role was simply to advise on films with military themes and assist whenever necessary. "I don't think anyone can question the industry's patriotism," said Mellett, "and we are willing and anxious to cooperate with the government in any way to further the war [effort]."[9] Most famously, for each production, the OWI wanted Hollywood to consider, "Will this picture help win the war?"[10] The OWI also asked studios to avoid mischaracterizing the United States and its allies, to be aware of how movies create understanding around the world, and to recognize how quickly the world can change in the time it takes for a project to progress from script to screen. Of course, Warner Bros. had long been considering these issues, as proved by its production record.

One of the most popular films of the war years was the George M. Cohan musical biography *Yankee Doodle Dandy* (1942). Cohan was awarded the Medal of Honor for his World War I songs "It's a Grand Old Flag" and "Over There." The film stars James Cagney showcasing his masterful dancing skills, a welcome assignment after playing gangsters for more than a decade. The film got off to a rocky start, including Cagney's initial disinterest due to Cohan's antiunion labor views. Another wrinkle was Cagney's image issues, which began in 1940 when former Communist Party member John Leech presented a laundry list of major Hollywood names who were communist sympathizers to a grand jury in Los Angeles. The list included actors James Cagney, Humphrey Bogart, Fredric March, and Francis Lederer; director Gregory La Cava; and writers Clifford Odets, Lester Cole, and Budd Schulberg. The

Screen Actors Guild issued a statement that its members "hate Nazism, Communism, and fifth-columnists . . . the present smear campaign against certain prominent actors is playing squarely into the hands of real fifth columnists, whom America must smash."[11] Bill Cagney, the actor's brother, producing partner, and manager, contacted Martin Dies, the current front man of the House Un-American Activities Committee (HUAC), and set up a time for James to testify and clear his name. When Jack Warner expressed interest in furthering Cagney's image as a patriot, Bill told him James would play "the damndest patriotic man in the country." When Jack asked who that was, Bill quickly replied, "George M. Cohan."[12]

To studio boss Jack Warner and director Michael Curtiz, the film's overt patriotism was not phony. For many immigrants whose homelands had been torn to shreds, there was no such thing as jingoism. *Yankee Doodle Dandy* was already in production when Germany declared war on the United States on December 11, 1941. Studio employees spoke of the growing passions on the set as the crew realized that they were making a special and timely picture. Joan Leslie recalled that Cagney's contagious emotions impacted everyone, from the cast in front of the cameras to the lighting technicians up in the rafters. The "Grand Old Flag" number was particularly important to Curtiz, and it was rehearsed in front of producer Hal Wallis and Jack and Harry Warner.[13] Today, some may see *Yankee Doodle Dandy* as an overly simplistic flag-waver, but the moment it was released, it struck a chord with the moviegoing public and critics alike. The film's ability to inspire unity is as traditional as it is timeless.

When *Yankee Doodle Dandy* premiered in New York City at the Hollywood Theater on Broadway, advance ticket sales—which were donated for war bonds—totaled $5.45 million.[14] Many seats sold for thousands of dollars apiece. Albert and Harry Warner both purchased sections of seats, as did the Bloomingdales, Al Jolson, and Eddie Cantor, as well as civic groups such as Musicians Union Local 802, the Teamsters Joint Council, and many others. The Warner public relations push incorporated women's groups such as True Sisters and the Jewish Federation of Women. Also in attendance was former Vitagraph producer Alfred E. Smith, New York City mayor Fiorello LaGuardia, and New York governor Herbert Lehman. The theater was decorated with large banners and cardboard cutouts in the lobby, all star-spangled to fit the occasion. The film was a financial success for Warner Bros. and served the brothers' interest in boosting morale during the war.

Yankee Doodle Dandy premiere.

Even with fewer productions, Warner Bros. cast a wide net during the war. *Kings Row* and *Juke Girl* proved to be fine vehicles for Ann Sheridan and Ronald Reagan. The latter film continued the studio's rebellious commentary on labor issues, siding with exploited farmers in Florida. *Juke Girl* director Curtis Bernhardt later recalled that Jack Warner was always eager to green-light controversial stories and would say, "At Warner Bros. you could make a film like this. MGM would never make something like this."[15] Bernhardt acknowledged that *Juke Girl* could be seen as radical, but this was the kind of movie audiences expected from Warner Bros. The Warners had both a standard house style and a reputation for engaging in difficult subject matter. Although the studio kept war-related themes at the forefront, it did not ignore the reliable genres on which the Warner name had been built.

The studio's service films, including the nearly one hundred training films promised to the OWI in 1943, were a testament to the Warners' dedication to the war effort. *Casablanca* saw a limited release in 1942 and broke wide open the following year. Looking forward, the studio was particularly excited about its 1943 lineup of war-related films, including *Air Force, Watch on the Rhine, Mission to Moscow, Action in the North Atlantic, This Is the Army, Edge of Darkness,* and *Background to Danger.* Puffing its 1943 programming, Warner Bros. reminded readers of *Variety* that the studio had been pushing antifascist and pro-freedom fare long before the attack on Pearl Harbor. As the war raged on, it was important to remember that "laughter and romance have their place in war, no less than in time of peace. Now, more than ever, pure entertainment is needed to lighten dark days."[16] Examples included the Frank Capra–directed and Epstein brothers–penned *Arsenic and Old Lace* (1944); *The Corn Is Green* (1945), a Bette Davis–driven melodrama about a teacher working to increase education in a mining town; and *Rhapsody in Blue* (1945), a musical biography of composer George Gershwin.

Harry Warner's vision was a Hollywood that could both "entertain and inform." During times of war, "hysteria and emotion are much a part of the individual and he must not only discipline his own thought but receive from cogent sources all the guidance possible." Pushing back against a massive infestation of propaganda from fascist nations made Hollywood's responsibilities both "honorable" and "frightening." Harry commended his brother Jack for his leadership at the studio, which was full of talented directors, writers, actors, and technicians. "Long ago, when the crooked cross of Germany first became apparent on a horizon in turmoil, we sat down all of us together and mapped a course. At the time we pledged ourselves, no matter what history and fate brought to us, to carry out this course." The Warners had led the charge against fascism since 1933, a badge of honor for the studio. Deviating slightly from his usual proud promotion of Warner Bros. films, Harry argued that wartime obligations required "much more than a photographic mirroring of the times." The studio's name had been built on of-the-moment storytelling, which still rang true, although the context had changed since the Depression years.

Harry mused about cinema's ability to be an influence for good and to offer a powerful riposte to pro-Nazi propaganda. "In a motion picture theater, in less than two hours, a person today can inform himself, can start preparing his thinking for the future." And, Harry continued, "while this critically needed information is coming to him in the fastest, clearest way possible, he is also being entertained." With the studio's finger always on the pulse of the surrounding culture, Warner boasted that *Casablanca* had been finished before North Africa was invaded, and it provided a useful perspective on Vichy France. Currently in the editing room was *Edge of Darkness* (1943), about the Nazi occupation of Norway. Warner believed the upcoming *Air Force* would be the studio's most important war film thus far and noted that all profits for *This Is the Army* (1943) would be donated to the Army Emergency Relief Fund. During a screening of *Casablanca* for some bigwigs in Washington, DC, Jack had been approached by someone who asked where the studio got its directives and whether it had hushed the crew into secrecy. Harry responded, "Our only directives are those which come from an informed staff which has voluntarily read and soaked in all that is printed about our times, which observes trends, which weighs truths

Filming *This Is the Army.*

against more propaganda, and which, finally, has come to value the intan-
gibles." Harry was pressed about *Mission to Moscow,* based on ambassador
Joseph E. Davies's experiences in Russia, and was asked whether it was wise
to put a Russia-friendly story into production. Harry defended the picture,
of course, noting that the studio wanted to do all it could for America's allies.

The end of the *Variety* memo pivots toward what can be described as
quintessential Harry Warner condescension toward Hollywood excess, which
his brother Jack reveled in. "The glamor era has vanished. Glamor belonged
to a decade which brought us this war. We ought to leave it far behind and
forget it as quickly as possible." Harry was ecstatic to find no more "days of
swimming pools and fast cars and bathing suited cuties chasing right young
men into honorable marriage." The "cuties," as Harry called them, were now
"standing over airplane parts, or welding or riveting. Or they are living quietly
in a small room existing on a soldier's pay and thinking day and night in
terms of how to win and win quickly." This was the bottom line for Harry:

every single person must be focused on winning the war. "These are realistic days," Warner declared, "the screen also has arrived at true realism." One could argue that Warner Bros. films had been hammering realism for more than a decade, but Harry's mission was to ensure that audiences were acutely aware of what was at stake.

Through it all, Warner retained a glimmer of hope for the future. "In the peace to come, the cuties may shuck themselves of their overalls and go back to being lovely young creatures. We may once more look upon the playboy as a source of amusement and gaiety." For now, however, it was time to tell war stories to boost morale and inform those not already engaged in the global battle against fascism. Understanding the full potential of motion pictures, Warner concluded, "I like to think that to some appreciable degree these pictures, having given escape and entertainment in crowded, dark times, also have given counsel and wisdom to meet the history that is just around the corner." Harry knew that happiness could follow darkness, having lived through the process himself, and true to form, Harry left his audience with a sense of optimism.

One of the most famous films in Warner Bros. history, *Casablanca* premiered in New York City in November 1942, just after US tanks tore into the Moroccan city then occupied by German-allied Vichy France. As it expanded into wide release in early 1943, *Casablanca* gained popularity as the Axis occupation of North Africa ended. The film gained additional publicity when FDR and Winston Churchill held a meeting in Casablanca to plan the next phase of the war, which led to a demand for the unconditional surrender of the Axis powers. Commenting in the *Los Angeles Times,* Edwin Schallert observed that *Casablanca* was "one of those lucky pictures which happens to be linked right with the headlines." "Regardless of the latest arresting happenings linked with the war," he wrote, "the picture would unquestionably thrive on account of its general timeliness. The topical nail is binged right on the head."[17] *Casablanca* was so popular in London that crowds continued to pack theaters after the sounding of air-raid alarms.

Casablanca presented exactly what Harry Warner desired: a film that both entertains, with a story about a love triangle involving disgruntled expatriate Rick (Humphrey Bogart), Nazi resistance fighter Laszlo (Paul Henreid), and his girlfriend Ilsa (Ingrid Bergman), and educates audiences about pivotal movements of Allied and Axis forces, resistance fighters, and disloyal Nazis such as Captain Renault (Claude Rains). *Casablanca*'s memorable supporting cast includes Conrad Veidt, Sydney Greenstreet, Peter Lorre, and Dooley Wilson. The timeliness of the film was not lost on the cast, made up largely of European immigrants who had fled the terror. In short, these players were playing themselves. Most of the seventy-five actors in *Casablanca* were immigrants, and "of the fourteen who were given screen credit only Humphrey Bogart, Dooley Wilson, and Joy Page were born in America."[18] Although Jack Warner would later steal credit for the film, Hal Wallis produced it.

The relationship between Jack and Wallis became increasingly tense, largely due to contract and assignment disputes. *Casablanca*'s production was turbulent, but it would go on to win the Academy Award for Best Picture. In his memoir, Wallis vividly described the Oscar ceremony: "I started up the aisle to receive my award," because, after all, Best Picture Oscars go to the producers, and "to my astonishment, Jack Warner leapt to his feet, ran to the stage, and received it ahead of me." Jack's face bore a "broad, flashing smile and a look of great self-satisfaction" as the "audience gasped." It is one of the most infamous events in Oscar history, as Jack literally stole credit on Hollywood's biggest night. "Almost forty years later," Wallis wrote, "I still haven't recovered from the shock."[19] The next morning, Wallis went to Warner's office to collect the award, but Jack refused to turn it over; he insisted that the producer be photographed only with the Thalberg award (which Wallis had also won). The dispute made it into Schallert's *Los Angeles Times* column, where he noted that sometimes a studio boss can accept an award, but titles mean nothing; it all depends on "who swings the biggest wallop at the moment in rampageous studio politics."[20] History has sided with Wallis, acknowledging that Jack Warner's spotlight grab was a bad move. Wallis soon left Warner Bros., making him the second major producer to abandon the company for greener pastures.

Wallis got due credit for *Air Force* (1943), directed by Howard Hawks. According to Hawks, the idea for the film came from Major General Hap Arnold, the same man who gave Jack Warner his vaunted rank of lieutenant colonel. Arnold suggested the story of a fleet of B-17s that leave California and are over the Pacific when Japan hits Pearl Harbor. Jack Warner intended to have the film premiere on December 7, 1942, the one-year anniversary of the attack. However, it took a couple months longer, thanks to OWI concerns about a line stating that the United States could win the war alone. The PCA also had several problems with the script. Joseph Breen wired Jack Warner in October 1942, concerned that the PCA had not yet received a full script for *Air Force*. He also sent numerous memos, complaining about some of the script's lines. The PCA had a list of banned words, phrases, and gestures, which included "hold your hats, boys," "lousy," and the act of nose-thumbing.

The biggest point of contention over the film's dialogue was the phrase "damn 'em," despite the approved final line of *Gone with the Wind* three years earlier: "I don't give a damn." This was a wartime picture, and Jack Warner wanted it to be as tough as possible. Warner wired Breen at the end of November 1942: "Will appreciate your group giving consideration to our scene in *Air Force* where Garfield sees Pearl Harbor burning and says 'Damn 'em.'" Jack knew that softening the language of the crew on a bomber plane would sound phony to audiences. He wrote, "Being strictly a man's picture, we want to keep this in the picture and if necessary will put it to the board of directors. Hope this won't be necessary as I know you realize the importance of this picture which was made with the cooperation of our air forces."[21] The PCA finally approved the film on January 27, 1943, although the lines in question were censored locally around the country.

Air Force hit the big screen in February 1943, filling the spot freshly vacated after *Casablanca*'s three-month run at the Hollywood Theater in New York. Like other Warner Bros. war pictures, *Air Force* was tied to a large promotional and bond-buying campaign. The film stood easily on its own merits, with a screenplay by Dudley Nichols and solid performances from John Garfield, Harry Carey, Arthur Kennedy, and others. The *Hollywood Reporter* billed *Air Force* as "the great American aviation picture of World War II."[22] Hawks's biographer appropriately described the film as "equal parts physics, action, and emotion, all balanced by the master engineer [the director] to run beautifully together, even if on the spare parts of propaganda, nationalism, and expediency."[23] Whip-fast production was Warner's strength, nationalism was part of the Warner brothers' mold, and the feel of propaganda was a side effect of many war-era films. It is impossible to miss the post–Pearl Harbor animosity with a line like "They have a lot to pay for" as bomber pilots rattle bullets at Japanese fighter planes. As the war progressed, Warner Bros. films mirrored the evolution of both the mission and home-front attitudes.

The Regrettable *Mission to Moscow* and the Turn toward Victory

Mission to Moscow was perhaps the only film Jack Warner regretted. The Germans invaded Russia, taking Stalingrad in the summer of 1942. According to legend, President Roosevelt spoke with former US ambassador to Russia Joseph E. Davies about fast-tracking a book he was writing about his time in Russia (1936–1938). Roosevelt also spoke with Jack and Harry Warner and, according to producer Robert Buckner, "brainwashed" them into making the film.[24] Jack told Buckner the film was a favor for the president. "FDR had a tremendous ability to twist your wrist," Buckner said years later; the Warner brothers "were so impressed with being in the White House, and they were trying to be good, loyal Americans."[25] Buckner read the book in June 1942 on his way to New York, where he met with Harry Warner before traveling to Washington, DC, to discuss the project with Davies. Buckner knew the score and never fully trusted Davies; he asked Jack Warner if the purpose of the film was to "influence . . . public psychology for reasons of state."[26] Buckner's suspicion was correct. This became clear when Harry Warner assigned Michael Curtiz to direct the film. The director declared, "You know I am anti-communist." "So am I," Warner replied, "but the Russians are now our allies and President Roosevelt would like us to make the picture."[27] Jack Warner assured Curtiz that the film would be an important addition to the director's canon. Davies wanted a more famous director (*Casablanca* was not yet a classic), but Jack stood firm, knowing that Curtiz was one of the most reliable directors on the lot.

The production of *Mission to Moscow* ran into trouble when Davies demanded revisions to Howard Koch's script. Curtiz biographer Alan Rode also cites memos back and forth between the director and Jack Warner regarding the overuse of film stock. Jack wrote, "You know there is a war on, Mike, and you must conserve film." The director pointed a finger at Walter Huston, who played Davies in the film and kept flubbing his lines. "These things occur and are really beyond my control," replied Curtiz. "Of our 130,000,000 Americans, I am foremost in the desire to win the war."[28]

Buckner and Curtiz had the sense that Davies was not being fully forthcoming when he claimed that any script changes were direct requests from President Roosevelt. They knew Davies had fabricated events to make the

Russians look good, such as adding that the USSR did not invade Finland (which it did in November 1939). Buckner recalled, "Davies was variously helpful or a damn nuisance, with his final OK of everything in his contract." Davies was given the red-carpet treatment because the Warners saw this film as a favor to Roosevelt. "Curtiz, who had a notoriously short temper on the set, was often furious with Davies' petty objections," Buckner explained, "and I had to restrain him on several occasions, although I shared his [the director's] feelings."[29] Because *Mission to Moscow* was produced during the short-lived alliance between the United States and Russia, the OWI's Bureau of Motion Pictures quickly approved the film and spoke highly of its potential to offset Axis propaganda.

Davies arranged a screening of *Mission to Moscow* at the White House in April 1943 before being granted authority to present the film to Joseph Stalin in Russia. Davies wired Harry Warner after showing the film to top Russian leaders at the Kremlin and claimed that Soviet marshal Georgy Zhukov and premier Vyacheslav Molotov "were generous in their praise of the picture."[30] Davies oversold the event because, two days later, Stalin hosted a dinner for Davies, and the film was shown again at the Kremlin. Ambassador William Standley wrote to Secretary of State Cordell Hull and confirmed that the Russians' reaction to *Mission to Moscow* was "glum curiosity" and that they "will not desire to give publicity to the film." In closing, Standley argued that "the film will not contribute to better understanding between the two countries."[31] Even worse, Buckner was told that Stalin and his cronies laughed continuously during the film.

Mission to Moscow premiered in Washington, DC, and New York City on April 28–29 and was set for wide release on May 22. The "tough, hard-boiled audience" at the Washington premiere consisted of nearly four thousand politicians and members of the press, but according to the *Hollywood Reporter,* the film "won tumultuous applause and unanimous acclaim."[32] *Mission to Moscow* packed two screenings to capacity at the National Press Club, with a third screening scheduled to satisfy the thousands turned away from the first two. At a luncheon, Davies commended the Warners for having faith in his story and said the film had "the purpose of serving the peace."[33] Felix Cotton, president of the National Press Club, commended the Warner brothers, saying, "We newspaper men believe that *Mission to Moscow* constitutes a very important piece of news and the fact that Warner Bros. has acceded to our request to view it in advance, so that we may report on it to the world at large, brings greater dignity to our profession and in turn dignifies your own."[34] Cotton was adamant that motion pictures were news events and should be covered as such, especially when they tackled topical narratives.

Buckner knew the film was a mistake. A petition began to circulate accusing *Mission to Moscow* of containing "historical falsifications" that were "characteristic of totalitarian propaganda."[35] The petition argued that *Mission to Moscow* whitewashed Stalin's 1936–1938 purge trials, which were fast-tracked executions of political enemies, and presented the Russian government as misunderstood. Days before *Mission to Moscow*'s wide release, Harry Warner responded to increased chatter about the public's exhaustion with war films. He announced that his studio would not be "intimidated or coerced" by "persons who are not wholeheartedly behind our war effort" and are pushing to keep the reality of fascism from audiences.[36] Warner was the first producer to comment on this issue, and as expected, he thought Hollywood had an obligation to continue to produce war-related films. Schallert's *Los Angeles Times* coverage quoted the mogul's strong words: "Any arbitrary exclusion of war pictures either to satisfy a small appeaser element or for personal reasons without regard to the general public interest is equivalent to sabotage." Warner's passion for the war effort had not waned. Harry stated, "If the screen does not help prepare members of the younger generation to understand why they are being called upon to fight, and to inform those at home how our vast production of war material is being used in battle it would be evading its obligation."[37]

In hindsight, *Mission to Moscow* was a bad move. Both the book and the film were hastily produced, based on hurried wartime decisions. At the end of 1943, the *Hollywood Reporter*'s representatives at a laudatory Washington, DC, event published a less than complimentary review: "When J. L. Warner gave the order to go ahead . . . Joseph E. Davies . . . calmly declared that Hitler would never take Stalingrad, that Russia's valiant resistance would rise to greater heights than ever. Warner Bros. took his word for it."[38] The Warner brothers, who had followed Roosevelt's lead since 1933, stuck with a game plan that had worked for a decade. But *Mission to Moscow* was seen as an opportunistic and shortsighted film, and it would raise the ire of the anticommunist crusaders who were just around the corner. Astute film critics could see through the wartime veil of a temporary alliance with Russia.

Knowing that *Mission to Moscow* might not age well, screenwriter Howard Koch mounted a defense. He maintained that he "had very few clear convictions for or against the Soviet Union. Perhaps that's why Mr. Warner gave me the assignment—because he believed I would approach the problem as a dramatist and not as a political partisan." Koch knew that there were many opinions regarding the Soviet Union, but he remained unclear about the role it played in the world. Koch had liked Davies's account and thought he could trust the former ambassador's experiences, which Koch described as "brilliant, legalistic fact-finding and reporting." Koch stood by his research on the purge trials, which he had undertaken in search of a theme and a lesson regarding Russia's internal affairs. He had condensed two purge trials into one, simplifying them for story purposes. Characters had to be invented or amended to create a story arc, but the confessions of the defendants remained the same: "treasonable fifth column activities under the leadership of Trotsky in concert with Germany and Japan to overthrow the government of the Soviet Union." Koch defended Davies's slow understanding of the trials because "he was too careful of an observer to jump at a premature conclusion." Understanding that American audiences might be put off by the standard Russian demeanor, Koch noted that the "Slavic temperament of the Russian is sometimes taciturn and secretive." The screenwriter was later gray-listed for his work on *Mission to Moscow*, largely a result of Jack Warner's refusal to clear his name.[39]

Jack Warner was the likely author of a letter written to Joseph Stalin on May 1, 1943. An unsigned copy of this letter is archived in the studio's legal files, but the content and perspective are that of a high-ranking studio executive. "I have asked our mutual friend, Mr. Joseph E. Davies, to present you with my compliments a print of the motion picture *Mission to Moscow*, which has been adapted from Mr. Davies's book," the letter explains. "When you view this picture, I am sure you will agree that it is the first attempt by a foreigner to portray on the screen the foresight and sound judgement of the statesmen of the U.S.S.R. relative to the Nazi menace." The only Warner brother with so little political acumen that he would refer to Stalin's Russia as having "sound judgement" was Jack. The letter continues, "If this film, in conveying its message, shall clear up to even a small degree the misconceptions and misunderstandings about Russia which have already existed too long, then my effort in the production of the picture will have been rewarded a thousand-fold." The vague olive branch offered in this letter has Jack Warner written all over it. One can imagine him writing a letter to Stalin just to have a good story to share at cocktail parties. The letter concludes, "In closing, may I express to you my great admiration for the soul-stirring fight which the Army and the Citizens of the U.S.S.R. are waging for the destruction of our common foe."[40]

The fall release schedule from Warner Bros. was less controversial and more focused on boosting national confidence. *This Is the Army,* based on Irving Berlin's stage play, was another well-timed morale booster that raised $5 million for the Army Emergency Relief Fund when Warner Bros. donated the film's profits. *Thank Your Lucky Stars,* a musical romanticizing the United States, featured songs such as "God Bless America." *Edge of Darkness, Background to Danger,* and *Adventure in Iraq* filled the need for relevant war-related thrillers.

Toward the End of War

Jack and Harry Warner shared their optimism with studio employees in the December 1943 issue of *Warner Club News.* "I believe our darkest hours are behind us," wrote Harry. "Each day will see the future horizon becoming brighter and brighter. It is up to every one of us, every man, woman and child, whether in uniform or not, to work and fight together as a United Nation."[41] Harry's bright view of the future included an ongoing battle for "the Victory of Good over the forces of Evil and Intolerance, so that the World will actually live and practice the teaching of Christ, Peace on Earth—Good Will Toward Men." Harry was entirely sincere in his drive for the betterment of humanity. He argued that Americans should not "rest on any laurels" but should "carry on the fight with all our energies, with all our money which we can so wisely invest in War Bonds, and with all our faith and hope and charity." Referring to the multifaith celebrations at year's end, Harry added, "This is the season for rejoicing. We should rejoice, then, in new and renewed opportunities to serve our neighborhoods and our country. This could bring important dividends in satisfaction before the new year ends."

Jack's words were simple. He saw the end of the war on the horizon. "Our defeats are becoming victories. America has come of age. Democracy is on the march." He took every opportunity to tell employees that the studio was essential to the war effort. "Never forget that our pictures are a direct contribution toward winning the war. Our jobs this year are more important, therefore, than ever before." Jack reminded employees that this was the third Christmas of the war, but "it is by far the most encouraging one. We have

Hollywood Canteen advertisement in *Photoplay*.

not completed the tremendous and arduous task in which our country is engaged, but we have a right to feel pride without overconfidence." Jack and Harry regularly used the holiday issue of *Warner Club News* to share words of wisdom with studio employees at all levels.

Because Warner Bros. was both conserving materials and donating them to the war effort, the studio's output dropped to nineteen feature films in 1944, down from the usual fifty. Notable Warner Bros. films of 1944 included *Destination Tokyo, Arsenic and Old Lace, Passage to Marseilles, Mr. Skeffington,* and *Hollywood Canteen.*

In June 1944 the SS *Benjamin Warner* set out to sea from Richmond, California. A large model of the Statue of Liberty was unveiled at the shipyard, containing a plaque that read: "The Pacific Coast Shrine of Liberty. At this shipyard was built the S.S. Benjamin Warner, the last Liberty ship launched from the Pacific coast in World War II. Built by order of the U.S. Maritime Commission."[42] In attendance were Harry and Jack, Lita, Anna (now married to Dave Robbins), and Sadie (now married to Louis Halper) and her son, Sam. Speaking at the ceremony, Harry said, "Benjamin Warner knew the meaning of liberty better than we can know it because he had the bitter experience of oppression. He also knew the value of unity."[43] Harry's father had always told him that as long as the brothers were together, the family would be strong. "That, I feel, would also be Benjamin Warner's message to our country today."[44] In covering the Richmond launch, *Motion Picture Herald* noted Harry Warner's recent comments about studios' responsibility to ensure that their films have a positive impact on audiences. "A lot of the customers know that, too," it agreed. "Responsibility runs from studio stage to theater screen."[45] The brothers continued to receive accolades for their work during the war years, and their ability to read the culture extended well beyond the war.

On July 28, 1944, Jack Warner received an award at a luncheon hosted by the Hollywood division of the War Activities Committee, where the US and Canadian governments paid tribute to the motion picture industry. Warner extolled cinema's purpose during wartime: "The use that our war government and our armed services have made of the motion picture and the extent to which they have called upon us for assistance constitutes a milestone in the development of the film as a means of carrying information and inspiration to large numbers of people." Warner spoke of his studio's dedication not only to feature filmmaking for the betterment of the war effort but also to producing training and recruitment films for the armed services, noting that "the services rendered by our actors and actresses through the Hollywood Victory Committee constitute a great record of unselfish and patriotic devotion." Warner Bros. employees involved with the Hollywood Victory Committee included Olivia de Havilland, Errol Flynn, John Garfield, Sydney Greenstreet, Alan Hale, Walter Huston, Joan Leslie, Gene Lockhart, John Loder, Irene Manning, Dennis Morgan, Ann Sheridan, Alexis Smith, George Tobias, Jane Wyman, Jack Carson, Dinah Shore, Humphrey Bogart, George Brent, Paul Henreid, Claude Rains, Edward G. Robinson, S. W. Sakall, Joan Crawford, Bette Davis, Geraldine Fitzgerald, Hattie McDaniel, and Cheryl Walker.[46]

After years of global conflict, Jack Warner lauded motion pictures for their ability to "provide some recreation, some escape from the terrible tragedy of war, and [keep] alive the meaning of the war and the high purposes for which we fight." Jack highlighted *Confessions of a Nazi Spy* and its warnings about espionage and propaganda, while also giving kudos to MGM for *Mrs. Miniver* (1942), which "made us realize the meaning of human sacrifice." Warner continued by noting that the film industry would have to consider what kind of films would be needed in the future, films to "carry the great truths of our times." Certainly, Warner Bros. films had been imparting social and political truths for well over a decade. Stark realism was part of the Warner brand. However, Jack thought the entire industry should refocus as the country prepared for the postwar years.

Warner offered six essential postwar principles: (1) "Every one of us is responsible for safeguarding our great American heritage of freedom." (2) "Every one of us must remember that freedom, if taken for granted, can be lost." (3) "We must be quick to recognize the forces that will destroy freedom." (4) "We must be physically able to put down those forces if they attack us." (5) "We must be morally able to keep them from developing within our country." (6) "We must never forget that the world cannot exist half-slave and half-free." These six principles could have been cribbed from one of Harry Warner's speeches, but they perfectly represented the Warner brand of filmmaking as a social duty. Jack argued that postwar films "must keep these lessons of the war alive . . . we are fighting not just to win a fight, but to win a world in which our children and their children can know the security of peace and freedom." World War II was truly a battle for freedom, and the brothers used their production facilities to support the cause.

Jack closed by correctly anticipating the imminent criticism of motion pictures in the HUAC trials of 1947 and beyond. Jack knew that movies would always be a target of political and religious warriors. "In the post-war world, motion pictures must have the same freedom of expression as is guaranteed to the press and the spoken word," he said. "We must be constantly on the alert to resist all forms of dictation or attempted regulation. We must refuse to be intimidated from expressing our honest convictions on the screen." The Warners always defended their films while also defending the nature of motion pictures. Hollywood would face its strongest enemy in the postwar years, but until then, it was business as usual on the production front.

A high point for Warner Bros. was *Hollywood Canteen,* released on New Year's Eve 1944. The film celebrates the Los Angeles club for servicemen cofounded by Warner's own Bette Davis, John Garfield, and Music Corporation of America founder Jules Stein. The club was operated by Hollywood talent and supported by trade unions, including several chapters of the International Alliance of Theatrical Stage Employees (IATSE). Set directors and studio carpenters rehabilitated a dilapidated old club known as the Barn and brought it back to life as the Hollywood Canteen. Community members donated materials for the kitchen and decorations for the main room; additional renovations were funded by gifts. Three thousand Hollywood players, including many from Warner Bros. (e.g., Olivia de Havilland and Mervyn LeRoy), worked at the club as hosts, busboys, cooks, and many other roles. Big-name bands played every night. Opening night in 1942 was emceed by Eddie Cantor and featured Duke Ellington, Rudy Vallee, Abbott and Costello, Eleanor Powell, Dinah Shore, Betty Hutton, and others. Admission was granted only to those in military uniform, although many stars and executives, Jack Warner among them, paid $50 for an admission ticket on opening night. The food was warm, the stars were A-list, the bands were national acts, and the dance floor was swinging with jitterbugs every evening.

It is no coincidence that the Hollywood Canteen was spearheaded by Bette Davis, a Warner megastar who held so much sway at the studio that she was often referred to as the fifth Warner brother. Despite her spats with the studio, Davis's progressive nature was a perfect fit. She took her talent and ambition into the community for a great cause. Davis devised specific instructions for the volunteers, including guidelines on how to address wounded soldiers. "Forget the wounds, remember the man," she directed.[47] In addition, the Hollywood Canteen was known for its inclusivity. During

Harry Warner, Bette Davis, and Jack Warner. (Author's personal collection)

an era still marred by segregation, the club had no restrictions based on race. When objections were raised about "mixed couples" dancing at the canteen in January 1943, Davis responded unequivocally, "Let them dance if they want to." A syndicated column celebrated Davis's stance on race relations, noting, "One more blow was landed on color prejudice and an example was set by one of the most famous Hollywood celebrities."[48] When *Hollywood Canteen* failed to depict the club's positive influence on race relations, Warner Bros. caught flak for the film's whitewashing; similar concerns were raised about the use of blackface in *Thank Your Lucky Stars*.[49] After the studio's great strides with Dooley Wilson's role in *Casablanca, Hollywood Canteen* was a step back. That said, a close look at Warner Bros. background scenes shows a wider range of mixed races than any other studio. The acknowledgment of difference was integral to the Warner brothers, and that sentiment trickled into many of the studio's films.

Regardless of some negative press surrounding *Hollywood Canteen,* it was popular with audiences. The club itself, unmarred by negative film reviews, hosted more than two million servicemen and -women during its short period of operation. The film allowed the country to experience an onscreen version of the club, which had gained a national reputation for its wartime service. The premiere of *Hollywood Canteen* at the Strand in Albany, New York, raised $24 million in war bond sales, thanks to a massive publicity campaign.[50] The film was also a great way to take advantage of Davis's stardom, as she played a charming version of herself. But not everyone was complimentary. Warner star Joan Crawford called *Hollywood Canteen* "a very pleasant pile of shit for wartime audiences."[51] And not all servicemen enjoyed the happy-go-lucky depiction of soldiers so late in the war, when just about every community had lost someone killed in action. Even so, the soldiers continued to enjoy the time they spent at the Hollywood Canteen. Joan Leslie, star of the film and a regular on Warner Bros. nights (Tuesdays) at the canteen, remembered "the faces of the servicemen: young men thrilled at this glimpse of Hollywood glamour, deliriously happy on liberty, and yet willing to be sent out the next day to the other side of the world."[52]

During the holiday season in 1944–1945, *Warner Club News* shared more words of wisdom from the studio's fearless leaders. "On this, the fourth Christmas of the war, our first thoughts are of our friends and loved ones abroad with the armed forces," wrote Harry. "The realization of what they have endured so that we might live in peace should make all of us humble and grateful." With the weight of the war felt across the nation, Harry sympathized with the toll taken in every community. "I know that there is scarcely one of you who has not been touched in some way by the war. Yet, through all the difficulties and inconveniences, and despite anxieties and sorrows, you have carried on with your work in a way that is worthy of the best traditions of our country." Warner would have been remiss if he had not mentioned the role of film during the war, but he was fast to credit the entire company for its success. "Each of you has had a part in the development of this great medium, and each of you shares in the credit for its achievements." Harry ended with his usual brand of optimism, likely a welcome shaft of light for a community operating under the shadow of war. "I am confident that in the future, the motion picture will be of even greater service to mankind," wrote Warner, "bringing education, inspiration and understanding to millions. I know that I can count on all of you to help us attain this great ideal."[53]

In September 1945 Jack Warner took out a multipage ad in *Showmen's Trade Review* to highlight the studio's war service and make a pledge for the coming years. On the first page he wrote, "Peace: A challenge already met by the company which led the industry in meeting the challenge of war!" The studio's wartime policy, he noted, "was expressed in Warner Bros. pictures that inspired tens of millions of Americans to their war-winning tasks, and brought new prestige to exhibitors." This was followed by a pledge for peacetime: "We shall continue to combine 'good picture-making with good citizenship' by providing glorious entertainment for millions of free men working to reap the happy fruits of victory." The next several pages highlighted the studio's service-related films, including *Confessions of a Nazi Spy, Underground, Air Force, Yankee Doodle Dandy*, and *Hollywood Canteen*, among others. Warner concluded, "With this policy, with this pledge, and with this product, Warner Bros. points the industry's way to a new day of peace, progress, and prosperity."[54] The Warners had reason to be proud of their ability to engage audiences in important topics through motion pictures. The studio's films evolved with the war, beginning with the hoorah adventures of *Desperate Journey* to the somber *Objective, Burma!* (1945), which irked English audiences because it overlooked British contributions in the Pacific. After Germany surrendered on May 9, 1945, followed by Japan's surrender on September 2, World War II was over, and Jack Warner needed to make good on his peacetime pledge.

As the war was winding down, Warner Bros. produced films that spoke to the pathos of late war. For example, *Hotel Berlin*, adapted from Vicki Baum's novel of the same name, tells the story of people living in a bombed-out hotel toward the end of the war. *Objective, Burma!* and *Pride of the Marines* present different themes related to the costs of war. *Appointment in Tokyo*, a short documentary made in conjunction with the War Activities Committee, covers General Douglas MacArthur's war record from the Philippines in 1942 to the surrender of Japan in 1945. *Variety* described the documentary as "a graphic portrayal of the glorious fight back," noting that "it strikes out with dramatic suddenness with no preliminary warmup, to keep one frozen in one's seat for 54 minutes of awe-inspiring warfare on film."[55] The Warners ended the war as they had begun it—by keeping the evolving war narrative front and center with feature films and documentaries distributed through the studio's exhibition network.

Warner Bros. won an Oscar for the short subject *Hitler Lives*, released at the end of 1945. The film is an aggressive attack on the Nazis still living in Germany. In his memoir, Jack Warner said he had been motivated to produce

Warner Bros. wartime advertisement.

a documentary about how fascism lived on after Hitler's death. "After the war I made a tour as General Eisenhower's guest," he wrote, "and it was obvious that Nazism had still not been obliterated."[56] On his tour with Eisenhower, Warner took notes and photographs that could be developed into a script. The short film was directed by a young Don Siegel and went into wide release in early 1946. Critics applauded the studio's reminder that "Hitler lives today even in the thinking of Americans placed as high as Congress itself, and it advises us not to allow this influence or German deception to fool us into treating the enemy too lightly."[57] A reference to men of the cloth pushing fascism was a clear allusion to Father Coughlin. Bosley Crowther's *New York Times* review called the film "a real stimulant of public thought."[58] The film reminded viewers that fascist thought could rise up again, "which is why we occupy Germany," thundered narrator Knox Manning.

The Hollywood Foreign Correspondents Association presented Jack Warner with an award for *Hitler Lives.* Upon accepting the award, Warner warned the global audience about the danger of communism, fascism, and other isms. The United States had witnessed its own dangerous version of Americanism, as the America First movement championed xenophobia and anti-Semitism. *Hitler Lives* highlights Germany's history of conquest and reminds audiences that, as a country full of Nazi fellow travelers, Germany continues to be an enemy to humanity. The largest threat, the film argues, are the children of Germany. "They know no other system but the one that poisoned their minds. They're soaked in it. Trained to win by cheating. Trained to pick on the weak. They've heard no free speeches, read no free press." Nazi children "were brought up on straight propaganda . . . the worst educational crime in the history of the world. They believe they are masters and we were born to be their slaves. Germans are not sorry they caused the war, only sorry they lost it. We cannot accept a German apology with an open hand when that was the hand that hailed Hitler . . . the hand that murdered, massacred . . . dedicated to the ruthless use of force."[59] Jack Warner wrote, "I wish Adolf Hitler, Goebbels, and the rest of the Nazi hoods had lived long enough to see the film."[60]

In 1945 Warner Bros. produced just under twenty films, down from the fifty-plus in 1935. Despite the low numbers, the studio produced several memorable films that year. *Mildred Pierce,* based on the novel by legendary crime writer James M. Cain, is a female melodrama–suspense thriller full of sex, violence, and betrayal seen through the eyes of a divorced mother (an unforgettable Joan Crawford) who opens a restaurant to support her family. Joseph Breen wanted to shelve the film, believing it could not pass the Production Code and would likely irk many groups around the country. *Mildred Pierce* was another example of the Warner ability to identify cultural trends, as the nation was contemplating the role of women in the workforce, following women's wartime participation in jobs previously reserved for men. The film landed Crawford an Oscar for Best Actress.

Another notable film from 1945 was *Christmas in Connecticut,* starring Barbara Stanwyck as a reporter; it remains a holiday classic. *To Have and Have Not,* loosely based on Ernest Hemingway's novel, brought together what would become one of the most famous romances in film history both onscreen and off: Humphrey Bogart, whose marriage to actress Mayo Methot was on the rocks, and Lauren Bacall, a nineteen-year-old model who would soon be a major star. Bacall also starred in *Confidential Agent* alongside Charles Boyer and Peter Lorre.

Battles at Home

The war years offered Warner Bros. much to celebrate, but the brothers themselves had their share of home-front battles. While he was enjoying peak stardom, Errol Flynn found himself accused of multiple counts of statutory rape, irrevocably damaging his status as a matinee idol. Jack Warner summoned Los Angeles attorney Jerry Geisler to fight the charges and promised Geisler $40,000 to take Flynn's case. When Warner asked if Flynn could get acquitted, Geisler said, "If he's telling the truth."[61] In February 1943 Flynn was acquitted by a jury of nine women and three men. One of the accusers, Peggy Satterlee, said of the women on the jury, "They just sat there and looked at him adoringly . . . they never did believe he was guilty."[62] Jack knew that Flynn's lifestyle of sex and booze was wreaking havoc on the actor's health. In his memoir, Jack joked that sex never killed anyone, which, he observed, "must be true, otherwise many of the biggest stars in Hollywood would have been laid away long ago instead of falling ill or dying from such dull ailments as goofball addictions, overindulgence in schnapps, or anemia of the box office."[63] That said, Warner believed Flynn was speeding toward an early grave, which he certainly was.

In November 1943 Harry Warner testified in federal court against labor mobster Willie Bioff. After being charged with tax evasion, extortion, and racketeering, Bioff squealed on his mob buddies Johnny Rosselli and Frank

Nitti in return for a reduced sentence. If Bioff was willing to rat out some of the cruelest gangsters around, there was no telling what he might do to a Hollywood mogul. Warner testified in court that he carried a gun and had hired extra personal security out of fear of the racketeer. Defense counsel James Murray asked why Warner had not reached out to the police for protection. "They couldn't help me if I was dead," answered Harry. "You mean all the law enforcement agencies couldn't keep you from getting killed?" asked Murray. "No," Warner shot back, "not after I was dead. No sir." Murray also asked why Warner had not been more forthcoming in 1937 when asked about Bioff. Harry answered that he feared for his life. He was on the hook in this extortion plot, and Bioff "had the power to close my business or do me bodily harm, or both, and this persuaded me to give it [payments] to him."[64] Harry and Murray locked horns numerous times throughout the day, forcing the government's counsel to step in.

Murray also flung accusations at Albert Warner. "Don't rush me," fired Albert after Murray accused him of being Bioff's willing accomplice.[65] Albert too feared Bioff and spoke of his frustration with the labor leader. After reluctantly paying dues to avoid labor strikes, he then learned he was on the hook for constant bribes. The entire industry was victimized by Bioff's exploitation. Both Harry and Albert had refused to hand Bioff any money personally. In an attempt to pin Harry as Bioff's friend, Murray accused Warner of sending orchids to Mrs. Bioff as a good-bye gift before a Rio de Janeiro vacation. "I never sent orchids to Mrs. Bioff, or any other woman, including my wife," quipped Harry.[66] He claimed he had not paid anything to Bioff since 1937, when, just before Christmas, the gangster had asked for $20,000 as a Christmas gift for his bosses in Chicago. In total, Warner Bros. sank $100,000 into Bioff's scheme. One day in 1955 Bioff got into his vehicle, turned the key, and in true mob hit fashion was blown to bits.

The Warner Bros. lot saw its share of battles as well. After spats with James Cagney and Bette Davis over contracts and scripts in the 1930s, Olivia de Havilland became the biggest thorn in Jack Warner's side. Like Davis, de Havilland started to reject scripts, leading to numerous suspensions. Warner called de Havilland's claims "ridiculous," given the many successful Warner roles that had made her a star.[67] If de Havilland wanted to compare every role to her part in *Gone with the Wind*, Jack volunteered to get every major producer to tell her that was a bad idea. De Havilland had been loaned to David O. Selznick for that film because she pleaded with Jack's wife, Ann, to speak up on her behalf. After all, it was Ann who had lobbied for Jack to take a chance on a young Errol Flynn. As de Havilland's biographer argued, "It's a pity Jack didn't listen to his wife more often."[68] By June 1944, Harry told Jack to stop suspending the talent if they did not comply with their assignments. "If they don't want to work in one picture, make some other picture with them, but for goodness sake make a picture." The frugal Harry knew that it made no sense to sit on top talent. He reminded Jack that with all the liberty and freedom talk going on, the talent wanted more control. "When the war is over and all the actors and help have come back, you can at that time suspend anyone you want—including me, but right now don't cut your nose to spite your face."[69]

Jack wrote back, arguing that if they let the actors pick their roles, the studio wouldn't "be in business very long." Jack told Harry that actors often pushed back on a film as a ploy to get a raise or renegotiate the terms of their contract. "Everybody isn't suspended every time because they don't play a picture," reasoned Jack. "If they were, we wouldn't be making pictures at all. We play ball with them but when people become ornery like Bogart, De Havilland, this type, you haven't any alternative."[70] One of the problems with suspensions was that the time was added to the end of an actor's contract. De Havilland, like others who had tried and failed before her, filed a lawsuit in 1943 to get out of her contract with Warner Bros. She had been on suspension five times in seven years, so, according to Jack, she had time to make up. De Havilland took the case to the California Supreme Court in December 1943, which ruled in her favor. The seven-year contract maximum is still referred to as the de Havilland law. Besting Jack Warner was a turning point for de Havilland and set an example for other stars who wanted more control over their own careers.

Actors were not the only ones pushing for more control. IATSE and the Conference of Studio Unions (CSU) were feuding over union representation of set decorators. CSU leader Herbert Sorrell had orchestrated the Disney animators' walkout in 1941. As the CSU organized strikes, "the producers began to hire scabs," recalled Sorrell. "There was violence, but not enough." It was time to "pick one studio and hammer it good . . . we finally decided on Warner brothers."[71] What Sorrell did not realize was that the studio had the capacity to hammer back.

The CSU and Sorrell had pickets set up shop at the Warner Bros. main entrance on October 5, 1945. Dozens had gathered at the lot by 5:00 a.m.;

this ballooned to three hundred by 6:00, and an hour later, there were around seven hundred protesters who grew unruly fast. Word spread quickly across the Associated Press wires about a "melee of fire hoses, tear gas, bombs, and bottles."[72] By noon, the studio's police force was spraying the rioters with three fire hoses, knocking them off their feet. The stunned picketers then became an angry mob and rushed the police, who quickly launched tear gas into the crowd. The mob retaliated by heaving bottles, causing many of their own number to be injured by glass shards.

Studio law enforcement constructed barricades, likely out of leftover material from air-raid preparations. A riot squad from the Los Angeles Police Department arrived by bus, assembled into two brigades, and cleared the studio's front gate. The *Los Angeles Times* reported that "one striker who swung his fist at a policeman was felled with a club and dragged away. Another who grabbed a motorcycle officer's revolver from its holster was subdued by the policeman with the barrel of his recovered weapon."[73] There were numerous fistfights, several stabbings, and three overturned cars, one of which belonged to a studio police officer. Sorrell was in police custody by the end of the day. The event is known as Hollywood Black Friday. Strikes took place on other lots, including Paramount, RKO, and Universal. The protests did not end until Will Hays's replacement at the Motion Picture Association of America (MPAA; formerly MPPDA), Eric Johnston, negotiated with the American Federation of Labor to reorganize the CSU.

In addition to taking the brunt of the strike, Jack Warner was the victim of CSU anti-Semitism. CSU supporter L. T. Sheppard wrote to Jack, calling the Warners "a pack of real kikes," "real dirt Jews," and "cheap Jew bastards."[74] Warner was irate, feeling pressure from all sides and ready to erupt over the turmoil on his lot. John Wexley, who penned *Angels with Dirty Faces* and *Confessions of a Nazi Spy* for Warner Bros., remembered the aftermath of October 5. Wexley had always liked Warner, but after the strikes, the mogul sounded off, "I saw you on the goddamn picket line. Stop striking. Fuck off!"[75] The strikes continued into 1946 and had a lasting effect on the Warner brothers, particularly Jack. Tensions were so high that Jack's daughter remembered someone sending a note to their house "threatening to scatter our bones all over our golf course; a map was enclosed to show where the different pieces would be buried."[76]

Roy Brewer, an IATSE representative, remembered working with Ronald Reagan to counter communist forces in the trade unions. Reagan was a contract player at Warner Bros. and head of the Screen Actors Guild. Many believe that this period solidified Reagan's move from the political left to the political right. Brewer maintained that the communists orchestrated the violence on Black Friday, but Ring Lardner Jr., who was working on the script for *Cloak and Dagger* (a 1946 thriller set in Nazi Germany), remembered it differently. "The head of the Warner studio police, Blayney Matthews, was an American fascist type, very much against unions, and he led this business of attacking the picket lines when there was no real cause for it," the screenwriter said. "That made Warner brothers a particular target for liberals and radicals."[77] What was once seen as the most progressive studio in Hollywood had become a target for the political left. Matthews, a former investigator for the Los Angeles district attorney, maintained a range of connections and was a force to be reckoned with on the lot.

A major blow to the Warners was the death of President Roosevelt in April 1945. FDR had been the Warner brothers' political and, in some sense, moral leader since the Great Depression. Warner Bros. put more faith in FDR than any public official before or since. Jack Warner's statement on the president's passing began, "This is a day of reverence in memory of our late dearly beloved President Franklin Delano Roosevelt." Warner saw Roosevelt's vision of victory as the most important influence in winning the war, and "his memory will always remain enshrined in our hearts—his spirit of constant inspiration in a better world." It was time to welcome a new era where "tyranny and injustice will be no more" and where there is no space for "rabble-rousers and demagogues who would set class against class, creed against creed, and race against race." Warner hoped Roosevelt's memory would bring attention to America's freedoms—"freedom from fear and want, freedom of thought and religious conviction. For THAT we fought this war [and] for that we must work in peace."[78] The postwar years in Hollywood would find none of that peace. The ripple effects of the labor strikes were felt as the industry struggled to maintain its own narrative.

That same month, Jack Warner toured Europe with other industry leaders, including Darryl Zanuck and Harry Cohn. The purpose of the trip was mostly to rub elbows with top military and government officials after years of aiding the war effort. The most impactful part of the tour was visiting liberated concentration camps. General Dwight D. Eisenhower insisted that the media document the atrocities, and Jack Warner insisted on visiting "to visually record and educate the American people to the bitter fruits of race hatred."[79] The Hollywood brass toured the gas chambers and furnaces. When Harry learned of the enormity of the evil, he wired his brother, "How long have I been telling you to make a picture showing the atrocities?"[80] Harry had been the first in Hollywood to sound the alarm about the Nazis, and now the world was left with the ruins of their genocide. Unfortunately, depicting the death camps was beyond what the censorship office would allow. Still, Jack made sure to relay the horrifying details when he arrived back on the Warner Bros. lot.

As the war ended and the victory over fascism was celebrated, it was clear that the landscape of the United States had been forever altered. Hollywood in 1945 has been aptly described as a place where "politics, profits, and propaganda could reinforce each other to create symbols of a unified, harmonious society. But the new world ushered in by the war—a world of increasing diversity both nationally and internationally—doomed the old Hollywood and its message."[81] Following the victory, the nation's next chapter would be filled with fear and contention. The US government, which had already filtered out communists within its ranks, began to investigate numerous industries for subversive activities. Unfortunately for Hollywood, it would soon be sweating under HUAC's heat lamps.

6

Postwar Politics, HUAC, and the Blacklist

1946–1947

In January 1946 Jack and Harry Warner shared their hopes and desires for the postwar years in *Warner Club News*. Harry emphasized the need to rejoice after the war but reminded everyone that "to us, the victors, belongs the responsibility for rebuilding the peace of the world. Europe is in ruins. Millions of liberated people are homeless and starving. Voices of dissension are already heard again in the world, seeking to ferment new strife and to breed new hatreds." Despite living in the safety and comfort of the United States and now residing in a place of privilege, Harry never forgot how easily hatred can spread if it goes unchallenged. In addition, he worried about the new and terrifying technology highlighted by the bombing of Hiroshima and Nagasaki. "Overshadowing everything is the tremendous new discovery of atomic power," said Warner, "so devastating that we may well destroy ourselves with it." Harry remained a realist who knew that freedom requires constant and diligent management. Though he had been optimistic about the Allies winning the war, he was concerned about the ripple effects of the social and political strife in the United States that divided so many. "Everywhere men and women are seeking answers to the terrible questions left in the wake of the war." Jack Warner added, "This is our Victory Christmas." After noting that many had not come home from the war, Jack declared, "That is our task for 1946 and the years ahead: to promote understanding between nations, races and creeds, to put an end to hatreds, to build a way of life in which war will be a crime."[1]

Writing in *Motion Picture Herald*, Terry Ramsaye published a lengthy celebration of the twentieth anniversary of synchronized sound. Twenty years prior, Warner Bros. premiered *Don Juan* and a series of Vitaphone shorts that revolutionized the industry. Ramsaye wrote, "The motion picture, by gift of speech and music, has grown to a new dominance among the media of expression and to command of the greatest audience in all the history of entertainment." Cosponsoring the anniversary were the many other companies that had helped propel sound cinema into existence, including American Telephone and Telegraph (AT&T), Bell Telephone Laboratories, Western Electric, Eastman Kodak, RCA Victor, Radio Corporation of America (RCA), the Society of Motion Picture Engineers, and the Edison Company. Because of Sam Warner's insight, the brothers were able to strike at the right time. Without Sam, Warner Bros. would not have been the 160-acre production powerhouse it had become by 1946. The brothers also used their 1,200-acre ranch in Calabasas for outdoor location shooting. When production was humming at normal capacity, as many as thirty-five hundred people worked on the Warner Bros. lot. Already famous was Stage 21, which could be flooded with four million gallons of water. "Errol Flynn and Humphrey Bogart have guided many a fabled ship across the Pacific and Atlantic by way of this lake," observed Ramsaye.[2]

Harry enjoyed a "presidential cottage office," but its walls were not filled with expensive art, like many other Hollywood offices. Instead, Harry decorated his office with photographs of the evolution of Warner Bros., from the early days through the recent years of award-winning films. Looking back at the struggle to solidify his company in Hollywood, Harry noted, "The number of unbelievers was more than a thousand to one against us."[3] Without those who did believe in the brothers, "a wonderful new medium of entertainment, education, culture and world understanding might have remained on the shelf for many more years." Harry was especially appreciative of "those pioneer exhibitors, and the inventors, the engineers and all other pioneers who helped, as well as to the pioneer patrons of talking pictures." He concluded, "Jack, Albert and I want to salute them on this Twentieth Anniversary of Talking Pictures. And I know that Sam, if he were still with us, would too."

Jack marveled at how quickly two decades had passed "since the screen became articulate." "In the quality of pictures and in the expansion of our influence for public good, we have made more progress in the past six years than in the preceding forty-five years." For Jack, the medium was better than ever and had a bright future. "Today's talking picture is not the last horizon for us. There are new and brighter ones ahead." Warner Bros. would soon use wide-screen and 3D technologies as it navigated the 1950s and competed with television.

City of Sound

ACRES OF WORDS AND MUSIC–THE WARNER
STUDIOS AT BURBANK IN CALIFORNIA

WARNER BROTHER
WEST COAST STUDIO.

The original Warner Brothers studio in
Hollywood.

Warner Bros. lot, 1946.

Albert noted that talking pictures led to new respect for feature films, something Lewis Warner had surmised before his untimely death. "Educators began to find the screen a great help in their work," he explained. Remembering the massive counteroffensive launched by religious leaders around the country, Albert observed that "churchmen, who at one time admonished their congregations to stay away, began to find sermons in current films." Although Albert was largely occupied by the financial workings of the family business, he understood how the medium had changed over the last twenty years. "National and world leaders seeking to influence public opinion sought to do it through the medium of the screen." Albert was especially grateful for the increased interest in the film business by the banking and investment sectors. As sound cinema became popular, "investors multiplied rapidly and thus it was possible to finance the enormous expansion of our industry." Albert clearly understood the Warner studio's contribution to the industry, but he knew that for Warner Bros. to enjoy continued success, investors would

THE WARNER BROTHERS

need to recognize the value of the entire medium. "This recognition of our industry would never have come about if the screen had not been given a voice," Albert concluded.

Warner Bros. animation was also pushing the industry forward. Now operating on the much-improved Burbank lot, the animators still referred to their work space as Termite Terrace. The Looney Tunes and Merrie Melodies shorts had become increasingly popular thanks to the multitude of Mel Blanc characters. One of the most storied voice actors in the history of entertainment, Blanc created voices for most of the Warner Bros. animated characters, including Bugs Bunny, Elmer Fudd, Daffy Duck, Porky Pig, Tweety Pie, Sylvester, Foghorn Leghorn, and Road Runner. Bugs Bunny would top a fan poll of favorite short subjects in 1946, besting Disney, the Three Stooges, and *March of Time* newsreels. Blanc's bunny also beat Tom and Jerry and Popeye cartoons. Though Warner Bros. cartoons had been around for some time, their popularity grew during the war years with specials such as *Beyond the Line of Duty, I Won't Play, Give Me Liberty,* and *The Declaration of Independence.*

In his memoir, Blanc recalls starting at Warner Bros. in the "ramshackle cottage on Fernwood Avenue, near Van Ness Avenue," in the back corner of the Sunset studio.[4] Blanc thought his boss, Leon Schlesinger, knew that history was being made in that little building. The group often joked about the Warner brothers' limited knowledge of the animation department. Legend has it that Jack thought the studio produced Mickey Mouse. That misconception has also been attributed to Harry, but it sounds more like a Jack Warner flub. Blanc warmly recalled the days of storyboarding and ad-libbing that created some of animation's most iconic characters. Lines such as "What's up, doc?" were also created during these improvisation sessions.

During the war, Blanc's voices helped Americans cope. He wrote, "To a public outraged over Pearl Harbor and Nazi atrocities, headstrong, brain-dead Elmer symbolized the brutish Axis powers. Cocky, fearless Bugs, naturally, was the quintessential Yank." Bugs was modeled after leading stars of the day. According to Blanc, "Bugs possessed [Clark] Gable's impertinence, [Humphrey] Bogart's cool-headedness, and [James] Cagney's New York–bred toughness."[5] Warner's cartoon characters were familiar enough to be used for comedic wartime propaganda, but a new character was created just for the war. Private Snafu, voiced by Blanc, was billed as "the goofiest soldier." Theodor "Dr. Seuss" Geisel was one of the writers for the series of Snafu shorts. (Snafu, of course, is military slang for *situation normal all fouled up*, although the *F* often stands for a more colorful word.) These shorts were a hit with GIs, as they "assured servicemen that discipline and military procedure wasn't instituted to make their life miserable, but served the dual purpose of achieving victory while increasing their odds of survival."[6]

Ongoing Labor Wars

Following the 1945 riots on the Warner lot, Herbert Sorrell was found guilty of contempt of court and failure to disperse for his role in the unrest. Labor strikes continued at many studios in 1946. Someone was stabbed during a protest at Universal, fights regularly broke out at MGM, and pickets were mainstays at 20th Century–Fox, RKO, Paramount, and Columbia. Sorrell led hundreds of picketers back to the Warner Bros. lot in September 1946. Speaking through a megaphone, he announced, "There may be men hurt, there may be men killed before this is over, but we're in no mood to be pushed around anymore!" The *Los Angeles Times* reported that thousands of pickets were preventing employees from entering the Warner lot.[7] Having learned a lesson from the previous year's strikes, Warner Bros. was not about to let the spectacle continue. When Sorrell's group arrived shortly after 4:00 a.m., strikebreakers were ready with "chains, bolts, hammers, six-inch pipes, brass knuckles, wooden mallets, and battery cables." Blayney Matthews, known as the "head of Warner Bros. private gestapo," brought in county officers to help break the strike. The picketers were ready, though, donning the white air-raid helmets that had been so prominent during the war. The strikebreakers drove cars into the crowd, while the strikers tried to stop vehicles from getting onto the lot. Overturned automobiles eventually prevented workers from gaining access. Fire hoses and tear gas were used, once again, to disperse the crowd. Sorrell described the scene as "slaughter."[8]

The *Los Angeles Times* estimated that only about half the strikers were employed in the film industry; the rest were union members from other industries. A leaflet was found, written by the North Hollywood chapter of the Communist Party, leading to rumors of communist infiltration. The Conference of Studio Unions (CSU) changed tactics. Instead of convincing the workers to strike, it used force to keep employees off the lot. Jack Warner eventually asked employees who had been able to leave the lot to come back. He called Arthur Silver and asked, "How are we going to win the strike if

everybody stays out?"⁹ Employees sneaked onto the lot through a storm
drain connected to the Los Angeles River. Those who made it back to the
studio had to stay there for days. One worker claimed that someone threw
acid at them. Shots were fired by the Burbank police. Labor relations were so
bad that the Epstein brothers joked the Warners should change their slogan
from "combining good picture making with good citizenship" to "combining
good picture making with good marksmanship."¹⁰ Sheriff Eugene Biscailuz
assigned more than 120 officers to guard the studio in the days following the
violence. Sorrell and his accomplices faced a $3 million lawsuit; they were
charged with "conspiracy to ruin the film company by strikes and by pickets
keeping it closed both last year and this year on various occasions."¹¹ Sorrell
was also accused of inciting a riot, but he would eventually be acquitted of
that charge. The nearly yearlong series of strikes and studio shutdowns deeply
impacted Jack Warner, who began to reconsider his progressive feelings
about the "little guy."

To address the Hollywood labor strikes of 1946, particularly the violent
unrest at Warner Bros., state senators Jack B. Tenney and Hugh M. Burns
and assemblyman Fred H. Kraft organized a subcommittee of California's
Un-American Activities Committee to advise Governor Earl Warren on subversive activity. Its report read: "After [a] thorough investigation of [the] juris-
dictional situation at Warner Bros. studio," the subcommittee "is convinced
that the strike is Communist inspired and dominated." According to the
Tenney Committee, the strike was not about wages or working conditions; it
was simply "a long-range communist strategy to control [the] motion picture
industry as [a] potent medium for propaganda." The committee was appalled
at strikers who disobeyed all "lawful orders," and it urged the governor to
"personally investigate this deplorable revolutionary situation immediately
in order that you may take proper executive action."¹² Tenney became one
of California's leading anticommunists as the red scare swept the nation.

As president of the Screen Actors Guild (SAG), Warner employee Ronald
Reagan worked diligently with George Murphy and Robert Montgomery to
keep the CSU from controlling their union. Montgomery was concerned that
if more unions joined the CSU, the studios would shut down, putting many
thousands of people out of work. Reagan and Montgomery sided with the
International Alliance of Theatrical Stage Employees (IATSE), which had
kept its members working and helped fill the vacancies left by strikers. They
knew that pushing the narrative of a "red CSU" could hobble the striking

union. Meanwhile, the CSU gave Sterling Hayden the task of convincing SAG to support the strikes. When Reagan and William Holden attended a meeting at Ida Lupino's house in October 1946, they saw Hayden making the CSU's case, with support from John Garfield, Howard Da Silva, and others. Holden prevented Reagan from making a scene. The next day, Reagan got a phone call on the set, which turned out to be a credible threat of violence. Blayney Matthews, the notorious Warner Bros. police officer, handed Reagan a permit to carry a .32 Smith & Wesson. Reagan remembered, "I mounted the holstered gun religiously every morning and took it off the last thing at night."[13] The constant protests, coupled with the increasing violence and threats, had a lasting effect on Reagan.

During the strikes, Jack Warner spoke in support of Reagan, who "turned out to be a tower of strength, not only for the actors but for the whole industry."[14] Reagan was proud of his role but frustrated by the result, writing in his autobiography, "We stopped the Communists cold in Hollywood, but there was a dark side to the battle . . . some members of the House Un-American Activities Committee came to Hollywood searching more for personal publicity than they were for Communists. Many fine people were accused wrongly of being Communists simply because they were liberals."[15] Although Jack Warner supported Reagan's role in muscling the unions, he was not so keen about the actor's political future. Writer-producer Robert Buckner was on the lot when the studio boss first heard of Reagan's interest in running for governor. "No, no," Warner quipped, "Spencer Tracy for Governor, Reagan for his best friend."[16]

Postwar Film Trends

Writing in the January 1947 *Warner Club News*, Harry Warner lamented the difficulty of attaining peace: "If we are honest with ourselves we must admit that in the world there is much religion but little faith; many opinions, but little tolerance; many worthy causes, but little sincerity." Harry's strength was always boiling down complex ideas into reflective musings. "We have led ourselves to believe that we are somehow entitled to peace as a matter of right. We have forgotten that this blessing comes only from hard work and an unselfish devotion to the welfare of mankind," wrote Warner. "Faith, tolerance, and sincerity" were Harry's keys to peace. Jack observed, "Peace is more than a laying down of arms. It is more than a writing of treaties. It

Warners Entertains Variety

On stage 2 of the Warner Bros. studios last Saturday, Jack L. Warner was host to more than 1,200 delegates to the Variety International convention. The occasion was the annual Humanitarian dinner, and the studio went all out with entertainment and hospitality. Here are some photos taken at party.

Entering the Gay Nineties mood, left to right, are: Jack Carson, who was master of ceremonies; Charles Skouras, president of National Theatres; Jack L. Warner, WB's production chief; R. J. O'Donnell, chief barker; and Dennis Morgan, Warner star.

Jack Warner in a jovial mood greets John Harris, Variety's Big Boss.

Alan Hale (L) asks Milton Schwaber, Tent 19, Baltimore, to try some of the popcorn.

Carson and Morgan in a bit of horseplay with James Coston, WB Theatre executive.

Veteran Monte Blue as a barker points out the attractions to (L to R) A. B. Paterson and E. V. Richards Jr. of New Orleans; George Bowser, Fox West Coast general manager; and Oscar Oldknow, Los Angeles.

From production and distribution, (L to R) Jack Karp, Paramount production executive; Charles M. Reagan, Paramount distribution chief; Hal Roach, producer; LeRoy Prinz, WB dance director; Henry Ginsberg, Paramount production head.

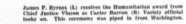

The impressive scene on stage No. 2 at the Warner Bros. studio where the dinner was held. Over 1,200 guests were seated. Outside, studio streets depicted a midway.

James P. Byrnes (L) receives the Humanitarian award from Chief Justice Vinson as Carter Barron (R) Variety official looks on. This ceremony was piped in from Washington.

Jack Warner and company entertaining twelve hundred on Stage 2 for the Variety International convention.

can be achieved and kept only in a spirit of 'good will to men,' and it is the sacred trust and responsibility to all men of good will."[17]

Variety reported that Warner Bros. had amassed record earnings in the past nine months, totaling $19,134,000 by the end of July 1947.[18] Albert Warner had been busy acquiring Warner stock with the studio's profits; shareholders were selling high, and the studio could afford to invest in more stock. As part of his dealings, Albert donated twenty-nine hundred shares, valued at $47,000, to Jewish charities: two thousand shares to the United Jewish Appeal and nine hundred to the Federation of Jewish Philanthropies of New York.[19]

As postwar profits soared, Warner Bros. shifted toward dark crime films and a renaissance of musicals. During this time, Michael Curtiz discovered band singer Doris Day, who was riding high from her hit song "Sentimental Journey" with Les Brown and His Band of Renown. He signed Day to his own Michael Curtiz Productions, which he was operating within Warner Bros. (a growing trend in the postwar years). Day starred alongside Janis Paige, Jack Carson, and Don Defore in *Romance on the High Seas* (1948), a musical directed by Curtiz. Day was not the only musical personality at Warner Bros., but she pumped out enough films to signify a second coming of Warner musicals since the genre had last peaked on the lot in 1933. *Young Man with a Horn* (1950), a film about a jazz musician directed by Curtiz and starring Kirk Douglas and Lauren Bacall, continued Day's streak of musicals at Warner Bros., including *Tea for Two* (1950), *I'll See You in My Dreams* (1951), *On Moonlight Bay* (1951), *By the Light of the Silvery Moon* (1953), and *Calamity Jane* (1953). Although the MGM musicals of the postwar era certainly had more historical significance—Arthur Freed was producing films such as *Easter Parade* (1948), *On the Town* (1949), *Annie Get Your Gun* (1950), *An American in Paris* (1951), and *Singin' in the Rain* (1952)—it is worth noting that Jack Warner did not limit his studio to the dark, cynical films that populated the late 1940s and 1950s. Like it had in the 1930s, Warner Bros. balanced its crime films with a series of musicals and other genres.

That said, Warner's postwar cycle of crime films was notable. As historian Thomas Schatz observes, "Warner's on-screen style in the mid-1940s . . . more than any other studio was keyed to the industry trend toward film noir."[20] Following *The Maltese Falcon* and *Mildred Pierce*, Warner Bros. continued its slick crime thrillers, combining the talents of Bogart and Bacall. *The Big Sleep* (1946), based on Raymond Chandler's novel and directed by Howard Hawks, became a quintessential film noir known for both its stylish presentation and its complicated plot. *Dark Passage* (1947), written and directed by Delmer Daves, continued the Hollywood power couple's chemistry. Their final film together, *Key Largo* (1948), added the talents of Lionel Barrymore, Claire Trevor, Monte Blue (whose work at Warner Bros. dated to the silent era), and Edward G. Robinson, who reprised his iconic gangster persona. While John Huston was writing the script with Richard Brooks, the director recalled that "the high hopes and idealism of the Roosevelt years were slipping away, and the underworld—as represented by Edward G. Robinson and his hoods—was once again on the move, taking advantage of social apathy."[21]

Other productions included *Of Human Bondage* (1946), a remake of the 1934 Bette Davis film (Jack purchased the rights from RKO after Davis pushed hard for better roles). Joan Crawford starred in the female melodrama *Humoresque* (1946) with John Garfield. *Cloak and Dagger* (1946), directed by Fritz Lang and produced by Milton Sperling (Betty Warner's husband), was an Office of Strategic Services (OSS) film about subversion and espionage. The script was written by Lester Cole and Ring Lardner Jr. during the labor strikes at Warner Bros. in late 1945. Both were subpoenaed to testify before the House Un-American Activities Committee (HUAC) in 1947 as unfriendly witnesses. Other top productions included a foray into the growing trend of psychological westerns with *Pursued* (1947), starring Robert Mitchum and Theresa Wright and directed by Raoul Walsh. Joan Crawford also starred in *Possessed* (1947), a psychological drama about a mentally unstable woman's struggle with obsession, taking advantage of the growing interest in Freudian psychology. The previous year, Humphrey Bogart starred in *Conflict*, a psychological thriller about a man who killed his wife—or did he?

The Unsuspected (1947), directed by Michael Curtiz and starring Claude Rains, Audrey Totter, and Constance Bennett, offers a masterful example of the postwar crime film. As Curtiz's biographer notes, *The Unsuspected* "is a template for the chiaroscuro lighting style associated with Eagle-Lion films noirs made by Anthony Mann and the cinematographer John Alton that began production in late 1947."[22] The mystery-thriller films Warner Bros. released were, as usual, representative of the studio's ability to gauge the culture and cater to the growing postwar pessimism. Despite the Bogart and Bacall chemistry in *Dark Passage* (1947), about a convict who escapes from prison and hopes to hide after undergoing plastic surgery, the *Chicago Daily Tribune* saw through the wild tale. As fans of noir know, these films often have convoluted and confusing plots that are overshadowed by great performances and visuals. The *Tribune* opened its review of *Dark Passage* this way: "If you have the right friends, it really is a simple matter to break out of San Quentin . . . have your face remodeled so completely that even your closest acquaintance won't recognize you . . . avoid implication despite being on the scene when three different people die, and retire to live happily ever after."[23]

Vincent Sherman was set to direct an adaptation of James M. Cain's *Serenade,* about a young male singer who has an affair with an older man. The singer begins to lose his timbre as he falls in love. Then he meets a woman (reestablishing his manhood), who eventually kills the older man. Sherman and Cain discussed how they could make the film work, given that the Production Code would likely require them to write out the homosexual elements. Sherman came up with a treatment and ran it by Jack Warner, who asked, "What the fuck kind of story is that?" Warner already had a cast and crew ready to go, so he quickly pivoted to film *The Unfaithful,* a remake of *The Letter* about a cheating wife during World War II starring Warner's "oomph" girl Ann Sheridan. Shooting was scheduled to begin in two weeks, and production began with only twenty pages of script. A nervous Warner kept tabs on the production, and when the film was finished, he screened it at his house. Warner then called Sherman to his office and said, "Any sonofabitch that can make a picture without a script and make it come out like that can stay here as long as he likes." Sherman promptly asked for a contract extension and a raise, both of which were immediately granted.[24]

The dark, cynical films of the first postwar years were as relevant as they were prophetic. Hollywood would soon be under the government's microscope once again, this time for alleged communist infiltration. Like the war pictures, many of the dark noir films were written and/or directed by left-wing artists who were perfect targets for government officials' anticommunist crusade. Warner Bros. had its share of employees investigated by the FBI. There were rumors of the studio spying on private gatherings (likely through Blayney Matthews) and writing down the license plate numbers of attendees. The postwar culture was tense, and it was about to get tenser.

Road to the Blacklist

Hollywood Reporter publisher Billy Wilkerson wanted to expose Hollywood as a hotbed of communists. He and his friend Howard Hughes conspired to name names in the press. According to legend, which may very well be true, the largely nonreligious Wilkerson found himself at the Holy Sacrament Catholic Church on Sunset Boulevard on July 6, 1946, confessing the sins he was so desperate to commit to Father Cornelius J. McCoy. Wilkerson's longtime secretary George Kennedy thought that, despite being hell bent on attacking Hollywood, Wilkerson knew people and careers would be destroyed, so he sought "spiritual confirmation." After Wilkerson explained his intention to battle Hollywood and the Communist Party, Father McCoy reportedly said, "Castrate those Commie sons of bitches, Billy!"[25]

Wilkerson began his war on July 6. "There is a very high, insidious effort being exerted by the 'commies' and their 'fronters' here in Hollywood," his front-page essay began. Wilkerson believed that many Hollywood writers took their orders directly from the Kremlin, "in hopes of communizing the whole world."[26] Three weeks later, on July 29, Wilkerson was ready to name names on the front page of his *Hollywood Reporter.* His biggest beef was with the Screen Writers Guild, a union he accused of adopting the American Authors Authority position that all properties must be sold through the proper channels. Wilkerson referred to this policy as the "thought police," three years before George Orwell's *1984* made that phrase popular. Under the guise of combating the guild's control over properties, Wilkerson named Dalton Trumbo, Maurice Rapf, Lester Cole, Howard Koch, Harold Buchman, John Wexley, Ring Lardner Jr., Harold Salemson, Henry Meyers, Theodore Strauss, and John Howard Lawson as communists.

The concern for the Warners was that most of these men had recently penned scripts, including major films, for Warner Bros.: Wexley (*Angels with Dirty Faces, City for Conquest, Confessions of a Nazi Spy*), Lardner (*Cloak and Dagger*), Trumbo (who began as a reader at Warner Bros.), Lawson (*Action in the North Atlantic*), Koch (*Casablanca, Sergeant York, Mission to Moscow*), and Cole (*Objective, Burma!*). Warner Bros. was painted with the brush of communism by proxy. Wilkerson believed that freedom of speech was at stake and argued that "the United States is at present embroiled in an ideological war with a Communist philosophy that repudiates those freedoms."[27] Wilkerson was close with FBI director J. Edgar Hoover, which is likely how he acquired the ID numbers of Communist Party members, which he also published in his industry rag. The front-page assault continued on August 8, 1946, when the *Hollywood Reporter*'s front-page headline read "Pix Control U.S. Minds—Reds." The article cited Ilya Ehrenburg, who wrote for the Russian newspaper *Izvestia.* According to Ehrenburg, the typical American is convinced that he or she is a free-thinker but only "repeats what he has read in the newspaper, heard on the radio or seen on the screen."[28] There was no going back. The industry would be forced to make an impossible choice: admit the ideological leanings of some employees or cast them out as a way to save the business. For the red-baiters, there was no nuance: one was either with them or against them.

Betty Warner remembered that her father, Harry, was not afraid of HUAC. After all, Harry had stood up to the senators who claimed that Hollywood was pushing propaganda to pull the United States into the European war in 1941. "All our friends were being accused of writing propaganda and being communist and running cells," recalled Betty. "It was terrifying."[29] Harry knew how to fight back, but Jack lacked his brother's political savvy. Given the hysteria, anger, and paranoia following the riots on the Warner lot, Jack did what he thought was right and testified in front of HUAC. Harry saw through the fear and understood that these investigations had always had an anti-Semitic slant. In this sense, HUAC was not much different from Senate Resolution 152. In 1941 the isolationist senators had wanted to exert their power over Hollywood, as they thought the movies had too much influence. Harry knew that HUAC was cut from the same cloth; its only interest was publicity and control. Unfortunately, Jack was unable to see through Hoover's accusations.

When Hoover testified in front of HUAC in March 1947, he was sure Hollywood was a haven for communists. The labor strikes reeked of left-wing radicalism, and *Mission to Moscow* was a prime example of communist influence onscreen. Of course, Hoover failed to understand that the USSR was the United States' ally in 1943, and a number of films were soft on Russia for purposes of the war effort. This was widely known at the time, but factual amnesia worked well for Hoover's case. The new president of the Motion Picture Association of America (MPAA), Eric Johnston, defended the industry, refuted Hoover, and argued that "if the Communists set out to capture Hollywood, they have suffered an overwhelming defeat."[30] The argument went nowhere with Hoover and HUAC. Lee Garling, writing in *Box Office,* noted Hoover's disagreement with Johnston and reported that HUAC "may never get around to a probe of the film colony. Reason: too many other more important probes into alleged left-wing and pinko activities."[31] Sadly, Garling was wrong.

Jack Warner volunteered to testify at a secret HUAC hearing, but the Los Angeles location made it difficult to avoid the industry press. Ambassador

Davies got wind of Warner's testimony and wired committee chairman J. Parnell Thomas (R-NJ) on June 10, 1947, to defend the film *Mission to Moscow*. Davies said he did not believe Warner Bros. had been coerced into making the film. Davies denied carrying orders for FDR and reminded Thomas that the United States had been allied with Russia at the time. The former ambassador claimed that numerous studios had approached him with an offer, but he preferred Warner Bros. based on its reputation for political engagement.

The FBI had been quietly investigating Hollywood for some time. Files dating back to July 8, 1943, show a seventeen-page memo to Hoover regarding *Mission to Moscow*. Walter Huston's attendance at an event at the Shrine Auditorium in Los Angeles celebrating the twenty-fifth anniversary of the Soviet Republic was questioned. Huston's membership on the Hollywood Democratic Committee, believed to be a communist front group, was also noted. Additional suspicion was raised by Huston's friendship with Joris Ivens, a filmmaker known for the antifascist (which, to the FBI, presumably meant pro-communist) documentary *This Spanish Earth* (1937). Ivens had recently done work for the War Department, including *Our Russian Front* (1942), which Huston narrated. The memo connected these associations back to Jack Warner, who was accused of forging positive press for *Mission to Moscow*. Warner's ad copy for the film was declared "Communist propaganda." And the Los Angeles Public Library apparently had a table of books to be read in conjunction with *Mission to Moscow*. According to the FBI file, "There can be little doubt that this was a well-planned scheme to broaden the field of Russian and Communist propaganda."[32]

The *Mission to Moscow* FBI file also includes a letter from publishing magnate William Randolph Hearst to Jack Warner dated May 19, 1943. Hearst had published criticism of the film in his newspapers. Jack wired Hearst on May 17 to offer a defense of *Mission to Moscow* from an American perspective, written by Dr. Arthur Upham Pope. Warner wrote, "In view of our long friendship am submitting to you that reproduction of the Pope letter in your papers would only be fair to all concerned."[33] Curiously, Warner's letter is not in the FBI file, but Hearst's response is. After Hearst maliciously reprinted Warner's letter in his newspapers, the publisher claimed that criticism of *Mission to Moscow* was the real American viewpoint because the film "gives the other side of the case—the Communist side—quite completely." Hearst continued, "I am sorry that we disagree on the proper function of the press, and of the moving picture." He assured Warner that any criticism of his studio was "guided by no personal unfriendliness, but merely by a sense of public duty."[34] In his autobiography, Warner begrudgingly stated, "There are some controversial subjects that are so explosive and so open to misinterpretation by well-meaning supporters of one side or the other, that it doesn't pay for anyone to be a hero or martyr. You're a dead pigeon either way."[35] Even with the approval of FDR, the film was a losing proposition.

An FBI memo dated May 14, 1943, rightfully criticized *Mission to Moscow* for minimizing the evils of Stalin's purge trials, which killed nearly one million people. The agent, whose name was redacted, believed the film does not "try to create friendship between the Russian and American people but is devoted to blotting out the murderous reputation which Stalin bears and the building up of a Stalin regime which has the appearance of being most democratic and beneficent."[36] Bureau files from July 31, 1943, contained the names of many people who were or had been affiliated with Warner Bros. One report stated that Los Angeles FBI special agent Richard B. Hood learned that Donald K. King of the Warner Bros. publicity department had attempted to recruit someone (the name was redacted) into the Communist Party. HUAC files from the early 1940s included detailed dirt on many studios, but the July 1943 memos indicated significant interest in the Warners, largely due to suspicions surrounding *Mission to Moscow*. Individuals of interest who worked for or were affiliated with those who worked for Warner Bros. were Arnold Albert, assistant producer of shorts at Warner Bros.; Robert H. Buckner, producer; Julius Epstein, producer and writer; Irving Fein, head of publicity at Columbia and brother-in-law of Charles Einfeld, who was vice president of advertising at Warner Bros.; John Garfield; Olivia de Havilland; John Huston; Jules Levine, friend of Einfeld and currently serving in the US Navy; Dr. Herman Lissauer, head of the research division at Warner; Vern Parten, publicity; and Robert Rossen, who wrote *They Won't Forget, The Roaring Twenties, The Sea Wolf,* and *Edge of Darkness* at Warner Bros.[37] The documents focused on writers' organizations, which were broken into branches: Hollywood, Sunset, Beverly-Westwood, and Fairfax. Their goals were supposedly to open bookstores and hold gatherings where "communists can function openly."[38]

An FBI document dated February 12, 1944, described Walter Huston, star of *Mission to Moscow,* as a "fanatical follower" of the Communist Party, in addition to being a member of various front groups. Vincent Sherman, Jack's friend and director of *Underground,* was labeled an active member of the League of American Writers and a "close follower of the Communist party line."[39] According to the FBI, the Communist International (Comintern) realized in 1933 that movies were a perfect vehicle for propaganda, and in 1935 the Communist Party initiated a major effort to attract cultural groups, writers, artists, actors, actresses, and others to the communist cause. At the same time, the Communist Party infiltrated many labor fields in the film industry.

Another document dated March 20, 1944, questioned the loyalty of Jerry Wald, producer of *Destination Tokyo*. According to the file, Wald "has shown sympathy with Communists in the motion picture industry." Regarding Albert Maltz, the film's coauthor, the FBI file was unequivocal, declaring, "A Communist wrote the screenplay. Maltz's record as a Communist is well-known and he has been active for many years. He is fanatically devoted to the cause." The document also claimed that "Delmer Daves, Director [of *Destination Tokyo*], has shown Communist sympathy." Finally, "Cary Grant and John Garfield, co-stars of the picture, have both been active in Communist circles. Garfield, particularly, has a long record of such activity. He has just returned from Italy, where he had been sent on a military forces entertainment tour."[40] An FBI memo from July 9, 1945, questioned the affiliation of the Independent Citizens Committee of Art, Sciences, and Professions. It named Warner stars Edward G. Robinson and Olivia de Havilland and questioned the loyalty of California attorney general Robert W. Kenny.

An astonishing number of Warner Bros. employees, including Jack, were named in FBI investigations that were turned over to HUAC. It is unclear whether Jack was aware of this. In any case, Jack, unlike Harry, was terrified of what might happen if he did not cooperate with the government. Business was good, but the culture was shifting. The New Deal chic that had made Warner Bros. look edgy and progressive in previous years was now raising questions among government officials who were anxious to expose treasonous activity. When MPAA president Johnston was unable to shift the government's red lens away from Hollywood, Jack Warner panicked. He was the first to testify at the October 1947 HUAC hearings on the communist infiltration of Hollywood. The move was unsurprising, given Warner's constant and desperate defense of *Mission to Moscow*. On the day before he testified, the *Chicago Daily Tribune* rightfully predicted that Warner would be questioned about the pro-Soviet film described as "shot thru with Communist propaganda . . . which sought to explain the reasons for the Hitler-Stalin Pact of August 23,

1943 . . . which gave Hitler the green light for his invasion of Poland."[41] The newspaper also noted HUAC's interest in Ambassador Davies and acknowledged Roosevelt's order to make the film, but understanding the context did not matter much in a country suffering from red fever. Having outed alleged industry subversives, the *Hollywood Reporter* geared up for the show, which it promised would be an "all-out fight to protect freedom of the screen."[42]

Jack Warner's "Pest-Removal Fund"

HUAC chairman J. Parnell Thomas wrote to President Truman in April 1947 about the seriousness of communist infiltration in the United States. "It is a menace that is so serious," wrote Thomas, "that unless it is dealt with by the law enforcement agencies of the Federal Government, the time may well arrive when the very security of our country will be impaired by this fifth column within our midst."[43] Thomas noted the May 15 testimony of Jack Warner and Adolphe Menjou, proudly telling the press that "both of these men named names. Based on testimony taken so far, I have come to believe that the industry itself can clean house." Rupert Hughes, novelist, producer, and brother of the famous aviator Howard, told the committee that the industry "was lousy with Communists, some of them making $3,000 to $5,000 weekly and whom you couldn't get to go to Russia in a million years." Reports surfaced that Warner had told the committee he was forced to make *Mission to Moscow*, as Ambassador Davies had brought direct orders from President Roosevelt. Warner's story changed when he testified on the national stage, but this kept the rumor mill busy until the October hearings. President Truman, who had supported loyalty checks during the war, assured federal employees that such inquiries would not become a "witch hunt."[44] Truman hoped to set an example from the top by assigning a political opponent to oversee the program. The goodwill maneuver went nowhere with Thomas's committee, made up of Robert Stripling (chief investigator), Benjamin Mandel (director of research), Karl Mundt (R-SD), John McDowell, (R-PA), Richard Nixon (R-CA), Richard Vail (R-IL), John Wood (D-GA), John Rankin (D-MS), J. Hardin Peterson (D-FL), and Herbert Bonner (D-NC).

On October 20, 1947, five newsreel cameras and one television camera flanked the audience in a packed Washington courtroom illuminated by rows of klieg lights. Journalists had anticipated this day for months, and by 9:00 a.m., the line of spectators hoping to get a seat stretched through the

House Office Building. A total of ninety-four people gained admittance to the first day's session. The star-studded affair included Warner Bros. vice president Jack Warner, MGM studio boss Louis B. Mayer, director and producer Sam Wood (*The Pride of the Yankees, Kings Row*), and antiauthoritarian author Ayn Rand (*Atlas Shrugged, The Fountainhead*). As Thomas entered the caucus room, flashbulbs lit the room. The chairman held up his hand to halt the cameras, surveyed his domain, and gazed approvingly over the stage he had set.

A smirking Jack sat alongside stern-faced industry counsel Paul V. McNutt. When McNutt asked if he would be able to cross-examine witnesses, Thomas informed him, "You will not have that right. You are no different than anyone else." Ironically, after McNutt was muzzled, Thomas went on to expound on the fairness of this investigation and his belief that the majority of Hollywood was made up of "patriotic and loyal Americans."[45] Thomas, whose snorting and gavel-breaking would soon become the stuff of legend, then welcomed Jack Warner.

Following the opening elucidations, Jack Warner read a statement that varied little from the one he had made in May. He quickly made it clear that he believed "our American way of life is under attack from without and from within our national borders."[46] The mogul hammered the "dictator-trained wrecking crews" that had ravaged much of Europe. The most frequently cited section of Warner's statement came early on: "It is my firm conviction that the free American screen has taken its rightful place with the free American press in the first line of defense. Ideological termites have burrowed into many American industries, organizations, and societies. Wherever they may be, I say let us dig them out and get rid of them. My brothers and I will be happy to subscribe to a pest-removal fund. We are willing to establish such a fund to ship to Russia the people who don't like our American system of government and prefer the communistic system to ours."

With his anticommunism firmly established, Warner assured the committee that not a single Warner Bros. film could be viewed as anti-American or pro-communist. Knowing that *Mission to Moscow* would come up, Warner called the accusations of White House pressure (which he had supposedly admitted in May) pure "fantasy." The film, he argued, "was made to fulfil the same wartime purpose for which we made such other pictures as *Air Force, This Is the Army, Objective Burma, Destination Tokyo, Action in the North Atlantic,* and a great many more." If producing *Mission to Moscow*

IN the House of Representatives caucus room this week.

HOLLYWOOD GOES TO WASHINGTON

JACK L. WARNER, vice-president in charge of production for Warner Brothers, was the first witness on Monday.

LOUIS B. MAYER, MGM production chief, takes the oath.

Jack Warner and Louis B. Mayer under oath.

was subversive, Warner claimed, "then the American Liberty ships which carried food and guns to Russian allies and the American naval vessels which convoyed them were likewise engaged in subversive activities." His studio always practiced "positive Americanism," he said, and if someone wanted to take issue with one of its films, so be it. But if that meant attempting to destroy a studio or an entire industry, that violated freedom of expression.

Interestingly, Jack maintained, "I have never seen a Communist and I wouldn't know one if I saw one." At this point, Stripling read from the transcript of Warner's May statement, where Jack spoke of communist infiltration. For the most part, his accusations involved writers. Warner was careful to avoid words like "blacklist" and "wrongful termination" when describing how he refused to rehire writers he felt were un-American. Stripling asked Warner if by un-American he meant communist, and Jack tried to dodge: "I say un-American propaganda. If you want to use the word Communist, naturally you have that prerogative." Stripling continued to read Warner's earlier statement, where the mogul described not renewing Gordon Kahn's contract after learning of the writer's communist sympathies. The May statement also included a reference to studio enforcer Blayney Matthews, who regularly investigated subversive activities by Warner Bros. employees. Warner viewed the *Hollywood Reporter*'s accusations as "hearsay" but seemed to follow Wilkerson's line of reasoning anyway.

Jack Warner listening to a statement from J. Parnell Thomas. (Author's personal collection)

Stripling read the list of names Warner had given in May, many of whom had already been named by Wilkerson: Alvah Bessie, Gordon Kahn, Howard Koch, Ring Lardner Jr., John Howard Lawson, Albert Maltz, Robert Rossen, Dalton Trumbo, Irwin Shaw, John Wexley, Julius and Philip Epstein, and Clifford Odets, among others. Warner spoke of the war service of many of these writers, several of whom had written war pictures for Warner Bros. Then he pleaded ignorance about certain brands of subversive writing. Some content might go over his head, Warner admitted, "because you can't be superhuman. Some of these lines have innuendos and double meanings . . . and you have to take 8 or 10 Harvard law courses to find out what they mean." Stripling agreed that subversive writing could be quite subtle. Warner noted that writer John Howard Lawson had "tried to swing a lot of things" into scripts. He did not provide specifics, but he also mentioned the Epsteins as good writers "who fell off." Even after pointing out writers who might have been worthy of questioning, Warner argued that "these people whom I have mentioned have not written Communist doctrines or endeavored to put in Communist stories."

Chairman Thomas sought clarification of Warner's previous testimony, where the mogul noted he had "detected slanted lines" and "discharged a number of employees." Warner denied such firings, which would have been an admission of blacklisting, and instead said, "I have had them fulfill their legal obligations [to the studio] and then didn't renew their options." After detailing the destruction he had witnessed on a European trip, Warner said that he was "in favor of making [communism] an illegal organization." He answered a series of Nixon's questions by advocating open communication, contrary to Germany and Italy, which had controlled the flow of all information during the war. Nixon asked about the patriotic duty of Hollywood studios, and Warner responded by submitting a list of pro-American films made and distributed by Warner Bros. Warner's list of forty-three films dated back to *My Four Years in Germany* (1918), as well as the more recent *The Dawn Patrol* (1930), *Black Legion* (1937), *Casablanca* (1943), and *Pride of the Marines* (1945). In addition, Nixon mentioned the list of thirty-nine short subjects, all pro-American, produced by Warner Bros. since 1936. Warner made sure to mention the studio's latest short, *The Last Bomb* (1945), a Technicolor production made in alliance with the Army Air Force about the bombing of Japan. "I think I can see why you have been so successful in selling your pictures to the American public," observed Nixon, who commended Warner for his anti-Nazi films. The question remained, however: had the studio produced any anticommunist films? Warner noted one, *Up until Now,* which was in development.

Inevitably, *Mission to Moscow* was brought up again. Stripling asked Warner his opinion about how to deal with communist infiltration. "Don't let them get off the boat," he responded, during a discussion about immigration. Stripling then returned to *Mission to Moscow* and asked Warner who had spearheaded the film project. This time, Jack blamed Harry, claiming his brother had contacted Ambassador Davies. Stripling recalled the committee's back-and-forth with Jack in May, when he maintained that *Mission to Moscow* was simply fulfilling the studio's wartime mission. Of course, much had changed by 1947, and Thomas asked, "Do you believe the film is pro-Communist?" and "Would you release the film now?" Warner quickly backpedaled, stating that the studio would not make the film in 1947, but only "because of the way Russia is handling international affairs since the cessation of war." Stripling continued to pressure Warner to name some government official who had insisted on making the movie. Warner claimed the idea that someone had coerced Warner Bros. to make the film was nothing more than hearsay. When asked if *Mission to Moscow* accurately depicted Stalin's purge trials, Warner pleaded ignorance. At one point, when McNutt leaned

Jack Warner holding the *New York Times* in front of HUAC.

in to whisper something to Warner, Thomas "stared down" and "rapped the handle of his gavel reprovingly."[47]

Stripling then tried to get Warner to respond to *The Curtain Rises* (1944), written by war correspondent Quentin Reynolds, an editor for *Collier's Weekly*. Warner would not entertain any discussion of the book, as it had been published after *Mission to Moscow* and had nothing to do with the time Davies spent in Russia in the late 1930s. An irritated Warner fired back, "I am on record about 40 times or more that I have never been in Russia. I don't know what Russia was like in 1937 or 1944 or 1947, so how can I tell you if [*Mission to Moscow*] was right or wrong?"[48] When Stripling asked if producing a film that portrayed Russia in a positive light put the studio on dangerous ground, Warner interrupted and said, "We were not on dangerous ground in 1942, when we produced it. There was a war on. The world was at stake." When Stripling resumed, Warner broke in again, saying, "We made the film to aid the war effort, which I believe I have already stated." Stripling continued to press, calling the film "fraud of fact" and insisting that the government was behind the production. "I want to correct you, very vehemently," blasted Warner. "There was no cooperation of the government." Warner reminded the committee of his studio's impressive war record: "You couldn't be more courageous, to help the war effort, than we." Stripling had no more questions and submitted Warner's May 15 testimony for the record.

Most important, Warner stated, "I can't, for the life of me, figure where men could get together and try in any form, shape, or manner to deprive a man of a livelihood because of his political beliefs." With all the prior circuitous discussion, this was direct and to the point. Warner did not like the idea of a blacklist. Johnston had rejected the idea, and now Warner had as well.

In the end, Congressman Vail asked Warner if he saw communism as a serious threat. "I certainly do recognize it," said Warner. It is "a threat not only to the United States but to many of the European and the far-eastern countries." Vail followed by pointing out the high salaries enjoyed by many of the writers who had been branded communists. Warner asked for more details, such as proof of such claims, but Vail simply added that those in Hollywood should know the real story. "You have failed to act for lack of supporting proof," Vail continued. "Would you act if proof were supplied?" "We would act very effectively if we had the proof," responded Warner. The following days were filled with "friendly witnesses" denouncing communism and "unfriendly witnesses" pleading the Fifth. One wonders how the first day would have differed if it had been Harry Warner testifying in front of the committee following his defense of the industry in 1941.

The next day, the *Hollywood Reporter* described Jack Warner's testimony as "crackling denials" of communist infiltration of his studio, despite the dismissal of writers because of their ideological views.[49] McNutt charged that HUAC was trying "to dictate and control, through the device of the hearings, what goes on the screens of America."[50] The idea that HUAC was interested in censorship and control percolated through Hollywood.

Irwin Shaw, screenwriter for the 1941 Warner Bros. film *Out of the Fog*, released a statement to the press repudiating Jack Warner. Shaw was one of the writers whose contract had not been renewed based on "un-American" activities. Perhaps the writer's refusal to join the army was interpreted as subversive. But according to Shaw, Warner had enjoyed the noir melodrama *Out of the Fog* so much that he offered him another contract for double his previous salary. Going further, Shaw wrote that Warner "attempted to hire me again and again at constantly increasing prices." Shaw said he was offered a film by "one of their leading producers who knows my work and my politics"; it was a "pro-democratic, anti-fascist and anti-Communist picture which they had contemplated making."[51] Perhaps he was referring to *Up until Now*, which Warner had mentioned during his testimony. Delmer Daves was supposed to direct the film, but it never happened. *Up until Now* may have been just an attempt to placate HUAC.

It is important to note that not everyone in Hollywood was automatically on board with the anticommunist investigations. Reporting from Washington, Red Kann expressed frustration that HUAC was unable to provide a list of questionable films (as the Senate committee had done in 1941 with anti-Nazi films). "When this committee refuses to submit a list, it rests on ground so uncertain that the investigative structure which it seeks to erect faces collapse." Kann noted that only three films were questionable—*Song of Russia* (MGM, 1944), *The North Star* (RKO, 1943), and *Mission to Moscow*—but all of them had been made during the wartime alliance with Russia. Put simply, Kann wrote, "times change and views on motion pictures change with them."[52] Kann was an old pro who had been covering Hollywood for years. He spoke approvingly of Warner Bros.'s courageous films of the 1930s. He understood the value of making movies for the moment, but unfortunately, the politicians in Washington did not know enough about the industry to ask intelligent questions.

Gordon Kahn, one of the individuals Jack Warner named in his HUAC testimony, had plenty to say about Jack in his book *Hollywood on Trial: The Story of the Ten Who Were Indicted*. As Kahn described the scene, "The city of Washington wore a tense air, like that on the event of a coronation—or an important hanging."[53] Interestingly, Kahn inquired why nobody seemed to notice the absence of an American flag in the room used to investigate un-American activity. Kahn was also curious why Warner had not absolved Howard Koch, screenwriter for *Mission to Moscow*, the film Warner had defended ad nauseam as a patriotic war picture. The rumor in Hollywood was that the strikes of 1945–1946 had broken Jack Warner, and he was through making tough, socially conscious movies because he felt betrayed by the people he thought were his allies. Warner had hired a good speechwriter to compose his opening statement, which defended Hollywood and denied the ability to ferret out communists, but he crumbled under questioning. Kahn gave Warner credit for trying, and he understood that Vail was pushing hardest for a blacklist. After the October 20 hearings, the feeling was that there would be no blacklist.

Looking back, Jack Jr. saw the difference between his father and Harry more clearly than ever in 1947. Harry was honorable and knew how to put up a fight, but he also knew what real oppression was like, having lived in Poland. Speaking of the Warner family, Jack Jr. wrote, "They have history" in their Polish communities, where "daughters were grabbed and raped, the sons were put into the army in labor battalions where they'd all be killed. This was not based on fear alone but on experience."[54] Harry had known real oppression, which probably explained his fearlessness in the United States. There was anti-Semitism, but nobody was coming to take your children away. Being born in Canada and then moving to America, Jack lacked his elder brother's insight. Jack Jr. described his father's HUAC testimony as being riddled with "humiliation," caught up in "a time you couldn't really think straight, just a time of hysteria."[55]

Jack and Ann's daughter Barbara was attending school in Europe when her father testified. She was isolated from the Hollywood debates but knew her father was terrified of communists. Decades later, Barbara saw footage of her father arguing to rid the country of termites and became incredibly disconcerted. She remembered Jack being so proud of what he and his brothers had accomplished as American citizens "that he would have done anything for the government, including things he shouldn't have. Depriving people of their livelihood is the worst thing my father could have done."[56] Lacking Harry's political savvy, Jack was unable to see the ripple effects of his participation in the government's witch hunt.

Harry's daughter Betty remembered her father speaking with Jack about HUAC. "All of our friends were being accused of writing propaganda and being communist and running cells," recalled Betty. "It was terrifying."[57] As the hysteria mounted, Jack acted out of fear and did what he thought was right. Harry had defended his studio and the film industry in 1941; now it was Jack's turn to do the same. However, the game had changed, and right and wrong were not so easily distinguished. Warner's defense of his studio and a general denunciation of communism devolved into a shouting match between congressmen and Hollywood writers. "Are you now or have you ever been a member of the Communist Party" was billed as the $64 question posed to the ten "unfriendly" witnesses.

The Committee for the First Amendment (CFA), founded in September 1947 to protest HUAC and defend the Hollywood Ten, included Warner Bros. employees Humphrey Bogart, Lauren Bacall, Edward G. Robinson, John Huston, John Garfield, and Paul Henreid. The organization's membership also boasted other A-list talent such as Katharine Hepburn, Gene Kelly, Burt Lancaster, Groucho Marx, Frank Sinatra, Judy Garland, Billy Wilder, Jane Wyatt, and Marsha Hunt. On October 23 the CFA took out an advertisement in the *Hollywood Reporter* that cited the "abundance of unsubstantiated charges" during the first two days of testimony and examination. The CFA agreed that Hollywood should be investigated if there were proof of movies being made to undermine the government, but the examples of pro-communist films were vague at best and absurd at worst. The CFA knew that Chairman Thomas's real goal was publicity. As the *Hollywood Reporter* advertisement stated, "He has brought forth nothing to make the whole affair seem anything more than an attempt to seek personal aggrandizement on the tax-payer's funds."[58]

The idea to crash HUAC's party in Washington came while Humphrey Bogart, Lauren Bacall, William Wyler, and John Huston were enjoying coffee on the morning of October 24. They chartered a small plane and invited a few of their friends, including Jane Wyatt, Paul Henreid, Danny Kaye, Evelyn Keyes, June Havoc, Geraldine Brooks, Richard Conte, Sterling Hayden, Marsha Hunt, Sheppard Strudwick, and Gene Kelly. The group attracted press at each stop on the way to Washington. When the CFA representatives arrived at the caucus room in DC, they found that the day's events had been rearranged; instead of MPAA president Eric Johnston, John Howard Lawson (*Action in the North Atlantic*) was set to be questioned. Lawson was a known communist who never hid his feelings or his politics. The schedule change made it appear that the CFA was "the cheering section for the first of the unfriendly witnesses."[59] The CFA's nonpolitical support was quickly branded as being sympathetic to communism. When the HUAC sessions ended, Hollywood looked weak and out of touch. The Hollywood Ten were indicted for contempt and faced fines and jail time. Red hysteria was sweeping the nation, and the moguls had some decisions to make.

In the meantime, Warner Bros. star Lauren Bacall offered a statement about why she had attended the HUAC hearings. The essay titled "Why I Came to Washington" was composed while Bacall was "pacing up and down the hotel room in her stocking feet, dictat[ing] this story to a hunt-and-peck typist. Every word of the story is hers. No ghost-writer or press agent had anything to do with it."[60] Bacall attended two sessions and was terrified by what she saw. She was concerned that the witnesses were allowed to answer only yes or no and were not permitted to adequately defend themselves. "It starts with us, but I'm sorry to say I don't think it will end with us," she wrote. "If this committee succeeds in indicting people without giving them a chance to defend themselves, then they can stretch out their arms and reach all industries all over the United States." There was fear on both sides of the red hysteria: either there were communists around every corner or the red hunters might be coming for you next. This was the culture in which the moguls had to navigate their next moves.

On November 25, 1947, Jack and Albert Warner found themselves at the Waldorf-Astoria in New York City among Hollywood's top brass. Attendees included Barney Balaban (Paramount), Nicholas Schenck (MGM), Louis B. Mayer (MGM), Eddie Mannix (MGM), Harry Cohn (Columbia), Dore Shary (RKO), Spyros Skouras (20th Century–Fox), J. Cheever Cowdin (Universal), James Grainger (Republic), Walter Wanger, William Levy (Disney), and Samuel Goldwyn. A team of industry attorneys was also present, including Paul McNutt and longtime MGM counsel Mendel Silberberg. Some historians have added Harry Warner to the list, as it seems likely that he would have been present. After two days of deliberation, Eric Johnston released a statement to *Variety* and the *Motion Picture Herald* known today as the infamous Waldorf Statement. The document outlined the industry's decision to fire the Hollywood Ten and promised to "not reemploy any of the 10 until such time as he is acquitted or has purged himself of contempt and declared under oath that he is not a Communist." It continued, "We will not knowingly employ a Communist or a member of any party or group which advocates the overthrow of the Government of the United States by force or by any illegal or unconstitutional methods."[61]

Thus the blacklist began. The Waldorf Statement declared that the industry would not "be swayed by hysteria" but "recognize[d] that such a policy involves dangers of hurting innocent people. Creative work at its best cannot be carried on in an atmosphere of fear."[62] The entire statement gives the impression of an industry that was backed into a corner. There are many reports of major producers and studio heads speaking out against any type of blacklist prior to the HUAC hearings. Most producers did not care about their employees' politics. Darryl Zanuck, interestingly, did not even attend the Waldorf-Astoria meeting. Jack Warner, as evidenced by his testimony and cross-examination, was scared. Albert, always mindful of the bottom line, knew that if Warner Bros. or any other studio backed the Hollywood Ten, the government could push for censorship or even a boycott of Hollywood. The postwar hysteria seems irrational today, but for those who lived it, the terror sweeping the nation was real.

Lester Cole, who wrote *Objective, Burma!* for Warner Bros., was one of the Hollywood Ten convicted of contempt and sentenced to one year in prison. In his autobiography, Cole rehashed a story Dalton Trumbo had told him about Jack Warner. When Warner fired Trumbo in 1936 over the writer's activity in the new Screen Writers Guild, Trumbo accused Warner of blacklisting. "Sure, it's blacklisting," he replied. "But you can't prove it since we got no list; we do it by phone." Cole would work for Warner Bros. during the blacklist using an alias. Warner bought a story from Cole that eventually became *Chain Lightning* and allowed the writer to receive screen credit as "J. Redmond Prior."[63] As fate would have it, J. Parnell Thomas would be convicted of corruption for falsifying employment records—making up fake employees and taking their salaries for himself. Ironically, Thomas served time in the same jail as Cole and Ring Lardner Jr.

Harry Warner was uncharacteristically quiet during the HUAC investigation. It is possible that he thought HUAC would go no further than the Senate had in 1941. Harry kept his focus on philanthropy. On December 5, 1947, the Hollywood Foreign Correspondents Association presented Harry with its annual humanitarian award for his work on the Friendship Train. The Friendship Train was the brainchild of journalist Drew Pearson, who wanted to get food to those who were rebuilding postwar Europe. The idea was simple: the train would travel across the country, making stops in various communities that donated food and supplies. The train departed Los Angeles on November 7 with eight carloads and traveled to New York, where it dropped off more than two hundred cars full of food. A ceremony was held in Battery Park as the food was being prepared to ship across the Atlantic. While Jack had been ducking and weaving blows from HUAC, Harry had been orchestrating a national undertaking to support the starving people in war-torn Europe. "Hunger and ignorance are the chief allies of totalitarianism,"

Harry Warner and his colleagues working on the Friendship Train.

said Harry as he accepted his humanitarian award.[64] While much of the film industry was caught up in the debates over communism, Harry's altruistic public service was true to form.

Harry was spending an increasing amount of time at his 1,100-acre ranch north of Los Angeles. Horses and horse racing were a useful distraction from the politics of Hollywood. Harry enjoyed quiet walks around the ranch, often with his children. The usually stoic Harry became loose and relaxed, smiling and goofing around with his family and his beloved animals. Harry became interested in breeding racehorses, but his investments in that venture resulted in minimal payback. He made headlines when he purchased two of Louis B. Mayer's star Thoroughbreds. Mayer was auctioning sixty horses, and Harry bought two of the top performers—Stepfather for $200,000 (bidding started at $50,000) and Honeymoon for $135,000 (bidding started at $75,000)—along with another young horse named Captain Flagg for $30,000. It was clear that Harry's eyes were on the racetrack, a welcome distraction from arguing with his brother or the US government over the content of Hollywood films. Harry also purchased property for another ranch near Woodland Hills, between Ventura Boulevard and Vanowen Street. He bought 753 acres from the estate of Harry Chandler (*Los Angeles Times* publisher), in addition to two smaller lots connected to the property.

While Harry was distancing himself from Jack, he found himself once again negotiating with Sam's widow, Lina Basquette. Lita was about to get married, and Harry had approved her request to see her mother in New York after nearly two decades apart. Following their meeting, Lina got to thinking about how wealthy the Warner family was. Sam's stock in the company was now worth $15 million. A *Los Angeles Times* headline read "Lina Basquette Wants Share of Movie Millions." Lina believed her $100,000 trust was fraudulent because the probate had occurred in New York and not California, where Sam lived and where widows received a larger share of their husbands' estates. Harry ultimately paid Lina $100,000 in cash in return for her promise not to write anything about the Warners in her tell-all book. It is doubtful that Harry was afraid of anything Basquette might write; more likely he was simply tired of dealing with such matters.

The war years brought other changes to the Warner family. Harry's daughter Doris ended her marriage to director Mervyn LeRoy. The separation was amicable, as LeRoy described in his memoir: "There was no particular reason, no one major bone of contention, just a gradual falling out of love."[65] Doris had taken a job with the coordinator of inter-American affairs in New York, which allowed the marriage to die a natural death without fireworks. Harry, as expected, disagreed with the divorce on principle but understood that the two had simply grown apart. Mervyn and Doris remained friendly, and the director eventually returned to Warner Bros. for future projects. Doris married director Charles Vidor in 1945 in a ceremony at the Beverly Hills Hotel. The marriage lasted until his death in 1959.

Harry had spent the last two years forging a relationship with President Truman. Between 1946 and 1947, Harry held several conferences with the president, beginning with his request that Truman sponsor emergency legislation to open up Alaska for those displaced by the European war. Always practical, Harry recognized that Alaska's current population was less than 100,000, yet the landmass was big enough to hold millions. Truman was open to a discussion of the matter, and when the two men met in July 1946, Harry learned that efforts were under way to relocate 300,000 displaced Jews to Palestine, Brazil, and South Africa. Warner informed the president that he wanted to help everyone impacted by the war, not just Jews. Harry made his case for using Alaska as a haven for displaced persons, including regulations to ensure that everyone in Alaska did not move down to the lower United States all at once. Harry assured the president that people "living in barbed-wire fences would certainly be glad to be given the opportunity to have space where they could build homes for their families."[66] Warner described the prejudice his family had endured in Poland and the opportunities they had been granted in the United States. Harry wanted to do the same for many others.

Harry revisited his concerns in another meeting with Truman on May 9, 1947. This time, Harry advised the president that only 20 percent of those in displaced persons camps were Jewish; the rest were Christians. He reminded the president that most immigrants in recent history had been refugees of some kind. He then presented the president with research on how different countries achieved their immigration quotas, as well as a detailed breakdown of the number of displaced persons per European country (e.g., 31,336 in the French zone of Germany, and 288,204 in the British zone). President Truman later wired Harry, "I wish it might be possible, as you say, for the heart of man and the mind of man to get land and people together."[67] Truman assured Warner that he would send his suggestions to the Department of State. This might have been glad-handing on the president's part; however, Harry offered to fund the entire operation in Alaska. The two continued to communicate, and Warner sent cameras to the displaced persons camps to document conditions there.

At the end of another tumultuous year, Harry and Jack once again addressed their employees in the December 1947 issue of the *Warner Club News*. Harry wrote about a world looking for answers and looking for peace. "There is peace in fact, but not in spirit," he observed. "Many lands are ridden by dissension, suspicion, and fear. Distrust and discouragement are nourished by hunger."[68] Harry hoped that Americans could find joy in simple virtues. "Because of our great resources and the example of our working, prospering democracy, we are able to build for a free world. By providing aid and showing the way, we can effectively fight the forces of destruction." The Friendship Train was one of many ways Harry led by example, giving to those in need. "Let us not listen to those who think in terms of hate, who want to destroy," said Harry. "If we set an example, now and in the future of faith and tolerance and sincerity, other peoples will know how to build for themselves." Jack, as usual, had a shorter message that echoed his brother's: "Our land is unscarred by war; its resources are still plentiful; its people are strong. Best of all, its ideals are still bright." Jack also shared some post-HUAC feelings, writing that "the structure of Americanism stands out more clearly than ever, contrasted as it is against dark clouds on the international horizon." Those dark clouds were undoubtedly a reference to Jack's fear of communist infiltration. Anyone who knew the studio boss understood that he was caught up in Cold War paranoia. The next few years found Warner Bros. putting out anticommunist films and big-budget prestige pictures, finding its place in a world changed by the advent of television. And the Warner family would be dealing with the most coldhearted move in Hollywood history.

7

Last Gasp of Old Hollywood
1948–1955

As the dust settled around the blacklist, Hollywood was dealt two more serious blows: antitrust legislation and the growth of television. The Federal Trade Commission (FTC) had known about the movie business's monopolistic practices since at least 1921, but the FTC finally gained traction on its case when exhibition practices were reexamined in 1944. The five largest studios (Paramount, RKO, MGM, Fox, and Warner Bros.) owned 3,137 of 18,076 theaters. This may not seem like a lot, but as postwar Hollywood expert Drew Casper notes, "70 percent were first-run city-center movie houses that commanded 47 percent of the yearly box-office take."[1]

The Supreme Court decision on May 3, 1948, that the Hollywood studios were in violation of the Sherman Antitrust Act settled the long debate over the industry's vertical integration and the studios' large stakes in film production, distribution, and exhibition. The decision forced the studios to sell off one of the three arms, and they decided to divest their theater chains, given the uncertainty following the HUAC hearings and the growing interest in television. Harry Warner initially rejected the antitrust ruling, and as late as November 1, 1949, the Warner brothers were in Washington trying to negotiate a compromise. The government held firm, however, and in one fell swoop upended the Hollywood studio system that had created the powerhouse industry. Theater chains were sold off, block booking (requiring blocks of films to be purchased as a package) would be highly regulated, and blind buying (forcing exhibitors to take packages of unscreened films to obtain the most desirable productions) would be outlawed and replaced with screenings for exhibition executives.

In May 1949 Harry Warner knew he would have to divest his theater chains and was angling to buy KLAC-TV, a Los Angeles television station owned by Dorothy Thackery. Warner was willing to spend just over $1 million

211

for KLAC and its affiliated stations, with additional investments dedicated to producing films for television. The Federal Communications Commission (FCC) held up its decision on the sale in light of Warner Bros.'s antitrust violations. In fact, 20th Century–Fox and Paramount were also awaiting FCC rulings on deals of their own. Thackery even pushed the FCC to approve the sale; otherwise, she might be on the hook for money Warner Bros. had already invested in television operations.

As the FCC dragged its feet and rumors spread that Warner was trying to purchase television stations in every major city in the country, Harry pushed back. "We are not planning to create a monopolistic television network," he said. "We are limiting our television station applications to just three cities—Los Angeles, New York, and Chicago." Warner showed no interest in television on a large scale; instead, he was motivated "by the use we can make of this great means of communication for the good of all mankind."[2] Once again, Harry was looking to use new technology to combine good citizenship with good picture making. He boasted about his family's accomplishments in bringing movies into the modern sound age, arguing that not allowing Warner Bros. to experiment with this new technology would be an assault on free enterprise. "I am now 68 years of age," he wrote. "I want to assure my countrymen that my goal in this new field is not a commercial one. I would like to make use of my age and experience in this hectic world of today to do the things that may make it a better world to live in. Through television I hope to make this contribution."

Warner highlighted his studio's historic influence on mass media. "Through sound films we brought a universal language into being and we propose to further this greatly through television." Movies had become universal—a great equalizer of sorts that was accessible to people of all means. Live theater catered to the upper class, with the most prestigious plays performed only in major cities, while movies could entertain people around the world for reasonable prices. Such a meaningful purpose was a defining motivation for Harry. Money was not the main appeal, as it was for Jack, who had just purchased a villa in the South of France. Harry was proud of his humanitarian efforts and had received the Cross of the French Legion of Honor for outstanding service to the French Gratitude Train (follow-up to the Friendship Train), presented by French consul Alexandre de Manziarly and Captain Pierre Lancelot, naval attaché at the French embassy in Washington. Harry referenced his "United We Stand, Divided We Fall" speech from 1940, reiterating his point that one must have faith, regardless of what that faith might be. Harry always encouraged others to believe in something larger than themselves. He was still driven by his dedication to bring entertaining and educational material to the world through mass media. If this were not true, Harry assured readers, "I would remain on my farm and have a few years of peace in my old age."

When the FCC still refused to rule, Harry Warner publicly pulled out of the deal, stating that the FCC's lack of action would result in the end of a $50 million television operation. Some thought this was a ploy to force a decision by the FCC, but Warner maintained that he had a contract with Thackery for one year and wanted to either make good on it or move on. The Justice Department decided that the Warners had to choose between production and distribution, and purchasing a television network meant they would still be involved in distribution after selling off their theaters. The ownership shares in either the production or the distribution operations had to be placed in a trust so that the brothers lost voting rights—and the Justice Department would be watching closely. By the end of 1949, the decision was made to sell the Warner theaters. The move was bittersweet, as the brothers' first venture into the film business had been their theater operation all those years ago. With assistance from Lehman Brothers, the studio put its exhibition operations on the market for $20 million. Serge Semenenko was looking to purchase the theater operations for $80 million, but he would soon have his eye on the entire company.

Growing frustrated with his inability to shield his company from government interference, Harry Warner began looking for a way to cash out. He sold most of his racehorses and much of his land. Liquidating assets is always a sign of things to come. Meanwhile, Jack and Ann Warner did the opposite: they purchased a ten thousand–acre cattle ranch in southern Arizona, complete with a thousand head of cattle. While Jack was increasingly interested in vacations, including trips to France, Harry and Abe were laser-focused on keeping Warner Bros. stable.

Prior to the antitrust decision, Warner Bros's feature film production had been declining for various reasons, dropping from forty-five in 1940 to twenty-five in 1949. Despite this reduction, the Warners decided to boost the studio's star power with a feature in *Motion Picture Daily*. Jack Warner boasted that the studio's resources would be increased. Harry promised that the studio's goal was "quality pictures produced in quantity" to meet the changing

Jack, Albert, and Harry, 1949.

demands of the audience.[3] With television's future uncertain, Warner Bros. doubled down on its in-house talent. Joan Crawford was cast in *Flamingo Road,* and an adaptation of Ayn Rand's best-selling novel *The Fountainhead* was put into production starring Gary Cooper and Patricia Neal.

Humphrey Bogart, arguably the studio's biggest star, was cast in the aviation thriller *Chain Lightning.* Other major stars working on Warner Bros. projects included James Cagney (returning to the studio for a three-picture deal), Danny Kaye, Bette Davis, Errol Flynn, Virginia Mayo, and Jane Wyman. John Garfield, Kirk Douglas, Burt Lancaster, John Wayne, Randolph Scott, Marlene Dietrich, and Ginger Rogers had all signed to star in upcoming Warner films. Several stars were partnered with other production companies that were utilizing Warner Bros. for distribution, including Alfred Hitchcock (Transatlantic Pictures), James Cagney (Cagney Productions), Burt Lancaster (Bryan Foy Productions), Doris Day (Arwin Productions), and John Garfield (Roberts Productions).

Another notable film was the classic adventure *Treasure of the Sierra Madre* (1948), starring Humphrey Bogart and directed by John Huston. Joseph Breen wrote several letters to Jack Warner imploring him to ensure that the film, about men searching for gold in 1920s Mexico, was not offensive to our neighbor to the south. *Key Largo* (1948) would be the last Bogart and Bacall vehicle, directed by Huston and featuring a fantastic supporting cast that included Edward G. Robinson, Claire Trevor (who won the

Best Supporting Actress Oscar), Lionel Barrymore, and Monte Blue. Errol Flynn, whose peak swashbuckling days were long behind him, starred in *The Adventures of Don Juan* (1948). The western *Colorado Territory* (1949) served as a respectable remake of *High Sierra*. Cagney reprised his iconic gangster persona for *White Heat* (1949), playing the most psychotic of all his tough-guy roles. The line "Made it Ma, top of the world" was forever etched into the popular imagination. Although the late 1940s saw less output from the studio, several Warner Bros. films became classics. It was one last hurrah for the Old Guard stars at Warner. Flynn and Bogart died before the end of the next decade. Cagney was tired of Hollywood and would soon be semiretired, spending most of his time on the East Coast. Sadly, major stars like Bette Davis and Joan Crawford would soon be considered outdated and out of style. Though both women made some strong films in the 1950s, they would soon be relegated to low-budget horror films (at a time when horror was still viewed as second tier).

Trustworthy Warner Bros. director Raoul Walsh helmed the Technicolor aviation film *Fighter Squadron* (1948), made in cooperation with the National Guard. Continuing the studio's track record of puffing the armed forces, Jack Warner used his government connections to get permission to use actual combat footage. Walsh wrote in his autobiography, "There are people who say Jack Warner is extremely cautious with a buck. I never found that to be true. In fact, he gave me a couple of big bonuses for bringing pictures in under budget, and once I got three pay raises in one year."[4] There are plenty of stories to support the brothers' frugality, such as Jack's complaints about the lights being turned on during the day, but the Warners spared no expense if they truly believed in a film. As evidenced by the studio's wartime productions, the company was happy to bankroll something that benefited the nation, even if it meant a financial loss for the studio.

Not to be outdone by his brother's humanitarianism, Jack hosted an event for the United Jewish Welfare Fund. The affair took place on Warner Bros. Stage 7, with two hundred people in attendance. The crowd raised $11 million for ongoing assistance to immigrants and those displaced by the war. "To put it bluntly, it's a matter of life—or a slow, terrible death," said Warner as he addressed the crowd. "At the rate of a thousand persons a day these survivors of the concentrated hate of Hitlerism are entering the one place in all this world where they are wanted—where they are taken in with no questions asked. If we fail them, there is nothing but hate and barbed

The Warners touting their new stars and productions.

wire to return to."[5] Warner also reminded listeners that local hospitals and welfare centers were in need of assistance. Although the event was held to support the United Jewish Welfare Fund, Warner boasted that the money donated would help a range of people, not just those of Jewish background. For the next few years, Jack continued to raise funds for the United Jewish Welfare Fund, encouraging major Hollywood players such as Harry Cohn, Dore Schary, Joseph Schenck, and Music Corporation of America (MCA) chairman Lew Wasserman to contribute. Warner also produced a short film for the cause, financed by donations from Warner Bros. employees—Harry Warner ($103,559.86), Jack Warner ($120,000), Michael Curtiz ($5,000), and Milton Sperling ($7,500). Many others contributed smaller amounts. By 1953, Warner Bros. was the leading donor to the United Jewish Welfare Fund, with 555 employees donating a total of $67,308 in that year alone.

Rounding out 1949, Jack received the Navy Distinguished Public Service Award for producing *Task Force,* starring Gary Cooper and directed by Delmer Daves. The film details the advent of the aircraft carrier and its role in national defense. The award was presented by undersecretary of the navy Dan Kimball, who commended Jack for adding "to the public's fuller understanding of the Navy and its part in national security."[6] *Task Force* had a two-ocean premiere. The Atlantic premiere was aboard the USS *Midway* in Gravesend Bay, and the Pacific premiere was aboard the *Valley Forge* near Long Beach. Both events were attended by top navy officers and local politicians.

Jack was an old soul clinging to the heyday of film. In early 1950 he would decry television, asserting that "the only screens which will carry Warner Bros. products will be the screens of motion picture theaters the world over."[7] His statement was likely fueled by animosity toward the FCC for stalling the Warners' television ventures. The studio needed something to keep it going. With Harry looking to the future and getting resistance, Jack clutching to the films of yesteryear, and Albert glued to managing the company's stock, the brothers needed to find a new path forward.

Entering the Long 1950s

In January 1950 the cover of the *Warner Club News* depicted the Statue of Liberty next to the Star of Bethlehem, both sitting above a crowded planet earth with the headline "The Hope of the World."[8] Harry Warner described the symbolic cover: "The Star of Bethlehem brings light and hope to people of all faiths. It isn't important as to what one's faith is—but it is important that one have a faith. No religion teaches bad—all religions teach good." Always the optimist, Harry spoke glowingly about the United States and the freedom enjoyed by all. "The rays of our Statue of Liberty light up our land. So strong are the lights from the Star of Bethlehem and our Statue of Liberty that they must eventually pierce the iron curtains of despotism, and light up the darkest corners of the earth so that men everywhere will live in peace and dignity." Warner urged readers to "guard well our precious heritage of freedom lest power-drunken forces extinguish the Star of Bethlehem and darken the light of our own Freedom's torch which are today the only hope of a helpless world." By 1950, the power-drunken forces were largely viewed as the communists around the globe and, of course, those looking to subvert the American way of life.

Jack Warner reiterated his brother's words and asked for more good deeds. "We must have a sense of obligation to our associates in a great industry and responsibility as citizens of the only nation where contentment and plenty can be found." Jack was certainly living a plentiful life, but his humanitarian streak was commendable (if only not to be outdone by Harry). "We should again dedicate ourselves to the service of industry, country, and humanity," Jack concluded. Hollywood was still a powerful cultural and political force, despite being hobbled by antitrust decrees. Even if movies had to compete with television, audiences would still be drawn to movie stars. There was no question of Hollywood's social and political power. The question was how the industry would navigate an era with new technology and conflicting political winds.

With Hollywood working feverishly to establish a firm footing after the antitrust case, the time was ripe for outside investors to buy out the aging moguls. Warner Bros. was no exception. The brothers got offers to buy the studio, but the deals went nowhere. They sold their radio station, KFWB, to Harry Maizlish, who had managed the station for fourteen years. KFWB had been important dating back to the anti-Nazi years and had been useful in publicizing the studio's stars, but television was becoming the shiny new vehicle for promotion. The studio halted operations for short periods while upper management focused on transitioning to new ventures. Jack Warner defended the shutdowns as brief time-outs while future strategy was solidified. Many people in Hollywood were turning an eye toward independent production, including Jack Warner Jr., whose Phoenix Productions began to grab headlines. The 1950s was a rough decade for the founding moguls, and many would not live to see the end of it.

The fear of communism was spreading as Alger Hiss, a government employee and alleged Soviet spy, was convicted of perjury in 1950. That same year, Wisconsin junior senator Joseph McCarthy made his infamous claim that he had the names of 205 communists employed by the US State Department. Hollywood responded with dozens of anticommunist films; most of them were not successful, but they satisfied the government's desire to have Hollywood take up the cause. Warner Bros. made some of the more popular red scare films, such as *Big Jim McLain*, which greatly benefited from John Wayne's star power.

Red fever soared as *Billboard* ran a series of anticommunist editorials. Harry Warner expressed his support and welcomed the publication "to the ranks of those of our industry who are determined to prevent either its infection or assimilation by subversive interests of any kind." Warner also shared his favorite quote: "Eternal vigilance is the price of liberty." It has been attributed to multiple people, including Thomas Jefferson, but it originated in

Thomas U. P. Charlton's 1809 book *The Life of Major General James Jackson*. Regardless of where Warner found it, his eternal vigilance in defending both his industry and his homeland was unquestionable. "I hope all of us who are trying to guard the sacred prerogatives of liberty and peace will remain vigilant until the whole world is convinced that Democracy is here to stay."[9] While many were swept up in the paranoia, Harry Warner was coming from a place of experience. His family had left Poland because of the threat of totalitarianism, so he did whatever he could to make sure it did not happen in the United States.

The Warner Bros. president cautioned his employees about the red menace. Harry called a thirty-minute meeting for all employees and told them to watch for "organized communist conspirators who would threaten the peace and security of this country." Just as he had rejected radicalism leading up to World War II, Warner did not want to employ anyone "who belongs to any Communist, Fascist, or other un-American organization . . . don't allow these bullies to bully you. Get rid of them." Harry offered to pay the fare for any subversive players who wanted to go back to Russia. This was not grandstanding. He really would have ponied up the money to send anyone who did not appreciate the United States anywhere else in the world. Warner ended the meeting by playing the patriotic short titled *Teddy, the Rough Rider,* in which Roosevelt warns about saboteurs in America. The *Hollywood Reporter*'s Billy Wilkerson commended Warner and noted the deep communist infiltration of the industry. Local FBI agents were delighted to hear that many of the guilds had instituted loyalty oaths and asked members to fill out anticommunist affidavits.[10]

Harry was getting tired of fighting with Jack. According to one largely corroborated studio legend, Harry found Jack philandering with one of the studio's starlets. The scene became so heated that Harry chased Jack around the lot with a lead pipe screaming, "I'll kill you, you son-of-a-bitch." Milton Sperling, Harry's son-in-law and Warner Bros. producer, verified the story. "I spent most of my time on the Warner lot carrying truce flags back and forth between them," he remembered, "just to keep them from tearing the studio apart."[11] Jack and Harry's spats peaked in the 1950s, testing Ben Warner's lesson about family unity. Jack was never loyal to his family, his wives, or his children, plus he was absent from the studio during extended stays in France. Despite their personal differences, Harry had once been able to trust Jack with studio operations. Now that trust was in serious doubt.

Harry called a meeting at Warner Bros. to discuss how the studio could assist the FBI with its ongoing investigations. He also met with bosses at each major studio and learned that everyone was interested in getting an inside line on subversive activities in Hollywood. Part of this maneuver, to be sure, had to do with the desire to stay ahead of any news that could cause the studio harm. The industry had long succeeded in staying ahead of headlines that might put Hollywood in a negative light, but the task had become increasingly difficult. An FBI report from September 5, 1950, described Warner's enthusiasm for assisting the bureau, but the local agent was not overly optimistic about the usefulness of any information the Hollywood studios might provide.

The FBI report also highlighted an advertisement in the *Hollywood Reporter* funded by the top brass at multiple studios, including Samuel Goldwyn, Louis B. Mayer, Joseph Schenck, Darryl F. Zanuck, Albert Warner, Harry Warner, Jack Warner, and Y. Frank Freeman, as well as actor John Wayne and director Cecil B. DeMille. Titled "Let Us Make No Mistake about It," the ad addressed the growing concern over the United States' war effort in Korea. It stated that American citizens were looking at the Korean War "with equal parts of fury, incredulity, confusion, and frustration." The United States stood on the side of South Korea's republic and against North Korea's dictator and its Chinese and Russian allies. "It's a war we don't want and have tried in every way to avoid. Two world wars would seem to be enough. Now we have a third." The Cold War tensions led many to believe that the loss of South Korea would be the first step toward handing the world over to the Russians. If the Soviets pushed west, the ad posited, the United States would be justified in dropping more atomic bombs. "The atom bomb is still ours and is holding the Russians at their borders." For those in Hollywood, the Korean War was the next front line of freedom's defense.[12]

Harry Warner told the FBI that the Russians wanted to purchase about fifty films from Hollywood studios that dealt with a range of social issues. Specific Warner Bros. titles pursued by the Russians included *The Adventures of Mark Twain, The Sea Hawk, The Sea Wolf,* and *The Life of Emile Zola.* According to a report by Los Angeles FBI agent Hood, "Mr. Warner stated that he was very much against the selling of any films to the Russians, inasmuch as they can make inserts and do other things to them to direct propaganda against this Country, and we would never know the difference. He reported confidentially that he has been informed that the President is in favor of selling these 50 motion pictures to that Government. Mr. Warner said that his firm will not sell Warner Brothers pictures to the Soviets until he considers the matter further, reviews the pictures and sees just what the possibilities are in them."[13]

It is possible that President Truman was willing to let the Russians buy the films to track their propaganda operations. Truman was not a fan of the fear tactics of the red scare, famously responding to the political climate at a 1950 Federal Bar Association gathering by stating, "We will not turn this into a right-wing totalitarian country to combat a left-wing totalitarian threat."[14] The films in question were a mix of standard American adventure fare, suggesting that the Russians wanted to study how to engage audiences through exciting narratives that could be edited to subvert their original message. The inclusion of *The Life of Emile Zola,* dealing with the Dreyfus affair, suggests that the Russians were interested in inverting the Warner Bros. story and finding a creative way to produce a cinematic frame-up for political purposes.

Warner Bros. was humming along at a strong but less productive clip than in previous years. Coming on the heels of the explosive *White Heat* (1949), James Cagney played another nasty gangster on a crime spree in *Kiss Tomorrow Goodbye* (1950), produced by Bill Cagney and distributed by Warner Bros. Socially conscious filmmaking was on full display in *Storm Warning* (1950), an indictment of the Ku Klux Klan in the same vein as *Black Legion. Variety* called the film a "tough melodrama" that worked because it "avoids shouting its points."[15] Starring Ginger Rogers, Ronald Reagan, Steve Cochran, and a young Doris Day, *Storm Warning* offered postwar antifascism branded with the red scare fear of naming names and pointing fingers. *Storm Warning* was made in the style of a socially conscious 1930s Warner Bros. thriller (such as *Black Legion* and *They Won't Forget*), updated for the 1950s and billed as "fresh as the ink on tomorrow's headlines!"

The new decade offered something for the Old Guard while making room for the next generation of filmmakers cut from a different cloth. They were the first generation to grow up on motion pictures. Directors such as Elia Kazan, who got his start on the New York stage, came of age watching Hollywood films. Kazan remembered coming to the Warner Bros. lot to play a supporting role in *City for Conquest* (1938) and was in awe of the star power there—Paul Muni, Errol Flynn, Humphrey Bogart, Bette Davis, Gary Cooper. More than anyone, though, Kazan was wowed by James Cagney, who was starring in *City for Conquest* alongside Ann Sheridan. By the time Fox

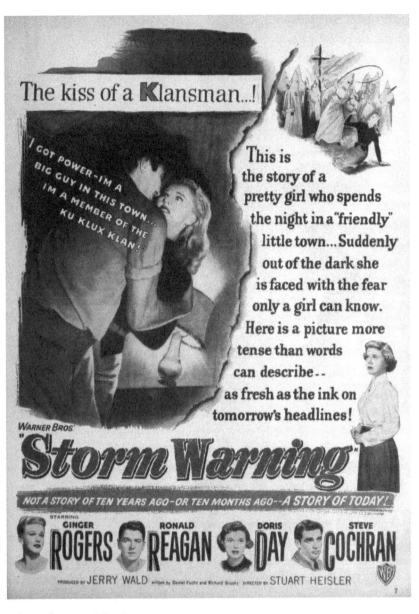

Ad copy for *Storm Warning.*

loaned Kazan to Warner Bros. in 1951, he was already an accomplished director whose credits included the family melodrama *A Tree Grows in Brooklyn*
(1945), the tight noir thriller *Boomerang!* (1947), and the social problem film
Gentleman's Agreement (1947), which won Oscars for Best Director (Kazan),
Best Supporting Actress (Celeste Holm), and Best Picture.

At Warner Bros., Kazan used his talents to adapt a stage play into a feature film: *A Streetcar Named Desire* (1951), produced by Charles K. Feldman
Productions. That family melodrama would usher in a new era of directors
and onscreen talent, earning Oscars for Best Actress (Vivien Leigh), Best
Supporting Actor (Karl Malden), Best Supporting Actress (Kim Hunter),
and Best Art Direction (Richard Day and George James Hopkins). Marlon
Brando popularized the Stanislavsky method of character acting that would
define many stars in the coming years. When Kazan finished the film, he
complimented Jack Warner on the talent that graced his lot. In particular,
Kazan was impressed with editor Dave Weisbart, who had helped the director fine-tune the emotions needed for the film. Kazan considered Weisbart's
contribution so significant that he asked Warner to bump his credit from
film editor to associate producer. Although that did not happen, Weisbart did
begin producing films at Warner Bros. Jack's decision to promote Weisbart
was likely due in part to Kazan's adamant support.

The primary reason Kazan enjoyed working for Jack Warner was his
willingness to defend the studio's films against censorship. Warner had promised Kazan that *A Streetcar Named Desire* would be released at the director-
approved length of two hours and fourteen minutes. However, the Legion of
Decency was considering a C rating, condemning the film. Being condemned
by the Legion of Decency meant that distribution would be impossible in
numerous parts of the United States and overseas. Perhaps the problem was
that HUAC had been circling Kazan. "It was at this time I became aware of
the similarity of the Catholic Church to the Communist Party," the director
wrote in his memoir, "particularly in the 'underground' nature of their operation."[16] Warner Bros. ultimately shaved several scenes, totaling four minutes,
to placate the censors and avoid condemnation by the legion.

Alfred Hitchcock began his tenure at the studio by directing two color
productions: *Rope* and *Under Capricorn*. Hitchcock first came to Warner
Bros. as part of a distribution deal with Sidney Bernstein and Transatlantic
Productions. *Rope* was a modest success, but the two films did not do well
enough at the box office to boost Transatlantic. Jack Warner did not want to

Jack, Harry, and Albert, 1951.

lose a big name like Hitchcock, so he offered the director a separate deal to make *Stage Fright* (1950), *Strangers on a Train* (1951), *I Confess* (1953), and *Dial M for Murder* (1954), produced and distributed through Warner Bros.

Hitchcock reached a new level of stardom while at Warner Bros., and the press started to refer to him as the "master of suspense." For years, Hitchcock had been a "name above the title" in the Frank Capra sense. He was a member of the old-school silent filmmakers who survived the transition to sound. Hitchcock was also a rare animal, in that he was both a director and a star—something that became more common in the coming decades. Jack Warner, who always controlled his studio's films, gave Hitchcock free rein as a producer while keeping final script and casting approval for himself. Warner and Hitchcock managed to get along quite well. Their mutual respect paid off, and any differences were worked out with relative ease (unlike Hitchcock's interactions with producer David O. Selznick).

During the early stages of *Strangers on a Train,* Joseph Breen wrote to Jack Warner almost daily. Breen was largely concerned about the flippant portrayal of marriage, as two men agree to murder each other's spouses. Other issues included the brutality of the fight scenes, the consumption of alcohol, sarcastic use of the phrase "thank God," and frustration over the studio's ignoring the Production Code Administration's request to make Guy (Farley Granger) less sympathetic because of his wife's infidelities. The PCA also asked that the scene showing a reflection of Bruno (Robert Walker) strangling Miriam (Kasey Rogers) be removed. The scene stayed in but was censored locally in some areas. What the censors missed completely was the homosexual subtext throughout the film.

Not every executive at Warner Bros. was enthusiastic about *I Confess,* the story of a priest who refuses to break the sanctity of the confessional to solve a murder and absolve himself in the process. The original story and the first version of the script ended with the priest being executed. Jack Warner understood how personal this film was to Hitchcock, who had a lifelong fascination with murder and devotion to his faith. Warner allowed the director to travel with screenwriter George Tabori and producer Sidney Bernstein to Quebec to find a church that would allow the crew to use it as a location for the film (one of many trips made during preproduction). Father La Couline, an area priest with a doctorate in theology, was hired as a consultant—a move that really paid off. As Hitchcock biographer Patrick McGilligan explains, "Father La Couline bridged the discussions with the Church, reading the script to authenticate the ecclesiastical reality and recommending terms to avoid censorship."[17] *I Confess* proved to Jack Warner that finding allies within the church hierarchy was essential for this kind of production. Years later, Warner would spearhead a major support campaign, starting with the Archdiocese of Los Angeles, for *The Nun's Story* (1959).

The studio largely agreed with the church's concerns over filming the execution of a priest. The ending of *I Confess* was amended to have the priest acquitted after a trial, the killer shot by police, and the priest hearing his confession. There was also concern over the priest's having an out-of-wedlock child. Hitchcock argued that because the affair occurred before the priest took his vows and the woman did not tell him she was married, the child was not illegitimate.

Warner did not like Hitchcock's casting options, which included James Stewart and Laurence Olivier. Warner wanted an American star, so Montgomery Clift was chosen because he was coming off an Oscar nomination for *A Place in the Sun* (1951). Hitchcock wanted Swedish actress Anita Bjork for the female lead, which Warner initially approved to appeal to European markets. However, when the married Bjork showed up with a new boyfriend and an out-of-wedlock child, a phone call was placed to Jack Warner. As McGilligan describes, "Warner recommended that Bjork obtain a quickie divorce and marry the child's father," which she refused to do. "Warner then insisted that Bjork be replaced and simply paid off."[18] The role went to American actress Anne Baxter.

Hitchcock filmed *Dial M for Murder* quickly and got little interference from the censors. Hitchcock's Warner Bros. years were good for the studio

Alfred Hitchcock and Jack Warner. (Author's personal collection)

and great for the director, who was gearing up for some of the best films of his career. He worked gratis (but kept a percentage of the profits) on *The Wrong Man* (1956) as thanks to Jack Warner for his support on *I Confess*.

John Wayne was another presence on the Warner lot, starring in *Operation Pacific* (1951), one of the studio's armed forces epics. Wayne was the top box-office star in 1950, 1951, and 1954. The studio continued to distribute a series of films produced by Milton Sperling's United States Pictures, including the war film *Retreat, Hell* (1952), an early entry in the Korean War film cycle. *The Enforcer* (1951) was a Humphrey Bogart thriller about a district attorney hunting a killer.

Harry's January 1951 *Warner Club News* message was curt: "That momentous quotation 'peace on earth and good will toward men' has come back a mockery."[19] Pessimism was a change of pace for Harry, and it may have been evidence of his increasing exhaustion. His note was not totally without hope, however. He wrote, "Remember that it is always darkest before the dawn. If united we keep our faith in our country and are willing to fight for America, then we can look forward to a world where once again 'peace on earth and good will toward men' will have meaning." Having grown up in a land full of hate and despair, watching synagogues burn in Poland, Harry was disheartened to see similar situations happening around the globe. More than anything, Harry wanted a world with less conflict.

Jack was more verbose than usual in his January note: "It is not easy to reconcile the traditional peaceful spirit of the holiday season with the militant attitude that must be ours in the face of a world reverberating with the cries of war." With the Korean conflict grabbing headlines and stoking fears of communism, Warner wrote, "The foes of peace have conspired again to set the world in flames, and with the honor-given strength that is the precious weapon of peace-loving people, we must not fail . . . to direct our energies to stamping out this ruinous fire." Looking forward to a future without war, Jack reminded his readers about American exceptionalism: "So let us make this holiday season a time not just for the grateful observance of the good way of life that America almost alone still represents, but also a time to renew our resolution that we will fight always to preserve that way of life." For Jack, the best way to fight was to make good on his promise to HUAC and produce anticommunist films.

As soon as FBI informant Matt Cvetic sold his story to the *Saturday Evening Post,* Jack Warner snatched up the film rights. *I Was a Communist for the FBI* was a hot-off-the-press story, just as *Confessions of a Nazi Spy* had been in 1939, and Warner regularly connected the two films in press statements. *I Was a Communist for the FBI* presented Cvetic as a hero, but he was actually a troubled man who fell into an opportunity to inform for the feds and had a hard time keeping his cover when he was drinking. The film painted communists as anti-Semitic and anti-Black. The censors wanted the n-word deleted from the script, but it stayed in the film. Censors also objected to the brutality of the riot scenes, including a lead pipe wrapped in a newspaper. After dealing with violent strikes on his lot, the last thing Jack Warner wanted to do was sugarcoat the reality of labor riots. Breen sent numerous letters directly to Warner, but his requests for changes were largely ignored.

The press took the anticommunist bait when the film was released in May 1951. *Motion Picture Daily* wrote, "A thorn adding to the dismayed annoying of Communists here is the knowledge that within the inner circle of the party are agents of the F.B.I." Understanding the significance of the film's timing, the review continued: "There is a happy appropriateness to the film. At a time when the House Un-American Activities Committee is exposing Communist infiltration in isolated segments of the industry, the

Ad copy for *I Was a Communist for the FBI*.

picture shows where the industry as a whole stands on the question." In true Warner Bros. style, "patrons will recognize a lot of occurrences as coming right out of the newspaper headlines." Readers of the *Saturday Evening Post* finally saw the serialized story on the big screen. *Variety* described the film as "excellent exploitation" and as "timely as today's newspaper headlines." The *Hollywood Reporter* appreciated some of the film's nuances, observing, "The script is careful in showing that not all union men and not all members of minority races are blind to the threat of Communism, and in this respect, the subject can expect the fullest support of these groups." Sadly, the differences between dangerous radicals and intellectual writers were not appreciated before industry leaders got together to blacklist suspected subversives.[20]

At the end of 1951 the Warner brothers were given the Pioneers of the Year award by the Motion Picture Pioneers. Five hundred leaders of American industry attended the event at the Waldorf-Astoria Starlight Roof in New York City. Among the notables were Henry Ford (Ford Motor Company), David Sarnoff (RCA), Frank Folsom (NBC, International Atomic Energy Agency), and Eric Johnston (MPAA). Accepting the award, Harry Warner said: "I don't presume to have any quick solution for the very serious problems of the world outside our industry, but I am concerned with the impact and effect of our business on the world itself. Motion pictures can have a tremendous effect, both in this country and beyond our borders. They can portray the spirit and meaning of America, in a way that nothing else can. But, to do that, we must seek and find the spirit within ourselves—the spirit of hope and vision."[21] At nearly seventy years old, Harry refused to give up his idealistic view of the cinema.

As the HUAC hearings continued to grip the country, Warner Bros. made *Big Jim McLain* (1952), starring John Wayne and Nancy Olson and produced by Robert Fellows and Wayne's production company. A combination of drawing from the headlines and fulfilling Jack Warner's promise to make anticommunist films, *Big Jim McLain* was shot quickly and efficiently in Hawaii, the gorgeous location offering a delightful counterimage to the static sets on television. Like *I Was a Communist for the FBI,* the film was a low-budget production but with star power. Both films are largely forgettable, time-stamped tales of fear and paranoia that are useful cultural documents for those looking to get a sense of the era's distrust and hysteria. John Wayne made several films through his production company, such as *Island in the Sky* (1953), *Hondo* (1953), and *The High and the Mighty* (1954), all of which were distributed by Warner Bros.

A new era began in January 1953 when General Dwight D. Eisenhower was sworn in as president of the United States. The long years of Roosevelt and Truman, both of whom the Warners had supported, gave way to a Republican era that matched the brothers' (and the motion picture industry's) political shift to the right. Jack Warner served a central role with the Entertainment Industry Joint Committee for the Eisenhower-Nixon administration. Jack, like many others in Hollywood, was completely on board with Eisenhower's small-government platform after so many years of Roosevelt-led and -inspired big-government programs. Or so the story goes. More than anything, it could be argued, the industry's rightward shift was an attempt to avoid additional government interference during the height of McCarthyism.

In addition, the Warner brothers were part of an old generation that was undoubtedly important as industry founders, but they were not the visionaries they once were. Harry, Jack, and Albert were men of a different time, cut from a different cloth than the new generation of agents and producer-stars. Like the other moguls, the Warners considered retirement. Some, like Louis B. Mayer, were simply forced out of the business. Others, like Darryl F. Zanuck, valiantly fought against the changing tides until the very end. The Warner brothers soon faced the retirement question head-on. Until then, it was business as usual.

In October 1953 Jack Warner chaired an award ceremony for director Mervyn LeRoy. Those who could not attend sent apologies and kind words. Sam Goldwyn wrote, "You can count on me for the fullest cooperation not only because I am always delighted to work on any committee you head but because I have always had great respect and admiration for Mervyn's stature as a splendid citizen and the many fine things he has consistently done."[22] Jack responded with a spirited telegram when Columbia's Harry Cohn sent his regrets: "Sorry you cannot come for lunch today because you have no relations here. Did you mean relatives or business relations? If you mean either of them you are mistaken because I found a cousin of yours working here. If you mean business relations this is news to me. The lunch is being held for something that concerns us as Americans and it is my opinion that everyone in our business should find the time to participate in this type of good citizenship." Jack concluded, "Expect you at the lunch at one o'clock."[23]

LeRoy was awarded the World Brotherhood trophy on behalf of the National Conference of Christians and Jews. LeRoy was directing at MGM at the time, but his friendship with the Warners dated long before he married (and later divorced) Harry's daughter Doris. The event was held at the Beverly Hill Hotel in front of four hundred Hollywood leaders. The award was presented by Louis B. Mayer, and among the speakers were Greer Garson, Walter Pidgeon, Edward G. Robinson, Dore Shary, Jesse L. Lasky, and Jack Warner, with Jack Benny as master of ceremonies. The World Brotherhood award, the first to go to a member of the film industry, was for "25 years of service to greater world understanding through motion pictures."[24] President of the World Brotherhood's American branch, Dr. Everett R. Clincy, said, "The motion picture industry has a warm heart for human welfare, which only those who have worked with the film corporations and individuals can understand."[25] Those were interesting words for anyone involved in the blacklist, but true in terms of the humanitarianism of so much of the work put out by Warner Bros.

When it was Jack Warner's turn to celebrate his friend, he mused, "It seems rather tragic that many people look out the window when asked to attend an affair such as this. Little do they realize that America is one of the few places left in this world where there can be gatherings like this and where freedom of speech, freedom of religion and other freedoms are still enjoyed."[26] Warner recalled some of LeRoy's significant contributions to the studio's edgy, ripped-from-the-headlines style. *Little Caesar, I Am a Fugitive from a Chain Gang,* and *They Won't Forget* were entries in the studio's record of fearlessly engaging the culture with a powerful celluloid punch. "Let no one be fooled," said Warner, "it is easy to be complacent and say, 'I am doing my share' for this and that, but we privileged people can never do enough. I am sure that is the reason all of us are here tonight—to help those who are not as fortunate as we are." It was easy to see Jack as the selfish, shallow brother when compared with Harry, but he had an honest, humanitarian side that often got lost in his ostentatious social presence.

Jack regaled the audience with the story of how he met LeRoy when Mervyn was a young assistant cameraman at Famous Players–Lasky Studio (before it became Paramount). Jack next encountered LeRoy as an actor in *Little Johnny Jones* (1923), when the director was absent one day and Jack stepped in. When Warner Bros. purchased First National, LeRoy had just been fired as a director and Jack rehired him. Jack remembered that Mervyn was "young when I introduced him to Eddie Robinson, Paul Muni, and Fredric March. Each time they asked 'is this kid the director or the prop man?' It wasn't long before they learned he really was a fine director and he still is." LeRoy had established himself as a master of many genres and made several more films for Warner Bros., including *Mister Roberts* (1955), *The Bad Seed* (1956), and *The FBI Story* (1959).

Jack Warner considered producing an adaptation of Kathryn Hulme's 1956 novel *The Nun's Story* shortly after it was published. It tells the tale of a woman who joins a convent of nursing nuns, struggles with obedience, and ultimately leaves to fight the Nazis. The studio's history of producing stories that irked the Catholic Legion of Decency—not to mention Jack's history of pushing back against his family's religious traditions—made Warner Bros. the logical home for a story about a woman who rebels against her Catholic faith. Warner had been in talks with Jack Vizzard at the Production Code office about the story's numerous censorship issues.

High Noon (1952) director Fred Zinnemann wrote a long letter of appreciation to Jack Warner on July 21, 1958, thanking him for spending so much time trying to find allies for *The Nun's Story*. "I know that I am not exaggerating when I say that without you we would have had very little cooperation from the Church. It was only through your intervention with Father Lunders and thanks to the many hours of patient discussions which you had with him, that we were able to get a sympathetic hearing and cooperation."[27] Lunders and Warner spoke with church officials in Rome, and through his connections there, the priest was able to obtain global Catholic support for the film.

Producer Henry Blanke also met with the archbishop of Los Angeles. The archbishop's opinion was that the novel had been received with trepidation in Belgium, which could signify similar problems elsewhere. The story "can easily be harmful to religious vocations" because it "disregards the intrinsic beauty and consolations of a life dedicated to religion."[28] Blanke organized a meeting with Zinnemann and John J. Devlin, the diocesan director of the Legion of Decency. Devlin was much more open-minded about the film and felt the director and producer had created an intelligent and sympathetic adaptation of the novel. The Legion of Decency ultimately gave the film an A-11 rating, meaning it was suitable for adults but might be morally objectionable to some. The MPAA approved *The Nun's Story* for release on October 29, 1958.

While Warner Bros. continued to churn out adventure films (*Island in the Sky, The High and the Mighty*) and crime thrillers (*The Blue Gardenia, Crime Wave*), Jack Warner began to explore horror and science fiction. The studio entered big-monster science fiction with *Beast of 20,000 Fathoms*. Although Warner Bros. was not known for its horror films, the studio had a respectable run in the 1930s with *Doctor X* (1932) and *Mystery of the Wax Museum* (1933), both utilizing two-strip Technicolor film stock. In 1953 Jack green-lit the 3D film *House of Wax*. Animator Chuck Jones recalled that Warner hired Andre De Toth to direct *House of Wax*. But De Toth "had only one eye [and therefore couldn't see in 3D] . . . typical of Jack Warner."[29] The film was a smashing success, and soon Warner wanted everything in 3D, including the western *The Moonlighter,* reuniting legendary screen team Barbara Stanwyck and Fred MacMurray. Shortly thereafter, Hitchcock's *Dial M for Murder* was given the 3D treatment too. It should be noted that this practice was short-lived, as the non-3D versions were more successful. For example, *Dial M for Murder* played for one week in 3D, and after it was given a traditional "flat" release, the box office picked up.

Despite Jack Warner's reluctance to adopt wide-screen technology, *The Command* was the studio's first wide-screen feature, filmed in CinemaScope (marketed as WarnerScope). One of the studio's high-profile productions of 1954 was the Judy Garland and James Mason musical remake of *A Star Is*

Born. The director, George Cukor, had directed its predecessor *What Price Hollywood?* (1932). The film was a comeback vehicle for Sid Luft's wife, Judy Garland, who had been dealing with a number of health issues. Jack Warner agreed to sink $5 million into the film, which initially ran more than three hours. The length of the premiere, enthusiastically praised in *Motion Picture Herald,* was 182 minutes. Even with the positive press in other outlets such as *Time* and the *Hollywood Reporter,* the studio cut the film down to 154 minutes, likely to allow exhibitors to present more screenings.

The large price tag for *A Star Is Born* was indicative of many future Warner Bros. productions, as Jack sought to acquire a range of best-selling novels, stage plays, and musicals. He landed a string of major novels that he turned into films, such as John Steinbeck's *East of Eden* (1954), directed by Elia Kazan and starring James Dean; Ernest Hemingway's *Old Man and the Sea* (1958); and Irving Rapper's *Marjorie Morningstar* (1958), an adaptation of Herman Wouk's novel. All three films were photographed in Warner-Color. James Wong Howe won an Oscar for cinematography on *Old Man and the Sea.*

Sayonara (1957), a romance set against the backdrop of the Korean War, starred Marlon Brando and won supporting actor and actress Oscars for Red Buttons and Miyoshi Umeki. The film was photographed using Technirama, Technicolor's contribution to the new wide-screen technology. The goal was to fine-tune the anamorphic aspects of the camera to capture greater color and depth in a wide lens. Aligning with the studio's rich history of films dealing with prejudice, *Sayonara* was praised for tackling racism in the US armed forces head-on. In the film, an American serviceman and his Japanese bride commit suicide because of US military harassment of soldiers married to Japanese women. The film remains a strong argument in favor of interracial marriage from the early civil rights era. *Sayonara* is a solid example of Warner Bros. in peak postwar form. The film was nominated for ten Academy Awards.

Many of Warner Bros.'s top productions now utilized CinemaScope, although Kazan protested its use for *East of Eden.* There were too many close-ups, he argued, but Jack Warner insisted that the director use the latest in wide-screen technology for this high-priced adaptation. Kazan and Warner got along fairly well—well enough that Kazan stayed primarily on the Warner lot during the coming years, directing *Baby Doll* (1956), *A Face in the Crowd* (1957), *Splendor in the Grass* (1961), and *America America* (1963); he even stuck around for *The Arrangement* (1969), after Warner Bros. was purchased by Seven Arts. Other major adaptations ordered by Jack Warner at the end of the 1950s included the musicals *The Pajama Game* (1957) and *Damn Yankees* (1958), the war film *The Naked and the Dead* (1958, produced by RKO and distributed by Warner Bros.), the farces *No Time for Sergeants* (1958) and *Auntie Mame* (1958), the drama *Home before Dark* (1958), the male melodrama *The Young Philadelphians* (1959), the family melodrama *A Summer Place* (1959), and, as previously discussed, *The Nun's Story* (1959).

New Politics

Jack and Harry opened 1954 with their usual *Warner Club News* wisdom. "We should seek to spread our message throughout the world, and pray for decency and understanding and peace wherever there are men and women," wrote the always optimistic Harry. He saw the light at the end of the tunnel, as his statements and speeches became much shorter than usual. Jack told his employees, "This isn't a time for weak promises and idle intention, but rather a time for strong decisions and confident goal-setting. Let's make those decisions and set those goals with utter faith in each other and in our national destiny." Jack's words may have landed soundly in years past, but speaking of "national destiny" during the tumultuous postwar years when the national identity was up for debate was a difficult task.[30]

Harry continued his philanthropy, winning the Los Angeles Phi Lambda Kappa Medical Achievements Award for donating hundreds of thousands of dollars to hospitals over the years "without regard to race or creed to aid in their building funds and in research (St. Johns, St. Joseph, Cedars of Lebanon, and City of Hope Hospitals)."[31] Meanwhile, Jack continued to make connections with new political candidates. In 1954 he sought support for Mildred Younger's campaign for state senator. Younger was a rising Republican star and historically important because she would have been the first female senator, but she lost in a close election. Mildred then became the political mind behind her husband Evelle (Los Angeles district attorney, California attorney general). On September 27 Jack sent a letter to director George Stevens, a Democrat, asking him to donate to the Republican's campaign. Stevens responded on October 8: "Sorry—some mistake here. I am a Democrat. Please call on me for contributions to the 'Joe Must Go' [referring to Senator Joe McCarthy] and things of that nature."[32] Younger thanked Warner for his help, as his networking had led to additional support from Steve Trilling, Henry Blanke, Roy Obringer, Mervyn LeRoy, Elia Kazan, Victor Saville (whom isolationists had branded a British spy in the early 1940s), Billy Wilder, George Stevens (perhaps he donated after all?), Lew Wasserman, Harry Warner, Milton Sperling, Virginia Mayo, Alan Ladd, and others. During this time, Warner also supported Goodwin J. Knight for California governor, Thomas H. Kuchel for US senator, and Eisenhower for president. Amidst all this politicking, Jack would soon find his studio accused of contributing to juvenile delinquency by the US Senate.

One reason for Hollywood's new range of potentially objectionable content was the retirement of Joseph Breen. Geoffrey Shurlock had been Breen's assistant for many years, beginning as part of the Studio Relations Committee and landing a role in the Production Code Administration in 1934. As an English Protestant, Shurlock did not share Breen's hard-edged adherence to Catholic mores. Postwar Hollywood expert Drew Casper writes that "the appointment of the moderate liberal, sympathetic to the idea of movies for adults, displeased the Legion [of Decency], fearing that its mutual reciprocity with the PCA might be jeopardized."[33] Another factor was the highly regulated medium of television. What was deemed unacceptable for TV could be an asset for studios willing to produce narratives made for adults only.

Trouble with the US Senate, Again

Senator Estes Kefauver (D-TN) became prominent in the early 1950s when he chaired a Senate subcommittee that investigated organized crime. Notable defendants were Joe Adonis, cofounder of the Cosa Nostra crime organization, and Frank Costello, boss of the Luciano crime family. Costello made headlines when, in response to being asked what he had done to his credit as an American citizen, the mobster famously quipped, "Paid my tax." These gangsters were not afraid. After all, they had skirted the legal system for generations. The investigation led the FBI to formally acknowledge the existence of organized crime, which resulted in a series of laws focused on gambling and racketeering. Then Kefauver pivoted to juvenile delinquency. He took a shot at the comic book industry in 1954, nearly sinking the business in the process. The Comics Code Authority, modeled after Hollywood's Production Code Administration, offered a self-censoring body that kept the senatorial crusaders at bay. In 1955 Kefauver looked at movies as a prime source of deviance among America's youth, paralleling the Payne Fund studies decades prior. One of the Hollywood targets was Jack Warner.

On June 16 the Subcommittee to Investigate Juvenile Delinquency convened at 10:10 a.m. in room 518 of the Los Angeles Courthouse. Kefauver presided, along with attorney James Bobo and lobbyists William Haddad and Carl Perian, suspiciously billed as "consultants." The witness stand was flanked by movie posters deemed lewd by subcommittee members. The same tactic had been used against the comic book industry, aiming to paint the witnesses as agitating delinquency before they opened their mouths. Still, the senator assured the packed courtroom that he had no prejudices or preconceived notions about movies, nor was he interested in increasing censorship in Hollywood. "We honestly believe that the majority of the people in the film-making business, the great majority, are sincere in their efforts to make good products," commented Kefauver.[34] The senator explained that the film industry had become more understanding of the government's concerns following the cooperation of Eric Johnston. However, Kefauver described receiving many letters from "intelligent people throughout the country" who were "concerned about an increase in what is felt to be unnecessary movie violence," which included "excessive brutality, sadism, and illicit sexual behavior." The senator admitted that one cannot point to a single film as the direct cause of youthful behavior. However, he argued, "we do feel that with the prevailing world conditions, with the uncertainty of the draft, with the lurking thought of atomic destruction, with all of these as background an atmosphere of violence is being conveyed by the mass media." The problem, according to the senator, was that too much violence in the media had the potential to negatively impact children, especially those in unstable situations. Similar concerns were expressed about advertising for movies, which often featured weapons, criminals on the run, and lurid sexual images. Kefauver's goal was to determine the efficiency of current censorship strictures. Given the senator's interest in films as "performance of a greater good," one might have expected Harry Warner to be first in line to testify. However, this time, Jack took the hot seat.

Before Warner took the stand, he listened to the testimony of William Mooring, a Catholic journalist who cited several films he considered socially dangerous. The list included *The Wild One* (Columbia, 1953), *Blackboard Jungle* (MGM, 1955), *Big House, U.S.A.* (United Artists, 1955), *Kiss Me Deadly* (United Artists, 1955), *Black Tuesday* (United Artists, 1954), and *Cell 2455*

Death Row (Columbia, 1955). Mooring complained that youths wore leather jackets like Marlon Brando and hats like Davy Crockett, while "millions of children play gangsters with wooden guns and with an Edward G. Robinson smile." Of course, that last line implicated Warner Bros. without naming either the studio or its films. Mooring attacked Hollywood by asserting that "as sure as marijuana leads to heroin, morally vicious pictures create a desire for pornography." He mentioned that the Los Angeles police chief, who also testified in front of Kefauver's subcommittee, had growing concerns about the influence of movies on both juvenile and adult crime. Like the critics in the early 1930s, Mooring claimed that the Production Code was either ineffective or improperly enforced.

Also testifying was Ronald Reagan, who defended the industry and the dramatic necessity of striking content. Dr. Frederick Hacker and Dr. Marcel Frym (of the Hacker Foundation) argued that movies instigated delinquency and that film advertisements were often more offensive than the films themselves. MGM vice president of production Dore Schary claimed the industry's treatment of gangster films had changed with public opinion. After all, there was a big difference between Cagney's role as an impressionable victim of circumstance in *The Public Enemy* (1931) and his portrayal of the unequivocally psychotic criminal in *White Heat* (1949). Frank Freeman, president of Paramount, predictably defended the industry and, like Schary, spent time explaining the production process to the curious Kefauver and company. It was following this mix of accusation and resistance that Jack Warner began his testimony.

Senator Kefauver introduced Jack Warner by presenting a biography of the mogul that included "all the good and bad things you have done."[35] This suggestive statement, intimating that Warner should be worried, did not stir the studio chief. He made several corrections to Kefauver's introduction, such as the year the Warner brothers started in the film business—1905, not 1918—and Jack's origins—born in Ontario and then moving to Lynchburg, Virginia. Knowing Kefauver was from the South, Warner wanted to establish his southern credentials—the part of the country Kefauver called "Davy Crockett territory." Warner quipped that Crockett "has a corner on all the coonskin caps" before changing his tone to deliver a serious statement.

Warner opened by pointing to the Prohibition era as a recent period that had changed the fabric of society. Warner Bros. made many films mirroring and interpreting the cultural milieu to engage audiences during the

Prohibition and Depression years. Jack named *The Public Enemy* and *Little Caesar* as films with "social contact." As society began to push back against the increase in crime in 1933 and 1934, Warner Bros. produced *G-Men* (1935), a film about the origins of the FBI, with Cagney playing a character on the right side of the law this time. The film helped showcase why federal officials needed to carry firearms. The *New York Times* called *G-Men* a film "combining good citizenship with good picture making," a slogan the brothers had used ever since. "Pictures certainly have a great impact on the kind of citizens, good or bad, that we are going to have," responded Kefauver.

For Warner, the seeds of juvenile delinquency had been planted in the last forty to fifty years of war and depression. The proper response to social ills, he argued, was education. Warner's answer, as always, was to use motion pictures to promote good. "I have very rarely ever seen a film that hasn't had some kind of moral, either for good or bad, but they have some kind of moral." He added, "Motion pictures must be entertaining and therefore, must have dramatic content. You cannot make motion pictures about a tranquil world or a utopia because it just does not exist. When you make films, you have to show the bad and how good triumphs." Warner cited *Confessions of a Nazi Spy,* which took on fascists both at home and abroad, and the more recent *I Was a Communist for the FBI,* a timely testament to the studio's anticommunism, as two films that tackled important real-world issues through entertainment. Jack also pointed out that a lack of parental guidance was a problem. This was a central theme in the studio's forthcoming *Rebel without a Cause* (1955), which he referred to as depicting the "juvenile delinquency of parents." Kefauver informed the mogul that, based on early reports, the film was "not a good picture from the viewpoint of influence on young people." "They must be working from radar," quipped Warner, "because I myself haven't seen it put together. You mustn't believe everything you get by call—I guess you know that by now." Kefauver maintained that his information was reliable but offered little evidence as to why he believed so. Warner joked that the senator's snitch must be someone from a competing studio. Kefauver was not amused. Pushing further, he asked the mogul what types of experts were consulted on each film. Warner boasted the presence of national defense personnel, when necessary, and stated that attention to detail was applied to nearly every film. Warner then provided a list of experts in juvenile psychology who were regularly consulted, which included the following:

Dr. Douglas Kelley, criminologist, University of California–
Berkeley; chief examining psychiatrist for the US Army at the
Nuremberg war trials; lecturer and adviser to police departments
Dr. H. R. Brickman, California Youth Authority
Dr. Coudley, chief psychiatrist at juvenile hall
Judge William B. McKesson
Dr. David Bogen, director of juvenile hall
Mr. Gentilly of the boys' group movement
Carl Holton, probation officer
Captain Ben Stein, California Youth Authority

While Warner was on the stand, Jack Young, a small-time cinematographer, stood and asked to speak. He told the subcommittee that Warner
Bros. "has made more gangster pictures than all major studios combined,
so much so that the churches throughout the country had gotten together
and preached to the congregation not to attend these pictures." This was only
partially true; all the studios made films that were objectionable to those who
were deeply religious. Warner Bros. was certainly a thorn in Breen's side,
but Young intimated that it was the sole reason Hollywood ended up with a
stricter Production Code in 1934. Young commended Mooring's testimony
before Kefauver interrupted, wondering whether there was a question amidst
the lecture. Young argued that the Hollywood studios stopped complying with
the Production Code after Will Hays's retirement (he passed away in 1954).
Warner countered that every studio negotiated with the censor's office and
every Warner Bros. film was released with the proper Production Code seal
of approval. Kefauver saw no reason to continue this line of inquiry once he
learned that the censors and studios usually reached an agreement before a
film was released.

A woman identified as Mrs. S. George spoke out about films such as
Blackboard Jungle, which depict youth "with turbulent emotions and crazy
upside-down patterns of life," and she asked Warner why he wanted to "profit
by horror things." Kefauver reminded the woman that Warner Bros. did not
make *Blackboard Jungle,* and Jack added that such films bring important
issues to the forefront. Kefauver mentioned one Warner Bros. film, *I Died a
Thousand Times,* that was objectionable. Warner minimized the film's impact;
however, looking at the advertising, one can see why it would have irked a
subcommittee focused on brutality.

Ad copy for *I Died a Thousand Times.*

Another man, Nathan Small, asked how many of Warner's last thirty films depicted "excess[ive] drinking and smoking by women and juveniles?" Warner found it hard to take the question seriously and indulged in a heavy sigh before saying, "I can only answer that by [asking] 'why do you beat your wife?' It is the same thing." The studios had endured criticism for depicting drinking during the Prohibition years, but that was decades ago. Warner continued, "You must be living in a backwoods country, boy, because everybody is smoking and drinking nowadays in some form. You [only] drink water or something?" Kefauver would not allow Jack to continue haggling with Small and ended the session. Other witnesses followed, including studio executive Jerry Wald and Geoffrey Shurlock, Breen's successor at the PCA, who explained that nearly every film released in the United States had to go through his office.

Following Warner's day in the spotlight, the press weighed in. Martin Quigley Jr., publisher and editor of *Motion Picture Herald,* thought Senator Kefauver was hoping to recapture the spotlight by going after Hollywood. Quigley mockingly wrote, "The Senator from Tennessee, Davy Crockett fashion, is out to 'shoot 'im a b'ar.'" Kefauver's probe into Hollywood films, searching for the roots of juvenile delinquency, was nothing more than a "wild goose chase." The origins of many social problems vary considerably, observed Quigley, and "juvenile delinquency is not going to be solved by Hollywood headline hearings."[36]

Writing in the *Hollywood Reporter*, Jim Henaghan argued that "Kefauver got what he came for" by forcing the Hollywood brass to answer lengthy questions "that translated might have sounded like 'wouldn't you consider yourself a horrible person if you pole-axed your wife—whom, of course, you love deeply."[37] Many journalists jumped on Kefauver for continuing the investigation even though he found no direct link between movies and juvenile delinquency. Others, such as Thomas Pryor in the *New York Times,* noted that "the fact that the hearing was inconclusive is no cause for optimism in Hollywood because its critics now have fresh ammunition to fire."[38] It was the third time in two decades that Hollywood's top executives were forced to defend their industry on the national stage. In 1941 the propaganda hearings had been thwarted by the attack on Pearl Harbor. In 1947 Hollywood had made the difficult decision to establish a blacklist as a means of maintaining the public's trust in movies (while keeping the government at bay). In 1955 the industry continued to read the culture, which was increasingly interested in films that depicted new ideas.

Because Jack Warner's tiffs with the government always made headlines, the mogul received a stream of letters following his testimony. B. J. Glaser, a maintenance engineer in Glendale, argued that "showing all those filthy, dirty things in pictures to our children and others should be stopped and only good clean educational and religious pictures should be permitted."[39] The Reverend John Kulp, minister at Swathmore Methodist Church in Pennsylvania, complained in July about *Rebel without a Cause,* a film he could not have seen because it would not be released until October. Kulp opined, "This kind of film inevitably and eventually does infinite more harm than good . . . the border-line impressionable adolescents accept new, damaging ideas from our studios as if they were charmed endorsements of their latent animalisms."[40] William Mooring responded to an essay in the *Los Angeles Examiner* supporting the moguls, and his June 17 letter ended up on Jack Warner's desk. He argued, "There is so much good in so many stories that could truly be shown with great pride. What's the matter, have the minds of these producers become so stale and filth laden that nothing matters except money?"[41] A letter from Senator Kefauver thanked Warner for his time and his assistance in helping the subcommittee better understand the film business.

Changes on the Horizon

The press-averse Albert Warner grabbed headlines when he was given an award by the United Jewish Appeal (UJA) at the Hotel Pierre in New York in front of 250 people. Barney Balaban, president of Paramount Pictures, presented Albert with the award for his "leadership in humanitarian causes and his renowned and yet quiet philanthropies."[42] Everyone knew that Albert avoided the spotlight whenever possible, which was even more reason to highlight his long dedication to charity and goodwill causes. Albert was presented with a silver-bound Bible, handmade in Israel, with an inscription that acknowledged his dedication to "follow[ing] the precepts in the book." Upon accepting the award, Warner spoke of UJA's role in defending democracy for all people: "It is never a job which is finished, for the rights and privileges of mankind are eternal. By helping UJA, we are furthering the cause of freedom all over the world." UJA aimed to raise $1 million, which would be distributed to the United Israel Appeal, New York Association for New Americans, National Jewish Welfare Board, and American Jewish Congress.

Albert made front-page headlines in the trade press when he spoke at a shareholders' meeting about the expected upswing for the film business. The savvy mogul may have been shy of publicity, but he was always on point as the company's controller. "Today more than any other period in the history of this business," said Warner, "it is the excellence of the product that counts." Albert understood that the industry's progress created the desire for a better product, a responsibility the Warner brothers always took seriously. He saw Hollywood as a forward-looking industry, and he was quite proud to be a part of it after fifty years in the business. Albert was more optimistic than ever and was "encouraged by what I see happening under my brother Jack's direction at our studio." He also addressed the "prophets of gloom" who seemed to be present during every transitional period. Certainly, Albert remembered the pessimists who said talking pictures would "upset the economic applecart." During the Great Depression, Hollywood "defied the signs of the times and came out of that period with renewed strength." Albert boasted of the studio's ability to constantly improve filmmaking and projection and said, "We have met the greatest challenge of all by bringing to our studio the kind of superlative talent that can only result in a flow of the best and most successful pictures this company has ever made."[43]

Albert Warner receiving an award from the United Jewish Appeal, 1955.

Despite Kefauver's hearsay-informed concern about *Rebel without a Cause,* Jack Warner took out an ad in the trade press to brag about the film's popularity in preview screenings. Its stars, James Dean and Natalie Wood, were knockout young performers. Using the image of a Warner Bros. memo signed by Jack, the ad claimed the film "had the most outstanding preview" at the Paramount Theater in Los Angeles. All the top critics "milled around in [the] lobby for over half [an] hour after [the] preview was over and heaped praise upon praise not only upon Jimmy Dean and Natalie Wood but [the] entire picture."[44] Warner noted that the spellbound audience stayed through the entire preview (studios always expected a few walkouts, as not every film will be enjoyed by every viewer). *Rebel without a Cause* was ushering in a new era of filmmaking and star power. James Dean was already a shining star in the epic CinemaScope family melodrama *East of Eden* (1954), and his status was cemented after his untimely death in a car accident in September. Dean had just finished filming his scenes for *Giant* (1956) and was eager to get behind the wheel of his new Porsche Spyder. On his way to the Salinas racetrack, Dean's high-speed shenanigans led to the fatal crash.

Jack Warner scrambled to find a replacement for his young idol. The answer was Tab Hunter, a young, handsome, gay man who could easily be transformed into the innocent boy next door. Hunter accompanied Natalie Wood to the Audience Awards in November at the Beverly Hilton. Some of the photographers ribbed Hunter, who had been featured in the tabloid rag *Confidential* the previous September. He was embarrassed, knowing full well that he was a stand-in for the immortal James Dean. Hunter won his own Audience Award that night, but the unenthusiastic response from the crowd was painful. "Say what you will about Jack Warner," wrote Hunter in his autobiography, "and Lord knows terrible things have been said, but I'll always remember him most for what he did next." Warner found his way to the winner's circle, put his arm around Hunter, and dropped his famous quip: "C'mere Tab. Remember this: today's headlines—tomorrow's toilet paper."[45] Warner knew that the number of people who read *Confidential* paled in comparison to those who read *Variety* and *Photoplay* or bought tickets to *Battle Cry* (1955), the Raoul Walsh–directed Warner Bros. war melodrama featuring the young actor alongside Van Heflin and Nancy Olson. Hunter and Warner would have some contractual spats over the years, which was par for the course, but Warner's encouragement and his perspective on bad press had a lasting impact on Hunter.

George Stevens Jr., son of *Giant* director George Stevens, remembered spending time on the Warner Bros. lot prior to Dean's death. The studio was changing, as was the industry. Directors like Stevens landed production deals that granted them full creative freedom and even control over the final cut. Stevens Jr. recalled Jack Warner's reputation for ending arguments by asking, "Whose name do you see on that water tower?" Stevens and Warner knew that *Giant* had massive potential, but Jack was deeply concerned about the length of the script. He wanted the director to make a two-hour film that maintained the dramatic arc of the 178-page script. According to Stevens Jr., Jack "could be jovial and was known for telling lame jokes, but he wielded the hammer at Warner Bros."[46] During location filming in Virginia, Jack sent Stevens a telegram complaining about the director's multiple takes. Stevens responded in kind, promising to pick up the pace.

When the film premiered at the California Theater in San Diego, Jack Warner sat in the back row with his yes-men from New York. The house was packed with people eager to see James Dean's last, posthumous film. The addition of Elizabeth Taylor and Rock Hudson to the cast did not hurt

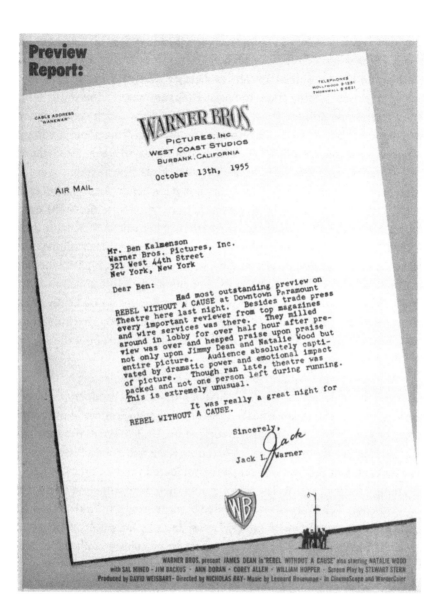

Preview Report:

WARNER BROS.

PICTURES, INC.
WEST COAST STUDIOS
BURBANK, CALIFORNIA

October 13th, 1955

AIR MAIL

Mr. Ben Kalmenson
Warner Bros. Pictures, Inc.
321 West 44th Street
New York, New York

Dear Ben:

Had most outstanding preview on REBEL WITHOUT A CAUSE at Downtown Paramount Theatre here last night. Besides trade press every important reviewer from top magazines and wire services was there. They milled around in lobby for over half hour after preview was over and heaped praise upon praise not only upon Jimmy Dean and Natalie Wood but entire picture. Audience absolutely captivated by dramatic power and emotional impact of picture. Though ran late, theatre was packed and not one person left during running. This is extremely unusual.

It was really a great night for REBEL WITHOUT A CAUSE.

Sincerely,

Jack

Jack L. Warner

Jack Warner's ad puffing *Rebel without a Cause*.

attendance either. When the film was over, the preview cards filled out by the audience rated *Giant:* 307 excellent, 64 good, and only 3 poor. When Stevens and his son walked upstairs to meet Jack, Ben Kalmenson, head of advertising, was gabbing about the numerous communist ideas in the film. With Hollywood still feeling the taint of the blacklist, such commentary was expected, but many producers were tired of worrying about ideology when there was big box office to be had. Jack downplayed Kalmenson's claim and invited Stevens for drinks to discuss some ideas. The next day, Warner wired Stevens, "Believe me, in my estimation it is a better picture than *Gone with the Wind,* and I'm glad the preview patrons agree with me."[47] The only problem with the film was the scene where Bick Benedict and Senator Bale Clinch discuss the depletion allowance on oil revenue. Warner wanted the scene removed because he was in talks with oil investor Serge Semenenko to purchase Warner Bros. Apparently, Semenenko had threatened to slash Warner's line of credit if the scene was not cut, but Stevens refused, fully exercising the creative control he had lobbied for. Jack Warner received numerous calls from the American Petroleum Institute complaining about the scene, but the furor was not enough to scare away Semenenko.

Albert was right: Warner Bros. profits were on the upswing by the end of 1955. One major factor was the influx of independent productions. After the war, audience attendance peaked and then began to decline. To offset the rising costs of producing and distributing a film, United Artists brought in a management team run by attorneys Arthur B. Krim and Robert S. Benjamin. The independent production company shouldered production costs while retaining creative control. The major studio then distributed the film at its own expense. Jack Warner saw the value in partnering with independents, as he had done recently with James Cagney and Elia Kazan.

In 1956 Warner Bros. distributed one of the most historically important westerns, *The Searchers,* a John Wayne–led adventure about tracking two kidnapped girls following an Indian raid. Today, the film is important for its unself-conscious embrace of interracial marriage, its display of the rich culture of indigenous people (though not entirely devoid of stereotypes), and Wayne's portrayal of a conflicted man of the West, mirroring the actor's struggles with the racist views prevalent in his era. *The Searchers* may be one of the most important Warner Bros. films produced during Hollywood's golden age and deserves a pedestal next to films like *Casablanca.*

The film was produced by C. V. Whitney Pictures. Cornelius Vanderbilt Whitney, a businessman, government official, and beneficiary of the Whitney and Vanderbilt fortunes, was also a major shareholder in the Technicolor Corporation. He helped fund *Gone with the Wind* (1939) and established his own production company many years later, which made only one film with Warner Bros. Sharing the financial risk allowed director John Ford, actor John Wayne, and Warner Bros. studio to take a chance on a dark western that cast superstar Wayne against his usual clear-cut heroic role. Ethan Edwards, a flawed hero who battles deep-seated prejudices, would become one of Wayne's most iconic characters.

The trade-off was having to deal with the eccentricities of a millionaire. As journalist Glenn Frankel wrote about the production, "If the requirement was that he tolerate the flights of fancy of a spoiled rich man, it was a price John Ford was willing to pay."[48] Both Ford and Warner received regular suggestions from Whitney about how the film should sell the American Dream (a far cry from the story's actual purpose). At one point, Whitney insisted that the title be changed to "The Searchers for Freedom," which did not mesh with the story of a Civil War veteran searching for the surviving members of his family following a Comanche raid. Both Ford and Warner ignored Whitney, resulting in a successful film that has become a classic.

With the studio capitalizing on new production trends, the time was ripe to sell the company, and the brothers seriously considered cashing in their chips. Harry was tired, and Albert wanted to spend more time at the beach in Florida. Jack remained the wild card. The coming year would be an unforgettable one for the brothers, with ripple effects that would be felt for generations. The Warners would experience their most difficult test yet—one that might rupture the family forever. Jack's son and Harry's granddaughter would later refer to 1956 as the year of the "betrayal."[49]

8

End of the Studio, End of the Family

1956–1959

Harry Warner's secretary, Lois McGrew, began in the music department at Warner Bros. in the mid-1950s. By 1956, she was working in the studio president's office. Lois recalled Harry's office being rather quiet. He usually arrived at 11:00 a.m., had lunch in the commissary next door (making sure to finish before Jack arrived), and was gone by the afternoon, often making an appearance at the racetrack. Lois remembered Harry as a complete gentleman with a nice personality. Although many considered Harry the most stoic of the Warners, Lois spoke warmly of his lighthearted personality, seen only by those closest to him. Harry would tease Lois about her earrings, saying that ladies did not need to "dress up their ears."[1] Harry also clowned with the delivery boys who dropped in, who were often in awe of the millionaire. Harry always told them, "You have youth, something money can't buy." Given his formal nature, Harry always dressed as if he were meeting the president of the United States. According to Lois, some people were intimidated by his mere presence.

Lois gleaned much from Harry, including his perspective on the studio president's proper place on the lot. "I don't hang out at the stages because that's where you get in trouble," Harry said. This was no doubt a poke at his brother Jack, who was known to wander the lot—not necessarily to oversee productions but more likely to meet the young starlets. Jack always had multiple girlfriends. Lois said, "He got around but Harry did not." Harry's wife stopped by the studio often. Lois fondly recalled how well Harry and Rea got along after so many years together. The two were very generous and gave employees turkeys at Thanksgiving and substantial gifts at Christmas. Harry's sisters Anna and Sadie also came by regularly. The mogul's short office hours, usually full of family visitors with a little business mixed in, were a reminder that Harry's interests were largely outside the studio. Lois wondered whether most people on the Warner Bros. lot even knew who Harry was. She saw him losing interest in the film business as television became the talk of the town, and he understood that Hollywood would need to find a way to work with the blossoming technology.

Lois was also well acquainted with Harry's brothers. Unsurprisingly, Jack almost never came to Harry's office, although he bounded across the lot daily. But the days of taking high-profile partners on tours of the studio were a thing of the past. Whenever Albert came to town, Lois assisted him and took messages for him. Albert was quiet, even among Harry's small circle of colleagues, but he was always very nice to Lois. By this time, Jack was not so popular on the lot. According to Lois, he caught flak for laying people off during the holidays, only to hire them back after the first of the year.

Lois also witnessed the constant battles between Jack and his son. Jack regularly kicked Jack Jr. off the lot over minor tiffs. One day Jack Jr. was on his way to ask Harry to intervene, but the studio cops apprehended him first. Harry's mind may not have been focused on studio business, but he always looked after his employees. Lois told a story about Harry winning big at the track one afternoon. The following day he used his winnings to give everyone in the office a surprise bonus of a week's salary.

The Betrayal

The Warners, having been in the business for five decades, once again considered selling the studio. Harry insisted that they would not sell unless all the brothers agreed to the terms. They got into the film industry together, and they should leave together, respecting the wishes of their late father. The Warners were always strongest when they worked together, as history has proved. At the annual board meeting in February, Harry was reelected to serve as Warner Bros. president for another year. In May, the brothers finally agreed to sell 90 percent of their collective holdings to Serge Semenenko, a banker from Boston who had brokered several Hollywood studio reorganizations. His team of investors included Wall Streeter Charles Allen and theater owner Simon Fabian. Because of recent antitrust legislation, Fabian's role in the new organization would hinge on US Justice Department approval, and he was ultimately forced to sell his interest in the Stanley Warner theater chain to take on his new production role. On board with the new Warner Bros. leadership was Benjamin Kalmenson, longtime theater exchange manager who eventually worked his way up to general sales manager, and Samuel Schneider, who had served Warner Bros. in many capacities since the 1920s.

When it came time to sign the paperwork, Jack did not hesitate, but Harry and Albert were somber. Harry mumbled an apology to his late father as he signed over the company. The brothers agreed to stay on the board of directors to guide the company through the leadership changes. Despite any misgivings they might have had, the time was right to sell. Other studios, such as Paramount, were reorganizing. Aging studio bosses like Darryl Zanuck were leaving their posts, and MGM's Louis B. Mayer had been pushed from his position in 1951. The Warners had achieved success and riches never before seen in their family, and it was a moment to celebrate. However, something did not feel right, and Harry knew it.

Lois was there when Harry received the phone call that quickly turned the old, exhausted studio boss angrier than she had ever seen him. Harry asked Lois to get Jack on the phone, which she did. Lois remembered Harry pounding his fist on the table and yelling into the phone, "Over my dead body will you be president of this company!" Jack had brokered a deal with Semenenko to buy his way back into the company and serve as president, effectively taking over Harry's position. Jack clearly did not think much of his father's lessons about family partnership, which Harry saw as akin to blasphemy. "Mr. Warner got this attorney on the line and all hell broke loose that day," said Lois. But it was too late. There was no way to undo Jack's betrayal. It was one of the coldest moves in Hollywood history, and it shattered the Warner family forever. Harry suffered a minor heart attack, which he thought at first was just fatigue, but a checkup at the hospital confirmed the attack.

Harry was never the same after his brother's treachery. Lois remained in the office for another month, along with an accountant, to help Harry close everything down. Before he left, Harry shook Lois's hand long and hard. With deep sadness in his eyes, he said, "I will never step foot on this lot again." To her knowledge, he never did. Harry's health was deteriorating, and the stress of fighting with Jack had taken its toll. Rea was worried sick, and many feared that Jack's back-door deal to take Harry's job would be a fatal blow to the aging mogul. The trade press reported rumors about Harry's poor health. Meanwhile, Jack took the captain's chair at Warner Bros., and in July he issued a statement to the press as if nothing sinister had happened. "Our sole purpose in the future will be to supply an important and challenging output of pictures for the world market," wrote Jack, "and I am very happy that my brothers, the board of directors, and the distinguished financial group have placed under my direction the perpetuation of the company which our family pioneered."[2] Jack proudly puffed his family legacy after burning every last bridge he had with his brothers.

During this time, longtime Warner Bros. employee Samuel Schneider resigned after being with the company since its incorporation in 1923. Schneider had started as an accountant for the studio and worked his way up to vice president. When Jack took control of the company, he kept Schneider on as treasurer. Jack was cold, but he was not stupid. He knew he needed someone as fiscally savvy as his brothers. However, Schneider was loyal to Harry and Albert and found Jack's maneuvering distasteful, so he announced his resignation in July.

Ignoring his brothers' vital importance to the studio's history, Jack boasted that the company's foundation was "more solid today than ever before."[3] What Jack did not ignore was the changing landscape of film production. He saw films like *Giant,* the horror-thriller *The Bad Seed,* Elia Kazan's family melodrama *Baby Doll,* Alfred Hitchcock's *The Wrong Man,* and Billy Wilder's Charles Lindbergh biopic *The Spirit of St. Louis* as movies of the future. Of course, *The Spirit of St. Louis* was an odd choice, given Lindbergh's well-documented embrace of xenophobia, anti-Semitism, and eugenics. It is possible that Warner had forgotten the aviator's shortcomings and remembered only his historic 1927 transatlantic flight and the subsequent tragic and well-publicized kidnapping and death of his child. The fact that the film did not fare well at the box office may be evidence that the moviegoing public recognized that the famed aviator had devolved from an American hero into a racist ideologue.

Mervyn LeRoy suggested *The Bad Seed* to Jack Warner after seeing the Maxwell Anderson play on Broadway about a child who is a murderer. This signified a new trend in psychological horror. LeRoy got pushback from the censors; the new regime under Eric Johnston had "taken over as arbiters of film morals" and would not approve the original ending, which allowed the girl to get away with her crimes. LeRoy argued that the public would never seriously believe a young girl could act with such evil. He even asked young Patty McCormack, who had also played the character onstage, if she felt uncomfortable in the role. "Oh, Mr. LeRoy," she said, "I'm having so much fun."[4] LeRoy thought the audience would see how much fun young Patty was having and grin along with her character's misdeeds. Jack Warner, however, was not willing to take that risk and ordered a new ending for the film in which Rhoda dies to ensure that "crime doesn't pay," in accordance with the Production Code. Even with the forced ending, *The Bad Seed* paid off, earning $4 million against its $1 million budget. Warner would fight a much bigger censorship battle over another film.

Elia Kazan's *Baby Doll*, based on a one-act Tennessee Williams play, was arguably the most controversial film of the 1950s. The film's plot involves a bitter battle between two cotton gin owners in Mississippi. What caused conniptions in the Catholic Church was the sexually forward and scantily clad character named Baby Doll (Carroll Baker), whose thumb-sucking behavior and limited mental capacity would have earned the film complete condemnation from the Legion of Decency. Williams's black humor was completely lost on the film's harshest critics. Complicating matters, the Motion Picture Association of America (MPAA) issued the film a seal following the Production Code's 1956 revisions that loosened regulations regarding sex and drugs. The use of racial slurs was discouraged (but not banned), which opened the floodgates for many civil rights–era narratives. *Baby Doll* was filmed in Mississippi and depicted the racism prevalent in the Deep South in the year following the Emmett Till lynching.

Kazan produced the film as part of his own independent Newton Productions, but it was clear why he chose to set up shop at Warner Bros. Jack Warner never feared a battle with censors or religious leaders or the possibility of timid audiences. Film historian Jon Lewis put it best: "Williams intended the film as an affront to traditional moral standards and Kazan and Warner Brothers made the film in open disregard and defiance of the PCA."[5] Even the *Hollywood Reporter* saw the connection to Warner's history of gleefully bucking the censors, describing *Baby Doll* as "a typical Warner picture, of the same distinguished lineage as those realistic masterpieces of the thirties."[6] Kazan knew Warner would stand behind the film, so he asked for a marketing campaign that flaunted *Baby Doll* like P. T. Barnum touted his Greatest Show on Earth. The goal was to put a massive sign on the Victoria Theatre in New York City's Times Square because, as Kazan put it, such a bold advertisement would make the film "the talk of not only Broadway, but of the show world, of café society, of the literati, of the lowbrows, and everybody else."[7]

Kazan was keenly aware of Jack's love of performance. "What's wrong with show business is that its balls have been cut off," argued Kazan. "No one showboats anymore. There is no flash in it. It is too damn much like television." However, distinguishing movies from television was not an end in itself. "Now that we have this new era at Warner Bros., let's be bold. I repeat: let's be bold." At the end of his letter, Kazan offered a postscript detailing the early feedback he had received about daring advertising: "It's old-fashioned show business, man. . . . Remember when you were in vaudeville, Jack, and people weren't afraid to say: you gotta see this show!" What was described as the world's largest painted sign, featuring Baby Doll lying in her crib sucking her thumb, went up above the Victoria Theatre. Flaunting the lewdness of *Baby Doll* during Christmas season did not win favor with the Legion of Decency.

On December 1 the Legion of Decency issued a statement calling the film "morally repellent both in theme and treatment," warning of the story's "carnal suggestiveness," and branding the film "corruptive" to "traditional standards of morality."[8] Kazan and Warner Bros. quickly replied, reminding the legion that *Baby Doll* had received an MPAA seal and was intended strictly for adults. Speaking at St. Patrick's Cathedral in New York City, Cardinal Spellman denounced the film and warned Catholics (and everyone else) not to see *Baby Doll*. Church members who viewed the film were in danger of excommunication. Episcopal leader James A. Pike, dean of the Cathedral Church of St. John the Divine, did not agree with Spellman's vendetta and called it "the efforts of a minority group to impose its wishes on the city."[9] *Baby Doll* was advertised in Europe as "condemned by Cardinal Spellman." When British Jesuit J. A. V. Burke offered support of the film as a commentary on racial intolerance, he was promptly fired as director of the Catholic Film Institute. To the delight of the Legion of Decency, the film opened strong but then fizzled. However, the studio's defense of this daring film would not go unnoticed. Several of Hollywood's most controversial films would find a home at Warner Bros. in the coming years.

At the famed 21 Club in September 1956, Jack Warner hosted a luncheon for the New York metropolitan area trade and press representatives. Seated with Jack were Stanleigh P. Friedman, the new vice president of Warner Bros.; publisher Martin Quigley; and Warner executives William T. Orr, Ben Kalmenson, and Inez Robb. Warner explained to the group of seventy-five how the film market had changed, noting that these days, one big film can make the money of three major productions twenty-five years ago. Jack saw

Baby Doll advertisement at the Victoria Theatre.

Jack Warner with Ben Kalmenson and William Orr.

the industry shifting to what would eventually become a studio system that invested more money in a smaller number of films. Large-scale productions like *Giant* were attracting more public interest. "Only superior product has a chance. The public has not tired of pictures, but it will not buy inferior ones," said Jack. "We must fight for new and better entertainment to meet public demand. The wide screens have made a valuable contribution in that regard. We're in a race for our futures and it is essential that we create an atmosphere of excitement and interest. Enthusiasm is needed. That's what attracts the public."[10]

In an ironic twist, Jack received the 1957 Brotherhood Award from the National Conference of Christians and Jews. The awards banquet was held at the Waldorf-Astoria Hotel. Among the 1,240 people in attendance were investors Semenenko, Allen, and Fabian. Warner praised the industry and his studio and lauded Hollywood for once again using motion pictures to usher in a "new era of understanding." Certainly Warner Bros. films had always been on the cutting edge of social commentary, and this trend continued with a new generation of talent showcased in *Rebel without a Cause* (teen angst), *Giant* (race and class), *The Searchers* (race and family), *Baby Doll* (overt sexuality), and the soon-to-be-released *A Face in the Crowd* (media manipulation). Warner noted, "Many of the industry's films—features and short subjects—had dramatized the power of brotherhood in the historic highlights that have made the United States a great united nation. At our

Jack Warner with his Brotherhood Award.

own studios we have tried to present on film this record of accomplishment, the story of brotherhood behind the greatness of America."[11] But many of these historic highlights on film were actually the work of Harry Warner, who labored tirelessly to make sure people saw the studio's patriotic and historical short films.

Despite his declining health, Harry continued to write his messages for the *Warner Club News*. Perhaps they were now composed by Lois or another assistant, but these statements were usually consistent with Harry's carefully worded speeches of years past. His January 1957 note was short and a bit nostalgic: "Through my many years in the motion picture industry, I have seen Warner Bros. grow from a single nickelodeon to a world-wide organization and to leadership in a great industry. I know that all of us can be proud to be associated with a company whose influence is felt around the world and whose primary goal is to create happiness wherever pictures are shown."[12]

Harry had every reason to be proud of his life's work, but he would not let studio employees see the deep pain caused by Jack's betrayal. In June, Harry went to the hospital and was diagnosed with a "rundown condition," according to the *Hollywood Reporter*.[13] Although he improved, he was seen walking with a cane, but that did not stop him from going to the racetrack. Although Harry was in poor health and doctors prescribed rest, the aging mogul remained on the move.

Unable to make peace with Jack's deceit, Harry continued to distance himself from his former studio. He sold another bundle of stock to Semenenko, making $6 million on the deal. The old New York office was sold, and Harry urged his daughters Betty and Doris to sell their stock, which they did. It was sad to watch Harry liquidating his life's work. There was so much success to celebrate, but for Harry, it had all been marred by Jack's shifty move. Harry was defeated by a lifelong sibling rivalry that had soured every day since Sam's passing. Everyone knew that Jack could be a bit conniving, but even Harry thought Jack would not stoop so low. But there he was, still reeling in surprise and sadness.

On August 23, 1957, Harry and Rea celebrated fifty years of marriage. The original plan had been dinner at the Beverly Hills Hotel, but Harry's declining condition allowed only an at-home gathering. By this time, Harry and Rea had moved from the sprawling French château on Woodland Drive in Beverly Hills to a much smaller home on Copa de Oro Road in Bel Air. With his deteriorating mobility, Harry greeted his guests seated in an armchair. The surprise of the day was Jack's arrival. Guests could hear Jack cracking stupid jokes about Harry living with one woman for fifty years as he got out of his car. When the crowd of 125 guests stared at him in a combination of surprise and disgust, Jack gulped some champagne and quipped, "Where's H. M.? I'm bustin' my balls at the studio and he's livin' the good life!"[14] Nobody talked to Jack that day.

Another day, Jack Jr. was visiting Harry when Jack came strolling through the door. He "bounced into the room . . . exuding good cheer and jollity, his unnaturally black hair and thin mustache glistening."[15] Jack said something to Harry that Jack Jr. could not make out, but Harry's response spoke louder than words. The eldest brother, one-time president of Warner Bros., social and political fighter, defender of freedom and America, and loyal family man had nothing left to say to his brother. Harry closed his eyes as tight as he could, tears dripping down his cheeks. True to form, Jack was oblivious to his brother's discomfort, but when he finally noticed, he turned toward the door and left. Jack Jr. held Harry's hand for some time to comfort him.

With what little strength Harry had left, he managed to provide a holiday message for Warner Bros. employees in December 1957. He wrote, "My thoughts and interests as always are close to the world-wide fraternity of men and women associated with Warner Bros." Harry continued, "May the holiday season be one of happiness and cheer for all of our families and may we all remember with gratitude our priceless privilege of enjoying the blessings of living and working in a free land."[16] It was his last message to the studio.

Jack Jr. was about to leave for Hawaii when Harry had his last stroke. When Jack saw his son at the studio the next day and asked why he wasn't in Hawaii, Jack Jr. explained, "I couldn't leave Uncle Harry so sick." Jack responded coldly, "Why not? He's not your father."[17] On July 25, 1958, seventy-six-year-old Harry Warner died at his home. The cause of death was cerebral occlusion. His doctor, Myron Prinzmetal, was treating Warner at his bedside at the time of his death. Within the previous year, several founding Hollywood moguls had passed, including Louis B. Mayer (1957), Jesse L. Lasky (1958), Harry Cohn (1958), and Vitagraph cofounder Albert E. Smith (1958).

The loss of Harry Warner was felt throughout the nation as newspapers carried lengthy obituaries celebrating his life and achievements. Harry's story was an inspiration: the oldest of twelve in an immigrant family who came to the United States with nothing but dreams of opportunity. More than anything, Harry was proud of his family, which is why Jack's final betrayal hurt so much. Despite their differences, Rea contacted Jack at his French villa on Cap d'Antibes, but Jack told her point-blank that he would not attend Harry's funeral. Rea hoped he would come to his senses and at least travel home to support his family. Jack Jr. also wired his father in France, urging him to return. The message went unanswered. The coldhearted Jack stayed in France. At the funeral, Rea made her feelings clear: "Harry didn't die. Jack killed him."[18]

One thousand people attended Harry's funeral at the Wilshire Boulevard Temple in Los Angeles. Albert escorted Rea to and from the synagogue. Hollywood's favorite rabbi, Edgar Magnin, described Harry as "a plain man, a simple man, a man who loved above all else being a farmer." Harry loved spending time on the ranch, and Betty and Lita cherished their memories of riding horses, feeding the chickens, and exploring the grounds with him. "He will be remembered not only as a cinema pioneer," Magnin said, "but because he was Harry Warner as a human being, a good Jew, a good American, and a dear, sweet person."[19] It was nearly impossible to find anyone (with the exception of Jack) who did not have deep respect for Harry. The pallbearers were Michael Curtiz, William Demarest, Herbert Freson, Blayney Matthews, Edward G. Robinson, Steve Trilling, Bertram Tuttle, and J. C. Yost. As they carried Harry's casket out of the temple, Rea, Albert, Doris, Betty, and Lita left through a side exit to avoid the press melee. The group traveled to the Home of Peace Memorial Park mausoleum, where Harry was laid to rest next to his brother Sam and their parents, Ben and Pearl.

The coming days saw an outpouring of condolences. *Motion Picture Daily* published a long obituary and a series of tributes from Hollywood leaders. Sherwin Kane wrote that Harry's death was another reminder of how quickly the founding moguls were passing from this world. Kane lauded Harry's ideal that motion pictures should both educate and entertain. In addition to his monumental contributions to the film industry, Harry was a humanitarian hero, and Kane listed many of Warner's awards from the National Red Cross, the Veterans of Foreign Wars, and the American Legion. Wolfe Cohen, president of Warner Bros. International Corporation, wrote that Harry "personified the era of the motion picture industry during which it developed into the most important medium of communication and understanding between all peoples."[20] MPAA president Eric Johnston saw Harry as a "great pioneer," and United Artists president Arthur Krim called Harry's death a "tremendous blow to the motion picture industry." Paramount president Barney Balaban, who had defended Hollywood's anti-Nazi films alongside Harry in 1941, noted Warner's courage in the early days of cinema. "He knew that the motion picture had incalculable potential," said Balaban. "At the moment when Vitaphone appeared, permitting the silent film to find a voice, he lent courage and vision to the project and the motion picture surged forward."

Spyros Skouras, president of 20th Century–Fox, praised Harry for shepherding cinema's transformation into a "great American institution" that worked as a "servant of mankind and a medium of entertainment and enlightenment." Columbia president Abe Schneider recalled Harry's courage and the "dignity of his life." Charles Einfeld, vice president of 20th Century–Fox, said that although Harry's passing left the entire industry "shaken," it would move forward thanks to Warner's "heritage of wisdom and courage that will [continue as a] source of perpetual inspiration." In a business where enemies were made daily, Harry managed to make many friends.

Rea Warner lived until 1970, when she passed of colon cancer. After Harry's death she moved into a condominium near Beverly Hills. Rea continued to attend social events, and she especially enjoyed Dodgers baseball. One of her primary activities was working with the Los Angeles Jewish Home for the Aged, where she had served in key roles for three decades and was still a trustee and chair of hostesses for major events when she died. Rea had first been recruited by Ida Mayer Cummings, sister of Louis B. Mayer.[21] Rabbi Magnin conducted Rea's funeral from the Wilshire Boulevard Temple and Home of Peace Memorial Park.

While the rest of the family was in mourning for Harry, Jack Warner was living large in France. The gambling and drinking caught up with him in early August when he was driving home from an all-night gambling binge. On a road between Cannes and Nice, Jack crashed into a coal truck and was thrown out of his Alfa-Romeo, cracking his skull and fracturing several ribs. Luckily, witnesses took him to a nearby hospital in Cannes. Early press accounts downplayed the severity of the accident, but Jack spent several weeks in the hospital, and speech and movement were difficult. Doctors were concerned when there was minimal improvement over the first week, but Jack eventually recovered enough to receive outpatient care closer to his villa. Warner did not return to the United States until the end of November. His sister Sadie was so angry at him that she promised to tell Jack the car wreck had been God's punishment.

Warner Bros. employee Johnny O'Steen believed Jack survived the accident only because he refused to let anyone else take over his empire. O'Steen understood all the gripes against Jack but wrote in his unpublished memoir about the man's human side. One day, recalled O'Steen, Warner heard that a man who worked in the shoe parlor on the lot was in the hospital and could not afford to pay, so Jack covered the bills himself. Jack also kept many of the studio's first employees on the payroll throughout their later years. There were many sides to Jack Warner. Now sixty-six years old, he was atop the Warner Bros. pedestal, and it was up to him to call the shots.

Jack's desire to live like a king, focusing on riches and excess, was affecting his marriage. He and Ann had grown apart, and according to some sources, Ann was seeing an air force veteran named Patrick Foulk. Jack, of course, also had a mistress ensconced at the Beverly Carlton Hotel. The affair was facilitated by a man named Richard Gully—sometimes billed as Jack Warner's pimp. Gully had served in World War II making training films for Hal Roach Studios. After the war, Jack hired him as a special assistant. Gully had a way of inserting himself into the inner circles of Hollywood. A suave and cultured man, Gully seemingly knew everyone, including gangster Bugsy Siegel, studio boss Louis B. Mayer, and actress Grace Kelly. Gully also helped out on the set whenever special assistance was needed. For example, Warner sent Gully to the *Giant* set when they were shooting in Texas, where Gully "struggled valiantly to curb Rock Hudson's randy adventures with the neighborhood cowboys."[22] Gully was also the man at Warner Bros. who looked after the young stars and starlets, facilitating or masking their relationships. Some called him Cupid, but a more accurate term was "fixer." Richard Gully likely took over many of the roles previously performed by Blayney Matthews. Harry hated that Jack put Gully on the Warner Bros. payroll, but he lived with it. Perhaps Harry did not fully appreciate Gully's "fixer" status, which was an essential role at every studio during Hollywood's golden age.

Gully's thick Rolodex and English charm meant that he was liked and admired everywhere, and he was trusted by powerful people in high places. Gully was, in many ways, Jack and Ann's guide to living like royalty, but Ann eventually tired of that life. Jack took Gully everywhere with him, but sometimes he sent Gully with Ann to monitor her spending. According to Gully, in 1958 "Ann fired me, out of aggravation. She was sick of Jack having a mistress, and the three of us having more fun than she. She couldn't fire her husband, so she fired me." On a couple of occasions, Ann and Gully came close to having an affair themselves but backed off—not that Jack deserved the respect. Gully knew exactly what Jack was: "A playboy. He lived like royalty and thought in terms of royalty."[23] By this time in his life, Jack had few real friends, and it was very lonely at the top.

Back at the studio, Jack's old friends distanced themselves from him. Vincent Sherman, one of the most reliable directors on the lot, became despondent when Jack refused to help him during the HUAC years. "I felt that in that time when I couldn't work he could have helped me, but he didn't; even after I was supposed to have been cleared."[24] The two men later met in London and reconciled, and Warner invited Sherman to come back to the studio. Warner set up a meeting for Sherman with studio executive Steve Trilling. Although the salary Sherman was offered was not great, there would be a bonus after the first film was completed. Sherman accepted.

Others, such as *The Spirit of St. Louis* scribe Wendell Mayes, remembered Jack quite simply. "If you ask me what kind of person Jack Warner was," Mayes told an interviewer, "my answer will be a cliché: he was a showman. Zanuck was a showman. Harry Cohn was a showman. All these people were showmen, and that's the only way to describe them. They were in business from the time they were sixteen years old; they grew up in it, and they had the feel and scent of show business about them, which doesn't exist now." Mayes understood that, despite all his faults, Jack Warner had a great talent for choosing movie material. "Jack Warner would make a decision about a piece of material, not because the studio would make a lot of money, but because he liked it as a story," Mayes continued. "If you look at the studio's

Jack Warner looking
confident about his future.

record of motion pictures, it's a fascinating record. And Jack Warner was the
person to say yes to all of them." Mayes was right; Jack deserves credit for
the many great and even courageous films he green-lit. Though Jack could
be tough, if not outright crude, when dealing with his employees, Mayes
remembered that the mogul was kind to him as a young writer. "You went
and sat in his office. He had read the script, and he had notes in the margin
of his copy for you. He told you what he liked and he didn't like. Look, Jack
was a very astute, hard-nosed businessman," said Mayes. "A lot of people
who didn't like Jack Warner were the people who didn't get what they wanted
from Jack Warner."[25]

　　While shareholders were elated in early 1959 when Warner Bros. stock
soared to record highs, Jack Warner Jr. found himself the target of his father's
wrath. The relationship between them had always been turbulent. Despite
having a wonderful example of familial support growing up, Jack did not
know how to be a father or how to treat his family. He continued to push

END OF THE STUDIO, END OF THE FAMILY

his son away. Maybe Jack was offended that Jack Jr. actually cared for the rest of the Warner family. It did not help that there was no love lost between Ann and her stepson. Jack Jr.'s support for Harry in the end may have been too much for Jack. Now, with Jack ruling the kingdom, the Warner Bros. president was out for blood.

An argument broke out between Jack and his son in January 1959. The dispute was so severe that the *Los Angeles Times* ran the story on the front page: "Studio Bars Young Jack Warner as Family Feud Breaks into Open." Jack Jr. was serving as vice president of commercial and industrial films, in addition to filling multiple roles related to the studio's investment in television production. Rumors circulated that Jack Jr. had been physically thrown off the lot. It was true, up to a point, as the studio cops always felt bad whenever they were ordered to remove Jack's son. Usually, Jack Jr. would willingly leave with the officers and go across the street for coffee and commiseration. This time, Jack Jr. told his side of the story to the press: "I went out to the studio this morning just like a normal business day and was denied admittance to my office." Custodians were removing Jack Jr.'s name from his office door. "I have practically grown up in this studio," he said. "I have worked here almost all of my life."[26]

The battles were rarely about business. What irked Jack Jr. most was that his father regularly lampooned the rest of the family in front of employees. The attacks against Harry were one thing when the elder Warner had been alive to defend himself or willingly ignore the barbs, but now that Harry was gone, the jokes felt outright cruel. Jack Jr. got fed up and confronted his father, and Jack threw his son off the lot. When this happened while Harry was still alive, he would tell Jack to bring Jack Jr. back or pack his own bags as well. But now Jack ruled with an angry iron fist. "Power corrupts. Absolute power corrupts absolutely," Jack Jr. later mused. "I always think of my father when I hear that. He was the man who fights to get up the trail to the mountaintop and when he gets there [he] rolls rocks down the trail to keep other people from joining him."[27] Harry, Sam, and Albert had always been confident enough to share their success with others. Jack, in contrast, always feared losing his place and would do anything and everything to exclude others—even his own family. Jack's old joke to Einstein about never hiring a relative was sadly prophetic for a man who refused to trust those closest to him.

In another strange twist of fate, amidst Jack's family feud, the Los Angeles City Council declared February 22–29 "Jack L. Warner Week." Councilmen

Jack Warner with his Irving Thalberg Award.

Harold A. Henry and Earl D. Baker submitted and seconded the motion, respectively, and it was quickly approved. The resolution described Jack as "a man whose record of accomplishment will stand as a major force in the progress and power of the screen."[28] As one of the last of the founding moguls, Jack received award after award, and he loved accepting them. With his brothers out of the picture, Jack reached a new level of self-centeredness.

In March, Jack received the vaunted Irving Thalberg Award from the Motion Picture Academy. Named after the late boy-genius producer, the honorary award was presented in recognition of recent years of service (today, it is awarded for lifetime achievement in the motion picture industry). The inaugural winner was Darryl F. Zanuck, followed by David O. Selznick and Walt Disney. According to biographer Bob Thomas, Jack "had long grumbled that the Academy had given the Thalberg Award twice to Hal Wallis and three times to Darryl Zanuck, but had never bestowed the honor to the man who hired them both."[29] That year, the Oscars were hosted by popular slapstick comedian Jerry Lewis. The Thalberg Award was presented by its previous recipient, Buddy Adler, who had recently replaced Zanuck as head of 20th Century–Fox. Jack accepted graciously, spoke warmly of his memories of Irving Thalberg, and walked offstage.

Toward the end of 1959 Jack lost another friend with the passing of Errol Flynn. Jack had recently brought the struggling actor back to Warner Bros. to play his idol, John Barrymore, in a film aptly titled *Too Much, Too Soon* (1958). Flynn was eternally grateful for Warner's willingness to give him a chance when much of Hollywood had looked the other way. Jack wrote in his autobiography about Flynn's concerning gray appearance, as well as his constant struggle to remember his lines. The film's title "should have been carved on a tombstone at the time," Jack noted, "for he was one of the living dead."[30] Hollywood's reaction to Flynn's death was mixed. Like Jack, Flynn had lived a life of self-inflicted isolation, and his reputation had been tarnished by his constant womanizing. Jack likely felt a kinship with Flynn because they shared a similar loneliness. Jack's eulogy described the star as "a man who laughed at himself, but never at acting, or his audience." Flynn had lived a life of excitement, some of which backfired, but through it all, the actor "was a warm and generous human being."[31] Pallbearers included Jack Oakie, Mickey Rooney, and Raoul Walsh. Jack claimed the bronze casket was lined with bourbon bottles—difficult to validate, but possibly true. One memory that Jack shared, corroborated by Johnny O'Steen, who was also in attendance, was that someone jokingly asked lawyer Jerry Geisler if he could get Flynn out of his current predicament. Naturally, Jack later took credit for the line (though it sounds like something he would have said).

By the end of the year, Jack was focused on hosting three hundred people at a reception for Vice President Richard Nixon. The event was held in the Nordic Room at the Beverly Hilton. Nixon spent the day golfing at the Bel

Air Country Club with actors George Murphy and Adolphe Menjou before attending the gala. Political organizing, previously Harry's forte, became an increasing interest of Jack's throughout the 1960s. With Albert in retirement, Jack could finally be *the* Warner brother. Powerful people responded to his name, but a new generation of filmmakers, producers, and agents was waiting in the wings to push the Warner Bros. president out to pasture.

9

A New Hollywood Rises
1960-1978

Jack knew his day was coming. Most of his contemporaries were gone. He had spoken with Louis B. Mayer the day he was pushed out of MGM, and Mayer had apparently spilled all the secrets that sent him to the grave shortly thereafter. Warner kept Mayer's secrets. "As I run through my engagement calendar these days, it seems to me that more and more I am becoming one of the principal players in a scary game of musical chairs. Slow music and funeral-parlor chairs. It is getting to the point where I am having to run like hell to avoid being on a bier instead of grabbing a spectator's chair." In his 1964 memoir, Jack listed many people he respected who had already passed, including Al Jolson, Dick Powell, Humphrey Bogart, John Garfield, Michael Curtiz, Marion Davies, William Randolph Hearst, Franklin D. Roosevelt, and Joseph Schenck. Warner still vividly remembered "our banking friend Motley Flint, without whose confidence there would have been no Warner Brothers." Flint, who was shot and killed in a courtroom many years ago, "never saw the full growth of the motion picture empire his loans had built."[1] Jack was one of the last men standing.

By 1960, the Warner Bros. lot was full of new stars. A young James Garner remembered Jack's short fuse and described him as "crude, rude, and over-bearing." One day, the studio president shouted, "I never want to see that man on the lot again . . . until we need him!" Perhaps Warner was hard on talent because he was afraid of actors, Garner posited. "I think Errol Flynn picked him up once and shook him. Threatened to throw him out the window. . . . I think Warner thought I was the same kind of guy who would pick him up and shake him . . . and he could have been right." The memories were not all bad, however. For instance, Garner recalled that Jack once replaced a director for him, for the film *Cash McCall* (1960) with Natalie Wood. "Warner was great in that respect. He could make a decision like that," said Garner, snapping

Jack Warner and Natalie Wood during *Cash McCall*.

his fingers. "I would almost rather deal with the mogul than the committee. Anything run by a committee is going to get screwed up, no doubt about it."[2]

Hollywood was moving into an era where more money was spent on fewer productions, and the studio's output was only a fraction of what it used to be, with fewer than twenty films per year. Warner Bros. continued Hollywood's trend of big productions with Fred Zinnemann's *The Sundowners* (1960), starring Deborah Kerr and Robert Mitchum. John Ford put actor Woody Strode front and center in *Sergeant Rutledge* (1960), a powerful western that tackled racial prejudice in a story about a guilty white man who accuses an innocent Black man (played by Strode) of rape and murder. Warner Bros. also released big-budget fun in the Rat Pack caper *Ocean's Eleven* (1960). William Inge won an Oscar for Best Original Screenplay for his work on the romantic melodrama *Splendor in the Grass* (1961), starring Warren Beatty and Natalie Wood. Jack Warner continued to produce a long list of adaptations of popular novels and plays: *The Bramble Bush* (1960), *Tall Story* (1960), *Dark at the Top of the Stairs* (1960), *Parrish* (1961), *A Majority of One* (1961), *Fanny* (1961), *The Sins of Rachel Cade* (1961), *The Chapman Report* (1962), *The Music Man* (1962), *Gypsy* (1962), *PT 109* (1963), *Act One* (1963), *Critic's Choice* (1963), *Spencer's Mountain* (1963), *Youngblood Hawke* (1964), *My Fair Lady* (1964), and *Who's Afraid of Virginia Woolf?* (1966).

Jack's Politicking

In the 1960 presidential election, Jack Warner supported Republicans Richard Nixon and Henry Cabot Lodge over popular Democrats John F. Kennedy and Lyndon B. Johnson. Trying to muster the political confidence of his late brother Harry, Jack took out ad space in the *Los Angeles Times* and wrote a lengthy statement in support of Nixon and Lodge. It read in full:

> An OPEN LETTER:
> This is an open letter to the voters of both parties . . . and an expression of the concern felt by almost everyone for the progress and prosperity of our country.
> As a citizen may I add one more voice in urging you to VOTE. As an American, concerned as we all are, with the problems confronting the nation and the world, may I urge you to vote for NIXON and LODGE.
> No Election has ever been so important, no time so critical. Your individual vote has never been so vital. Your lives, your continuing liberty, your very future will be affected by the vote you cast.
> In the dangerous days and months ahead the nation needs to be led with experience, wisdom and integrity. The nation needs to be strong. It needs NIXON and LODGE.
> In the interest of a sure and stable economy that will continue to provide opportunity for all Americans . . . as the best assurance of continuing *peace* in an explosive world . . . vote for NIXON and LODGE.
> With an awareness of the dangers of possible inflation, and its tragic shrinkage of fixed income, savings and pensions if the nation is not wisely led . . . with concern for the future of your children and mine . . . and their children . . . and with a prayer that the opportunity each individual has today will also be

available to them . . . I urge you in the strongest possible manner
to cast your vote on Tuesday for NIXON and LODGE.

As individuals and as a team, Richard Nixon and Henry Cabot
Lodge represent the experienced, trained, and tested leadership so
vital to our national *safety.*

They are men of integrity, courage and ability who have proved
their leadership at the highest national and international levels.
They are the right leaders at the hour most needed. They have
fought the international conspiracy of communism from the
streets of Moscow to the Halls of the United Nations.

Richard Nixon and Henry Cabot Lodge believe in the strength,
honor and future of the United States of America. They have the
qualifications and the will to continue American leadership based
on moral strength, military might and unshakable faith in our
national destiny.

Jack L. Warner[3]

Jack received many letters of support but an equal number of negative comments. Some questioned whether Warner Bros. had paid for the ad, which
could irk stockholders. Several concerned citizens sent the open letter back
to Jack and included their written feedback. One suggested that Jack should
"shove this up your ass!" Similarly, someone else suggested that Warner wipe
his ass with it. After Kennedy's victory, one reader sent the ad back with a
note that reminded Jack, "the better one won." Another colorful response
suggested that Jack "go paddle your own canoe." Yet another complained that
Republicans had done nothing for Jews, so Jack should not support them.
Jack's political shift was in line with many of the old Hollywood players, who
were still feeling the effects of the HUAC years. Warner supported outgoing
president Dwight D. Eisenhower and hosted a "Dinner with Ike" event in early
1960. Jack also got behind Thomas Kuchel for the California Senate. Kuchel
was gearing up for his run at civil rights legislation, which he cosponsored in
1964. Warner was often tapped for star-studded fund-raisers for the Republican National Committee, which was nearly out of cash, according to Kuchel.

Warner hosted a "Road to Victory" dinner in honor of Richard Nixon
in May 1961. The event was arranged by the United Republican Finance
Entertainment Committee, which was cochaired by Jack Warner, Walt Disney,
and George Murphy. In the coming years, Jack also served on the Nixon

for Governor Finance Committee with Desi Arnaz, Gene Autry (who later backed out, saying he preferred to remain neutral), Roy and Walt Disney, Samuel Goldwyn, Bob Hope, Dick Powell, James Stewart, Ira Gershwin, Harold Lloyd, Alfred Hitchcock, and John Payne. By the end of 1961, Jack Warner had changed his mind about JFK. He had long admired Kennedy's speeches, and when the newly elected president was in Los Angeles, Jack made sure to get himself a table at the event. When the two met, Jack was introduced as the man who had taken out that lengthy pro-Nixon ad in the *Los Angeles Times,* but Kennedy was gracious. The entertainer in Warner appreciated Kennedy's charisma and contagious energy. The president had recently traveled to Latin America on a goodwill mission to help the region achieve progress and stability through land programs. Warner sent Kennedy a telegram on December 18 stating, "Your courageous visit to Caracas and Bogota and your forthright speeches had the positive effect of building solid relations in this hemisphere for many years. With Mrs. Kennedy you have shown the peoples of these lands the proper way to enhance their freedom for centuries to come. In addition, you have accomplished remarkable results for your own way of life."[4] The president responded briefly and in kind, as he would to all such correspondence from Jack.

After years of rolling his eyes at the thought of producing programs for television, if only because Harry had seen television as essential to the future of entertainment, Jack publicly endorsed the medium. Reading a statement to the press in June 1961, Warner stated that film and television should be "equal partners." The *Hollywood Reporter* noted that Warner was uncharacteristically serious during his address. "Our talents, our production resources are interchangeable," Warner stated. "We are one studio devoted to the one purpose of reaching the largest possible audience with the best possible film entertainment."[5] Warner introduced longtime studio employee William T. Orr as head of theatrical and TV production, with many of the usual suspects, such as Steve Trilling and Max Bercutt, as part of the team. The reporters were treated to a screening of *Fanny* (1961), followed by an interview with director and playwright Joshua Logan. The previous evening, the Delmer Daves–directed melodrama *Susan Slade* (1961) had been screened for the press in the Warner Bros. commissary. Jack knew how to wow the media, especially the out-of-towners who were easily wooed with special VIP access.

Warner Bros. continued to work with the US government to make short films, mostly in the form of "readiness narratives," in the early 1960s. One,

A Force in Readiness (1961), was narrated by television star and producer Jack Webb (who took over as head of Warner Bros. television in 1963). The twenty-six-minute film details the training and evolution of the US Marine Corps, showcasing the latest artillery and air and sea machinery. Vice President Johnson sent a telegram to Jack Warner on February 1, 1962, thanking him for his studio's work on the film. Johnson wrote, "The picture serves the splendid purpose of reassuring our American people and properly presenting the power for peace that is the Navy and Marine Corps. I would like to express my appreciation for your contribution to the picture and your constant readiness to participate in any activity that contributes to the good of the Nation."[6] Warner also continued his philanthropic efforts, giving to causes big (United Jewish Fund) and small (Junior Tennis League of Southern California).

A new decade also meant a new mistress for Jack. The little-known actress Jacquelyn Park, known as Jackie to her friends, is the best insight we have into Jack's later years. Jackie had dated Ronald Reagan and Cary Grant before getting a jump on the swinging 1960s when she met Jack Warner. After the two had been seeing each other for some time, the still-married Warner demanded that their relationship be exclusive. "Don't fuck around with love," he told Jackie.[7] She went along with it because Jack took care of her: an apartment in Sunset Towers and a $350 per week allowance. Whenever Jackie showed an interest in going to art school, Jack would respond by saying something like, "That's a waste of time, go work for the Red Cross."[8] Of course, Jack was cut from a different cloth. His generation had invented an industry, and there was no school for what he and his brothers did.

Old Jack, New Hollywood

Production numbers were down but profits were high, so the time was right to invest in a gripping thriller. After first declining to make the film, Warner Bros. released the infamous *What Ever Happened to Baby Jane?* (1962), a story about a deep family rift (a topic the studio president could relate to). Jack hosted a welcome-back lunch for stars Bette Davis and Joan Crawford, held in the studio's trophy room. Davis told the crowd of press and studio onlookers, "Oh, I've had my differences with Papa Jack. But he is the man who gave me my start in pictures, and I will be forever grateful to him." Crawford looked at Jack and said, "I can't exactly call you my father, Mr. Warner, because I give

Bette Davis, Jack Warner, and Joan Crawford. (Author's personal collection)

that credit to the late Louis B. Mayer. But you are my second father." Jack was elated at the recognition. The two legendary actresses spoke excitedly about the script, which told the story of a lifelong rift between two aged child stars. "This is wonderful for me," said Crawford. "I usually play the bitches. Now I can sit back in my wheelchair and watch Bette do it."[9]

The film's reception was mixed, but it made more than $9 million on a budget of less than $1 million and became a cultural milestone. Like Gloria Swanson's role as aging actress Norma Desmond in *Sunset Boulevard* (1950), *What Ever Happened to Baby Jane?* proved, once again, that older actresses could command the big screen and give powerful performances. Davis's Jane Hudson became one the most haunting roles of the decade, and her self-described look as "Mary Pickford in decay" was impossible to forget.[10] The film won the Oscar for Best Costume Design. The lasting and potentially negative impact of youthful celebrity became part of the cultural fabric thanks to Davis's Jane and Joan Crawford as her disabled sister Blanche. (The infamous scene of Jane kicking Blanche on the floor was removed in Great Britain and Australia.) Davis and Crawford revitalized their careers in memorable horror-of-personality films (popularized at Warner Bros. with *The Bad Seed*). Davis starred in *Dead Ringer* (1964) at Warner Bros. and *Hush . . . Hush, Sweet Charlotte* (1964) for 20th Century–Fox, while Crawford starred in William Castle Productions' *Strait-Jacket* (1964) and *I Saw What You Did* (1965). *What Ever Happened to Baby Jane?* was also significant because it was the first coproduction between Warner Bros. and Seven Arts. Seven Arts was testing the waters around Hollywood, and soon it would target Warner Bros. as its next major investment.

Seven Arts was founded by independent producers Ray Stark, Eliot Hyman, and Norman Katz. The company had partnered with Paramount Pictures (*Thunder under the Sun*, 1959), United Artists (*West Side Story*, 1961), MGM (*Lolita*, 1962), and 20th Century–Fox (*Gigot*, 1962), and it would later coproduce with Hammer Films (*Dracula: Prince of Darkness*, 1966). Seven Arts produced some of the most famous Warner Bros. films from the late 1960s, including *Bonnie and Clyde* (1967), *Wait until Dark* (1967), *Cool Hand Luke* (1968), *Bullitt* (1968), and *The Wild Bunch* (1969).

Because war films were still popular, Warner Bros. released *Merrill's Marauders* in 1962, but Jack had a pet project that he was eager to get rolling. He wrote to JFK on March 7, 1961, inquiring about the president's World War II experiences on PT 109.[11] Kennedy was commanding the torpedo boat on a rescue mission when it collided with a Japanese destroyer and sank. Kennedy led the crew several miles through the ocean to an island, where they embarked on their own journey of survival. The book, *PT 109: John F. Kennedy*, had just been released by Washington correspondent Robert J. Donavan, and Warner wanted to purchase the film rights. Warner biographer Bob Thomas tells a slightly different story, claiming that the president's father and former RKO owner Joseph P. Kennedy called Jack to suggest that he produce the film. Perhaps Warner wrote to the president after speaking to his father. In any case, JFK was excited to see the film made and wanted some of the proceeds to go to the surviving crew. *PT 109* was the first film about a sitting president.

By this point, there was regular communication between Warner and Kennedy. Warner's girlfriend Jackie remembered that when one of the Kennedys called, they identified themselves as "code K," in case there were reporters around. In August 1962 a call came into the house, and Jackie picked up one line as Jack picked up another. "It's code K, Marilyn [Monroe] is dead," said the caller.[12] The next day the papers were full of news about the iconic actress's death. There is an old tradition in Hollywood that when a star is in trouble, one calls the studio boss before the police. Monroe had been working with 20th Century–Fox before being fired from the production of *Something's Got to Give*. The studio was also going through a leadership change at the time. So it is possible that because the Kennedys were working with Warner Bros. on *PT 109*, they called Jack to seek advice about handling the publicity surrounding Monroe's death, given her connections to the president.

The production of *PT 109* was helmed by Bryan Foy, who had been with Warner since the early days and produced the studio's first all-talking picture. Naturally, the president wanted full approval of the actor that would play him in the film. Having recently watched *Splendor in the Grass*, Kennedy wanted Warren Beatty to star, but Beatty declined the role because he thought the script was not very good. Jack Warner was incensed and told Beatty he would never work in Hollywood again. Peter Fonda was tested for the role, but the part eventually went to Cliff Robertson. After watching numerous auditions, Kennedy felt Robertson best represented him, despite the minimal physical resemblance.

Kennedy also wanted a top director. Names like John Huston, Fred Zinnemann, and George Stevens were thrown around. Jack Warner wanted Raoul Walsh, who had a long track record of success with the studio. Kennedy considered Walsh until he screened *Marines, Let's Go!* (20th Century–Fox, 1961). Before it was over, Kennedy had the projectionist stop the film. He stood up and said, "Tell Jack Warner to go fuck himself."[13] Warner Bros. ultimately hired Lewis Milestone, director of the World War I classic *All Quiet on the Western Front* (1930). Milestone's name carried weight, but the director was a pain to work with and was eventually fired. Television director Leslie Martinson, currently directing episodes of *77 Sunset Strip* (1958–1964), was hired to finish the film. Ultimately, *PT 109* enjoyed meager success but underwhelmed the parties involved. The president appreciated Warner's effort, but Kennedy reportedly told Beatty, "You were right about that movie."[14] The movie opened in March 1963 and was taken out of circulation when Kennedy was assassinated in Dallas on November 22, 1963.

Warner's next investment was his biggest yet on a single property: more than $5 million. The film adaptation of *My Fair Lady* was a Warner Bros. picture in name, but it had everything in common with big-budget Arthur Freed–produced MGM musicals. The film cost $12 million, and Jack Warner produced it personally. His first casting picks were Cary Grant (Higgins), James Cagney (Doolittle), and Audrey Hepburn (Eliza). There was pressure to cast Julie Andrews, who had played Eliza onstage. Jack was open to the idea and offered Andrews a screen test, but she balked, expecting to get the role based on her stage experience. Warner argued that the studio needed to see how well she photographed onscreen. Andrews held her ground and let the part go. Audrey Hepburn got the role of Eliza, but she knew she had big shoes to fill.

Rex Harrison (who starred in the play) was cast as Higgins. In fact, Cary Grant (Jack's first choice) suggested that the film would not work without Harrison. Despite Grant's advice, Harrison got the role only because Warner could not entice Noel Coward, Michael Redgrave, or George Sanders. George Cukor, who had directed *A Star Is Born* for Warner Bros., was hired to direct. He was fresh off *The Chapman Report* (1962), about a doctor studying women's sexuality, ranging from nymphomania to frigidity—a film Jack Warner greatly enjoyed. *The Chapman Report* began as a project at 20th Century–Fox, where Jack's former production chief Darryl F. Zanuck was running the show from Europe. As a favor to his old friend, Warner agreed to distribute the film, with both studios sharing in the profits. *The Chapman Report* was just one example of Warner's involvement with socially liberal films even after his own politics had moved to the right.

Warner hosted a luncheon at the studio, catered by Dave Chasen, where the mogul introduced Hepburn, Harrison, Cukor, Sterling Holloway, Gladys Cooper, Cecil Beaton, Andre Previn, Hermes Pan, and Harry Stradling Sr. to the press. He spoke about being pressured to make the film in England and boasted, "We have the finest actors and technicians in the world and they're happier when they stay home." Warner also reminded the reporters that his studio had made "two successful sea pictures without going to sea. We built the ships on a sound stage and put them on rockers." "I abhor these ingrates," he continued, "who make their pile here, then make a couple of pictures abroad and start knocking the town where they made their name

Jack Warner, Audrey Hepburn, and Rex Harrison. (Author's personal collection)

and fortune." Hedda Hopper commended Warner in her column, writing, "If we had more like him, Hollywood would never have lost its magic."[15]

My Fair Lady would have lost some magic if Jack Warner had taken the role of Eliza's father himself. "Fortunately, Cukor talked him out of it," remembered Jack's daughter Barbara.[16] The film may have been personal to Jack, who could be seen as a version of Eliza Doolittle to Richard Gully's Higgins. Of course, Gully could never fully refine Jack. Warner may not have been as sophisticated as he thought, but *My Fair Lady* became one of the most consummate musicals ever made. During the reception to celebrate the opening of production, Warner spoke about the substantial cost, making a humorous comparison to 20th Century–Fox's recent budget overrun: "We're not going to be like *Cleopatra* (1963). We're gonna wear clothes in our picture."[17]

When *My Fair Lady* premiered at New York City's Criterion, Bosley Crowther wrote that Hepburn's "brilliance" as the "Cockney waif who is transformed by Prof. Henry Higgins into an elegant female façade . . . gives an extra touch of subtle magic and individuality to the film."[18] Multiple reviews

Jack Warner with his *My Fair Lady* crew.

in papers nationwide praised the film. *My Fair Lady* was nominated for twelve Oscars and won eight, including Best Picture. As veteran Hollywood journalist Bob Thomas wrote, "This time Jack Warner didn't need to rush to the stage to beat Hal Wallis. Warner was validated as producer."[19]

With so much investment tied up in *My Fair Lady*, the studio produced only about a dozen films in 1964—a far cry from the early days when production facilities pumped out eighty films a year. Other notable films in 1964 included the John Ford western *Cheyenne Autumn*; the male melodrama *Youngblood Hawke*, directed by Delmer Daves; *Dead Ringer*, a Bette Davis thriller directed by *Casablanca* star Paul Henreid; and *Sex and the Single Girl*, starring Tony Curtis, Natalie Wood, Henry Fonda, Lauren Bacall, and Mel Ferrer.

Another major shift in Warner Bros. leadership was the exit of Steve Trilling, who had been with the company since 1928. Over the years, Trilling had served as Warner's executive assistant and most recently as vice president of the company. The trade press reported that Trilling decided not to renew his contract to pursue the growing trend of independent filmmaking. Sadly, Trilling died shortly after leaving Warner Bros. The popular theory is that Trilling was fired while Jack was in France and then committed suicide, possibly because he had been pushed out of the studio.[20] What we can confirm is that Trilling had left the studio by February 11, 1964, as reported in *Variety*, and was dead by June 8, 1964, as reported in *Boxoffice*.[21] Jack Warner issued a statement in February after reluctantly accepting Trilling's resignation, lamenting "the studio's loss of his experience, judgement and executive knowhow."[22] With Trilling's departure and subsequent death, Warner's small inner circle got smaller.

One change that Warner welcomed was the new era of rule-breaking filmmakers who did not have to deal with the outdated censorship process that Jack derided as "hokey pokey."[23] This attitude served him well when he had to defend one of the studio's next films from the censors. The mid-1960s brought new faces to the Motion Picture Association of America, including Jack Valenti, who had a background in advertising, and Louis Nizer as legal counsel. Both men had been in JFK's inner circle.

As early as 1963, the Production Code Administration (PCA) told Jack Warner that it would not issue a seal to *Who's Afraid of Virginia Woolf?* Nizer met with Warner and his right-hand man, Ben Kalmenson, for three hours to discuss the difficulties of approving such a film. The script was full of foul language, blasphemy, and sexual innuendo, as well as scenes of seduction and infidelity, earning it a quick rejection. Even though the PCA was on its last legs, the office still reviewed every screenplay, and Ernest Lehman's script was cut to pieces, with phrases such as "screw," "goddamn," "angel tits," "son of a bitch," and "hump the hostess" earmarked for removal.

Valenti and Nizer were understandably frustrated to be faced with such a big challenge so early in their new roles. Jack Vizzard of the censorship office recalled that Valenti initially wanted to have it out with Jack Warner, assuming that such a conflict would be winnable. Both men underestimated Warner's ability to defend a film. He had been facing censor pushback for decades and knew there was always a way around a controversy. By the end of the conversation, the issue for Nizer and Valenti was not the dialogue in this film but the regulations that had been established in 1930 and enforced since 1934.

A black comedy about a deteriorating marriage, *Who's Afraid of Virginia Woolf?* was directed by Mike Nichols and starred Elizabeth Taylor and Richard Burton. The film was full of the stage production's harsh language, which made even the most seasoned theatergoers shift uncomfortably in their seats. Nichols did not film alternative scenes, which was common practice when shooting a controversial film. Studios generally liked to have extra scenes on hand in case they needed to negotiate with the censors. Because Nichols had no scenes he could substitute, the studio had no choice but to release the movie as filmed. What ultimately saved the film was the Catholic Legion of Decency, now known as the National Catholic Office for Motion Pictures.

One might have expected *Who's Afraid of Virginia Woolf?* to be condemned by the former Legion of Decency. When Jack Warner confirmed that the film would be released for adults only, meaning that nobody under the age of eighteen would be admitted, the National Catholic Office for Motion Pictures gave the film a rating of A-IV (for adults with reservations). Nichols biographer Mark Harris contributed another story to the mythos surrounding the film. According to Harris, Nichols asked Jaqueline Kennedy to attend the Catholic group's screening of *Who's Afraid of Virginia Woolf?* With Kennedy's approval, the film's rating was changed from "condemned" to "A-IV."[24]

The adults-only designation was initially approved as a special case for an important film. Valenti rightly predicted that the film's dialogue would "hit the American public like an angry fist."[25] Jack Warner told *Variety* about his support for the adults-only label, saying, "It has always been my opinion that motion pictures should be as varied as possible. I don't believe a controversial, mature subject should be watered down so that it is palatable for children."[26] Warner assured the industry that great care had been taken to remain faithful to Edward Albee's play and to produce a film of great importance to adult audiences. *Who's Afraid of Virginia Woolf?* was a huge success, despite its potentially offensive language, and it ushered in the new era of film standards. Valenti later referred to Jack Warner as "the father of the ratings system" because of his defense of the film.[27] *Who's Afraid of Virginia Woolf?* was nominated for nearly every Oscar, landing wins for Elizabeth Taylor (Best Actress) and Sandy Dennis (Best Supporting Actress), as well as Oscars for Best Art Direction, Costume Design, and Cinematography.

Valenti used the success of *Who's Afraid of Virginia Woolf?* as justification for the addition of a new category to the Production Code: "suggested for mature audiences." Two years later, in 1968, a new ratings system was implemented: G for general audiences, M for mature audiences, R for restricted (nobody under age sixteen admitted), and X for films that were too vulgar or sexual to be given a seal (i.e., pornography). Once again, Warner Bros. was at the center of progress and change.

By the end of 1966, Jack Warner reconsidered retirement. The studio was his life, but at seventy-four, the aging mogul could certainly do with fewer responsibilities. Just after Thanksgiving, the *Wall Street Journal* reported that Jack Warner was selling about 33 percent of his interest in Warner Bros. to

Warner Announces 38 Major Films In Various Stages Of Production

Hot 1966 Summer Line-up Includes
"Virginia Woolf," "Fine Madness," "Big Hand"

Warner

Jack still green-lighting projects.

Seven Arts Productions. The $32 million deal was set to be finalized in January, with a cash payout to Warner. Louis Nizer, Jack's attorney, told the press that "this transaction was in accordance with Mr. Warner's plan ultimately to diminish his responsibilities."[28] Jack's role was assumed by Ben Kalmenson, who had been lobbying for Warner to sell. Ann Warner had also pressed her husband to retire and get his estate in order. Unlike Harry, Jack was not one for personal planning. Although he no longer controlled the company he cofounded, Warner would continue to take an active role in certain productions. His greatest strength had always been as a production chief. However, the new generation did not have the same respect for Hollywood's founding fathers as previous generations had, despite their differences.

Jack's Last Stand

The most high-profile film of Jack's last years at the studio was *Bonnie and Clyde* (1967), a gangster film about the infamous bank-robbing Barrow gang that tore through the Midwest and Texas at the height of the Great Depression. Warren Beatty's career had stalled thanks to a series of poor project decisions, and he was trying to get Warner to finance the film, but Jack was still upset at Beatty's refusal to do *PT 109*. "He always hated me," Beatty told author Peter Biskind. "He said he was afraid to have a meeting with me alone because he thought that I would resort to some sort of physical violence."[29] It is unlikely that Warner was afraid of anyone in the film industry; more likely he did not want to deal with needy and demanding talent determined to produce their own pictures. Warner was increasingly irritated by the influx of agents and producer-actors trying to get more control and, annoyingly, more money from the studio. Jack was still throwing his name around, expecting it to squelch any debate, and he still used his longtime favorite way to assert power: pointing and asking, "Whose name do you see on that water tower?" Beatty had the best response to that question, which usually ended the conversation: "Well, it's got your name, but it's got my initials."[30] Warner used the same routine with *Camelot* (1967) producer Joel Freeman.

When the filming for *Bonnie and Clyde* was completed in Texas, the editing was finished by Dede Allen, who is responsible for the film's iconic breakneck pace and jarring jump cuts. When Jack Warner saw the film, he was skeptical to say the least. He thought gangster films went out of style when Cagney stopped making them. Director Arthur Penn, Warren Beatty, and Bill Orr attended the screening at Warner's Beverly Hills home. "I'll tell you something right now," Warner told Penn. "If I have to go pee, the picture stinks." The film was more than two hours long, and Warner got up to relieve himself multiple times. When it was over, Warner asked, "What the fuck is this?" Orr noted that fifteen minutes would be cut from the film. "That's the longest two hours and ten minutes I ever spent," yelled Warner. "It's a three-piss picture!" Beatty tried to convince Warner that the film was an "homage" to Warner's old gangster films. Warner responded, "What the fuck's a homage?"[31] Because Jack did not like the film, it began with a limited release in the United States and Canada. Following favorable reviews (despite Bosley Crowther's infamous pan), *Bonnie and Clyde* went into wide release and became a major success for Warner Bros.

Biskind observed that *Bonnie and Clyde* marked "a shift in mass culture of tectonic proportions, away from the proper, morally and aesthetically conservative official culture of the Eisenhower era toward the anything-goes, let-it-all-hang-out counterculture of the 1960s."[32] While the cultural power of *Bonnie and Clyde* cannot be overstated, it is important to remember that Jack Warner set the stage for such films to be made when he found a way to get *Who's Afraid of Virginia Woolf?* released without changes. If some other actor had played Clyde, Warner might have enjoyed the film because Beatty was right: *Bonnie and Clyde* is, in part, an homage to Warner's classic gangster films. It pushed through the cracking boundaries of the 1960s just like Cagney and Robinson did with their Prohibition-era characters in the 1930s.

Jack Warner finally gave up his post as production boss in June 1967. The newspapers celebrated him, along with Zanuck, as one of the last moguls. Warner's job went to thirty-eight-year-old Kenneth Hyman, son of the

Albert Warner watching the construction of Mt. Sinai Hospital. (Author's personal collection)

chairman of the newly merged Warner–Seven Arts. Vincent Canby wrote in the *New York Times* that Warner "was feared, respected and, behind his back, lampooned." A Warner Bros. executive told Canby, "This morning, all the studio people loved Jack. After the news came out, they were saying Jack who?"[33] Joking aside, Warner continued to be a presence on the lot, serving as an adviser to Hyman. The former studio boss never lost his knack for awkward commentary. Journalist Charles Champlin related a story about Jack after visiting the lot: Warner entered the office, lit his cigar, and looked at two men in the room smoking cigarettes. "Cigarettes," Jack said. "Too effeminate for me. Too many dames smoking 'em these days."[34]

On November 26, 1967, not long after Jack went into semiretirement, his brother Albert passed away at age eighty-four at his Miami mansion. Abe, or Major, as many called him, was always happy to let his brothers take the spotlight. He did his job quietly, and he did it well. Despite his lack of interest in media coverage, Albert's death made headlines across the country. Many obituaries celebrated Albert and Bessie's philanthropy. The couple donated $1 million to Miami's Mt. Sinai Hospital, which Albert cofounded. The new four-story Albert and Bessie Warner Pavilion added 150 beds. The funeral, held at the Bethel Chapel of Temple Emanuel in New York City, did not get anywhere near the coverage of Harry's, and Albert would have been very happy about that. Jack managed to attend and even had some polite conversations with Jack Jr. Albert was buried in a mausoleum originally purchased by Harry and then gifted to his brother. The previous spouses of Albert and Bessie were laid to rest at the same cemetery, and the couple had made plans to be buried together. Bessie died due to complications of influenza in 1970.

Nonmedia conglomerates were taking over Hollywood. Gulf and Western took over Paramount (1966), while Transamerica acquired United Artists (1967). Steve Ross of Kinney National Service purchased Warner–Seven Arts in 1969. Kinney specialized in parking lots and funeral parlors, reminding us that, strangely enough, the Warner brothers organized some of their first screenings with chairs borrowed from a funeral parlor. Following the lead of Lew Wasserman, Ross aimed to purchase enough property to create a media conglomerate and acquired Ashley Famous Agency and DC Comics. Recognizing the value of Ted Ashley's experience in the entertainment industry, Ross named him chairman and CEO of Warner Bros. Champlin described the scene in the executive dining room on the Warner Bros. lot following Ross's acquisition: the "one long table over which Warner had presided for so many years in baronial style was dismantled, as if to symbolize a new day had begun."[35] Ross's entertainment investments continued into the 1990s when Warner Communications merged with Time to create Time Warner Inc.

Jack tried to maintain his jovial personality, but after selling the studio he became lonely. He and his wife were living more or less separate lives, although they traveled together when invited to the Nixon White House.

When Jack relinquished his power at the studio, he lost all personal connections. His weekend tennis parties were poorly attended, revealing that these so-called friends were just the usual Hollywood players looking for favors. Jack often joked that there was no room for friends when you were at the top because everybody wanted something from you. But Harry and Albert were perfect counterexamples.

In November 1969 the studio's new chairman Ted Ashley and his colleagues at Kinney National hosted a farewell dinner for Jack. The event began with a cocktail reception on Stage 7, which was still full of sets from *Camelot.* The party later moved to Stage 1, where there was ample room for the nearly one thousand guests under the red-dressed chandeliers. The black-tie dinner was a star-studded affair. Among those in attendance were Busby Berkeley, Ruby Keeler, Mae Clark, Billie Dove, Jack Oakie, Pat O'Brien, Barbara Stanwyck, Miriam Hopkins, Joan Blondell, Otto Kruger, and Dennis Morgan. When California governor Ronald Reagan looked over the well-dressed crowd, he remarked to Jack, "My God, dress extras! This must be costing you a fortune!"[36] Also in the room were Loretta Young, Jane Wyman, Chill Wills, Andy Devine, Tab Hunter, Rock Hudson, Tony Curtis, Marie Windsor, Joseph Cotten, and even Warren Beatty. Frank Sinatra, who had become friendly with Warner in recent years, was master of ceremonies. On the dais with Warner were Edward G. Robinson, Rosalind Russell, and Efrem Zimbalist Jr., who narrated a series of iconic scenes from Warner Bros. pictures. Among them were Dooley Wilson singing "As Time Goes By" from *Casablanca* and Judy Garland singing "The Man Who Got Away" from *A Star Is Born.*

Numerous guests took the floor throughout the evening. Ashley commented on rumors that he would break up the studio, saying, "I don't intend to preside over the dissolution of Warner Bros. or the diminution of this industry." Warner offered his usual brand of performance consisting of odd jokes and warm remembrances. He was honored because no other retiring mogul had been given such a gala send-off. Noting the changing of the guard with corporate-owned Hollywood, Edward G. Robinson sardonically asked, "Can you imagine going to a banquet to honor a conglomerate?"[37] Covering the event, *Variety*'s Thomas Pryor asked, "But has it ever happened that 963 persons turned out to honor a monarch who abdicated his kingdom and no longer has gifts to bestow?" Pryor saw this as Jack Warner's "last hurrah," as well as "a night of triumph unequalled in Hollywood history" that was "unlikely to have a sequel."[38]

Jack Warner had many faces, all of which Pryor summed up quite well in his *Variety* column: "the frustrated comedian, the stern taskmaster, the patient counselor during lulls in creative turmoil, the gambler on talents yet unproven, the autocrat of Burbank, the bluff, hearty good companion of night frolicking."[39] Warner's send-off was significant not only because he was the last Warner brother but also because he was the last man alive who had built one of Hollywood's first studios from the ground up. (Darryl Zanuck was still alive, but he had risen to prominence through Warner Bros.) The significance of the evening was not lost on anyone in the room, as evidenced by the long list of major stars who showed up.

After Warner Bros.

Jack was named a trustee of the University of Southern California, to which he eventually donated his personal papers. He received an award for his "outstanding contribution as a philanthropist and pioneer" from the Sunair Home for Asthmatic Children. The humanitarian award was presented at a star-studded gala at the Beverly Hilton. George Jessel served as toastmaster, giving the event the feel of a Friar's Club roast. The evening's sharpest barbs were reportedly unsuitable for print in the press. On the dais with Jack were Leonard Firestone, former California governor Pat Brown, and former senator George Murphy, who said it was "the first time I've ever spoken at an X-rated banquet."[40] George Burns, Mervyn LeRoy, and Ginger Rogers shared stories. Hal Wallis, Edward G. Robinson, and Gregory Peck also attended with their wives.

Still keeping one foot in the entertainment business, Warner rented a suite at 1900 Avenue of the Stars in Century City. Bill Schaefer and a handful of former Warner Bros. employees came along for the ride, including the studio barber. Warner's office was small, but it was decorated with an array of awards and images from his former studio's major films. Oscars for *The Life of Emile Zola*, *Casablanca*, and *My Fair Lady*, as well as *The Jazz Singer*'s special Oscar, were displayed alongside the Thalberg Award and every medal presented to Warner by heads of state over the years. His dark, polished desk was kept immaculate to highlight a sterling silver blotter set with JLW engravings.

"Warner sometimes misses the gigantic apparatus he had at his disposal in the old days," wrote Wayne Warga in the *Los Angeles Times* after visiting Jack's new office. Warner reflected about working on the Columbia lot: "Let

Jack Warner in his Century City office. (Author's personal collection)

me tell you it's an odd feeling making a film on Harry Cohn's old stomping ground. I wonder if the dressing rooms are still wired? No, no they couldn't be today." Warga described Warner twirling his pen and "sitting at his desk, the one-time potentate of a large kingdom trying to get accustomed to the idea that filmmaking as a physical kingdom is an anachronism and on the way to becoming an abstract." Warner maintained that he no longer missed the studio he had once presided over. He spoke of Bette Davis as being "a bit distraught for a while," referring to their long tiffs, but concluded that Davis was "the greatest lady ever to step in front of a camera." Warga found it "difficult to imagine Jack Warner in his bedecked office, conservative tailor-made suit with a French Legion of Honor in the lapel, as a child, bone-poor working for his immigrant merchant father in Youngstown. Yet it's true and there he is."[41]

Among the films Warner produced through his Century City office were *1776* (1972), a musical about the founding fathers, and *Dirty Little*

Jack Warner and part of his *1776* crew.

Jack Warner on the set of *1776*. (Author's personal collection)

Billy (1972), a retelling of Billy the Kid's early days. Both films were released through Columbia Pictures and did lackluster business. Jack was showing his age, such as being unable to remember the name of Peter Hunt, who had directed *1776* on Broadway and had been brought to Hollywood to direct the film. Warner decided to call him Roscoe, after silent film comedian Roscoe "Fatty" Arbuckle, a good friend of Jack's. The film had a tumultuous time in postproduction when Jack insisted on editing it himself. Rumor has it that Warner screened *1776* at the White House, and he and President Nixon decided to cut scenes with a liberal bent.

As production got under way at the Columbia studios, Jack strolled the lot as if it were his own—a hard habit to break after reigning over his own kingdom for so many decades. The former mogul walked into closed sets, ruining takes as he waltzed in to socialize. Studio security often included people who used to work for Jack, and they found it hard to forget the old man's former power. Signs of aging were apparent, though. Jack's eyesight was going. If there was something of interest in the trade press, Bill Schaefer would read it to him. Jack no longer drove himself to work. He hitched a ride with either Schaefer or his barber, Don Johnson.

Jack gave some short interviews, something he had proudly avoided during his long career. Jack's first and only appearance on TV was *The Merv Griffin Show*. Warner and Griffin, a former contract player for Warner Bros., reminisced about the good old days—stories of Flynn, Bogart, Davis, and Jolson and parties at Warner's home in Beverly Hills. The interview was awkward because Jack's goofy personality did not mesh well with the television interview format, even though he was always at his best when he spoke on the fly. At one point, Griffin asked Warner about the changing content in films. Jack went on a tirade about pinko commies, and the red-scared audience ate it up. *The Merv Griffin Show* would be Jack Warner's last interview.

Final Years

By 1973, Jack had slowed down considerably, although he still cracked stupid jokes and never took life too seriously. Bill Schaefer was alarmed one day when Warner arrived at the office slightly confused. Don Johnson picked him up for work one day and Jack thought they were in New York. On another day, on their way to the Columbia lot, Jack asked why they were not headed to Burbank. Jack had suffered a stroke and was forced to take a few months off. Jack's wife, who had been avoiding people, including Jack, for many years, rose to the occasion to nurse her dying husband. Ann made sure that Jack saw the right doctors and got the necessary care. Schaefer would tell Jack about the goings-on at the office and assure him that there was no need for him to go in. Jack's last years played out basically like this, with good days and bad, times of relatively good health followed by physical setbacks.

By the 1970s, historians and fans were taking a greater interest in Hollywood's golden age. Writers Kevin Brownlow, Patrick McGilligan, and Joseph McBride and filmmaker Peter Bogdanovich worked tirelessly to interview surviving members of the period. Warner Bros. experienced a resurgence in popularity as theaters around the country ran a "Salute to Warners," a ten-week, thirty-six-movie retrospective featuring titles such as *Little Caesar, I Am a Fugitive from the Chain Gang, Treasure of the Sierra Madre,* and *The Fountainhead.* Champlin acknowledged the cultural importance of so many Warner films, describing them as "the kinds of movies that if they hadn't been made, three generations of night club impressionists would have died for lack of material." Impressions of Cagney, Robinson, Bogart, and Davis were commonplace in stand-up routines. Champlin reminded readers that the great Hal Wallis had produced twenty-three of the thirty-six films in the retrospective. Wallis told Champlin, "You can call them robber barons, and maybe they were, but Warner and Cohn and Mayer were picture-makers first, last, and always. They knew their stuff."[42]

In 1978 Jack went to Scripps Clinic, where doctors worked to repair damage done by a stroke. Louis Rosner, Jack's physician at Cedars-Sinai Hospital, said the aging studio titan's primary struggle "involved a loss of visual recognition—a condition called cortical blindness, in which the person can see but can't make sense out of what he's seeing." Rosner recalled Ann's dedication to her husband's care. She had begun to delve into various religions, looking for answers. One day, Ann came into the office boasting about a new savior in the form of a Tibetan healer; she also learned about Buddhism and Hinduism. When Rosner asked Ann what religion she practiced primarily, she answered playfully, "Darling, I'm anything you want me to be."[43] But she was sensitive to other people's problems. When she became aware of tensions in the doctor's marriage, Ann encouraged Larraine Rosner to move out of her family home and into the Warners' Beverly Hills mansion, giving the couple a respite in their relationship and helping to save the marriage. She also gained a friend and confidante, which she badly needed.

When Jack returned home, he was weak and mostly blind. Ann helped him walk around the pool and encouraged him to take physical therapy, but Jack was giving up. His few visitors were taken aback by the white and nearly lifeless face—a stark contrast to the man who had always been well-manicured, tan, and smiling. By August, Jack could no longer be cared for at home and was transferred to Cedars-Sinai Hospital. Ann was on the phone with Larraine Rosner when Jack had his final seizure. He was eighty-six when he passed, ultimately dying of inflammation of the heart. The last of Hollywood's founding fathers was gone.

Ann insisted on a small funeral, likely because of her own fear of public gatherings (she had rarely been seen in public in more than two decades). Max Bercutt, former Warner Bros. publicity chief, pushed for a big Hollywood funeral. It is safe to assume that Jack would have loved a massive production with his coffin flanked by famous faces. Instead, there was a small gathering presided over by Rabbi Magnin at the Wilshire Boulevard Temple. The funeral had a strict no-photo policy. Those invited to attend were Barbara Warner, Max Bercutt, Cy Howard, Bill and Joy Orr, Bill Schaefer, Don Johnson, and Jack Warner Jr. The funeral was the first time Jack Jr. had seen Ann since his father's car accident. Jack and Ann's daughter Barbara always thought her mother's anger at Jack Jr. was unjustified. He had often tried to build a bridge to his father and Ann, but to no avail. Jack was laid to rest not at the Warner family mausoleum at the Home of Peace Cemetery but about fifty yards away. Ann would later join her husband there, eternally estranged from the family.

Despite the small funeral, news of the death of Jack Warner spread through the national press like wildfire. "The Passing of an Era," read the *Los Angeles Times*.[44] "Jack L. Warner's Death Closes out Pioneer Clan of Talkies," read *Variety*.[45] Every obituary regaled readers with the Warners' storied history of immigrating from Poland in search of a better life. The *Globe and Mail* in Toronto, where Jack was born, wrote that the mogul was "known for foresight and bad jokes."[46] Many obituaries gave Jack primary credit for bringing sound to the big screen, forgetting (or never knowing) that the studio's transition to sound was mostly the work of Sam and Harry Warner. With both Sam and Harry long gone, journalists considered Jack Warner *the* Warner brother—something Jack, no doubt, appreciated.

One remembrance was published by J. Wallace Bastian, whose father had been hired as a sound technician at Warner Bros. in 1929. Bastian, who was sixteen years old at the time, recalled seeing the "Hollywoodland" sign from the window of their room at the Hollywood Plaza Hotel. "This was the era of great premieres," wrote Bastian. "The skies over Hollywood were frequently ablaze then with the beams of powerful searchlights advertising the opening of another super colossal production at Grauman's Chinese." Bastian had watched movies transition to sound and then witnessed "the tremendous development of special effects" in films such as *Star Wars* (20th Century–Fox, 1977) and *Close Encounters of the Third Kind* (Columbia, 1977). During the emerging era of summer blockbusters, Bastian could look back to a time when filmmaking first became a mass communication powerhouse. "We shall not see the Hollywood of Jack L. Warner and his associates again," concluded Bastian. "To me he is a symbol of times dear to my heart."[47]

Jack Warner's death marked the end of an era in which the Warner brothers accomplished the seemingly impossible. They created a film studio that did more than entertain, as Harry's ideal of combining education and entertainment drove nearly every production decision. The studio's down-to-earth, gritty house style was known worldwide and recognized for generations. As Champlin wrote in the *Los Angeles Times*, "The Warner Bros. look, with a heavy play of light and shadow, was distinct from the look of movies made anywhere else."[48] Even today, fans of old Hollywood know a Warner Bros. film when they see one on Turner Classic Movies. It was under the guidance of Harry, Albert, Sam, and Jack that so many talented people created timeless art that lives on long after they are gone.

Before Jack died, he kept an eye on what was published about his family history. After reading a *Los Angeles Times* review of James R. Silke's *Here's Looking at You, Kid: 50 Years of Fighting, Working, and Dreaming at Warner Bros.*, Jack responded with some words of criticism about printing legends that were not true. The reviewer, Lisa Mitchell, quoted this line from Silke's book: "When Harry would be in Burbank, he could be seen picking up nails on the sound stages and straightening them with his teeth, out of habit, an old one, dating back to the years in Youngstown and Baltimore."[49] Jack's letter to the editor, published in the *Los Angeles Times*, noted that "the use of teeth later in life for such an idiotic and impossible purpose would have driven up dental bills far beyond any dubious economic benefit derived."[50] To make matters worse, Mitchell had attributed this habit to Sam.

Warner was understandably frustrated that such old nonsense continued to surface, but during this period, much of film history was based on hearsay. Some authors managed to land useful interviews, but with so many people from Hollywood's golden age gone, it was difficult to write about the industry's history without access to the kind of archives available today. Jack continued to express his displeasure about both Silke's book and Mitchell's review of it: "In reviewing a book loaded with omissions, distortions, half-truth and biased nonsense, it is disheartening that your reviewer not only repeated one canard, but distorted it as well." Jack lamented, "A definitive, honest and complete book on the Warner Brothers and their times has yet to be written and the book with the clumsy title reviewed by Ms. Mitchell is far from being it."[51]

I hope enough time has passed, and enough material has surfaced, to construct a meaningful biography of the brothers. The story of the Warners is simultaneously an immigrant story, an American story, and a Hollywood story. The Warner brothers serve as a perfect cross section of substance, struggle, and success in Hollywood. Sam's technical genius is embodied by innumerable people in the film industry. Albert's quiet success is mirrored by many fantastic producers who shy away from the press. Without question, Hollywood is still full of Jack Warners who are talented and deeply flawed and think a little too highly of themselves. Most important, Harry's desire to combine good citizenship with good picture making is a high bar maintained by many of today's best filmmakers.

Coda

As Time Goes By

Los Angeles, 1980

They're all gone. All of Hollywood's founding movie moguls have passed. Names like Carl Laemmle, Louis B. Mayer, Harry Cohn, David O. Selznick, and Darryl F. Zanuck are now in the distant past. This group of innovators "created a powerful cluster of images and ideas—so powerful that, in a sense, they colonized the American imagination. No one could think about this country without thinking about the movies."[1] Jack Warner was the last of these visionaries and quite possibly the most outrageous and outspoken member of the group.

With the last of the Hollywood moguls gone, the Friends of the University of Southern California (USC) Libraries held an event titled "The Colonel: An Affectionate Remembrance of Jack L. Warner." Warner had been voted the university's first honorary alumnus in 1927. Jack's widow, Ann, was unable to attend but sent a warm letter offering her husband's memorabilia to the USC cinema archive. Program participants included Hal Kanter (moderator), Olivia de Havilland, Julius Epstein, Mervyn LeRoy, William Orr, Debbie Reynolds, and Mel Blanc, among others. The evening was full of fond memories, film montages, and much laughter. A large photograph of a smiling Jack hung above the stage.

USC president, war hero, and diplomat John R. Hubbard spoke at the event. He quoted Jack Benny, who once quipped, "Jack Warner would rather tell a bad joke than make a good movie."[2] Many no doubt rolled their eyes at the memory of Jack's many bad jokes, which were often followed by his own roaring laughter. But, Hubbard told the audience, Warner Bros. was synonymous with "innovation and trend setting." So, continued Hubbard, "we meet to honor a vigorous, original man, a man whose jokes may not have survived the lunch table or the banquet but whose movies are an unforgettable and undying contribution to the cultural history of the world."

William Conrad, former Warner Bros. actor, also recalled the studio dining hall—invitation only—with Jack Warner sitting at the head of the table and fourteen chairs on each side. Bill Schaefer, Jack's longtime executive assistant, spoke of the elite aura of the studio's private dining room. "In its way it was like the Algonquin Round Table in New York," said Schaefer. It hosted "the greats of the motion picture industry, world figures such as Albert Einstein, Madame Chiang Kai-shek, even Mussolini's son . . . politicians, Nelson Rockefeller, governors, senators, and the two Roosevelt boys, Elliot and Jimmy." Jack, like his older brother Harry, was always rubbing elbows with the powerful. William Orr, head of Warner Bros. television, noted that although Jack's bad jokes were legendary, he could often be genuinely funny. He was a "very funny raconteur," said Orr. Of course, not everyone found Jack funny. When Madame Chiang left the studio, Jack rattled off one of his cringe-worthy lines: "Well we had a really lovely visit, and now you can send out your laundry." When the audience laughed, perhaps presuming that Orr had fabricated the line on Jack's behalf, Orr clarified, "That is not a joke, folks."

Warner Bros. director Mervyn LeRoy, known for solidifying the studio's gritty house style with films like *Little Caesar* (1930), shared some of Warner's bad jokes. If you asked him how he was, Jack would say, "Like the bottom of a stove . . . grate!" If you asked what's new? Jack would respond, "New York, New Mexico, New Hampshire, pneumonia." LeRoy, who remained close with the Warners after his divorce from Doris, spoke glowingly of Jack's instincts—how he knew which films to green-light—unlike the committee decisions made in the new conglomerate Hollywood. "Those two initials J.W. stand for Jack Warner, and those two initials mean Just Wonderful. That's how I feel about him and always will." Applause filled the room.

Julius Epstein, studio scribe and cowriter of *Casablanca* (1942), pointed to the photograph of a smiling Jack Warner behind him. "This is exactly the look he had when he fired you," quipped Epstein. Writers did not adhere to the 9:00 to 5:00 schedules of other employees on the lot. Epstein maintained that he spent only two hours per day at his desk; the rest of the workday involved brainstorming and scribbling story details in notebooks. One day, Jack saw Epstein arriving on the lot at 2:30 p.m., which he often did. "Goddamn it, read your contract. You're coming in at 9:00 a.m. Bank presidents come in at 9:00. Railroad presidents come in at 9:00, and you're coming in at 9:00."

Epstein sent Jack a half-finished script with a note that said, "Have the bank president finish the script." On another occasion, Epstein recalled sending Jack a terribly written scene. "This is the worst scene I've ever read," Jack responded. "How can that be? It was written at 9:00 a.m.," quipped Epstein.

Jack had a commanding presence. When *42nd Street* (1933) composer Harry Warren first met Jack on the lot, they introduced themselves and Jack said, "I'm Mr. Warner." Warren responded, "Which one?" "You'll find out," Jack replied. Debbie Reynolds, who got her first break working for Warner Bros., remembered her screen test. Jack said of her, "She's skinny and ugly but she's funny . . . put her under contract cheap." With Reynolds, the frugal mogul landed one of the best new talents in town. Others remembered some of Jack's truly funny moments. When a discussion of X-rated films surfaced at a banquet, Jack chimed in, "If Errol Flynn could see the pictures today, he'd turn over in his grave." Standing at the mic, he noted, "Come to think of it, that would be a more natural position for Errol." The room erupted in laughter as Jack riffed on the actor's history of nefarious dalliances.

Some of the most notorious battles at Warner Bros. took place between Jack and Olivia de Havilland. The actress reminisced about her first Warner Bros. film, *A Midsummer Night's Dream* (1935). She expected to become a Shakespearean actress at Warner Bros., but then Jack cast her in a baseball picture with Joe E. Brown. The relationship between de Havilland and Warner included the actress having to fight to get loaned out to do *Gone with the Wind* and filing a historic lawsuit to try to get out of her contract. The last time de Havilland saw Jack was at one of the many events held in his name. She wanted to say something surprising but truthful, so she said, "You know, Jack, during all of our disputes and differences and our great historic battle, I was always very fond of you." Jack was overwhelmed, and the two hugged and kissed and made up at the end.

Jack was not always focused on upholding his power. Irving Rapper, director of *Now Voyager* (1942), remembered that Warner personally paid wages to aged stars who had been big names in the silent era. "Jack Warner held and paid these people from year to year. We had no Social Security, no pensions, and I thought that was one of the most human things I've ever felt in my life." Our view of the silent stars left behind may be summed up in *Sunset Boulevard* (1950), but it is nice to know that people like Jack Warner continued to appreciate the forgotten stars who helped build the industry.

Coda

Television producer Hal Kanter offered these closing words: "He was the last of the empire builders, the last of four brothers who changed the course of motion pictures, and in doing so helped change the history of humanity." Kanter advised the film students in attendance to study the founding members of Hollywood and not the contemporary lawyer-mogul types. Speaking specifically about Jack, he said, "The films for which he was responsible live on as a reminder forever that Jack Warner had taste and guts and imagination, that he did in a very real sense combine good picture-making with good citizenship and left a heritage of community involvement you have continued tonight in his name."

As the evening came to an end, Kanter got ready to pass the mic: "In parting, here is one final Warner Brothers star, with one final Warner Brothers word. Ladies and gentlemen, Mr. Mel Blanc." Blanc, who was the voice of Daffy Duck, Porky Pig, and Bugs Bunny, took the mic and said, "abeeabeea-beeabee . . . that's all folks!" The room erupted in applause. It was the official end of old Hollywood.

Afterword

As a blue-collar Jersey boy growing up in the 1950s and 1960s, I was firmly in the grip of Warner Bros. I was hooked! There were many cartoons on TV in those days, but nothing—and I mean *nothing*—compared to the chaos, insanity, attitude, and explosive fun of Warner's Merrie Melodies and Looney Toons. If truth be told (and an afterword to an authoritative book some sixty years later seems like the right place and time for the truth), at my very young age back then, I couldn't tell you the name of the company that made those cartoons. All I knew was that I loved them and craved them, and now I cherish them.

Skip to my teen years—before cable, videocassettes and VCRs, computers, the internet, social media, streaming, and digital downloads—when WOR-TV in New York City, channel 9, featured a program called *Million Dollar Movie*. It showed the same golden age of Hollywood movie five days straight (usually repeated at least twice a day) for an entire week, just like the neighborhood movie theater did. That was my sole exposure to what my friends and I called "old-time movies." That was how I learned that Warner Bros. was a major Hollywood studio that produced some of the greatest black-and-white movies I ever saw on my black-and-white TV screen. For me and my fellow baby boomers who were first-generation television addicts, our home-based world of entertainment was largely black and white back then. But I quickly realized that these classic, cool, violent, action-packed Warner Bros. crime dramas featured on *Million Dollar Movie* actually looked best in black and white. The shadows looked great! The city looked great! Even the scary close-ups of James Cagney and Edward G. Robinson looked great! Unlike MGM—the Tiffany's of the golden age film industry—which embraced color, Warner Bros. embraced a lack of color, and I fell in love with black-and-white movies forever. That love compelled me to write this afterword—a small token to Warner Bros. for a lifetime of entertainment at its most memorable and impactful.

Only when I went to college at Indiana University in Bloomington did I become a fan of Warner's incredible stable of stars. The university held film festivals on Friday or Saturday nights at the Indiana Memorial Union, Whittenberger Auditorium, and revered Woodburn Hall. Many of the films starred Errol Flynn, Humphrey Bogart, or the Marx Brothers. Two of the three belonged to Warner.

Up until that time, all my childhood heroes had come from comic books—Spandexed superheroes such as Batman, Superman, and Spider-Man—or from some other medium, such as Zorro, Tarzan, and the Lone Ranger. But now I was entranced by an actor who was undisputedly the best action hero of his day and beyond. He was Captain Blood, Robin Hood, George Armstrong Custer, the Sea Hawk, Don Juan, and William Tell! I became a lifelong fan of Errol Flynn, especially when he was teamed with the beautiful and regal Olivia de Havilland. Everything you need to know about Errol Flynn you can find in this very book or in the movie *My Favorite Year.*

While Errol Flynn was my favorite action hero, Humphrey Bogart became my favorite actor ever. He was everything I had ever wanted to be when I grew up. He was tough yet vulnerable. He was handsome yet craggy. He was smart, but his intelligence was deliberately overshadowed by his attitude. He infuriated women and made them fall in love with him. On my list of top hundred films, Bogart movies (and, therefore, Warner Bros. movies) are prominent. My favorite movie of all time is *Casablanca.* It is a near perfect movie. Warner Bros. adopted its well-known song "As Time Goes By" as the studio's official music. *Casablanca* is closely followed in the annals of movie history by *The Maltese Falcon, All through the Night, The African Queen, The Treasure of Sierra Madre, High Sierra, The Petrified Forest, Key Largo, To Have and Have Not, Sabrina, The Big Sleep, Dead End, We're No Angels,* and *The Caine Mutiny.* Even if Warner Bros. had done nothing but give us Humphrey Bogart movies, it would have earned its lofty place in film lore.

As both a movie buff and a comic book geek, my life was changed when Warner Bros. released Dick Donner's masterpieces of the 1970s: *Superman: The Movie* and *Superman 2,* starring Christopher Reeve. Donner and Warner Bros. blazed a new path for Superman and nudged open the door for other superheroes to fly from four-color comic books to the silver screen.

Inarguably, Warner Bros. changed my life forever. Arguably, the studio changed Hollywood and the movie industry forever with its 1989 release of a project born from my dreams: our first dark and serious *Batman* movie, directed by a young genius named Tim Burton. Its production designer was another genius, my dear friend Anton Furst. Our revolutionary film proved that comic book superheroes could, indeed, be taken seriously by global, mainstream audiences. And so, Warner Bros. presented *Batman*, which begat Michael Keaton's Bruce Wayne, Jack Nicholson's Joker, Christopher Nolan's Dark Knight Trilogy, Heath Ledger's Joker, Chris Miller and Phil Lord's *The Lego Movie*, Bruce Timm's *Batman: The Animated Series*, Todd Phillips's *Joker* and *Joker 2*, Joaquin Phoenix's Joker, and Matt Reeves's *The Batman*. Cumulatively, this is a legacy to be proud of. Thank you, Warner Bros.

So cue up the music. Play "As Time Goes By." Then say it! Say the magic words that define every Warner Bros. movie, every movie ever made, and Hollywood itself: "It's the stuff dreams are made of!"

Michael Uslan
Originator and executive producer of the *Batman* movie franchise
2022

Acknowledgments

The first time I felt something special in relation to the Warner Bros. shield was when I saw *Batman* (1989) as a kid at my hometown theater. Originally built in 1929, the movie house had been turned into a multiplex by the time I first set foot inside. All its beautiful history was hidden behind ugly painted drywall and carpeting. By 1989, I was well-versed in Looney Tunes, so the Warner logo was familiar, but seeing it on something dark and edgy was thrilling. Many years later, I met *Batman* producer Michael Uslan. In addition, I helped found a community board that raised over $4 million to refurbish that historic theater to its original glory. It is now a nationally registered historic single-screen-and-stage venue called The Bend. Since its reopening in 2020, I am happy to report that we have screened not only *Batman* but also many historically important films that played at the venue during their original runs in the twentieth century.

Years after *Batman,* as I was getting to know Martin Scorsese's work, I began to dive deeper. After watching *Goodfellas* (1990) and *Casino* (1995), I went back and watched *Mean Streets* (1973) and *Taxi Driver* (1976). I needed to know more about the director and his work. It was at this point that I searched for everything Scorsese had ever said or written about his relationship with old Hollywood. After watching *A Personal Journey through American Movies with Martin Scorsese,* I was dedicated to learning more about Warner Bros. and hooked on Hollywood history. Scorsese's enthusiasm about the old James Cagney and Edward G. Robinson films was contagious. I *had* to see those movies. And there it began—my lifelong fascination with the history of Hollywood and of Warner Bros. in particular.

The Warner Brothers would not have been possible without the assistance of many remarkable people. Southern Methodist University librarian Christina Jensen scanned a couple dozen interviews over the course of a few months at the peak of the COVID-19 pandemic. I am eternally thankful for her willingness to take on this task at a time when all our lives were so difficult. As always, Warren Sherk and Louise Hilton at the Margaret Herrick Library in Beverly Hills were essential resources. Warren was kind enough to take me out to lunch during my research trip before the pandemic hit. I'll return the favor the next time!

I am also grateful to the original Warner Archive crew led by George Feltenstein, D. W. Ferranti, and Matt Patterson. These three film lovers curated a home video collection made for movie fans. Each release was special, and their podcast offered fun conversations about their thoughts on new releases. The team was kind enough to have me on their podcast when my first book on Warner Bros. was published, which focused primarily on the studio during the 1930s. Listening to the podcast every week became a ritual, as their enthusiasm for film history was both entertaining and contagious. These guys also allowed me onto the Warner Bros. lot on several occasions. Matt was kind enough to take me and my wife to lunch at the studio, followed by a walking excursion where we discovered bits of history immortalized in the buildings and around the property.

I was floored when arguably the world's most important film historian, Kevin Brownlow, read and blurbed my last book, *Hollywood Hates Hitler*. During my research for this one, Kevin offered sage advice and shared his firsthand experiences with many individuals in Hollywood in the 1920s. His insight into Sam Warner's wife was particularly useful to me in the early writing stages. Kevin was kind and courageous enough to be the first to read the entire manuscript of *The Warner Brothers*. He offered praise and kind words, while politely nudging some corrections and suggesting areas for expansion. I am grateful for Kevin's inspiration and encouragement.

Freshly retired from the University of Southern California (USC), Drew Casper also read the manuscript in its entirety (twice!) and highlighted crucial parts of postwar Warner Bros. culture that I could elaborate on. As a result, I discovered multiple previously unpublished tales from the lot. Although I never attended USC as a student, Drew has always treated me like I had. Speaking of USC, Ned Comstock (also retired) has long been a champion of my work and the work of so many others. While I was writing my dissertation and my first book on Warner Bros., Ned was there to help. He has remained a steadfast ally, ensuring that I got the archival material I needed to complete whatever I was working on at the time. Brett Service, formerly at the Warner

Acknowledgments

Bros. Archives, was always kind and reliable and a great person to work with. I'll miss seeing him on my next visit to USC.

Ned Comstock has managed to get thanked in every volume of film history worth reading, and Eric Hoyt will likely be the next person worthy of such an honor. Eric's work cofounding and maintaining the Media History Digital Library (MHDL) and its Lantern search engine has already had a monumental impact on film and media history. I never would have been able to complete my dissertation or my first book without MHDL, as I was working at an institution that had few to no resources. In the years since then, Eric has become a friend and mentor I can always count on.

Another one of my mentors, Thomas Doherty, read sections of the manuscript and offered valuable feedback. Tom's work inspired my own long before I was fortunate enough to meet him at a conference in Montreal. In the field of social and political Hollywood history, few can rival Tom's work. I am grateful to have such a trustworthy resource in my corner. I'm not sure how I can ever repay all the favors and feedback he's given me over the years.

Regular chats over coffee with author David Fantle were a welcome break. He was fortunate enough to meet many stars of Hollywood's golden age before they were gone. His insights and experiences help keep this period of history alive and well in my imagination.

At the University of Wisconsin–Milwaukee, I relied on constant encouragement from two philosophy professors: Mark Peterson, who has taught two courses with me for several years, and Dean Kowalski, who has championed my work as chair of our unique interdisciplinary department. As this project got going, the university hired a new dean, Simon Bronner, who is an extraordinary scholar. Bronner encouraged me to apply for a fellowship at the University of Wisconsin–Madison's Institute for Research in the Humanities (IRH). I was fortunate enough to be awarded the fellowship, which released me from teaching in the fall of 2021, allowing me to complete the first draft of *The Warner Brothers,* present sections of the book to world-renowned scholars, and utilize the expansive resources in Madison to ensure that I left no stone unturned. At the IRH, director Steven Nadler and staff members Katie Aspey and Elizabeth Neary were a joy to work with. Other fellows who offered conversation and feedback on my work included Francine Hirsch, Sunny Yudkoff, Douglas Haynes, Lea Jacobs, Kat Lecky, and my UW-Milwaukee colleague Anne Widemayer.

303

Acknowledgments

Of course, I cannot think of Madison without mentioning Mary Huels-
beck at the Wisconsin Center for Film and Theater Research. Mary has been
a stalwart supporter of my work for many years. I look forward to many more
visits with her. Christina Rice, an author and historian in addition to her job
as a Los Angeles librarian, helped me find the addresses of properties owned
by the Warner brothers over the years.

I benefited from the conversation and collegiality of many other col-
leagues and friends, including Noah Isenberg, Andrew Patrick Nelson, Simon
Surowicz, Mike Kutz, Sam Wasson, Joel Berkowitz, Peter Gibeau, Cyrus
Nowrasteh, and Paul Seydor, among others I am likely forgetting.

I am also appreciative of my editors in the popular press who have both
encouraged me and allowed me to share my ideas and research, which helps
keep a writer engaged and motivated during the years it takes to complete
a book project. At the *Los Angeles Review of Books,* I am grateful to Boris
Dralyuk, who is always eager to hear more about Hollywood history, and
to Rob Latham and Tom Zoellner for their astute editing, keeping my prose
readable. At the *Hollywood Reporter,* I am indebted to Scott Feinberg and
Erik Hayden, both of whom keep an eye on Hollywood history while serving
in the trenches of today's entertainment journalism. They even allow me to
publish a piece every now and then.

There would have been no book without renowned biographer Patrick
McGilligan. I was planning to write a follow-up to my first book, but in the
midst of a campus merger and having a child, I was never going to meet my
deadline. When I met Pat at a book signing for his Mel Brooks biography,
he insisted we have lunch and talk writing. I had been a fan of Pat's work for
many years and had always wanted to meet him, so I was honored that he also
wanted to get to know me and my work. When I pitched a biography of Harry
Warner—someone I thought deserved a more central place in Hollywood
history—he suggested that I write a biography of all four Warner brothers
who went into the film business. This was a much more daunting task, but
under the guidance of a respected biographer like Pat, I agreed to tackle it.

At the University Press of Kentucky, I am grateful for the leadership of
Ashley Runyon and her team. She took over the press not long after Anne
Dean Dotson exited (who was wonderful to work with as well). Ashley has
easily been the best publisher I've worked with to date. She promptly responds
to emails, takes a true interest in her authors' work, and offers solid bourbon
suggestions. Ashley is a great example of how to lead from the top. The rest

304

of the press staff is nothing but pleasant and reliable. I would like to thank everyone at the University Press of Kentucky for being so attentive to this project and so generous with their time.

This book would have been impossible to complete without the many mornings or afternoons my daughter, June, spent with my parents (or, as she calls them, "Gamma" and "Pa"). During my fellowship in Madison, where I was required to be on campus each Monday, our dear friend Brad Spanbauer watched June while I was researching and attending lectures. When Brad (or "Uncle Boo") was busy, my mother-in-law Susan ("Gamma Suzie") stepped in. Last and most important, I am grateful to my wife, Caitlin, and to June for their humor and support. The amount of time we spend laughing surely rivals the laughter produced by the best comedy clubs in the country. Anyone who has written a book understands the stresses that come with the territory, and I find any time spent with my family is relaxing and invigorating and always leaves my mind rested. This helped make any writing time, often occurring in small bursts, productive.

With that, *The Warner Brothers* is dedicated to my loving family, as well as to the four brothers who overcame impossible odds and prejudice to create what I believe is the greatest film studio in history.

Notes

Prologue

1. W. R. Wilkerson, "Rambling Reporter," *Hollywood Reporter,* December 10, 1938, 1.

2. Louis Nizer, "Pen Sketch of Harry M. Warner," *Exhibitor,* December 10, 1932, G.

3. Neal Gabler, *An Empire of Their Own: How the Jews Invented Hollywood* (New York: Crown, 1988), 1–4.

4. Max Bercutt, notes from an undated speech, David I. Zeitlin Papers, Warner, Jack, f. 183, Margaret Herrick Library, Beverly Hills, CA.

5. Nizer, "Pen Sketch of Harry M. Warner."

6. For more on Koverman, see Steven J. Ross, *Hollywood Left and Right: How Movie Stars Shaped American Politics* (New York: Basic Books, 2017), and Jacqueline R. Braitman, *She Damn Near Ran the Studio: The Extraordinary Lives of Ida R. Koverman* (Jackson: University Press of Mississippi, 2020).

7. Charles Higham, *Warner Brothers: A History of the Studio; Its Pictures, Stars, and Personalities* (New York: Scribners, 1975), 2.

8. "Warner Brothers," *Fortune,* December 1937, 111.

1. Manifest Destiny

1. Bob Thomas, *Clown Prince of Hollywood: The Antic Life and Times of Jack L. Warner* (New York: McGraw-Hill, 1990), 10.

2. Thomas, 11.

3. Neal Gabler, *An Empire of Their Own: How the Jews Invented Hollywood* (New York: Crown, 1988), 123.

4. Cass Warner, interview with Betty Warner-Sheinbaum, https://thebrothers warner.com/interview/betty-warner-sheinbaum/.

5. Jack Warner with Dean Jennings, *My First Hundred Years in Hollywood: An Autobiography* (New York: Random House, 1964), 17.

6. Warner, 29.

7. Warner, 35–36.

8. Esther Hamilton was born in 1897 in New Castle, Pennsylvania. She moved to Youngstown in 1918, after the Warners moved west. Hamilton became a prominent writer of science fiction, as well as a reporter for the *Youngstown Telegram* and later the *Youngstown Vindicator*. For seven decades, Hamilton wrote weekly columns, reported on the radio, or both. Being from towns where the Warner brothers had lived gave her the necessary credentials to cover their story.

9. Esther Hamilton, "Amazing Career of the Warner Brothers: Shoe Shop to Movie Empire Is Story of Former Youngstown Family," 1–2, Warner Bros. Archives, University of Southern California.

10. Jean Stein, *West of Eden: An American Place* (New York: Random House, 2016), 50.

11. Thomas, *Clown Prince of Hollywood*, 13.

12. Hamilton, "Amazing Career of the Warner Brothers," 4.

13. Cass Warner, interview with John Steel, https://thebrotherswarner.com/interview/john-steel/.

14. Edward Wagenknecht, *The Movies in the Age of Innocence* (Norman: University of Oklahoma Press, 1962), 13.

15. Terry Ramsaye, *A Million and One Nights: A Modern Classic* (1926; reprint, New York: Simon and Schuster, 1954), 429.

16. John S. Spargo, "Warner Brothers' Fight to the Top," *Exhibitors Herald,* June 6, 1925, 29.

17. Charles Musser, *The Emergence of Cinema: The American Screen to 1907* (New York: Charles Scribner's Sons, 1990), 367.

18. Hamilton, "Amazing Career of the Warner Brothers," 15.

19. Cass Warner Sperling with Cork Millner and Jack Warner Jr., *Hollywood Be Thy Name: The Warner Brothers Story* (Rocklin, CA: Prima Publishing, 1994), 13.

20. Tom Gunning, "An Aesthetic of Astonishment: Early Film and the (In)credulous Spectator," in *Film Theory and Criticism,* ed. Leo Braudy and Marshall Cohen (New York: Oxford University Press, 2004), 869.

21. Hamilton, "Amazing Career of the Warner Brothers," 13.

22. This date fluctuates by a year or two, depending on the source.

23. Sperling, *Hollywood Be Thy Name*, 35.

24. Sperling, 36.

25. Musser, *Emergence of Cinema*, 420.

26. Robert Sklar, *Movie-Made America: A Cultural History of American Movies* (New York: Vintage Books, 1994), 18.

27. Warner, *My First Hundred Years*, 54.

28. "Five Cent Moving Picture Theaters Prove Exceedingly Popular," *Moving Picture World,* October 5, 1907, 487.

29. Wagenknecht, *Movies in the Age of Innocence,* 15.

30. "Nickel Madness," *Moving Picture World,* October 5, 1907, 484.

31. Hamilton, "Amazing Career of the Warner Brothers," 9.

32. Sperling, *Hollywood Be Thy Name*, 41. The college is Duquesne University, a Catholic university founded in 1878.

33. "Skigie Sees Advanced Vaudeville," *Variety*, November 30, 1907, 12.

34. Terry Lindvall, "Sundays in Norfolk: Toward a Protestant Utopia through Film Exhibition in Norfolk, Virginia, 1910–1920," in *Going to the Movies: Hollywood and the Social Experience of Cinema*, ed. Richard Maltby, Melvyn Stokes, and Robert C. Allen (Exeter: University of Exeter Press, 2007), 77.

35. Sperling, *Hollywood Be Thy Name*, 44.

36. Alva Johnston, "Thrilling True Life Story of the Three Brothers Who Made Movies Talk," *Boston Sunday Post*, December 30, 1928, B-7.

37. Thomas, *Clown Prince of Hollywood*, 25.

38. Hamilton, "Amazing Career of the Warner Brothers," 17.

39. Hamilton, 9.

40. Hamilton, 19.

41. Sperling, *Hollywood Be Thy Name*, 45.

42. Hamilton, "Amazing Career of the Warner Brothers," 21.

43. Spargo, "Warner Brothers' Fight to the Top," 30.

44. Hamilton, "Amazing Career of the Warner Brothers," 22.

45. Sperling, *Hollywood Be Thy Name*, 52.

46. Sperling, 54.

47. Gretchen Bisplinghoff, "Gene Gauntier," Women Film Pioneers Project, https://wfpp.columbia.edu/pioneer/ccp-gene-gauntier/.

48. Letter from Lenore Coffee reproduced in Cari Beauchamp, *My First Time in Hollywood: An Anthology* (Los Angeles: Ashina and Wallace, 2015), 176.

49. Hamilton, "Amazing Career of the Warner Brothers," 23.

50. "Warner's Features, Inc.," *Moving Picture World*, July 11, 1914, 262.

51. Advertisement, *Motion Picture News*, July 11, 1914, 3.

52. Sperling, *Hollywood Be Thy Name*, 57.

53. Sperling, 60.

54. Sperling, 61.

55. Ramsaye, *A Million and One Nights*, 494.

56. Advertisement, *Exhibitors Herald and Motography*, July 20, 1918, 8–9.

57. Kevin Brownlow, *The War, the West, and the Wilderness* (New York: Alfred A. Knopf, 1979), 135.

58. Brownlow, 137.

59. Brownlow, 137.

60. "*Pershing's Crusaders* Blazes New Trail," *Motion Picture News*, September 14, 1918, 1707.

61. "Warner Tells Big Film Demand," *Motion Picture News*, October 26, 1918, 2675.

62. "Another Gerard Picture Is Coming," *Moving Picture World*, February 8, 1919, 735.

63. "Another Social Disease Film that Is Morbid and Unpleasant," *Wid's Daily*, July 6, 1919, 11.

64. "Open Your Eyes," *Variety*, July 4, 1919, 42.

65. Kevin Brownlow, *Behind the Mask of Innocence: Sex, Violence, Prejudice, Crime; Films of Social Conscience in the Silent Era* (New York: Alfred A. Knopf, 1990), 66.

66. Sperling, *Hollywood Be Thy Name*, 68.

67. Todd McCarthy, *Howard Hawks: The Grey Fox of Hollywood* (New York: Basic Books, 1997), 50.

68. "Monty Banks Begins New Series of Warner Films," *Exhibitors Herald*, October 29, 1921, 74.

69. Johnny O'Steen, "Were These the Golden Years?" (unpublished memoir, n.d., Margaret Herrick Library, Beverly Hills, CA), 11.

70. Warner, *My First Hundred Years,* 105.

71. Warner, 95–96.

72. Warner, 96.

73. "Warners to Build," *Film Daily*, June 7, 1920, 1–2.

74. "Stage Set for Frolic at Studio," *Los Angeles Times*, April 19, 1923.

75. O'Steen, "Were These the Golden Years?" 16.

76. "Jewish Control of the American Theater," *Dearborn Independent*, January 1, 1921, 8.

77. Advertisement for *Why Girls Leave Home, Exhibitors Herald*, November 26, 1921, 29.

78. Sperling, *Hollywood Be Thy Name*, 73.

79. "Fooling the Public an Injurious Policy," *Motion Picture News*, September 23, 1922, 1509.

80. William J. Reilly, "Will Hays Makes His Debut as Guardian of the 'Infant' that Is to Be Colossus," *Moving Picture World*, April 1, 1922, 453.

81. Harry M. Warner, "Why We Joined Will H. Hays," *Exhibitors Herald*, October 30, 1922, 57.

82. Harry M. Warner, "Warner Production Plans for 1923," *Motion Picture News*, September 23, 1922, 1509.

83. "Rapf for Big Productions," *Motion Picture News*, September 23, 1922, 1511.

84. "Huge Float to Tour from Coast to Coast," *Motion Picture News*, September 23, 1922, 1511.

85. "Warners Adopt a Trade Mark," *Moving Picture World*, December 30, 1922, 895.

86. Stein, *West of Eden*, 52.

87. Joe Adamson, *Byron Haskin: A Directors Guild of America Oral History* (Metuchen, NJ: Scarecrow Press, 1984).

2. Incorporation, Innovation, Triumph, and Tragedy

1. Johnny O'Steen, "Were These the Golden Years?" (unpublished memoir, n.d., Margaret Herrick Library, Beverly Hill, CA), 1.

2. "$50,000,000 Unit," *Film Daily*, April 6, 1923, 1, 8.

3. "That the booking and renting of all positive prints of each of said motion pictures shall be upon contracts separate and apart from the booking and renting of any other prints, films or pictures handled or controlled by the Exchange, and the booking or renting of any of said prints of the Producers' feature motion pictures shall not be made conditional or contingent upon the booking or renting of any other pictures, films or prints handled or controlled by the Exchange." Advertisement, *Exhibitors Trade Review,* March 17, 1923.

4. Advertisement, *Exhibitors Trade Review,* November 10, 1923.

5. "Three Warner Features Shown Consecutively for Three Weeks," *Moving Picture World,* July 7, 1923, 67.

6. "Keep Dates Open for Big Ones, H. M. Warner Advises Exhibitors," *Exhibitors Trade Review,* August 4, 1923, 426.

7. Albert Warner, "Raise Standard of Showmanship and Win," *Exhibitors Trade Review,* September 15, 1923, 707.

8. Warner, 707.

9. Bob Thomas, *Clown Prince of Hollywood: The Antic Life and Times of Jack L. Warner* (New York: McGraw-Hill, 1990), 42.

10. Hal Wallis and Charles Higham, *Starmaker* (New York: Macmillan, 1980), 7.

11. Hal Wallis, interview with Ronald L. Davis, Southern Methodist University Oral History Collection, 5.

12. Wallis and Higham, *Starmaker,* 10.

13. Wallis and Higham, 14.

14. Susan Orlean, *Rin Tin Tin: The Life and Legend* (New York: Simon and Schuster, 2011), 96.

15. Thomas, *Clown Prince of Hollywood,* 44.

16. Wallis and Higham, *Starmaker,* 12.

17. Thomas, *Clown Prince of Hollywood,* 45.

18. Alma Young (script girl at Warner Bros., 1923–1960), transcript of interview by Anthony Slide and Robert Gitt, January 30 and February 20, 1977, Margaret Herrick Library, Beverly Hills, CA.

19. Thomas, *Clown Prince of Hollywood,* 45.

20. Memo from Harry Warner to Jack Warner, May 15, 1926, Ernst Lubitsch Legal File—2729A, Warner Bros. Archives, University of Southern California.

21. Undated memo (presumably 1926) from Harry Warner to Ernst Lubitsch, Ernst Lubitsch Legal File—2729A, Warner Bros. Archives, University of Southern California.

22. Quoted in Joseph McBride, *How Did Lubitsch Do It?* (New York: Columbia University Press, 2018), 214.

23. Tino Balio, *The American Film Industry* (Madison: University of Wisconsin Press, 1985), 236.

24. Wallis and Higham, *Starmaker,* 14.

25. Wallis and Higham, 16.

26. O'Steen, "Were These the Golden Years?"

27. Young interview.

28. O'Steen, "Were These the Golden Years?" 33–34.

29. Joe Adamson, *Byron Haskin: A Directors Guild of America Oral History* (Metuchen, NJ: Scarecrow Press, 1984), 112.

30. Andrew A. Erish, *Vitagraph: America's First Great Motion Picture Studio* (Lexington: University Press of Kentucky, 2020), 16.

31. Erish, 14.

32. Erish, 24.

33. Donald Dewey, *Buccaneer: James Stewart Blackton and the Birth of American Movies* (Lanham, MD: Rowman and Littlefield, 2016), 12.

34. Albert E. Smith, *Two Reels and a Crank* (Garden City, NY: Doubleday, 1952), 11–12.

35. Anthony Slide, *Inside the Hollywood Fan Magazine: A History of Star Makers, Fabricators, and Gossip Mongers* (Jackson: University Press of Mississippi, 2010), 20.

36. Smith, *Two Reels and a Crank,* 276.

37. "Abe Warner Heads Vitagraph with Sale of Company to Warner Bros.," *Exhibitors Herald,* May 9, 1925, 23.

38. "Vitagraph Will Distribute Product," *Exhibitors Herald,* May 9, 1925, 24.

39. Douglas Gomery, *The Coming of Sound* (New York: Routledge, 2005), 36.

40. "Full Line-up of Warner's Forty Constitutes Notable Achievement," *Moving Picture World,* August 1, 1925, 542.

41. Gomery, *Coming of Sound,* 29.

42. "Warner Calls for Showdown," *Los Angeles Times,* May 14, 1925.

43. "Warner Calls for Showdown."

44. "Warner Calls for Showdown."

45. Sydney S. Cohen, "The Significance of Milwaukee," *Moving Picture World,* May 30, 1925, 516.

46. "Optimistic Statements: Sam Warner, Warner Brothers," *Moving Picture World,* May 30, 1925, 519.

47. Gomery, *Coming of Sound,* 36.

48. Kevin Brownlow, "Obituary: Lina Basquette," *Independent,* October 8, 1994.

49. Cass Warner Sperling with Cork Millner and Jack Warner Jr., *Hollywood Be Thy Name: The Warner Brothers Story* (Rocklin, CA: Prima Publishing, 1994), 96.

50. Lina Basquette, *Lina: DeMille's Godless Girl* (Fairfax, VA: Denlinger's Publishers, 1990), 42.

51. Brownlow, "Obituary."

52. Sperling, *Hollywood Be Thy Name,* 96.

53. Sperling, 98.

54. Basquette, *Lina,* 46.

55. Basquette, 46.

56. Basquette, 47.

57. Basquette, 54.

58. Basquette, 55.

59. Sperling, *Hollywood Be Thy Name,* 96.

60. Basquette, *Lina,* 56.

61. "Warner's 'Bonded Advertising' to Appear in 1,100 Newspapers," *Moving Picture World,* August 1, 1925, 546.

62. "Warner's 'Bonded Advertising' to Appear," 546.

63. Young interview.

64. Wallis and Higham, *Starmaker,* 17.

65. Scott Eyman, *The Speed of Sound: Hollywood and the Talkie Revolution 1926–1930* (New York: Simon and Schuster, 1997), 86.

66. Gomery, *Coming of Sound,* 38.

67. Jack Warner with Dean Jennings, *My First Hundred Years in Hollywood: An Autobiography* (New York: Random House, 1964), 168.

68. "Vitaphone Speech by Will H. Hays," *Motion Picture News,* August 21, 1926, 659.

69. Lee De Forest, "My Opinion of the Vitaphone," *Motion Picture News,* August 21, 1926, 661.

70. "The Greatest Line of All," *Moving Picture World,* August 28, 1926, 527.

71. John S. Spargo, "Vitaphone Perfections Seen at Premiere of Don Juan," *Exhibitors Herald,* August 14, 1926, 23.

72. "Vitaphone Bow Is Hailed as Marvel," *Variety,* August 11, 1926.

73. Terry Ramsaye, "Warners Mark 2 Decades of the Talking Picture," *Motion Picture Herald,* April 20, 1946, 25.

74. Kevin Brownlow, *The Parade's Gone By: A Vivid, Nostalgic, Immediate Portrait of an Art in the Making* (New York: Knopf, 1968), 569.

75. Ramsaye, "Warners Mark 2 Decades," 25.

76. The full letter is quoted in Warner, *My First Hundred Years,* 171.

77. Warner, 172.

78. Warner, 173.

79. David Nasaw, *The Patriarch: The Remarkable Life and Turbulent Times of Joseph P. Kennedy* (New York: Penguin Press, 2012), 101.

80. Joseph P. Kennedy, ed., *The Story of Films* (New Delhi: Isha Books, 2013), 13.

81. "Edison's Views Scorned by Harry Warner," *Motion Picture News,* March 18, 1927, 953.

82. "Edison Sees and Hears Himself in Movie; Prefers His Pictures in Silence, He Declares," *New York Times,* November 26, 1927, 1.

83. Harry Warner, "Future Developments," in Kennedy, *Story of Films,* 319–35.

84. Edwin Schallert, "Vitaphone in the Spotlight," *Los Angeles Times,* May 29, 1927, 13.

85. Edwin Schallert, "Vitaphone Activity in Hollywood," *Motion Picture News,* July 8, 1927, 35.

86. Warner, *My First Hundred Years,* 179–81. Until otherwise noted, subsequent quotations are from this source.

87. "HM Warner Goes to Ill Brother," *New York Times*, October 4, 1927, 22. Abe's presence on the train is based on Jack Warner's autobiography.

88. "Sam Warner Near Death in Hospital," *Los Angeles Times*, October 5, 1927, A13.

89. Thomas, *Clown Prince of Hollywood*, 62.

90. Basquette, *Lina*, 96.

91. Warner, *My First Hundred Years*, 181.

92. "The Romance of Vitaphone," *Screenland*, February 1928, 111.

93. Basquette, *Lina*, 100.

94. "Sam Warner Laid to Rest," *Los Angeles Times*, October 10, 1927, A1.

95. For a full list, see "Studio Will Pay Honor to Warner," *Los Angeles Times*, October 9, 1927, B11.

96. "Romance of Vitaphone," 111.

97. "Romance of Vitaphone," 111.

98. Sid Silverman, "The Jazz Singer," *Variety*, October 12, 1927.

99. Edward G. Robinson with Leonard Spigelgass, *All My Yesterdays: An Autobiography* (New York: Hawthorn Books, 1973), 100.

100. Mordaunt Hall, "The Screen: Al Jolson and the Vitaphone," *New York Times*, October 7, 1927, 24.

101. Norbert Lusk, "Jazz Singer Scores a Hit," *Los Angeles Times*, October 16, 1927, C13.

102. Donald Bogle, *Toms, Coons, Mulattoes, Mammies & Bucks: An Interpretive History of Blacks in American Films* (New York: Continuum International Publishing, 2001), 26.

103. For more about the transition to sound, see "Battle of the Giants: ERPI and RCA Consolidate Sound," https://www.encyclopedia.com/arts/culture-magazines/battle-giants-erpi-and-rca-consolidate-sound.

104. Brownlow, "Obituary."

105. Brownlow.

106. David Krause, "Longtime Aspen Fixture, Ballet Founder Lita Heller Passes away at California Home," *Aspen Times*, April 20, 2019.

107. William Wellman interview in *The Men Who Made the Movies*, ed. Richard Schickel (Chicago: Ivan R. Dee, 1975), 208.

108. For more information, see Chris Yogerst, *From the Headlines to Hollywood: The Birth and Boom of Warner Bros.* (Lanham, MD: Rowman and Littlefield, 2016).

109. Young interview.

110. Alan K. Rode, *Michael Curtiz: A Life in Film* (Lexington: University Press of Kentucky, 2017).

111. A. L. Wooldridge, "And Now the Deluge!" *Picture-Play Magazine*, September 1928, 24.

112. Rode, *Michael Curtiz*, 99.

113. Thomas, *Clown Prince of Hollywood*, 65.

114. O'Steen, "Were These the Golden Years?"

115. "Warner Gymnasium Is Given to Orphans," *New York Times,* October 1, 1928, 16.

116. Jean Stein, *West of Eden: An American Place* (New York: Random House, 2016), 44.

117. Stein, 44–45.

118. Stein, 51, 50.

3. Battling the Depression, Censors, and Stars

1. Thomas Doherty, *Pre-Code Hollywood: Sex, Immorality, and Insurrection in American Cinema 1930–1934* (New York: Columbia University Press, 1999), 55.

2. Casey Scharf, "The Julian Petroleum Scandal and the Murder of Hollywood Icon Motley Flint," *HuffPost,* July 17, 2013.

3. "Help Given by Flint to Films Cited: Jack L. Warner Asserts Banker Always Friendly to Picture Industry," *Los Angeles Times,* July 15, 1930, 4.

4. "Sound Film Discussed by Warner," *Los Angeles Times,* January 11, 1930, A2.

5. Cass Warner, interview with Betty Warner-Sheinbaum, https://thebrothers warner.com/interview/betty-warner-sheinbaum/.

6. "Harry Warner's Astounding Statement," *Harrison's Reports,* June 7, 1930, 92.

7. "Warners Vindicated in Court of Charges of Stockholder," *Exhibitor's Daily Review,* August 27, 1930, 1.

8. "Warners to Widen Stage Activities," *New York Times,* May 30, 1930, 25.

9. Cass Warner Sperling with Cork Millner and Jack Warner Jr., *Hollywood Be Thy Name: The Warner Brothers Story* (Rocklin, CA: Prima Publishing, 1994), 160.

10. Johnny O'Steen, "Were These the Golden Years?" (unpublished memoir, n.d., Margaret Herrick Library, Beverly Hills, CA), 46.

11. *Variety,* June 25, 1930, 1.

12. Lewis Warner, "Wedding of Screen and Stage," *Variety,* June 25, 1930, 4.

13. Harry Warner, "Warners—Past and Future," *Variety,* June 25, 1930, 2.

14. Albert Warner, "Warners and Finances," *Variety,* June 25, 1930, 6.

15. Jack Warner, "But a Few Short Years," *Variety,* June 25, 1930, 8, 28.

16. Spyros Skouras, "Operating Warner Theatres a Fast Project, Increasing as Theatre Holdings Expand," *Variety,* June 25, 1930, 16.

17. George Skouras, "Warners' Clean Pictures Are Profit Pictures, Says Skouras," *Variety,* June 25, 1930, 16.

18. Darryl F. Zanuck, "Building the Pictures," *Variety,* June 25, 1930, 8.

19. Hal B. Wallis, "Preparation for Value-Saving Production Is F.N.'s Safeguard," *Variety,* June 25, 1930, 20.

20. Jacob Wilk, "Purchasing Stories for Vitaphone Films," *Variety,* June 25, 1930, 4.

21. Chris Yogerst, *From the Headlines to Hollywood: The Birth and Boom of Warner Bros.* (Lanham, MD: Rowman and Littlefield, 2016), xxiii.

22. A. P. Waxman, "Warner Bros.," *Variety,* June 25, 1930, 98.

23. "What's Wrong with the Movies?" *Houston Chronicle,* July 10, 1930, MPPDA Digital Archive.

24. Memo from Will Hays to Harry, Albert, and Jack Warner, August 8, 1930, MPPDA Digital Archive.

25. Memo from Maurice McKenzie to Will Hays, September 9, 1930, MPPDA Digital Archive.

26. Mervyn LeRoy, as told to Dick Kleiner, *Mervyn LeRoy: Take One* (New York: Hawthorn Books, 1973), 93, 94.

27. Edward G. Robinson with Leonard Spigelgass, *All My Yesterdays: An Autobiography* (New York: Hawthorn Books, 1973), 117.

28. Leonard Hall, "What? No Guns?" *Photoplay,* January–June 1931, 56.

29. William Wellman Jr., *Wild Bill Wellman: Hollywood Rebel* (New York: Pantheon Books, 2015), 264.

30. William Wellman interview in *The Men Who Made the Movies,* ed. Richard Schickel (Chicago: Ivan R. Dee, 1975), 210.

31. Jack Warner with Dean Jennings, *My First Hundred Years in Hollywood: An Autobiography* (New York: Random House, 1964), 204.

32. Advertisement for the 1931–1932 Warner Bros. film lineup, *Photoplay,* August 1931, 3.

33. Warner, *My First Hundred Years,* 204.

34. Samantha Barbas, *The First Lady of Hollywood: A Biography of Louella Parsons* (Berkeley: University of California Press, 2005), 146.

35. Sperling, *Hollywood Be Thy Name,* 178.

36. "Lewis Warner Improves," *New York Times,* February 28, 1931, 12.

37. Sperling, *Hollywood Be Thy Name,* 179.

38. Sperling, 180.

39. Cass Warner, interview with Lita Heller, https://thebrotherswarner.com/interview/lita-heller/.

40. Warner, *My First Hundred Years,* 216.

41. Jean Stein, *West of Eden: An American Place* (New York: Random House, 2016), 55.

42. Stein, 52.

43. Tino Balio, *The American Film Industry* (Madison: University of Wisconsin Press, 1985), 255.

44. "Movies Still Need Pioneers," *Miami Daily News,* February 21, 1932, Harry Warner Collection, Margaret Herrick Library, Beverly Hills, CA.

45. "Film Magnate Warner Raps Agents for Stars," *Boston Globe,* August 6, 1932, Harry Warner Collection, Margaret Herrick Library.

46. "Thank Him for the Talkies! Pen Portrait of H. M. Warner, Whose Company Gave a Voice to the Films," *Screenland,* October 1932, 59, 91.

47. "R. E. Burns Escapes Georgia Chain Gang: Chicago Ex-Publisher, Serving Term for $4 Hold-up, Flees for Second Time," *New York Times,* September 5, 1930, 25.

48. For an overview of Burns's life story, see the introduction to the screenplay: John E. O'Connor, *I Am a Fugitive from a Chain Gang* (Madison: University of Wisconsin Press, 1981).

49. The agreement was $4,500 for the book rights, $3,750 within forty-five days, and another $3,750 in ninety days. See Warner Bros. Legal Files for *I Am a Fugitive from a Chain Gang,* Warner Bros. Archive, Wisconsin Center for Film and Theater Research.

50. Memo from Jacob Wilk to Darryl Zanuck, April 6, 1932, in Rudy Behlmer, *Inside Warner Bros. (1935-1951): The Battles, the Brainstorms, and the Bickering—From the Files of Hollywood's Greatest Studio* (New York: Simon and Schuster, 1987), 5.

51. LeRoy, *Mervyn LeRoy,* 111.

52. Scott Eyman, *The Speed of Sound: Hollywood and the Talkie Revolution 1926–1930* (New York: Simon and Schuster, 1997), 361.

53. Lina Basquette, *Lina: DeMille's Godless Girl* (Fairfax, VA: Denlinger's Publishers, 1990), 170.

54. Basquette, 166.

55. Basquette, 421.

56. Heller interview.

57. Louis Nizer, "Pen Sketch of Harry M. Warner," *Exhibitor,* December 10, 1932, G.

58. Giuliana Muscio, *Hollywood's New Deal* (Philadelphia: Temple University Press, 1997), 96.

59. "Itinerary Completed for 42nd Street Special," *Film Daily,* February 16, 1933, 1.

60. Warner Bros. advertising poster, reprinted with the script notes, in Rocco Fumento, *42nd Street* (Madison: University of Wisconsin Press, 1980), 39.

61. Warner Bros. advertisement, *Film Daily,* March 4, 1933, 3.

62. Wellman, *Wild Bill Wellman,* 277.

63. Marlys J. Harris, *The Zanucks of Hollywood: The Dark Side of an American Dynasty* (New York: Crown, 1989), 38.

64. Harris, 37–38.

65. "Zanuck Resigns from Warners," *Los Angeles Times,* April 15, 1933, A1.

66. Memo from Harry Warner to Will Hays, April 1, 1933, MPPDA Archive.

67. Bonner Lin, "Zanuck Reveals Reason Why He Teamed up with Schenck," *Hollywood Herald,* June 8, 1933.

68. Memo from Joe Schenck to Will Hays, June 12, 1933, MPPDA Archive.

69. "Warners Obey Academy: Will Accept the Emergency Committee Date and Restore Full Salaries from April 10," *Hollywood Reporter,* April 22, 1933, 5.

70. "Harry Warner as NIRA Propagandist," *Variety,* August 1, 1933, 5.

71. Quoted in Nancy Snow, "Confessions of a Hollywood Propagandist: Harry Warner, FDR, and Celluloid Persuasion," in *Warner's War: Politics, Pop Culture & Propaganda in Wartime Hollywood,* ed. Martin Kaplan and Johanna Blakley (Los Angeles: Norman Lear Center, 2004), 61.

72. "Producers Move to Tighten Production Code," *Film Daily,* June 23, 1934, 1.

73. Philip Kinsley, "Filthy Filmmakers Plan to Defy Reformers," *Chicago Daily Tribune*, June 18, 1934, 6.

74. Kinsley, 6.

75. "Copeland Joins Industry Defense at Senate Quiz on Crime Control," *Motion Picture Herald*, December 2, 1933, 52.

76. "Film Code Approved," *Los Angeles Times*, November 28, 1933, 1.

77. "Jack Warner Says Public Demands More Gayety in Pictures," *Film Daily*, January 12, 1934, 1.

78. Thomas Doherty, *Hollywood's Censor: Joseph I. Breen & the Production Code Administration* (New York: Columbia University Press, 2007), 53.

79. Doherty, 70.

80. LeRoy, *Mervyn LeRoy*, 113.

81. "Warner Marriage Filmed as Talkie," *New York Times*, January 3, 1934, 21.

82. LeRoy, *Mervyn LeRoy*, 113.

83. "Death Claims Mother of Four Warner Bros.," *Motion Picture Daily*, August 28, 1934, 1.

84. Sperling, *Hollywood Be Thy Name*, 198.

85. Warner, *My First Hundred Years*, 249.

86. "Hitler Lowdown Being Checked by Hays with Wash.," *Variety*, April 11, 1933, 13.

87. "W. B. Only Walk Out," *Variety*, April 25, 1933, 13.

88. Thomas Doherty, "Cold Case from the Film Archives," *History Today* 56, no. 1 (January 2006): 37.

89. Steven J. Ross, *Hitler and Los Angeles: How Jews Foiled Nazi Plots against Hollywood and America* (New York: Bloomsbury Press, 2017), 68.

90. "Osterberg, Foe of Maloy, Shot 4 Times," *Chicago Daily Tribune*, May 14, 1935, 1.

91. Alan K. Rode, *Michael Curtiz: A Life in Film* (Lexington: University Press of Kentucky, 2017), 159.

92. Rode, 159.

93. Sperling, *Hollywood Be Thy Name*, 211.

94. "Albert Warner Says He Feared and Paid Bioff," *Los Angeles Times*, November 5, 1943, 2.

95. "Attends Court on Stretcher: Court Faced by Berkeley Witness to Crash," *Los Angeles Times*, September 20, 1935, A2.

96. Jeffrey Spivak, *Buzz: The Life and Art of Busby Berkeley* (Lexington: University Press of Kentucky, 2011), 134.

97. "It's Open Season for Star-Studio Squabbles," *Motion Picture Herald*, March 14, 1936, 13.

98. James Cagney, *Cagney by Cagney* (Garden City, NY: Doubleday, 1976), 43.

99. John Kobal, "Joan Blondell," in *People Will Talk* (New York: Alfred A. Knopf, 1985), 188; "Loretta Young," in *People Will Talk*, 406.

100. Wellman, *Wild Bill Wellman*, 284.

101. S. J. Baiano, interview with Ronald L. Davis, August 12, 1986, Southern Methodist University Oral History Collection, 4.

102. Baiano interview, 62.

103. Warner-Sheinbaum interview.

4. Fighting Fascism, America Firsters, and the US Senate

1. Neal Gabler, *An Empire of Their Own* (New York: Crown, 1988), 193.

2. Joe Adamson, *Byron Haskin: A Directors Guild of America Oral History* (Metuchen, NJ: Scarecrow Press, 1984).

3. John Huston, *An Open Book* (New York: Da Capo Press, 1980), 72.

4. Robert Buckner, interview with Ronald L. Davis, Southern Methodist University Oral History Collection, 13.

5. Hal Wallis, interview with Ronald L. Davis, Southern Methodist University Oral History Collection, 7, 11.

6. "Nazi Consul's Warning Stirs Active Resentment," *Box Office*, April 24, 1937, 33.

7. Machel E. Birdwell, *Celluloid Soldiers: Warner Bros.'s Campaign against Nazism* (New York: New York University Press, 1999), 46.

8. "Many Murders Laid to Detroit Black Legion," *New York Herald Tribune*, May 24, 1936, 1.

9. "Black Legion Rises as 1936 Ku-Klux Klan," *New York Herald Tribune*, May 31, 1936, B1. See also Will Lissner, "Black Legion's Spread Surprising to Midwest," *New York Times*, May 31, 1936, E6.

10. "Black Legion's Killer Says He Obeyed Orders," *New York Herald Tribune*, June 4, 1936, 7. See also "Black Legion's Killer Tells of Poole Slaying," *Chicago Daily Tribune*, June 4, 1936, 1.

11. For a longer discussion of *Black Legion,* see Chris Yogerst, *From the Headlines to Hollywood: The Birth and Boom of Warner Bros.* (Lanham, MD: Rowman and Littlefield, 2016).

12. Red Kann, "A Fistful of Dynamite about *Black Legion,*" *Motion Picture Daily,* January 11, 1937, 6–7.

13. "Black Legion Film Causes Suit by Klan," *Chicago Defender* (national ed.), August 28, 1937, 9. See also "Ku Klux Sues Warners over Klan Nightshirts," *New York Herald Tribune,* August 11, 1937, 14.

14. Birdwell, *Celluloid Soldiers,* 49.

15. "Leo M. Frank, an Innocent Man, May Suffer a Disgraceful Death for Another's Crime," *New York Times,* March 15, 1914, 10.

16. Burton Rascoe, "Will the State of Georgia Hang an Innocent Man?" *Chicago Daily Tribune,* December 27, 1914, G1.

17. Frank S. Nugent, "The Strand's 'They Won't Forget' Is an Indictment of Intolerance and Hatred Juggernaut," *New York Times,* July 15, 1937, 16; Norbert Lust, "Tragic Film Hailed as Masterpiece," *Los Angeles Times,* July 25, 1937, C3.

18. "Death in the South," *Wall Street Journal,* July 15, 1937, 8.

19. "Warner Brothers," *Fortune,* December 1937, 215, 218.

20. "Warner Brothers," 110.

21. "Warner Brothers," *Fortune,* December 1937, reprinted in Rudy Behlmer, *Inside Warner Bros. (1935–1951): The Battles, Brainstorms, and the Bickering—From the Files of Hollywood's Greatest Studio* (New York: Simon and Schuster, 1985), 55–56.

22. "Warner Brothers," *Fortune,* 110, 111, 220.

23. Invitations from Harry Warner dated July 16, 1938, for a party on July 25, Community Relations Committee Collection, Warner Brothers Pictures Inc., 1938–1939, folder 17-47, California State University–Northridge.

24. July 26 memorandum from Harry Warner's party on July 25, 1938, Community Relations Committee Collection, Warner Brothers Pictures Inc., 1938–1939, folder 17-47, California State University–Northridge.

25. Morris S. Lazaron, *Common Ground: A Plea for Intelligent Americanism* (New York: Liverlight, 1938), 324.

26. Stephen Vaughn, *Ronald Reagan in Hollywood: Movies and Politics* (Madison: University of Wisconsin Press, 1994), 74.

27. Harry Warner, "A Tribute to the American Legion," Marty Weiser Collection, F809, Margaret Herrick Library, Beverly Hills, CA.

28. Warner, "Tribute to American Legion"; "Red Charge Is False, Warner Tells Legion," *Motion Picture Herald,* September 24, 1938, 16.

29. Vance King, "Patriotic Films," *Motion Picture Herald,* September 17, 1938, 35.

30. Thomas Doherty, *Hollywood and Hitler* (New York: Columbia University Press, 2013), 328.

31. Warner Bros. Studio Prior to 1940 (2 of 2), Margaret Herrick Library, Beverly Hills, CA.

32. "Press Supports Warner's Charge 'March of Time' Reel Is Pro-Nazi," *Motion Picture Herald,* February 5, 1938, 33.

33. Doherty, *Hollywood and Hitler,* 254.

34. "Now Come Educators with Plea for Films of 'Social Insight,'" *Motion Picture Herald,* March 5, 1938, 15.

35. "WB to Unloose Flood of Anti-Nazi Pix, Market Lost to Them, Anyway," *Variety,* December 6, 1938, 15.

36. Behlmer, *Inside Warner Bros.,* 82.

37. Quoted in Otto Friedrich, *City of Nets: A Portrait of Hollywood in the 1940s* (New York: Harper and Row, 1986), 49.

38. Friedrich, 50.

39. "50 Pictures on WB Schedule," *Showmen's Trade Review,* June 15, 1940, 7.

40. John Wexley, interview with Patrick McGilligan and Ken Mate, in *Tender Comrades: A Backstory of the Hollywood Blacklist,* ed. Patrick McGilligan and Paul Buhle (New York: St. Martin's Press, 1997), 713.

41. Steven J. Ross, "*Confessions of a Nazi Spy:* Warner Bros., Anti-Fascism, and the Politicization of Hollywood," in *Warner's War: Politics, Pop Culture & Propaganda in Wartime Hollywood,* ed. Martin Kaplan and Johanna Blakley (Los Angeles: Norman Lear Center Press, 2004), 52.

42. Ross, 54.

43. Saverio Giovacchini, *Hollywood Modernism: Film and Politics in the Age of the New Deal* (Philadelphia: Temple University Press, 2001), 100.

44. All the material in the pamphlet came from Leon Lewis's spy Joseph Roos. For more information, see Chris Yogerst, *Hollywood Hates Hitler! Jew-Baiting, Anti-Nazism, and the Senate Investigation into Warmongering in Motion Pictures* (Jackson: University Press of Mississippi, 2020), 17–18.

45. Advertisement in *Motion Picture Herald,* April 15, 1939, 51–54.

46. Ross, *Confessions,* 54.

47. Edwin Schallert, "Vigorous Film Document of Nazi-ism in America Shown," *Los Angeles Times,* April 28, 1939, 12.

48. Joseph Roos, memo to US Senate regarding attack on motion pictures, 1940, 34, Community Relations Committee Collection, folder 17-30, California State University–Northridge.

49. Roos, 35. The German vice consul was Herman Geistreich.

50. "War News Tangle," *Motion Picture Herald,* November 18, 1939, 8.

51. For a lengthy discussion of the production of and response to the film, see Doherty, *Hollywood and Hitler,* chap. 12.

52. Johnny O'Steen, "Were These the Golden Years?" (unpublished memoir, n.d., Margaret Herrick Library, Beverly Hills, CA), 160.

53. Maurice Kann, "Salute to Courage," *Box Office,* April 29, 1939, 3.

54. Press release from Jack Warner, box 635, WB Prior to 1940, Warner Bros. Archives, University of Southern California.

55. Vincent Sherman, interview with Ronald L. Davis, Southern Methodist University Oral History Collection, 20.

56. Vincent Sherman, *Studio Affairs: My Life as a Film Director* (Lexington: University Press of Kentucky, 1996), 92.

57. Sherman, 94–95.

58. Cass Warner Sperling with Cork Millner and Jack Warner Jr., *Hollywood Be Thy Name: The Warner Brothers Story* (Rocklin, CA: Prima Publishing, 1994), 232.

59. Sperling, 232.

60. "Americanism, Motion Pictures, and a Warner Creed," *Motion Picture Herald,* January 28, 1939, 12–13.

61. O'Steen, "Were These the Golden Years?" 42.

62. Harry M. Warner, "United We Stand, Divided We Fall," June 5, 1940, Warner Bros. Archives, University of Southern California. All subsequent quotes are from this speech until otherwise noted.

63. Raoul Walsh, *Each Man in His Time: The Life Story of a Director* (New York: Farrar, Straus and Giroux, 1974), 307.

64. For a book-length chronicle of Senate Resolution 152, see Yogerst, *Hollywood Hates Hitler!*

65. Gerald Nye, "Our Madness Increases as Our Emergency Shrinks," radio address, St. Louis, August 1, 1941, http://www.ibiblio.org/pha/policy/1941/1941-08-01c.html.

66. The text of Lindbergh's speech can be found at http://www.charleslindbergh.com/americanfirst/speech.asp.

67. David Welky, *The Moguls and the Dictators: Hollywood and the Coming of World War II* (Baltimore: Johns Hopkins University Press, 2008), 291.

68. Yogerst, *Hollywood Hates Hitler!* 69, 71.

69. Jack Moffitt, "Investigation in Deeper Bog," *Hollywood Reporter,* September 11, 1941.

70. Ed Ainsworth, "As You Might Say," *Los Angeles Times,* September 11, 1941.

71. "Underground Biz Spurred by Inquiry," *Film Daily,* September 23, 1941.

72. "Critics Nix Senate Charges," *Film Daily,* September 23, 1941.

73. Yogerst, *Hollywood Hates Hitler!* 139.

74. Yogerst, 140.

75. Yogerst, 142.

76. Yogerst, 146, 147, 148.

77. Jack Moffitt, "New Charges in Film Quiz Hurled," *Hollywood Reporter,* September 25, 1941.

78. O'Steen, "Were These the Golden Years?" 45.

79. Curtis Bernhardt, interview by Mary Kiersch, in *A Directors Guild of America Oral History* (Lanham, MD: Scarecrow Press, 1986), 90.

80. Memo from Alex Evelove to Carlisle Jones, n.d., War Pictures (1941) file, Margaret Herrick Library. All subsequent quotes are from this memo until otherwise noted.

81. A. M. Sperber and Eric Lax, *Bogart* (New York: William Morrow, 1997), 100.

82. Blayney Matthews, *The Specter of Sabotage* (Los Angeles: Lymanhouse, 1941), dedication page.

83. Matthews, 63.

84. Memo from Evelove to Jones.

5. The War Years

1. Working with Harry were Barney Balaban (president of Paramount), Harry Cohn (president of Columbia), Will Hays (president of MPPDA), Edward C. Raftery (president of United Artists), N. Peter Rathvon (president of RKO), Nicholas Schenck (president of Loew's), Nate J. Blumberg (president of Universal), Spyros P. Skouras (president of 20th Century–Fox), and James R. Grainger (president of Republic). Other representatives included George Stevens (president of the Screen Directors Guild), Robert Shannon (president of RCA manufacturing), G. S. Eyssell (managing director of Radio City Music Hall), and Thomas J. Hargrave (president of Eastman Kodak). Harry Warner's work as director of the Association of Motion Picture Producers is referenced in a memo from Herbert Freston to Y. Frank Freeman, July 8 1942, Motion Picture Association of America Hollywood Office Files f. 100—Warner Bros. Pictures—Miscellaneous, Margaret Herrick Library, Beverly Hills, CA.

2. A full list of Warner Bros. Victory Shorts and those produced by other studios can be found at Academy War Film Library Files, United Nations—War Activities Committee f. 70, Margaret Herrick Library.

3. Motion Picture Association of America World War II records, Hollywood Victory Committee—Correspondence f. 360, Margaret Herrick Library.

4. Warner Club News Collection, Warner Bros. Archives, University of Southern California.

5. Memo reprinted from *Hollywood Reporter,* December 31, 1942, Warner Bros. files, Margaret Herrick Library.

6. A. M. Sperber and Eric Lax, *Bogart* (New York: William Morrow, 1997), 193.

7. Sperber and Lax, 98.

8. John Huston, *An Open Book* (New York: Da Capo Press, 1994), 72.

9. "OWI Takes Step to Censor All Movie Scripts," *Chicago Daily Tribune,* December 20, 1942, 19.

10. Clayton R. Koppes and Gregory D. Black, *Hollywood Goes to War: How Politics, Profits, and Propaganda Shaped World War II Movies* (Berkeley: University of California Press, 1990), 66.

11. "Stars 'Humane Givers' Not Reds, Dies Holds," *Motion Picture Herald,* August 24, 1940, 48.

12. Patrick McGilligan, *Yankee Doodle Dandy,* Wisconsin/Warner Bros. Screenplay Series, ed. Tino Balio (Madison: University of Wisconsin Press, 1981), 16.

13. For background on *Yankee Doodle Dandy,* see Alan K. Rode, *Michael Curtiz: A Life in Film* (Lexington: University Press of Kentucky, 2017).

14. "War Bond Sale of $5,450,000 Sells out Show," *New York Herald Tribune,* May 28, 1942, 15.

15. Curtis Bernhardt, interview by Mary Kiersch, in *A Directors Guild of America Oral History* (Lanham, MD: Scarecrow Press, 1986), 88.

16. Harry Warner, memo to *Variety,* December 1942, Warner Bros. war files, Margaret Herrick Library. The memo was published in *Variety* on January 6, 1943. All subsequent quotations are from this memo until otherwise noted.

17. Edwin Schallert, "*Casablanca* Romantic, Highly Topical Event," *Los Angeles Times,* January 30, 1943, A7.

18. Aljean Harmetz, *Round up the Usual Suspects: The Making of Casablanca—Bogart, Bergman, and World War II* (New York: Hyperion, 1992), 212.

19. Hal Wallis with Charles Higham, *Starmaker: The Autobiography of Hal Wallis* (New York: Macmillan, 1980), 92–95.

20. Edwin Schallert, "Warner-Wallis Rivalry Intrigues at Film Fete," *Los Angeles Times,* March 4, 1944, 7.

21. Jack Warner to Joseph Breen, November 25, 1942, MPAA PCA Records, Air Force folder, Margaret Herrick Library.

22. "*Air Force* Magnificent; Fine Warner Achievement," *Hollywood Reporter,* February 3, 1943, 3.

23. Todd McCarthy, *Howard Hawks: The Grey Fox of Hollywood* (New York: Basic Books, 1997), 344.

24. David Culbert, *Mission to Moscow,* Wisconsin/Warner Bros. Screenplay Series, ed. Tino Balio (Madison: University of Wisconsin Press, 1980), 16.

25. Robert Buckner, interview with Ronald L. Davis, Southern Methodist University Oral History Collection, 46.

26. Culbert, *Mission to Moscow,* 17.

27. Rode, *Michael Curtiz,* 343.

28. Rode, 349.

29. Culbert, *Mission to Moscow,* 255.

30. Culbert, 261.

31. Culbert, 261–62.

32. "Capital Cheers for 'Moscow,'" *Hollywood Reporter,* April 29, 1943, 1.

33. "Capital Cheers for 'Moscow.'"

34. "Capital Cheers for 'Moscow.'"

35. Culbert, *Mission to Moscow,* 257–59.

36. "Harry Warner Upholds Films' War Themes," *Chicago Daily Tribune,* May 19, 1943, 19.

37. Edwin Schallert, "Harry M. Warner Criticizes Advocates of Escapist Entertainment on Screen," *Los Angeles Times,* May 20, 1943, 30.

38. *Hollywood Reporter,* December 31, 1943.

39. Response to *Mission to Moscow* criticism, n.d. [1943], Howard Koch Papers, Wisconsin Center for Film and Theater Research, University of Wisconsin–Madison.

40. Unsigned letter to Stalin, May 1, 1943, Warner Bros. Legal Files, Wisconsin Center for Film and Theater Research, University of Wisconsin–Madison.

41. *Warner Club News,* December 1943, Warner Club News Collection, Warner Bros. Archives, University of Southern California. All subsequent quotations are from this newsletter until otherwise noted.

42. "S.S. Benj. Warner to Be Launched at Richmond Saturday," *Hollywood Reporter,* June 28, 1944, 7.

43. Cass Warner Sperling with Cork Millner and Jack Warner Jr., *Hollywood Be Thy Name: The Warner Brothers Story* (Rocklin, CA: Prima Publishing, 1994), 255.

44. Sperling, 255.

45. "The Benjamin Warner," *Motion Picture Herald,* July 1, 1944, 7.

46. A full list of names for the Hollywood Victory Committee can be found in the Motion Picture Association of America World War II records—Hollywood Victory Committee—annual report mailing f. 167, Margaret Herrick Library. All quotes from Jack Warner's speech are from "Must Keep War Lessons Alive," *Motion Picture Herald,* August 5, 1944, 29.

47. Ed Sikov, *Dark Victory: The Life of Bette Davis* (New York: Henry Holt, 2007), 212.

48. "Bette Davis Vetoes Race Slur at Canteen," *New York Amsterdam Star-News,* January 9, 1943, 14.

49. Sherrie Tucker, *Dance Floor Democracy: The Social Geography of Memory at the Hollywood Canteen* (Durham, NC: Duke University Press, 2014), 292–95.

50. "*Canteen* Premiere in Albany Nets $24,000,000 Bond Sale," *Showman's Trade Review,* December 23, 1944, 9.

51. Sikov, *Dark Victory,* 221.

52. Joan Leslie, foreword to *The Hollywood Canteen: Where the Greatest Generation Danced with the Most Beautiful Girls in the World* (Duncan, GA: BearManor Media, 2012), 9.

53. *Warner Club News,* December 1944–January 1945, Warner Club News Collection, Warner Bros. Archives, University of Southern California.

54. Advertisement in *Showmen's Trade Review,* September 22, 1945, 10, 11.

55. "*Appointment in Tokyo* the Best Yet," *Variety,* November 28, 1945, 10.

56. Jack L. Warner with Dean Jennings, *My First Hundred Years in Hollywood: An Autobiography* (New York: Random House, 1965), 263.

57. "*Hitler Lives* Film Warns against Fascist Thinking," *New York Herald Tribune,* January 22, 1946, 23.

58. Bosley Crowther, "Public Opinion: A Further Word in the Discussion of Censorship—See *Hitler Lives,*" *New York Times,* January 27, 1946, X1.

59. Don Siegel, *Hitler Lives* (Warner Bros., 1945).

60. Warner, *My First Hundred Years,* 263.

61. Warner, 299.

62. "Jury Acquits Errol Flynn after 13 Hours," *New York Herald Tribune,* February 7, 1943, 25.

63. Warner, *My First Hundred Years,* 298.

64. "'Feared for Life'—H. M. Warner," *Hollywood Reporter,* November 8, 1943, 1.

65. "'Feared for Life,'" 8.

66. "Harry Warner Tells His Fear of Willie Bioff," *Los Angeles Times,* November 6, 1943, 2.

67. Undated memo, circa August 12, 1943, in Rudy Behlmer, *Inside Warner Bros. (1935–1951): The Battles, Brainstorms, and the Bickering—From the Files of Hollywood's Greatest Studio* (New York: Simon and Schuster, 1985), 234.

68. Victoria Amador, *Olivia de Havilland: Lady Triumphant* (Lexington: University Press of Kentucky, 2019), 94.

69. HM to JL, June 7, 1944, in Behlmer, *Inside Warner Bros.,* 235.

70. JL to HM, June 7, 1944, in Behlmer, *Inside Warner Bros.,* 235.

71. Quoted in Jean Stein, *West of Eden: An American Place* (New York: Random House, 2016), 70.

72. "Film Strikers Battle Police at Warner Studio," *New York Herald Tribune,* October 6, 1945, 3.

73. "Dozen Injured in Melee at Warner's Entrance," *Los Angeles Times,* October 6, 1945, 1.

74. Gerald Horne, *Class Struggle in Hollywood, 1930–1950: Moguls, Mobsters, Stars, Reds, and Trade Unionists* (Austin: University of Texas Press, 2001), 165.

75. John Wexley, interview with Patrick McGilligan and Ken Mate, in *Tender Comrades: A Backstory of the Hollywood Blacklist,* ed. Patrick McGilligan and Paul Buhle (New York: St. Martin's Press, 1997), 712.

76. Connie Bruck, *When Hollywood Had a King: The Reign of Lew Wasserman, Who Leveraged Talent into Power and Influence* (New York: Random House, 2003), 92.

77. Stein, *West of Eden,* 70–71.

78. "Warner Pays FDR Tribute in Visioning New Peace Era," *Hollywood Reporter,* August 17, 1945, 10.

79. Sperber and Lax, *Bogart,* 308.

80. Sperber and Lax, 308.

81. Clayton R. Koppes and Gregory D. Black, *Hollywood Goes to War: How Politics, Profits, and Propaganda Shaped World War II Movies* (Berkeley: University of California Press, 1990), 328.

6. Postwar Politics, HUAC, and the Blacklist

1. *Warner Club News,* January 1946, Warner Bros. Archives, University of Southern California.

2. Terry Ramsaye, "When Film Found Its Voice," *Motion Picture Herald,* August 3, 1946, 16, 26.

3. All quotations from Harry, Jack, and Albert are from Ramsaye's article until otherwise noted.

4. Mel Blanc, *That's Not All Folks! My Life in the Golden Age of Cartoons and Radio* (New York: Warner Books, 1988), 75.

5. Blanc, 89–90.

6. Larry Decuers, "Private Snafu Cartoon Series," National World War II Museum, New Orleans, https://www.nationalww2museum.org/war/articles/private-snafu-cartoon-series.

7. "Violence Opens Studio Strike," *Los Angeles Times,* September 27, 1946, 1.

8. Gerald Horne, *Class Struggle in Hollywood, 1930–1950: Moguls, Mobsters, Stars, Reds, and Trade Unionists* (Austin: University of Texas Press, 2001), 181.

9. Horne, 183.

10. Steven Vaughn, *Ronald Reagan in Hollywood: Movies and Politics* (Cambridge: Cambridge University Press, 1994), 139.

11. "$3,000,000 Warner Bros. Suit Names Unionists," *Los Angeles Times,* October 5, 1946, 8.

12. "Rioting in the Film Strike at Warner Bros. Studio," HUAC files, Margaret Herrick Library, Beverly Hills, CA.

13. Vaughn, *Ronald Reagan in Hollywood,* 140.

14. Vaughn, 133.

15. Ronald Reagan, *An American Life: The Autobiography* (New York: Simon and Schuster, 1990), 114.

16. Robert Buckner, interview by Ronald L. Davis, Southern Methodist University Oral History Collection, 28.

17. *Warner Club News,* January 1947, Warner Bros. Archives, University of Southern California.

18. "WB Skyrockets to $19,134,000 in 9-Mo. Earnings," *Variety,* July 30, 1947, 5.

19. "Albert Warner Gives 2,900 Shares to Charity," *Variety,* January 15, 1947, 9.

20. Thomas Schatz, *The Genius of the System: Hollywood Filmmaking in the Studio Era* (Minneapolis: University of Minnesota Press, 1996), 414.

21. John Huston, *An Open Book* (New York: Da Capo Press, 1994), 151.

22. Alan K. Rode, *Michael Curtiz: A Life in Film* (Lexington: University Press of Kentucky, 2017), 410.

23. Mae Tinee, "Newest Bogart and Bacall Film Is Far Fetched," *Chicago Daily Tribune,* October 31, 1947, 28.

24. John Kobal, "Vincent Sherman," in *People Will Talk* (New York: Alfred A. Knopf, 1985), 564–65.

25. W. R. Wilkerson III, *Hollywood Godfather: The Life and Crimes of Billy Wilkerson* (Chicago: Chicago Review Press, 2018), 218.

26. Billy Wilkerson, "Tradeviews," *Hollywood Reporter,* July 6, 1946, 1.

27. Billy Wilkerson, "A Vote for Joe Stalin," *Hollywood Reporter,* July 29, 1946, 4.

28. "Pix Control U.S. Minds—Reds," *Hollywood Reporter,* August 8, 1946, 9.

29. Quoted in Jean Stein, *West of Eden: An American Place* (New York: Random House, 2016), 73.

30. Quoted in Thomas Doherty, *Show Trial: HUAC, Hollywood, and the Birth of the Blacklist* (New York: Columbia University Press, 2018), 60.

31. Lee Garling, "Washington Report," *Box Office,* April 12, 1947, 28.

32. Memorandum regarding *Mission to Moscow,* dated July 2, 1943, and submitted July 8, 1943, HUAC files, Communist Activity in the Entertainment Industry Bureau Files, vol. 2, f. 2, 8–9, 13, Margaret Herrick Library.

33. Louis Pizzitola, *Hearst over Hollywood: Power, Passion, and Propaganda in the Movies* (New York: Columbia University Press, 2002), 407.

34. Memorandum regarding *Mission to Moscow,* 16.

35. Jack L. Warner with Dean Jennings, *My First Hundred Years in Hollywood: An Autobiography* (New York: Random House, 1965), 293.

36. FBI memo, May 14, 1943, HUAC files, Communist Activity in the Entertainment Industry Bureau Files, vol. 2, f. 2, 6, Margaret Herrick Library.

37. These names and more can be found in HUAC files, Communist Activity in the Entertainment Industry Bureau Files, vol. 2, f. 2, Margaret Herrick Library.

38. HUAC files, Communist Activity in the Entertainment Industry Bureau Files, vol. 2, f. 2, Margaret Herrick Library.

39. FBI document dated February 12, 1944, by Agent [redacted], HUAC files, Communist Activity in the Entertainment Industry Bureau Files, vol. 2, f. 2, Margaret Herrick Library.

40. FBI file dated March 20, 1944, HUAC files, Communist Activity in the Entertainment Industry Bureau Files, vol. 2, f. 2, 11, Margaret Herrick Library.

41. "Probers Call Top Film Brass in Red Inquiry: Jack Warner Faces Quiz on *Mission to Moscow,*" *Chicago Daily Tribune,* October 19, 1947, 10.

42. "Mayer, Warner on Stand First in Red Probe at Capital," *Hollywood Reporter,* October 16, 1947, 1.

43. J. Parnell Thomas to President Harry Truman, April 23, 1947, Truman Library, https://www.trumanlibrary.gov/public/2019-03/HUAC_DocumentSet.pdf.

44. "Adolphe Menjou, Jack Warner Name Names in Red Inquiry," *New York Herald Tribune,* May 16, 1947, 1, 16.

45. J. A. Otten, "Trying to Dictate and Control, Says McNutt," *Motion Picture Herald,* October 25, 1947, 14.

46. *Hearings Regarding the Communist Infiltration of the Motion Picture Industry, Hearings before the Committee on Un America Activities, House of Representatives, Eightieth Congress, First Session* (Washington, DC: US Government Printing Office, 1947), 7–54. All subsequent quotations are from this congressional record until otherwise noted.

47. Carl Levin, "14 Writers, 4 Directors, Named by Mayer, Wood, Warner in U.S. Inquiry," *New York Herald Tribune,* October 21, 1947, 1.

48. *Hearings Regarding the Communist Infiltration of the Motion Picture Industry.* All subsequent quotations are from this congressional record until otherwise noted.

49. "No Red in Films—Mayer, Warner," *Hollywood Reporter,* October 21, 1947, 1.

50. Otten, "Trying to Dictate and Control," 13.

51. "Irwin Shaw Denies Warner Statement," *New York Times,* October 25, 1947, 12.

52. Red Kann, "The Films Are the Pay-off," *Motion Picture Herald,* October 25, 1941, 16.

53. Gordon Kahn, *Hollywood on Trial: The Story of the Ten Who Were Indicted* (New York: Boni and Gaer, 1948), 4.

54. Stein, *West of Eden,* 73.

55. Stein, 73.

56. Stein, 74.

57. Stein, 73.

58. Advertisement for Committee for the First Amendment, *Hollywood Reporter,* October 23, 1947, 5.

59. Doherty, *Show Trial,* 217.

60. Lauren Bacall, "Why I Came to Washington," October 29, 1947, 1. All subsequent quotations are from this source until otherwise noted. See also Doherty, *Show Trial,* 226.

61. "Film Industry's Policy Defined," *Variety,* November 26, 1947, 3.

62. "Film Industry's Policy Defined," 3.

63. Lester Cole, *Hollywood Red: The Autobiography of Lester Cole* (Palo Alto, CA: Ramparts Press, 1981), 162, 296–97.

64. "Humanitarian Award Goes to Harry Warner," *Los Angeles Times*, December 6, 1947, A14.

65. Mervyn LeRoy, *Mervyn LeRoy: Take One* (New York: Hawthorne Books, 1974), 144.

66. Harry Warner's notes on conference with President Truman, July 10, 1946, Warner Bros. Archives, University of Southern California.

67. Harry Truman to Harry Warner, May 12, 1947, Memorandum of Conference with President Truman, May 9, 1947, Warner Bros. Archives, University of Southern California.

68. *Warner Club News,* December 1947, Warner Club News Collection, Warner Bros. Archives, University of Southern California. All subsequent quotations are from this publication.

7. Last Gasp of Old Hollywood

1. Drew Casper, *Postwar Hollywood: 1946–1962* (Malden, MA: Blackwell, 2007), 39.

2. "Warner Unveils Video Plans," *Hollywood Reporter,* March 21, 1949, 1, 7. All subsequent quotations are from this article until otherwise noted.

3. "Warner Boosts Schedule, Adds to Studio Star Power," *Motion Picture Daily,* April 21, 1949, 12.

4. Raoul Walsh, *Each Man in His Time: The Life Story of a Director* (New York: Farrar, Straus and Giroux, 1974), 360.

5. *Warner Club News,* August 1949, Warner Club News Collection, Warner Bros. Archives, University of Southern California.

6. "USN Kudoses J. L. Warner for *Task Force,*" *Variety,* September 21, 1949, 2.

7. Jack Warner quoted in Thomas Schatz, *Boom and Bust: American Cinema in the 1940s* (Berkeley: University of California Press, 1999), 442.

8. *Warner Club News,* January 1950, Warner Club News Collection, Warner Bros. Archives, University of Southern California. All subsequent quotations are from this issue until otherwise noted.

9. "Harry Warner & Anti-Red Drive," *Billboard* 62, no. 39 (September 30, 1950): 3.

10. "Warner Cautions Employees on Reds," *New York Times,* September 2, 1950, 22.

11. Cass Warner Sperling with Cork Millner and Jack Warner Jr., *Hollywood Be Thy Name: The Warner Brothers Story* (Rocklin, CA: Prima Publishing, 1994), 284.

12. "Let Us Make No Mistake about It," advertisement, *Hollywood Reporter,* August 30, 1950, 4–5.

13. FBI report on subversive activities in Hollywood, August 22, 1950, Communist Activity in the Entertainment Industry Bureau Files, vol. 24, f. 24, Margaret Herrick Library, Beverly Hills, CA.

14. Harry Truman, "Address at a Dinner of the Federal Bar Association," April 25, 1950, Harry S. Truman Library.

15. "Film Reviews: *Storm Warning,*" *Variety,* December 6, 1950, 15.

16. Elia Kazan, *A Life* (New York: Da Capo Press, 1997), 432.

17. Patrick McGilligan, *Alfred Hitchcock: A Life in Darkness and Light* (New York: Harper, 2003), 457.

18. McGilligan, 458.

19. *Warner Club News,* January 1951, Warner Club News Collection, Warner Bros. Archives, University of Southern California. All subsequent quotations are from this issue until otherwise noted.

20. All the reviews quoted are from *I Was a Communist for the F.B.I.* file, PCA files 1951, Margaret Herrick Library. All subsequent quotations are from this collection until otherwise noted.

21. The statement was reprinted in *Warner Club News,* December 1951, Warner Club News Collection, Warner Bros. Archives, University of Southern California.

22. Telegram from Sam Goldwyn to Jack Warner, September 24, 1953, National Conference—Christians and Jews folder 2949A—Jewish and Minority Causes, Warner Bros. Archives, University of Southern California.

23. Telegram from Jack Warner to Harry Cohn, September 24, 1953, National Conference—Christians and Jews folder 2949A—Jewish and Minority Causes, Warner Bros. Archives, University of Southern California.

24. Telegram from Jack Warner to Harry Cohn, September 24, 1953.

25. "Award of World Brotherhood Goes to LeRoy," *Los Angeles Times,* October 16, 1953, 19.

26. Telegram from Jack Warner to Harry Cohn, September 24, 1953. All subsequent quotations are from National Conference—Christians and Jews folder 2949A—Jewish and Minority Causes, Warner Bros. Archives, University of Southern California, until otherwise noted.

27. Fred Zinnemann to Jack Warner, July 21, 1958, *The Nun's Story* PCA file, Margaret Herrick Library Digital Collection.

28. Archbishop of Los Angeles to Henry Blanke, August 19, 1957, *The Nun's Story* PCA file, Margaret Herrick Library Digital Collection.

29. Interview with Chuck Jones, Television Academy Foundation, https://interviews.televisionacademy.com/interviews/chuck-jones?clip=55212#interview-clips.

30. *Warner Club News,* January 1954, Warner Club News Collection, Warner Bros. Archives, University of Southern California.

31. "Harry M. Warner: Recipient of the Los Angles P.L.K. Medical Achievements Award," *PLK Quarterly,* September 1954.

32. George Stevens to Jack Warner, October 8, 1954, Political—Jack L. Warner files, folder 2950B, Warner Bros. Archives, University of Southern California.

33. Casper, *Postwar Hollywood,* 137.

34. Juvenile Delinquency (Motion Pictures), Thursday, June 16, 1955, US Senate, Subcommittee of the Committee on the Judiciary to Investigate Juvenile Delinquency, Los Angeles. All subsequent quotations are from this file until otherwise noted.

35. "Statement of Jack L. Warner, Producer and Vice President, Warner Bros. Pictures, Inc., Hollywood Calif.," in *Hearings before the Subcommittee to Investigate Juvenile Delinquency of the Committee on the Judiciary United States Senate, Eighty-Fourth Congress, First Session, Senate Resolution 62,* Media History Digital Library. All subsequent quotations are from this file until otherwise noted.

36. Martin Quigley, "Kefauver in Hollywood," *Motion Picture Herald,* June 18, 1955, 7.

37. Jim Henaghan, "Rambling Reporter," *Hollywood Reporter,* June 17, 1955, 2.

38. Thomas Pryor, "Hollywood Test: Movies Defended, Assailed in Kefauver Probe of Films' Effect on Youth," *New York Times,* June 26, 1955, X5.

39. B. J. Glaser to Jack Warner, June 18, 1955, Political—Jack L. Warner files, folder 2951A Special (F005887), Warner Bros. Archives, University of Southern California.

40. John Kulp to Jack Warner, July 6, 1955, Political—Jack L. Warner files, folder 2951A Special (F005887), Warner Bros. Archives, University of Southern California.

41. Letter from William Mooring responding to an article in the *Los Angeles Examiner,* June 17, 1955, Political—Jack L. Warner files, folder 2951A Special (F005887), Warner Bros. Archives, University of Southern California.

42. "Honor Major Warner at UJA Lunch in New York," *Motion Picture Herald,* May 28, 1955, 23. All subsequent quotations are from this article until otherwise noted.

43. "Warner Points to 'Upsurge,'" *Motion Picture Daily,* October 24, 1955, 6.

44. Advertisement in *Motion Picture Herald,* October 20, 1955, 3.

45. Tab Hunter with Eddie Muller, *Tab Hunter Confidential: The Making of a Movie Star* (Chapel Hill, NC: Algonquin Books of Chapel Hill, 2005), 122.

46. George Stevens Jr., *My Place in the Sun: Life in the Golden Age of Hollywood and Washington* (Lexington: University Press of Kentucky, 2022), 142.

47. Stevens, 152.

48. Glenn Frankel, *The Searchers: The Making of an American Legend* (New York: Bloomsbury, 2013), 266.

49. Sperling, *Hollywood Be Thy Name,* 301.

8. End of the Studio, End of the Family

1. Cass Warner, interview with Lois McGrew, https://thebrotherswarner.com/interview/lois-mcgrew/. All subsequent quotations are from this interview until otherwise noted.

2. "Semenenko Warner Deal Completed," *Los Angeles Times,* July 12, 1956, B1.

3. "Warner Predicts New Era in Film Production," *Motion Picture Daily,* August 6, 1956, 1, 3.

4. Mervyn LeRoy with Dick Kleiner, *Mervyn LeRoy: Take One* (New York: Hawthorne Books, 1974), 198.

5. Jon Lewis, *Hollywood v. Hard Core: How the Struggle over Censorship Saved the Modern Film Industry* (New York: New York University Press, 2000), 124.

6. James Powers, "Baby Doll Has Makings of Box Office Blockbuster: Kazan Production Will Stir up Talk," *Hollywood Reporter,* December 5, 1956.

7. Elia Kazan to Jack Warner, July 25, 1956, in *The Selected Letters of Elia Kazan,* ed. Albert J. Devlin with Marlene J. Devlin (New York: Alfred A. Knopf, 2014), 338. All subsequent quotations are from this letter until otherwise noted.

8. "Legion Hits *Baby Doll* and Code," *Motion Picture Herald,* December 1, 1956, 27.

9. Jack Vizzard, *See No Evil: Life Inside a Hollywood Censor* (New York: Simon and Schuster, 1970), 209.

10. "Jack Warner Tells of Faith in Film Future," *Motion Picture Herald,* September 22, 1956, 30.

11. "Need of Brotherhood in Today's World Stressed by Warner," *Motion Picture Daily,* January 25, 1957, 1, 7.

12. *Warner Club News,* January 1957, Warner Club News Collection, Warner Bros. Archives, University of Southern California.

13. "H. M. Warner Improved," *Hollywood Reporter,* June 20, 1957, 2.

14. Cass Warner Sperling with Cork Millner and Jack Warner Jr., *Hollywood Be Thy Name: The Warner Brothers Story* (Rocklin, CA: Prima Publishing, 1994), 311.

15. Sperling, 312.

16. *Warner Club News,* December 1957, Warner Club News Collection, Warner Bros. Archives, University of Southern California.

17. Jean Stein, *West of Eden: An American Place* (New York: Random House, 2016), 96.

18. Sperling, *Hollywood Be Thy Name,* 313.

19. "1,000 Attend Services for Harry M. Warner," *Los Angeles Times,* July 28, 1958, B1.

20. "Industry-wide Tribute Paid to Harry M. Warner," *Motion Picture Daily,* July 29, 1958, 1, 6. All subsequent quotations are from this publication until otherwise noted.

21. "Home for the Aged Auxiliary Mourns Mrs. Harry M. Warner," *B'nai B'rith Messenger,* October 23, 1970, Harry M. Warner File, American Jewish Archives.

22. Amy Fine Collins, "The Man Hollywood Trusted," *Vanity Fair,* April 2001.

23. Collins.

24. John Kobal, "Vincent Sherman," in *People Will Talk* (New York: Alfred A. Knopf, 1985), 569.

25. Wendell Mayes, interview with Rui Nogueira, "Wendell Mayes: The Jobs Poured over Me," in *Backstory 3: Interviews with Screenwriters of the 1960s,* ed. Patrick McGilligan (Berkeley: University of California Press, 1997), 266, 267.

26. "Studio Bars Young Jack Warner as Family Feud Breaks into Open," *Los Angeles Times,* January 3, 1959, 1. All subsequent quotations are from this article until otherwise noted.

27. Stein, *West of Eden,* 94.

28. "L.A. City Fathers Cite Jack Warner," *Los Angeles Times,* February 19, 1959, 2.

29. Bob Thomas, *Clown Prince of Hollywood: The Antic Life and Times of Jack L. Warner* (New York: McGraw-Hill, 1990), 230.

30. Jack L. Warner with Dean Jennings, *My First Hundred Years in Hollywood: An Autobiography* (New York: Random House, 1964), 302.

31. "Many Seats Empty at Final Rites for Actor Errol Flynn," *Los Angeles Times*, October 20, 1959, 2.

9. A New Hollywood Rises

1. Jack L. Warner with Dean Jennings, *My First Hundred Years in Hollywood: An Autobiography* (New York: Random House, 1964), 303, 304.

2. Interview with James Garner, Television Academy website, https://interviews.televisionacademy.com/interviews/james-garner.

3. Jack L. Warner, "An Open Letter," *Los Angeles Times,* 1960, Political—Steve Trilling Collection ST 003-028, Warner Bros. Archives, University of Southern California. Subsequent quotations from responders to the letter are from the same file.

4. Telegram from Jack Warner to JFK, December 18, 1961, White House, Jack L. Warner files, 1961, folder 2952A (F015016), Warner Bros. Archives, University of Southern California.

5. "Motion Pictures, TV Equal Partners, Says Jack Warner," *Hollywood Reporter,* July 7, 1961, 1.

6. Telegram from Lyndon Johnson to Jack Warner, February 1, 1962, folder 2952, Warner Bros. Archives, University of Southern California.

7. Jean Stein, *West of Eden: An American Place* (New York: Random House, 2016), 104.

8. Stein, 105.

9. Shaun Considine, *Bette & Joan: The Divine Feud* (USA: Graymalkin Media, 2017), 336.

10. Considine, 342.

11. Jack Warner to John F. Kennedy, March 7, 1961, Political—1961, folder ST 003-031, Warner Bros. Governmental and Political Activity Special 2 of 2, Warner Bros. Archives, University of Southern California.

12. Stein, *West of Eden,* 105.

13. Bob Thomas, *Clown Prince of Hollywood: The Antic Life and Times of Jack L. Warner* (New York: McGraw-Hill, 1990), 240.

14. Ted Johnson, "Making of John F. Kennedy Biopic PT 109 Was Hardly Smooth Sailing," *Variety,* August 16, 2013.

15. Hedda Hopper, "Jack Warner Makes Pitch for Hollywood," *Chicago Daily Tribune,* June 7, 1963, C2.

16. Amy Fine Collins, "The Man Hollywood Trusted," *Vanity Fair,* April 2001.

17. Footage of 1963 Production Kick-off Dinner, special feature on *My Fair Lady* 4K Blu-ray, 2021.

18. Bosley Crowther, "Screen: Lots of Chocolates for Miss Eliza Doolittle," *New York Times*, October 22, 1964, 41.

19. Thomas, *Clown Prince of Hollywood*, 263.

20. David Thomson, *Warner Bros.: The Making of an American Movie Studio* (New Haven, CT: Yale University Press, 2017), 185.

21. "Departure from WB of Steve Trilling," *Variety*, February 12, 1964, 5; "Steven B. Trilling Is Dead; Former Warner Bros. V-P," *Boxoffice*, June 8, 1964, 12.

22. "Trilling Leaving WB after Three Decades," *Boxoffice*, February 10, 1964, W-2.

23. Footage of 1963 Production Kick-off Dinner.

24. Mark Harris, *Mike Nichols: A Life* (New York: Penguin Press, 2021), 194.

25. Harris, 194.

26. "Jack Warner Remarks Re 'Woolf,'" *Variety*, June 1, 1966, 1.

27. Thomas, *Clown Prince of Hollywood*, 278.

28. Leonard Sloane, "Jack L. Warner, President, Agrees to Sell His Interest in a $32-Million Deal," *New York Times*, November 15, 1966, 65.

29. Peter Biskind, *Easy Riders, Raging Bulls: How the Sex-Drugs-and-Rock n' Roll Generation Saved Hollywood* (New York: Simon and Schuster, 1998), 23.

30. Mark Harris, *Pictures at a Revolution: Five Movies and the Birth of the New Hollywood* (New York: Penguin Press, 2008), 192.

31. Biskind, *Easy Riders*, 35.

32. Peter Biskind, *Star: How Warren Beatty Seduced America* (New York: Simon and Schuster, 2010), 117.

33. Vincent Canby, "Jack Warner, 75, Resigns Top Job," *New York Times*, July 25, 1967, 31.

34. Charles Champlin, "Jack Warner: A Founding Father Who Carries On," *Los Angeles Times*, October 29, 1967, D1.

35. Charles Champlin, "Jack L. Warner Ends Ties with Movie-Making Studio," *Los Angeles Times*, September 12, 1969, C1.

36. Thomas, *Clown Prince of Hollywood*, 289.

37. Charles Champlin, "Retiring Jack Warner Feted by Golden Era's Who's Who," *Los Angeles Times*, November 22, 1969, A7.

38. Thomas M. Pryor, "Jack Warner, a Happy King Lear, Respected Even Though Abdicated," *Variety*, November 26, 1969, 1.

39. Pryor, 70.

40. Jody Jacobs, "New Camera Angle for Jack Warner," *Los Angeles Times*, January 25, 1972, F1.

41. Wayne Warga, "Jack L. Warner Getting His Second Wind at 79," *Los Angeles Times*, June 6, 1971, O1.

42. Charles Champlin, "Movie Wealth from Warners," *Los Angeles Times*, October 4, 1976, E1.

43. Stein, *West of Eden*, 109.

44. J. Wallace Bastian, "Death of Jack L. Warner and the Passing of an Era," *Los Angeles Times*, September 23, 1978, B5.

45. "Jack L. Warner's Death Closes out Pioneer Clan of Talkies," *Variety*, September 13, 1978, 2.

46. "Jack Warner Movie Mogul Known for Foresight and Bad Jokes," *Toronto Globe and Mail*, September 11, 1978, 15.

47. Bastian, "Death of Jack L. Warner," B5.

48. Charles Champlin, "Jack Warner: In Memoriam," *Los Angeles Times*, September 17, 1978, I33.

49. James R. Silke, *Here's Looking at You, Kid: 50 Years of Fighting, Working, and Dreaming at Warner Bros.* (Boston: Little, Brown, 1976), 38.

50. Jack Warner, "Disclaimer from a Warner," *Los Angeles Times*, January 16, 1977, S2.

51. Warner, S2.

Coda

1. Neal Gabler, *An Empire of Their Own: How the Jews Invented Hollywood* (New York: Crown, 1988), 7.

2. "The Colonel: An Affectionate Remembrance of Jack L. Warner," Friends of the USC Libraries, University of Southern California, 1980, Margaret Herrick Library, Beverly Hills, CA. All the following quotes are from this event.

Index

Across the Pacific (1942), 149–50
All through the Night (1942), 149, 299
American Legion, 121–23, 149, 259
anticommunism/anticommunist(s),
    2, 127, 161, 189, 196, 199, 202, 210,
    218–19, 227, 229, 238
antifascism/antifascist(s), 116, 118,
    121, 126, 192, 221
antifascist films, 114–45
Army Emergency Relief Fund, 154,
    163
Ashley, Ted, 285

Baby Doll (1956), 233, 251–55
Baby Face (1933), 96
Bacall, Lauren, 173, 187–88, 204–5,
    214, 278
Bad Seed, The (1956), 231, 251–52, 274
Baiano, S. J., 110–11
Banks, Monty, 32
Basquette, Gladys, 51–52, 67, 69
Basquette, Lina, 51–55, 60, 65–67,
    70–71, 92, 207–8
Beatty, Warren, 268, 275, 281–82, 285
Benjamin Warner, SS, 165
Bennett, Constance, 52, 188
Bercutt, Max, 4, 271, 291
Berkeley, Busby, 94, 96, 100, 108–9,
    114, 285
Bernhardt, Curtis, 142, 153
Big Jim McLain (1952), 218, 229

Bioff, Willie, 106–8, 173–74
Black Fury (1935), 107
Black Legion (1937), 114, 117–18, 120,
    126, 129, 199, 221
Black Legion (radical group), 116–18
blacklist, the, 179–85
Blackton, J. Stuart, 47–48
Blanc, Mel, 124, 159, 182, 294
Blanke, Henry, 115, 232, 235
Blondell, Joan, 96, 109–10, 285
Blue, Monte, 38, 41, 49, 55, 67, 188,
    215
Bogart, Humphrey, 85, 117, 134–35,
    150–51, 156–57, 166, 173, 175, 180,
    187–88, 204, 214–15, 221, 226, 267,
    289, 290, 299
Bonnie and Clyde (1967), 274, 281–82
Brando, Marlon, 223, 233, 237
Breen, Joseph, 2, 100–101, 127, 134,
    158, 173, 214, 224, 227, 235, 240
Brown, George, 106
brownshirts, 121
Buckner, Robert, 115, 159–61, 185, 193
Burbank Studio Lot, 4, 72–73, 77, 182,
    183–85
Burton, Richard, 279

Cagney, James, 2, 84–85, 94, 100, 106,
    109–10, 114, 119, 139, 143, 150–52,
    174, 182, 214–15, 237–38, 246, 276,
    282, 290, 298, 301

Index

Cagney, William "Bill," 152, 215
Cantwell, John J., 106
Casablanca (1942), 153–54, 156–57,
    159, 168, 190, 199, 246, 278,
    285–86, 295, 299
Cascade theater, 15–18
censorship, 90, 96, 100–101, 178,
    201, 223, 231, 252, 236, 279; self-
    censorship, 61, 100
Chandler, Harry, 136
CinemaScope, 232–33, 243
City for Conquest (1938), 190, 221
Cohn, Harry, 68, 92, 105, 107, 177,
    205, 216, 230, 258, 261, 290, 294
Committee for the First Amendment
    (CFA), 204
Conference of Studio Unions (CSU),
    175–76, 183–85
Confessions of a Nazi Spy (1939), 1–2,
    116, 126–30, 132, 137, 139–41, 149,
    170, 176, 190, 227, 238
Conway, Jack, 52–53
Coughlin, Father Charles, 117, 131,
    172
Covered Wagon, The (1912), 23
Crawford, Joan, 166, 169, 172–73, 188,
    214–15, 272–74
Curtiz, Michael, 53, 71, 85, 107, 124,
    139, 143, 152, 159–60, 187–88, 216,
    258, 267

Dante's Inferno (1911), 21–22
Daves, Delmer, 188, 194, 202, 216,
    271, 278
Davies, Joseph E., 159–62, 192, 195,
    199, 200
Davis, Bette, 106, 109, 114–15,
    134–35, 139, 143, 153, 166–69, 174,
    188, 214–15, 221, 272–74, 278, 287,
    289–90
Day, Doris, 2, 187, 214, 221
Dean, James, 233, 243–44

De Forest, Lee, 56–57, 67
de Havilland, Olivia, 85, 139, 166–67,
    174–75, 193–94, 294, 296, 299
DeMille, Cecil B., 34, 62, 68, 220
Desperate Journey (1942), 114, 145,
    150, 170
Dial M for Murder (1954), 224–25, 232
"Divided We Fall" speech, 131–34
Duquesne Amusement Supply
    Company, 18

Edison, Thomas, 6, 14, 20–21, 24,
    27–28, 49, 62–63, 67, 180
Eisenhower, Dwight D., 172, 177, 229,
    235, 270, 282
Epstein, Julius and Philip, 142–43, 153,
    184, 193, 198, 294–96

Federal Communications Commission
    (FCC), 212–13, 217
Federal Trade Commission (FTC), 211
First National, 10, 28, 49, 55, 70,
    72–73, 76–77, 80, 82, 231
Five Star Final (1931), 85–86
Flint, Motley, 34, 52, 76–77, 267
Flynn, Errol, 120, 139, 166, 173, 175,
    180, 214–15, 221, 265, 267, 289,
    296, 299
Flynn, John T., 135–37
Ford, Henry, 35, 84, 117, 228
42nd Street (1933), 94, 296
42nd Street Special, 94
Foy, Bryan, 2, 67, 71, 214, 275
Frank, Leo, 118–19
Friendship Train, 206–7
Friends of New Germany (FNG), 105

Garfield, John, 85, 143, 149, 158,
    166–67, 185, 188, 193–94, 214, 204,
    267
Garland, Judy, 204, 232–33, 285
Gauntier Feature Players, 23–24

Geisler, Jerry, 108, 173, 265
German-American Bund, 105, 126, 129, 133, 135, 150
Giant (1956), 243–44, 246, 251, 255, 260
Goebbels, Joseph, 129, 149, 172
Goldwyn, Sam, 205, 220, 230, 271
Grauman, Sid, 24, 60, 68
Great Depression, 75–86, 88–99
Gully, Richard, 260–61, 277
Gyssling, Georg, 116

Hamilton, Esther, 10, 20, 22
Haskin, Byron, 38, 46–47, 107, 114
Hawks, Howard, 32, 157–58, 187
Hays, Will, 36–37, 41, 57, 59, 61–62, 83, 85, 97–98, 101, 107, 127, 136, 176, 239
Hebrew Orphan Asylum, 74
Hepburn, Audrey, 276–77
Hitchcock, Alfred, 135, 214, 223–26, 232, 251, 271
Hitler, Adolf, 1, 84, 105–6, 127, 129–30, 133, 141, 161, 170, 172, 194–95
Hitler Lives (1945), 170–72
Hollywood Anti-Nazi League, 1, 105–6, 116, 125, 128
Hollywood Bowl, 136
Hollywood Canteen (club), 167–68
Hollywood Canteen (film), 167–70
Hollywood Foreign Correspondents Association, 172, 206
Hollywood Ten, 204–6
Home of Peace cemetery, 67, 102, 104, 258–59, 291
Hoover, J. Edgar, 9, 126, 190–92
House Un-American Activities Committee (HUAC), 122, 126, 152, 167, 188, 191, 193–95, 201–9, 211, 223, 227, 229, 261, 270
Hudson, Rock, 244, 285
Hunter, Tab, 244, 285

Huston, John, 115, 135, 142, 150, 188, 193, 204, 214, 275
Huston, Walter, 159, 166, 192–93

I Am a Fugitive from a Chain Gang (1932), 71, 90, 93, 140, 231
I Confess (1953), 224–26
Inside Nazi Germany (1938), 125
International Alliance of Theatrical Stage Employees (IATSE), 106–8, 167, 175–76, 184
investigations, Senate. *See under* United States Senate
I Was a Communist for the FBI (1951), 2, 227–29, 238

Jazz Singer, The (1927), 60, 63–65, 68–69, 73–74, 78, 286; New York premiere of, 66–69
Johnston, Eric, 176, 191, 194, 201, 204–5, 228, 236, 251, 259
juvenile delinquency, 235–44

Kahn, Gordon, 197–98, 202–3
Kalmenson, Ben, 246, 250, 253, 255, 279, 281
Kann, Red, 117, 129, 202
Kauffmann, Phil, 104–5
Kazan, Elia, 221, 223, 233, 235, 252–53, 256
Kefauver, Estes, 235–43
Kennedy, John Fitzgerald, 5, 269, 271, 274–76, 280
Kennedy, Joseph, 57, 61–62
KFWB (radio station), 46, 53, 106, 110, 147, 218
Koch, Howard, 159, 161–62, 190, 198, 202
Korean War, 220

Laemmle, Carl, 20, 26, 34, 50, 106, 294
Lardner, Ring, Jr., 177, 188, 190, 198, 206

Lasky, Jesse, 34, 230–31, 258
Lawson, John Howard, 190, 198, 204
Lazaron, Morris S., 121
Legion of Decency, 99, 101, 223,
    231–32, 252–53, 280
LeRoy, Mervyn, 83–84, 90–91, 94,
    101, 106, 111, 119, 120, 167, 208,
    230–31, 235, 251–52, 294–95
Levinson, Nathan, 18, 46, 50
Life of Emile Zola, The (1937), 75, 118,
    130, 140, 220–21, 286
Lights of New York (1928), 71
Lindbergh, Charles, 131, 135–36, 251
Looney Tunes, 81, 124, 182, 298, 301
Lost City, The (1920), 31–32
Lubitsch, Ernst, 45, 49, 54, 68, 105

Maltz, Albert, 194, 198
Marks, Joe, 14, 67
Matthews, Blayney, 144, 146, 177, 183,
    185, 189, 197, 258, 261
Mayer, Louis B., 44, 91–92, 99, 105,
    109, 129, 135, 196–97, 207, 220,
    229–30, 250, 258–60, 267, 273, 290,
    294
Mayo, Archie, 68
Mayo, Virginia, 214, 235
McCarthy, Joseph, 218, 234
McGrew, Lois, 248–51
Mellett, Lowell, 151
Menjou, Adolphe, 68, 195, 266
Meredyth, Bess, 53
Midsummer Night's Dream, A (1935),
    120, 296
Mission to Moscow (1943), 115, 150,
    153, 155, 190; HUAC hearings,
    190–96, 199–200, 202; production
    of, 159–63
Mizner, Wilson, 110
Moffitt, Jack, 137, 142
Motion Picture Association of
    America (MPAA), 191, 194, 204,
    228, 232, 252–53, 259

Motion Picture Patents Corporation
    (MPPC), 21
Motion Picture Producers and
    Directors Association (MPPDA),
    36, 41, 57, 61, 68, 127, 176
Motion Picture Relief Fund, 34
My Fair Lady (1964), 269, 276–78, 286
My Four Years in Germany (1918), 26,
    28–30, 199

Nichols, Mike, 279–80
Niles, Ohio, 15, 35
Nixon, Richard, 195, 199, 229, 265,
    269–71, 284, 289
Nizer, Louis, 92, 279, 281
Norfolk, Virginia, 19
Nun's Story, The (1959) 232, 234
Nye, Gerald, 135–37, 141

Office of War Information (OWI),
    147, 151, 153, 157
On with the Show (1929), 73
Open Your Eyes (1919), 31
O'Steen, Johnny, 39, 73, 79, 129, 132,
    142, 260, 265
Osterberg, Clyde, 107

Park, Jacquelyn "Jackie," 272, 275
Pittsburgh, Pennsylvania, 17–20
Production Code Administration
    (PCA), 127, 151, 158, 224, 235, 240,
    252, 279
Public Enemy, The (1931), 2, 82, 84,
    119, 237–38

Raiders on the Mexican Border (1912),
    23
Rapf, Harry, 35, 37, 41, 43, 67, 120,
    190
Reagan, Ronald, 2, 85, 153, 176, 184,
    185, 221, 237, 272, 285
Rebel without a Cause (1955), 238,
    241, 243, 255

Rin Tin Tin, 41–43, 45, 49, 55, 92
Rogers, Ginger, 2, 94, 106, 214, 221, 286
Roosevelt, Franklin Delano, 5, 47, 93–94, 90–100, 135, 140, 150, 156, 159–60, 177, 188, 192–93, 195, 219, 229, 267, 295
Ross, Steve, 284

Saville, Victor, 235
Sayonara (1957), 233
Schallert, Edwin, 64–65, 129, 156–57, 161
Schenck, Joseph, 34, 98, 107–8, 137, 205, 216, 220, 267
Schlesinger, Leon, 67, 75, 81, 101, 124, 182
Searchers, The (1956), 246–47, 255
self-censorship, 61, 100. *See also* censorship
Selig zoo, 32
Semenenko, Serge, 213, 246, 249–50, 255–56
Seven Arts, 234, 274, 281, 283–84
Shaw, Irwin, 198, 201–2
Sherman, Vincent, 130, 149–50, 189, 193, 261
Shurlock, Geoffrey, 235, 240
Smith, Albert E., 47, 258
Sorrell, Herbert, 175–76, 183–85
Sperling, Milton, 97, 131, 188, 216, 219, 226, 235
Stage Fright (1950), 224
Stanwyck, Barbara, 2, 75, 85, 173, 232, 285
Star Is Born, A (1954), 233, 276, 285
Strangers on a Train (1951), 224
Stripling, Robert, 195, 197–201
Sunset Studios, 32, 34, 46, 64, 67, 124, 182

Taylor, Elizabeth, 244, 279–80
Thalberg, Irving, 50, 105–6

They Won't Forget (1937), 111, 118–20, 126, 193, 221, 231
Thomas, J. Parnell, 192, 195–96, 198–200, 204, 206
Trilling, Steve, 235, 258, 261, 271, 278
Truman, Harry, 5, 195, 208–9, 221, 229
Trumbo, Dalton, 190, 198, 206
Turner, Lana, 111, 118

Unfaithful, The (1947), 189
United Jewish Appeal (UJA), 187, 242
United Jewish Welfare Fund, 215–16, 272
United States Senate: 1955 investigation of Hollywood for juvenile delinquency, 235–44; 1941 investigation of Hollywood for warmongering, 135–43

Vail, Richard, 195, 201, 203
Valenti, Jack, 279–80
Vitagraph, 21, 47–49, 56, 72, 89, 152, 258
Vitaphone, 46, 51, 54–66, 72, 77, 80–81, 124, 179, 259

Waldorf Statement, 205–6
Wallis, Hal, 41–43, 45–46, 56, 66, 68, 80, 82–84, 91, 97, 102, 107, 115–16, 119, 120, 126, 134, 150, 152, 157, 265, 278, 286, 290
Walsh, Raoul, 134, 188, 215, 244, 265, 275
War Activities Committee (WAC), 146
warmongering, 135–43
Warner, Albert: award from United Jewish Appeal, 242; donation to Miami hospital, 283–84; death, 284; early interviews with the trade press, 30–31; early years, 7–13; essay in *Variety*, 80; at Harry's funeral, 258; during Jack's betrayal,

Warner, Albert (*continued*)
249–51; marriages, 51; as president
of Warner Features, 23; on talking
pictures, 181–82; testifying against
Bioff, 108, 174; Waldorf Statement,
205
Warner, Anna, 12, 35, 53, 67, 74,
102–4, 165, 248
Warner, Ann Page, 102–4, 111, 113,
260–61, 263, 281, 290–91, 294;
marriage to Jack Warner, 111, 113
Warner, Barbara, 103, 113, 115, 203,
277, 291
Warner, Ben, 10, 14, 16–17, 20, 23, 26,
35, 52–53, 59–60, 67–68, 74, 101–4,
165, 219; SS *Benjamin Warner*, 165
Warner, Bessie (Krieger), 18, 51
Warner, Bessie (Siegal), 51, 103, 284
Warner, Betty, 8, 76, 86–87, 101–2,
111, 131, 188, 191, 203, 257–58
Warner, David, 35, 102–3
Warner, Doris, 87, 101–3, 131, 208,
230, 257–58, 295
Warner, Harry: antitrust legislation,
211–12; assisting FBI, 220;
competitive dance, 18; dealings
with and testifying against Bioff,
102–8, 173–74; declining health
and death, 256–59; "Divided We
Fall" speech, 131–34; donations
and philanthropy, 74, 87, 134,
152, 163, 167, 206, 212, 216, 234;
early years, 7–13; essays in *Warner
Club News*, 148, 163, 165, 169,
179, 185, 209, 217, 226, 234, 256;
firing Ernst Lubitsch, 45; first
jobs, 10–13; interest in movies for
public good, 36, 62–64, 71, 76–77,
91, 117–18, 120–22, 125, 143,
146, 161; Jack's betrayal, 258–51;
Lewis's illness, 86–88; life with Lita,
87, 89, 91–92, 101, 131, 165, 207,

258; making first movies, 23–24;
marriage to Rea (*see* Warner, Rea);
meetings with Harry Truman,
208–9; meeting with Roosevelt,
159; negotiating with Ambassador
Gerard, 27; purchasing First
National, 55; purchasing Vitagraph,
47–48; relationship with Judaism,
8; speech at Harvard, 61–64, 68;
testimony defending the industry
in 1941, 139–41; views of HUAC,
191; work with American Legion,
121–23
Warner, Irma, 24, 26, 53, 74, 88,
102–4, 111–13, 131
Warner, Jack: battles with Jack Jr. (*see*
Warner, Jack, Jr.); betraying his
brothers, 249–51; car accident,
260; dealing with censors (*see*
censorship); essays in *Warner
Club News*, 148, 163, 165, 169,
179, 185, 209, 217, 226, 234, 256;
HUAC testimony, 195–203; as
independent producer, 286–89;
involvement with the church on
behalf of *Baby Doll* (1956), 252–54;
involvement with the church on
behalf of *The Nun's Story* (1959),
225, 231; juvenile delinquency
hearings, 235–44; last years and
death, 290–91; late career battles,
281–86; making movies with Sam,
23–26; marriages (*see* Warner, Ann
Page; Warner, Irma); politics in
later life, 269–72; relationship with
Jacquelyn "Jackie" Park, 272, 275;
relationship with Judaism, 7–9;
remembrances, 291–97; selling
the company, 280–86; stealing
Academy Award from Hal Wallis,
157; as Warner Bros. president,
249–86

Warner, Jack, Jr., 26, 37, 74, 87–88, 103, 113, 203, 249, 257, 258, 263, 284, 291

Warner, Lewis, 18, 77–79, 86–88, 101, 104, 134, 181

Warner, Lita, 60, 70–71, 87, 89, 91–92, 101, 131, 165, 207, 258

Warner, Milton, 12, 74

Warner, Pearl, 7, 11–12, 16, 20, 23, 26, 35, 52, 53, 59–60, 66–68, 101–4, 258

Warner, Rea, 18, 86–87, 91–92, 101, 103, 248, 250, 257–59

Warner, Sadie, 10, 26, 67, 102, 104, 165, 248, 260

Warner, Sam: conflicts with Warner family, 52–53, 67; discovering *Dante's Inferno* (1911), 21–22; first movie projector, 14; life with Lina, 51–55, 60, 65; move to Los Angeles, 26–27; sickness and death, 64–68; work with Hale's Tours, 13; work with synchronized sound, 45–68

Warner Bros.: animation, 182–83; anniversary coverage in *Variety*, 79–83; anti-Nazism, 104–45; battling the Great Depression, 75–99; brothers sell the studio, 249–51; feature in *Fortune* magazine, 119–20; fighting the Production Code, 71, 75, 83, 96–97, 99–101, 127, 134, 223–25, 227, 239, 251–52, 279; first use of abbreviation, 32; incorporation, 39–41; Kefauver committee hearings on juvenile delinquency, 235–41; labor wars, 106–9, 173–78, 183–86; patriotic shorts, 123–24; postwar film trends, 185–88; role in the blacklist, 189–207; role in World War II, 146–73; transition to sound film, 45–74; US Senate attacks Warner Bros. for anti-Nazi films, 135–45

Warner Club News, 148, 163, 165, 169, 179, 185, 209, 217, 226, 234, 256

Warner Feature Film Company, 23–24

Warner's Features, 16, 24–26

Waters, Ethel, 73

Waxman, A. P., 82

Wayne, John, 75, 85, 91, 214, 218, 220, 226, 229, 246–47, 286, 300

Weber, Lois, 51

Western Electric, 46, 49, 51, 57, 59, 180

What Ever Happened to Baby Jane? (1962), 272–74

Who's Afraid of Virginia Woolf? (1966), 279–81

Why Girls Leave Home (1921), 35

Wild Boys of the Road (1933), 97

Wilkerson, Billy, 111, 189, 190, 198, 219

Willkie, Wendell, 136

Wood, Natalie, 243–44, 267–68

Wrong Man, The (1956), 226, 251

Yankee Doodle Dandy (1942), 115, 143, 151–53, 170

Young, Alma, 44–46, 56, 71

Youngstown, Ohio, 9–12, 15, 18, 20–21, 103, 287, 292

Zanuck, Darryl: first years at Warner Bros., 43–45; leaving Warner Bros., 97–99; producing headline-driven gangster films, 71, 83–85, 119; views of the brothers, 44; working with Robert Burns, 91; writing films, 49

Zinnemann, Fred, 231–32, 275

Screen Classics

Screen Classics is a series of critical biographies, film histories, and analytical studies focusing on neglected filmmakers and important screen artists and subjects, from the era of silent cinema through the golden age of Hollywood to the international generation of today. Books in the Screen Classics series are intended for scholars and general readers alike. The contributing authors are established figures in their respective fields. This series also serves the purpose of advancing scholarship on film personalities and themes with ties to Kentucky.

Series Editor
Patrick McGilligan

Books in the Series

Olivia de Havilland: Lady Triumphant
    Victoria Amador
Mae Murray: The Girl with the Bee-Stung Lips
    Michael G. Ankerich
Harry Dean Stanton: Hollywood's Zen Rebel
    Joseph B. Atkins
Hedy Lamarr: The Most Beautiful Woman in Film
    Ruth Barton
Rex Ingram: Visionary Director of the Silent Screen
    Ruth Barton
Conversations with Classic Film Stars: Interviews from Hollywood's Golden Era
    James Bawden and Ron Miller
Conversations with Legendary Television Stars: Interviews from the First Fifty Years
    James Bawden and Ron Miller
They Made the Movies: Conversations with Great Filmmakers
    James Bawden and Ron Miller
You Ain't Heard Nothin' Yet: Interviews with Stars from Hollywood's Golden Era
    James Bawden and Ron Miller
Charles Boyer: The French Lover
    John Baxter
Von Sternberg
    John Baxter
Hitchcock's Partner in Suspense: The Life of Screenwriter Charles Bennett
    Charles Bennett, edited by John Charles Bennett
Hitchcock and the Censors
    John Billheimer
A Uniquely American Epic: Intimacy and Action, Tenderness and Violence in Sam Peckinpah's The Wild Bunch
    Edited by Michael Bliss

My Life in Focus: A Photographer's Journey with Elizabeth Taylor and the Hollywood Jet Set
  Gianni Bozzacchi with Joey Tayler
Hollywood Divided: The 1950 Screen Directors Guild Meeting and the Impact of the Blacklist
  Kevin Brianton
He's Got Rhythm: The Life and Career of Gene Kelly
  Cynthia Brideson and Sara Brideson
Ziegfeld and His Follies: A Biography of Broadway's Greatest Producer
  Cynthia Brideson and Sara Brideson
Eleanor Powell: Born to Dance
  Paula Broussard and Lisa Royère
The Marxist and the Movies: A Biography of Paul Jarrico
  Larry Ceplair
Dalton Trumbo: Blacklisted Hollywood Radical
  Larry Ceplair and Christopher Trumbo
Warren Oates: A Wild Life
  Susan Compo
Improvising Out Loud: My Life Teaching Hollywood How to Act
  Jeff Corey with Emily Corey
Crane: Sex, Celebrity, and My Father's Unsolved Murder
  Robert Crane and Christopher Fryer
Jack Nicholson: The Early Years
  Robert Crane and Christopher Fryer
Anne Bancroft: A Life
  Douglass K. Daniel
Being Hal Ashby: Life of a Hollywood Rebel
  Nick Dawson
Bruce Dern: A Memoir
  Bruce Dern with Christopher Fryer and Robert Crane
Intrepid Laughter: Preston Sturges and the Movies
  Andrew Dickos
The Woman Who Dared: The Life and Times of Pearl White, Queen of the Serials
  William M. Drew
Miriam Hopkins: Life and Films of a Hollywood Rebel
  Allan R. Ellenberger
Vitagraph: America's First Great Motion Picture Studio
  Andrew A. Erish
Jayne Mansfield: The Girl Couldn't Help It
  Eve Golden
John Gilbert: The Last of the Silent Film Stars
  Eve Golden
Strictly Dynamite: The Sensational Life of Lupe Velez
  Eve Golden
Stuntwomen: The Untold Hollywood Story
  Mollie Gregory
Jean Gabin: The Actor Who Was France
  Joseph Harriss
Otto Preminger: The Man Who Would Be King, updated edition
  Foster Hirsch
Saul Bass: Anatomy of Film Design
  Jan-Christopher Horak
Lawrence Tierney: Hollywood's Real-Life Tough Guy
  Burt Kearns

Hitchcock Lost and Found: The Forgotten Films
  Alain Kerzoncuf and Charles Barr
Pola Negri: Hollywood's First Femme Fatale
  Mariusz Kotowski
Ernest Lehman: The Sweet Smell of Success
  Jon Krampner
Sidney J. Furie: Life and Films
  Daniel Kremer
Albert Capellani: Pioneer of the Silent Screen
  Christine Leteux
A Front Row Seat: An Intimate Look at Broadway, Hollywood, and the Age of Glamour
  Nancy Olson Livingston
Ridley Scott: A Biography
  Vincent LoBrutto
Mamoulian: Life on Stage and Screen
  David Luhrssen
Maureen O'Hara: The Biography
  Aubrey Malone
My Life as a Mankiewicz: An Insider's Journey through Hollywood
  Tom Mankiewicz and Robert Crane
Hawks on Hawks
  Joseph McBride
John Ford
  Joseph McBride and Michael Wilmington
Showman of the Screen: Joseph E. Levine and His Revolutions in Film Promotion
  A. T. McKenna
William Wyler: The Life and Films of Hollywood's Most Celebrated Director
  Gabriel Miller
Raoul Walsh: The True Adventures of Hollywood's Legendary Director
  Marilyn Ann Moss
Veit Harlan: The Life and Work of a Nazi Filmmaker
  Frank Noack
Harry Langdon: King of Silent Comedy
  Gabriella Oldham and Mabel Langdon
Mavericks: Interviews with the World's Iconoclast Filmmakers
  Gerald Peary
Charles Walters: The Director Who Made Hollywood Dance
  Brent Phillips
Some Like It Wilder: The Life and Controversial Films of Billy Wilder
  Gene D. Phillips
Ann Dvorak: Hollywood's Forgotten Rebel
  Christina Rice
Mean . . . Moody . . . Magnificent! Jane Russell and the Marketing of a Hollywood Legend
  Christina Rice
Fay Wray and Robert Riskin: A Hollywood Memoir
  Victoria Riskin
Lewis Milestone: Life and Films
  Harlow Robinson
Michael Curtiz: A Life in Film
  Alan K. Rode
Ryan's Daughter: The Making of an Irish Epic
  Paul Benedict Rowan

Arthur Penn: American Director
  Nat Segaloff
Film's First Family: The Untold Story of the Costellos
  Terry Chester Shulman
Claude Rains: An Actor's Voice
  David J. Skal with Jessica Rains
Barbara La Marr: The Girl Who Was Too Beautiful for Hollywood
  Sherri Snyder
Buzz: The Life and Art of Busby Berkeley
  Jeffrey Spivak
Victor Fleming: An American Movie Master
  Michael Sragow
Aline MacMahon: Hollywood, the Blacklist, and the Birth of Method Acting
  John Stangeland
My Place in the Sun: Life in the Golden Age of Hollywood and Washington
  George Stevens, Jr.
Hollywood Presents Jules Verne: The Father of Science Fiction on Screen
  Brian Taves
Thomas Ince: Hollywood's Independent Pioneer
  Brian Taves
Picturing Peter Bogdanovich: My Conversations with the New Hollywood Director
  Peter Tonguette
Jessica Lange: An Adventurer's Heart
  Anthony Uzarowski
Carl Theodor Dreyer and Ordet: *My Summer with the Danish Filmmaker*
  Jan Wahl
Wild Bill Wellman: Hollywood Rebel
  William Wellman Jr.
Harvard, Hollywood, Hitmen, and Holy Men: A Memoir
  Paul W. Williams
The Warner Brothers
  Chris Yogerst
Clarence Brown: Hollywood's Forgotten Master
  Gwenda Young
The Queen of Technicolor: Maria Montez in Hollywood
  Tom Zimmerman